Fallen Stars

Eleven Studies of Twentieth Century Military Disasters

Brassey's titles of related interest

THE FORGOTTEN VICTOR:
The Biography of General Sir Richard O'Connor
John Baynes

BRITAIN, FRANCE AND BELGIUM 1939–40
Brian Bond

THREE MARSHALS OF FRANCE
Anthony Clayton

GALLIPOLI 1915
Peter Liddle

HITLER'S GLADIATOR
Charles Messenger

THE LAST PRUSSIAN:
A Biography of Field Marshal Gerd von Rundstedt 1875–1953
Charles Messenger

WAVELL IN THE MIDDLE EAST, 1939–1941:
A Study in Generalship
Harold E Raugh

THE LIFEBLOOD OF WAR:
Logistics in Armed Conflict
Julian Thompson

Fallen Stars

Eleven Studies of Twentieth Century
Military Disasters

edited by
Brian Bond

BRASSEY'S (UK)

(A Member of the Maxwell Macmillan Group)
LONDON · WASHINGTON · NEW YORK

UK (Editorial)	Brassey's (UK) Ltd., 50 Fetter Lane, London EC4A 1AA, England
Orders, all except North America	Brassey's (UK) Ltd., Headington Hill Hall, Oxford OX3 0BW, England
USA (Editorial)	Brassey's (US) Inc., 8000 Westpark Drive, First Floor, McLean, Virginia 22102, USA
(Orders, North America)	Macmillan, Front and Brown Streets, Riverside, New Jersey 08075, USA Tel (toll free): 800 257 5755

First edition 1991

Library of Congress Cataloging-in-Publication Data
available

British Library Cataloguing in Publication Data
available

ISBN 0-08-040717 X

Typeset by Florencetype Ltd, Kewstoke, Avon
Printed in Great Britain by B.P.C.C. Wheatons Ltd., Exeter

Contents

1

Notes on Contributors

Brian Bond is Professor of Military History at King's College, London and President of the British Commission for Military History. His books include *War and Society in Europe, 1870–1970* (1984) and *Britian, France and Belgium, 1939–1940* (new edition, 1990).

Richard W Harrison is a graduate of Georgetown University, Washington, DC who is completing a doctorate in the Department of War Studies, King's College, London on Russian/Soviet Military Doctrine, 1904–37.

John Lee holds a Master's degree in War Studies at King's College, London and is working on a biography of Sir Ian Hamilton.

Anthony Clayton is a senior lecturer in the Department of War Studies at Sandhurst whose books include *The British Empire as a Superpower, 1919–1939* (1986) and *France, Soldiers and Africa* (1988).

Sir Anthony Farrar-Hockley is a retired British general and a military historian. His books include *The Somme* (1964) and *Goughie: the life of General Sir Hubert Gough* (1975), and he has recently completed the official history of the British forces in the Korean War.

Paul Harris is a senior lecturer in the Department of War Studies at Sandhurst. He has published several articles on the British Army in the 1930's and has edited (with Francis Toase) *Armoured Warfare* (1990).

Martin S Alexander is a lecturer in history at Southampton University. He has published numerous articles on French military history and a (forthcoming) biography of General Maurice Gamelin.

Wesley K Wark teaches in the history department of the University of Toronto. He is the author of *The Ultimate Enemy* (1985), and is working on the authorised biography of Field Marshal Lord Ironside.

Duncan Anderson is a senior lecturer in the Department of War Studies at Sandhurst. He has contributed to several volumes on military history and is revising his doctoral thesis on the English Militia in the 19th century as a book.

Julian Thompson is a retired major general who commanded 3 Commando Brigade in the Falklands War and described the experience in *No Picnic* (1985). He has also published *Ready for Anything: the Parachute Regiment at War, 1940–1982* (1989) and *The Lifeblood of War: Logistics in Armed Conflict* (Brassey's, 1991).

Louis Allen is a lecturer in French at Durham University. He served with British Intelligence in India and South East Asia in the Second World War and is a distinguished scholar of Japanese history and literature. His books include *Singapore, 1941–1942* (1977) and *Burma: the Longest War* (1984).

Charles Messenger is a former regular Army officer (Royal Tank Regiment) and author of numerous books including *The Art of Blitzkrieg* (1976) and *Hitler's Gladiator: the life and times of Sepp Dietrich* (1988). His biography of Field Marshal Von Rundstedt, *The Last Prussian*, has recently been published by Brassey's.

List of Maps

SYMBOLS

The formation symbols shown below have been used in this book. Where special symbols have been used, they are shown in the Key to the map in question.

Symbol	Name	Symbol	Name
	Army Group		Armoured
	Army		Infantry
	Corps		Airborne
	Division		Airfields

Introduction

Despite the complexities of modern warfare, the personality and performance of the battlefield commander remains of crucial significance. Responsibility for victory or defeat has often seemed deceptively clear cut at the time, with laurels awarded to the victor and obloquy or oblivion visited upon the loser. Even in cases where responsibility for success or failure is disputed, the commander knows that his reputation is at stake. As Marshal Joseph Joffre remarked 'I don't know who won the Battle of the Marne (in 1914), but if it had been lost, I know who would have lost it.'

The world, including historians, loves a winner and of course far more than the symbolic crown of laurels is involved. Successful British Commanders-in-Chief were traditionally awarded splendid country estates such as Blenheim, Stratfield Saye and Bemersyde; and Hitler's paladins also did well in this respect. Titles and financial grants have regularly marked the gratitude of government and nation. After the First World War, for example, Haig received an earldom and £100,000; French and Allenby £50,000 each; and most of the other army commanders (but excluding Gough) £30,000. The names of the German Generals of the Napoleonic era – Blücher, Scharnhorst, Gneisenau – were immortalised in modern battleships. Bronze statues have been raised to British service leaders of the Second World War. Institutions also perpetuate the names of successful Generals; thus Wellington College, the Mountbatten Centre at Southampton University; Monash University in Australia and the Marshal Foch Chair of French Studies at Oxford. Paris street names commemorating the military heroes of the Revolutionary Wars have their British counterparts in barracks, lecture theatres and public houses. Truly it may be recorded without irony of victorious Generals that 'their name liveth for evermore.'

In painful contrast, the once 'shining stars' who have suffered defeat, or been held accountable for failure, may be remembered only by military historians unless their names are inseparably linked to spectacular or controversial disasters such as Mack at Ulm, Samsonov at Tannenberg, Hamilton with Gallipoli and Gough with the German offensive of March 1918. Some 'fallen stars' such as Sir John French, Gough and Gamelin

1

vigorously defended their reputations in memoirs or polemics but others, such as Samsonov, Nivelle and Lucas, have had to rely on the reappraisals of a later generation of historians. Unfortunately for many of them, there is no certainty of reappraisal let alone of a more favourable verdict. Publishing incentives ensure that the likes of Wellington, Montgomery, Patton or Rommel will be constantly under attention, whereas it takes boldness and enterprise to attempt to rehabilitate a presumed failure, as for example, Christopher Hibbert did with his study *The Destruction of Lord Raglan*.

This volume is based on the assumptions that failure in battle can be interesting and instructive. Our selected subjects – eleven twentieth century commanders or leaders in land warfare – were all men of outstanding achievement or promise, so the circumstances of their 'fall' merit investigation. In 1915, for example, Sir Ian Hamilton was not merely the senior Lieutenant-General on the Army List, but also one of the most war experienced and innovative soldiers of his generation. Maurice Gamelin had been picked out as a rising star even before the First World War in which he was to excel as a staff officer. By 1940, he was immensely experienced, having been the French Army's Chief of Staff 1931–1935 and Commander-in-Chief 1935–1939. Gerd von Rundstedt, though on his own admission never scintillating, was already amongst the most senior German Generals when Hitler came to power; and although passed over, he was the Army's choice as Commander-in-Chief in 1938. Douglas MacArthur had already acquired a legendary reputation in the United States by the 1920's, and in the 1930's was commanding the Philippine Army with the rank of Field Marshal. By contrast, Hubert Gough had earned comparatively rapid, and Robert Nivelle meteoric, promotion in the First World War before both suffered sudden, and as it turned out, irreversible falls.

For obvious reasons, few Generals who have failed at a high level get a second chance; indeed some have suffered imprisonment, disgrace and even execution. Among our subjects Rundstedt was unusual in being *twice* recalled after removal from high command, but he had not been defeated in battle and remained useful to Hitler both for his qualities and his reputation in the Army. Another General given a second chance was Percy Hobart whose original 'fall' was due to personal failings rather than defeat in battle. In terms of rank and status his eclipse was the most spectacular: he was a Corporal in the Home Guard when 'rescued' by Churchill and given command of a division in 1942. Only Samsonov among our subjects summarily deprived himself of any chance of rehabilitation by committing suicide.

The main objective of our contributors has been to reassess the nature of their subject's fall and whether or not it was justified. There are numerous causes of failure in high command, including the following, which are not of course mutually exclusive. First, promotion above their career ceiling in terms of ability, experience or capacity to command the loyalty of passed-over subordinates. Nivelle may perhaps be placed in this category.

Secondly, incompetence for other reasons such as flaws of temperament which militate against co-operation in a group endeavour. Paul Harris makes a strong case that Hobart failed on this score. Mutaguchi failed in this respect but also himself took on a mission which was extremely ambitious. Thirdly, an able commander given an impossible mission or one that could only have been achieved with greater support from government and superiors than was actually forthcoming. John Lee would assign Sir Ian Hamilton to this category of honourable failures. Fourthly, commanders who are let down by subordinates and/or superiors in the course of battle. Martin Alexander makes a case for placing Gamelin in this group; Julian Thompson shows that Lucas had some grounds for criticism of both Mark Clark and Harold Alexander; while Gough was probably the hardest done-by on both counts. Finally, and this is a consideration which occurs in several of our contributions, there are Generals who, whatever their own failings, are in effect made scapegoats by their military superiors or their governments. Short of outright and undisguisable failure, this is probably the greatest hazard facing the military commander: that he will be removed for wider considerations of domestic politics, alliance requirements or simply *pour encourager les autres*. The studies in this volume amply bear out the pervasiveness of this pitfall.

The following editorial remarks are intended briefly to introduce the eleven subjects without anticipating their coverage of sources, arguments and conclusions in detail.

Samsonov's spectacular mishandling of the Russian Second Army at Tannenberg in August 1914 was one of the most obvious choices for a symposium such as this. Richard Harrison's essay, thoroughly based on Russian language publications, shows that there were extenuating circumstances for Samsonov's poor performance. He was in poor health and newly appointed to his command after several years 'on the shelf'. He was not properly briefed about the overall plan for the Russian invasion of East Prussia, communications and logistics were deplorable; his ill-trained army is described as 'a hungry mass'; and, not least important, his personal relations with the First Army commander Rennenkampf were, to say the least, cool. Indeed Harrison speculates that Rennenkampf may have deliberately slowed down his advance to make life difficult for Samsonov. If so, he certainly succeeded, but sympathy for Samsonov must be confined. He made at least three serious errors which seem inexcusable; namely in drastically altering the direction of his army's advance against the explicit orders of the front commander; in persisting with the offensive on his central front while knowing that both his corps on the flanks were being routed; and finally in abandoning his command for a 'fatalistic ride into oblivion'. Though Samsonov was ill-served by both superiors and subordinates he was in essentials the architect of his own downfall.

Sir Ian Hamilton certainly cannot be placed in the category of 'fallen stars' whose climactic campaign has been neglected by historians. On the contrary, Gallipoli has remained from 1915 to the present the most controversial campaign of a controversial war for reasons that are readily apparent. It was the outcome of an imaginative strategy based on Allied superior sea power designed to 'unlock' the Dardanelles, knock out Turkey and open up the Balkans. Moreover, although it ultimately failed, there were three occasions when the operations seemed on the brink of success. It is, therefore, *par excellence* a campaign of 'might have beens' which continue to fascinate historians.

Yet, despite an enormous bibliography, there is still no really satisfactory biography of Hamilton. John Lee makes a robust case in his defence, challenging the negative if not hostile opinions of Robert Rhodes James whose study, in some respects excellent, has held the field for more than twenty years. Hamilton was given an ambiguous and difficult, if not actually impossible, mission, but was partly to blame for accepting the challenge in a somewhat cavalier and romantic fashion. He was a truly tragic figure in that what would have been virtues in happier circumstances – imagination, loyalty to superiors and tolerant humanity to errant subordinates – helped to bring about his downfall. Lee contends that with a properly prepared force and with more consistent support during the operations Hamilton had the ability to succeed. He concludes that responsibility for failure lay ultimately in London, and particularly with Kitchener, whose death in June 1916 effectively deprived Hamilton of the opportunity to vindicate himself.

Robert Nivelle was also a tragic figure in the classical mould whose downfall was more directly due than Hamilton's to his own shortcomings which included over-optimism and arrogance. At the outbreak of war in 1914 Nivelle was commanding a regiment; by the end of 1915 he was commanding a corps; in April 1916 he took charge of Second Army at Verdun and in December he succeeded Joffre as Commander-in-Chief. He owed this ultimate step in promotion to his undertaking to achieve a sudden and decisive breakthrough on the Western Front in the spring of 1917. Quite apart from the formidable operational problems which he faced, Nivelle, as Anthony Clayton graphically shows, had two fatal handicaps. Even worse off than Hamilton, he lacked the full confidence of his own government and again, as in the Gallipoli operations, his intelligence security was appalling.

His offensive was not a complete failure by Western Front standards but it *was* a disaster in terms Nivelle's exaggerated claims, so much so that it destroyed the French soldiers' confidence in their commanders and contributed to the widespread mutinies that occurred soon afterwards. As Clayton concludes, Nivelle has found not real defenders and the best that can be argued in mitigation is that from the very outset his plan was undermined by political interference. Perhaps the contemporary realisation that in political terms he had had a raw deal accounts for the leniency with which he was treated in the few years that remained to him.

Unlike Nivelle, Hubert Gough did not fade away but lived to a great age, vigorously defending his own conduct and that of Fifth Army in several publications. While never actively re-employed after 1919, and not rewarded commensurately with the other Army Commanders, Gough at least had the satisfaction of seeing his conduct of the retreat in March 1918 largely exonerated, notably in the Official History.

Anthony Farrar-Hockley's essay, based on his biography *Goughie*, takes the view reached by other recent students of the German March 1918 offensive, that the Fifth Army commander performed well (indeed better than he and Fifth Army had done in 1917 during the Third Ypres campaign) and was, in effect, made the scapegoat for others' errors of omission and commission.

The evidence seems conclusive that in the weeks before the German offensive began on 21st March, Haig and GHQ believed that the main threat would be made much further north near Arras and would be directed towards the Channel ports. They also underestimated its strength. Consequently, Fifth Army's front was deliberately left thinly held (11 infantry and 3 cavalry divisions for 42 miles) compared with that of Byng's Third Army (14 infantry divisions for 28 miles). Even more remarkable, on 22 March, with the battle raging, Haig still expected the major attack to develop in the Arras sector. GHQ's subsequent explanation for the disproportionate strength of Third Army's as against Fifth Army's front, namely that the latter had been left weak because there was enough space behind it for the enemy's advance to lose momentum, does not survive a study of the orders given to Gough, which only allowed for a very gradual withdrawal. Not only was GHQ to blame for misreading the direction of the German threat and mishandling the chaotic retreat in the opening stages, but Byng's conduct was at least as open to criticism as Gough's. Yet it was Gough, who had remained calm throughout the critical period and fought the battle well, despite minimal support and understanding from GHQ, who was 'degummed' on 4 April.

There is general agreement among recent students of the campaign that the CIGS, Sir Henry Wilson, was the prime mover in getting Gough sacked. Wilson wished to remove Sir Henry Rawlinson as British Military Representative to the Supreme War Council at Versailles and transfer him to command of Fifth Army. But, according to Wilson's diary, Gough's removal was also urged by Lloyd George and Lord Milner. The same trio (Lloyd George, Milner and Wilson) were also keen to oust Haig but Lord Derby, the Secretary of State for War, threatened resignation if Haig were to be dismissed. Haig was reluctant to allow Gough to be made the scapegoat, but decided that it was likely to be a choice between the Fifth Army commander and himself, and his own services could not be spared. Haig and Lord Derby both promised Gough an enquiry into the causes of the initial enemy breakthrough, but none was every held. It was much to Gough's credit that he 'buried the hatchet' with Haig in the 1920's and Lloyd George in the 1930's.

Sir Percy Hobart ('Hobo'), forms our link between the two World Wars in that his 'star' shone brightest in the 1930's as one of the most promising British commanders of armoured forces. He is also anomalous in that his 'fall' was occasioned by disruptive conduct and consequent adverse personal reports. He was never destined to command in battle but was at least given a chance to retrieve his reputation after 1942.

Paul Harris' revisionist essay challenges the high reputation accorded to Hobart as an outstanding theorist of armoured warfare in the 1930's, notably by Liddell Hart but a favourable opinion endorsed by other historians, including myself. Harris contends that Hobart shared the British propensity to 'think small' in terms of mechanisation in that he favoured an all-tank or at least an all-armoured division which was beyond the technical reach of any army, including Germany's, in the 1930's. Even after the outbreak of war Hobart's conception of the armoured division was too 'heavy' in the number of tanks included, and too 'light' in the number of guns. George Lindsay is said to have displayed a sounder grasp of armoured organisation and operations than Hobart, who never really accepted the all-arms integrated division developed by the Germans. Hobart was not, on this evaluation, Britain's lost equivalent of Heinz Guderian. Harris also stresses his fits of depression, irritability and rudeness which dogged Hobart throughout his career and which surely did more to dim his prospects than any 'anti-tank conspiracy' on the part of the military establishment. Nevertheless at his best Hobart was an inspirational organiser and trainer of armoured forces: his compulsory retirement in 1940 was a loss to the army, but at least he was given a second chance which enabled him to make a significant contribution to the victorious campaign in Europe in 1944 and 1945. No one should underestimate the nature of that revival. Not only did he raise and train a brand new armoured division in a year, creating a spirit and level of efficiency that was to pay substantial dividends in battle, albeit under another commander, but he then accepted the challenge of creating, developing and training a division of specialised armour to breach the great West Wall in the invasion of Normandy. Even his critics would concede that only in Hobart did the Army possess a commander with the imagination, professional expertise and ruthless determination to carry through such a mission in 14 short months and then to mastermind its operations in support of other formations across the whole of the Allied front in north-west Europe. Whilst it is true that he never had tactical command in battle, his command of 79th Armoured Division throughout that campaign showed him to be a commander of a very special quality – yet it is the very fact that he was not in *tactical* command that has led to his important contribution to victory being gravely under-rated.

In our selection of 'fallen stars' from the Second World War it seems fitting that two very senior Anglo-French leaders (Gamelin and Ironside) should represent the catastrophic allied defeats of 1940; whereas a Japanese and a German general (Mutaguchi and Rundstedt) should represent the final phase of the Axis defeat. In between come Douglas MacArthur, whose performance in command in the Philippines has been criticised, though his 'star' certainly did not fall at the time; and John Lucas whose career was terminated by the Allied failure to break-out from the Anzio beachhead.

Maurice Gamelin is an ideal candidate for reconsideration as a 'fallen star'; highly respected – even by the Wehrmacht – as a brilliant staff officer and experienced military leader before the war, he suffered an ignominious dismissal in May 1940 and was thereafter to be ritually derided, by scholars as well as political partisans, as 'the man who lost the Battle of France'. Only in recent years have students of the final phase of the Third Republic begun to consider Gamelin more sympathetically, an approach which is boldly developed by Martin Alexander in his superb contribution.

First, Gamelin is depicted as 'the French high command's master impresario of bureaucratic politics' who, with Daladier, masterminded France's impressive rearmament effort between 1936 and 1939. Second, Gamelin was the architect of the plan, fully endorsed by the Allied governments, designed to ward off the enemy's initial blow whilst preparing for an eventual offensive. Much criticised after the debacle, Gamelin's efforts to bring neutral Belgium into the alliance and also to send military support to the Netherlands, were generally accepted in 1939. He was understandably unhappy about French participation in the Norwegian campaign, but was overruled by his bitter political opponent Reynaud, who emerges with far less credit from this account than in most British versions.

Thirdly, Alexander largely exonerates Gamelin of personal responsibility for the operational defeat in 1940. As Supreme Commander of the Allied forces (and all three French services), Gamelin's duties lay in the sphere of inter-allied politics and grand strategy. He was badly let down by the ineffectual commander of land operations, General Georges, who should have been retired earlier on health grounds. Gamelin was reluctant to interfere in the day-to-day command of operations, but had just resolved to do so when, on 19 May, he was dismissed by Reynaud. This caused a hiatus of two days at a crucial period when Gamelin had intended to organise a counter-offensive to cut off the narrow and vulnerable Panzer corridor to the Channel coast.

Finally, Alexander argues, Gamelin was made the scapegoat for what was essentially a failure of nerve on the politicians' part in the days immediately following the German breakthrough on the Meuse. Gamelin paid the price for the Allied defeat but it was Weygand and Pétain who sullied the honour of France in the remaining weeks of the campaign.

General Sir Edmund 'Tiny' Ironside owed his 'star' status mainly to his exploits in North Russia in late 1918 and 1919. His active career seemed to be over in 1938, but in the summer of 1939 he was recalled from Gibraltar to be Inspector General of the Forces. On the outbreak of war in September, he was surprisingly appointed Chief of the Imperial General Staff when Lord Gort insisted on vacating the post to command the Field Force. Whether or not Ironside would have done better than Gort in the latter role will never be known, but it was the appointment he had expected and felt qualified for. By contrast, on his own admission, he hated 'desk work' at the War Office and was suited neither by temperament nor experience to be CIGS. The documentary evidence, including his own published diaries, show that he got on badly with the War Minister, Hore-Belisha, and that neither GHQ in France nor his professional and political colleagues in Whitehall had much confidence in his judgement.

Wesley Wark, who is preparing the authorised biography, shows that Ironside's stock fell rapidly during the early months of 1940 over the discussions about operations in Norway followed by their disastrous implementation in April. To the general relief, Ironside was succeeded by Dill as CIGS at the end of May, but then was rather surprisingly made Commander-in-Chief Home Forces to prepare the land resistance to the anticipated German invasion. This appointment suggests that he still retained Churchill's confidence as a military commander, but his defensive plans soon ran into opposition and he was replaced by General Sir Alan Brooke, who had had the benefit of recent battle experience as a Corps Commander in France.

In the light of his lacklustre performance at Anzio, it may be difficult to envisage General John Lucas as a 'star', but soon after the American entry into the Second World War he was noted as such by George Marshall, and in October 1943 was promoted to command of US VI Corps in Italy. He took the Corps straight into battle, where he performed adequately but emerged physically and mentally exhausted. He repeatedly expressed apprehension of failure in his diary.

Combining thorough research with his own invaluable command experience in the Falklands War, Julian Thompson trenchantly explains that Lucas was not given a sufficiently large force (only two infantry divisions in the first wave) or the necessary armour if his mission was to break out, as distinct from consolidating a bridgehead. There are remarkable similarities between Lucas' role at Anzio and Stopford's at Suvla Bay in 1915, in that timid unenterprising corps commanders interpreted what appeared to be an offensive plan in a defensive way and were condoned in the interpretation by their force commanders, Mark Clark and Hamilton respectively. In the case of Anzio, after a promising first day on 23 January 1944, Mark Clark told Lucas not to take risks. Consequently, Lucas did little that was technically wrong but he was too passive and erred in leaving the British 1st Division in an exposed salient, only visiting the front on 10 February. The instructions which he then issued did not amount to orders but 'were more like a throw-away line in an indifferent war movie'. On 22 February he was replaced by the more dynamic Truscott.

Thompson concludes that both Clark and Alexander deserve criticism for overestimating what the Anzio landing could achieve with the forces allocated. Lucas' performance was so uninspiring that he had to be removed, but a more adventurous commander would have met with disaster had he attempted to push on to the Colli Laziali let alone to Rome. Lucas was 'the perfect scapegoat', but in this case it is impossible to feel that any great injustice was done.

Field Marshal von Rundstedt may seem a curious selection for inclusion in a study of 'fallen stars', but though luckier than many colleagues, he may be regarded as representative of the numerous German generals who were dismissed, not because they manifestly failed in battle, but because they defied Hitler's unrealistic orders or failed to retrieve situations which were irretrievable.

By 1938, Rundstedt was already the doyen of the German Generals and the chief hope of those conservatives who wished to resist Hitler's aggressive plans on purely professional grounds. Well aware of Rundstedt's potentially obstructive nuisance value, Hitler allowed him to retire in November 1938. However he was professionally resurrected in September 1939 and proved his 'star' quality by his successful command of Army Groups in Poland and in France. As Commander of Army Group South in *Operation Barbarossa* he survived until December 1941 when he suffered his first 'fall' because he permitted 1st Panzer Army to fall back in defiance of Hitler's orders. His judgement was soon vindicated and, in March 1942, he was appointed Commander-in-Chief West. By the time *Overlord* (the Allied invasion of Normandy) was launched his health was poor. He sought relief from depression about Germany's military prospects in heavy drinking and smoking. On 30 June 1944 he was relieved for not counter-attacking more vigorously, but was treated 'with kid gloves' by Hitler due to the respect he still enjoyed among senior officers. Reinstated as Commander-in-Chief West in September 1944, he saw his task as the defensive one of delaying the Allied advance to the Rhine. Consequently he had no sympathy with the reckless Ardennes offensive which, ironically, was often to be linked with his name. His final dismissal resulted from an oversight for which he was only nominally responsible; namely the American's capture of an intact bridge over the Rhine at Remagen on 7 March 1945.

Charles Messenger's appraisal, based on his recent biography, suggests that Montgomery exaggerated considerably in describing Rundstedt as 'the best German general I have come up against'. He was a sound professional commander of the old school, imbued with the Prussian concepts of duty, honour and loyalty. Indeed, so loyal was he that he agreed to preside over the Court of Honour which mercilessly examined the officers implicated in the 20th July plot against Hitler. Perhaps, it would have been better for Rundstedt had his dismissal in December 1941 been final because thereafter he was employed merely for his reputation as a focus for loyalty to the régime and an inspiration to continued resistance.

Douglas MacArthur would certainly receive the accolade of 'superstar' in any constellation of 20th century military commanders, but his reputation – and spectacular fall – are now inseparably linked with the Korean War. MacArthur, however, was hardly a failure in that war within the scope of this volume, so it seemed more interesting for Duncan Anderson to concentrate instead on the loss of the Philippines in 1942, for which he could more justly be criticised. Anderson shows how growing criticism in the later 1940's of MacArthur's role in the loss of the Philippines was stifled by the Korean war, only to revive with a new generation of scholars in the 1970's.

The new charges add up to a serious indictment, including as they do: failure to raise and train an effective native army; failure to appreciate the nature and seriousness of the Japanese threat; and failure to respond effectively when the invasion occurred. Whereas in early 1942 MacArthur seemed to be the only American general whose reputation had survived, or even been enhanced by, the initial Japanese conquests, his new critics would relegate him to 'failed actor. No better than Kimmel or Short'. In the eyes of these critics, MacArthur now 'looks less like a star than a supernova, a blaze of light without substance'.

Anderson finds this recent clutch of criticism uneven and unsatisfactory. MacArthur is blamed for aspects over which he had no control, such as the effectiveness of the Philippine Army, or changes in American policy towards Japan in general and the defence of the Philippines in particular. On the other hand he has been exonerated from failures for which he *was* personally responsible, such as the collapse of the logistical and administrative system in Bataan, and the plummeting morale of the troops there which was not helped by their commander's seclusion on Corregidor (hence the nick-name Dug-out Doug).

MacArthur concealed his inept handling of the defence of Bataan by a skilfully orchestrated press campaign, described as 'exciting, vivid and often wholly imaginary accounts of the campaign in which MacArthur was always accepted as a military genius, thwarting again and again Japan's evil designs'.

The resultant 'MacArthur-mania' in the United States made it impossible for the Joint Chiefs of Staff to leave the general to his fate on Corregidor. MacArthur ignored Marshall's orders to leave and attempted to dictate American strategy in the Pacific with a view to concentration on the speedy relief of the Philippines at the expense of other commitments. Eventually he received a direct order from the President to quit Corregidor for Melbourne where he would assume command of a new South-West Pacific theatre. This was 'one of the few orders MacArthur ever obeyed'.

Mutaguchi's 'star' ranking in the Japanese Army was confirmed by the exploits of his 18th Division in the conquest of Malaya. Promoted to the command of 15th Army in Burma in March 1943, he was inspired by Wingate's first raid into Japanese-occupied territory that year to contemplate an offensive through Assam into north-east India. As Louis Allen explains in his excellent contribution, based mainly on Japanese sources, higher Japanese headquarters were dubious about, if not downright opposed to, Mutaguchi's megalomaniac ambitions, but they allowed political considerations to overcome their well-founded logistical doubts, his trump card being the assumed revolutionary consequences of establishing Subhas Chandra Bose's National Army within India's borders.

Mutaguchi's was a classical case of hubris, albeit without the positive virtues to elicit sympathy. He ruthlessly overrode opposition and launched the campaign despite horrendous logistical problems, inadequate air support and faulty intelligence about the British reserves and their capacity to move them. Above all, he underestimated the enemy: he expected the British to cave in when surrounded, as they had done previously, thus making their supplies available for a drive into India. His reluctance to admit to this fundamental error caused the virtual annihilation of his army, around Imphal and in one of the most appalling retreats of the whole war. Mutaguchi and most of the other surviving Generals were dismissed in disgrace.

Not the least interesting aspect of Allen's essay is the post-war aftermath in which Mutaguchi tried to pass responsibility for failure on to Sato (31st Division) and Kawabe (GOC in Rangoon). Slim and the other British commanders thought at the time that the Japanese had missed a good opportunity to take Dimapur and hence to gain access to the rail link to India. Sato had indeed been insubordinate in failing to press on to Dimapur, but on a wider view Mutaguchi had paid the price of poor relations with all his divisional commanders, none of whom had any faith in his grandiose plan and were not above paying him out for earlier humiliations at his hands.

There was an ironic consequence. But for Wingate's first expedition it is doubtful if even Mutaguchi would have dared to attempt the invasion of India, given the daunting terrain and lack of supplies and air cover. However, Mutaguchi's complete failure and the obvious exhaustion of his overstretched divisions at the end of the battle for Imphal caused Slim to undertake what had previously seemed impossible: the reconquest of Burma from north to south by an overland campaign.

In the brief space available, it has only been possible to indicate a few points of special interest in each of these eleven case studies in twentieth century military failure. Readers may perhaps be stimulated to develop the comparisons and contrasts which have only been touched on in passing, or indeed to investigate the circumstances in which other military stars were dimmed in earlier wars. While a few individual failures – like Samsonov's – may be absolute and unmitigated, these case studies demonstrate that a longer perspective and fresh evidence (as with Hubert Gough) can put the assumed failure in a much better light. In other examples, such as that of Gamelin, the cooling of partisan fervour enables scholars to show that 'their' General has received a disproportionate share of the blame. These concluding remarks are not intended to encourage a new cult of military failures as a modern counterpart to the numerous traditional volumes of 'The Great Captains', but further studies on these lines would at least test the validity of the adage that more can be learned from defeat than from victory.

BRIAN BOND

King's College
London
March 1991

1

Samsonov and the Battle of Tannenberg, 1914

Richard W. Harrison

After more than 75 years, the events surrounding the Battle of Tannenberg continue to intrigue the military expert and layman alike. Like Waterloo, the disaster which befell General Samsonov's Second Russian Army in East Prussia has come to be regarded as the apotheosis of military defeat. This chapter examines the military and other factors which led to the Russian debacle and, in particular, the role which Samsonov's own personality played in these events.

Alesksandr Vasil'evich Samsonov was born on 14 November 1859, in Russian Central Asia. He began his military career in 1877 and saw service with a cavalry regiment in the Russo-Turkish War of 1877–78. Samsonov passed out of the General Staff Academy in 1884 and, for the next 20 years, he occupied a series of staff, command and educational posts throughout the empire. During the brief but disastrous war with Japan in 1904–05, he served with distinction in Manchuria, first as a cavalry brigade commander and then as commander of a Cossack cavalry division. In 1906, Samsonov was appointed Chief of Staff of the vital Warsaw Military District and a year later, was created *ataman* (chief) of the Don Cossacks. From 1909, he was simultaneously Governor-General of Turkestan and commander of the Turkestan Military District. The outbreak of war in 1914 found him on sick leave in the Crimea, where he was recuperating from a chronic asthmatic condition.

By all accounts, Samsonov was very much a 'soldier's General', well-regarded by his men and solicitous of their welfare. He was known for his personal courage under fire and preferred to direct his troops 'from the saddle', rather than from headquarters. For all his fine personal qualities, however, there is considerable doubt as to whether Samsonov's military skills in 1914 were equal to the task at hand. It had been nearly 10 years since he had commanded so much as a division in action, and he had spent

the ensuing time entirely on administrative assignments, remote from the
great changes taking place in military affairs. A British observer attached to
Samsonov's army at the beginning of the war had many of the same doubts.
He concluded that the General's career since the Russo-Japanese War had
been 'a poor preparation for the command of a large army in modern war'.[1]
What appears to have been an overall decline in his military prowess may
be linked to Samsonov's deteriorating health. One officer who saw him at a
1913 review described him as a 'human ruin'.[2]

Whatever the state of Samsonov's military skills, it should be borne in
mind that he was still only a part, albeit an important one, of a much larger
military machine with a bureaucratic life of its own. This giant apparatus
was in turn guided by a number of political and military imperatives which
determined to a significant degree the character and outcome of the Russian
invasion of East Prussia.

The central question facing Russia's military planners during the quarter-
century before 1914 was: in the event of war, should the army make its main
effort against Austria-Hungary or Germany? A number of political developments had made it almost inevitable that she would have to fight both her
neighbours simultaneously. This strategic dilemma remained a feature of
most Russian mobilisation plans right up to the beginning of the war, as the
locus of effort shifted first from one potential enemy to another. The final
prewar plan, adopted in 1912, contained two variants: Plan 'A' foresaw the
main effort against Austria-Hungary, while Plan 'G' posited Germany as
the chief enemy. Actual mobilisation in 1914 was carried out according to
Plan 'A'. In battlefield terms, this meant that instead of three armies being
directed against Germany, as called for in Plan 'G', there would now be
only two. By seeking to defeat both enemies simultaneously, the Russian
command fatally weakened the attack against Germany, which was universally recognized as the greater threat. This decision was to have disastrous
consequences for Samsonov and the Second Army.

Another serious impediment to the Russian effort was the slowness of the
country's mobilisation in the event of war. Since 1871, most European
nations had sought to emulate, to some degree, the Prussian system of a
cadre army backed by a large pool of trained reservists. The latter would be
called up upon the outbreak of war to swell the size of the regular army
enormously within a few weeks. However, mobilisation schedules varied
considerably from one country to another, and the pace of the Russian
mobilisation was by far the slowest of the major powers. While Germany
and Austria-Hungary could mobilise the bulk of their forces in about two
weeks, the Russians needed at least four, with some units taking even
longer.[3] However, the knowledge of these structural weaknesses did not
prevent General Ya G Zhilinskii, the Russian Chief of Staff, from rashly
promising his French counterpart in 1913 to put 800,000 men in the field
against Germany by the 15th day of mobilisation. Such a figure was far

beyond the Russians' capabilities and could only complicate the country's delicate mobilisation schedule at the moment of its greatest weakness.

Immediately upon the outbreak of war, the Russian deployment proceeded against its enemies in the form of two *fronts*, or army groups. The front was an organisational development designed as an intermediate command level between the field armies and supreme headquarters (*Stavka*). General N I Ivanov's Southwestern Front (Third, Fourth, Fifth and Eighth Armies) was directed against the Austro-Hungarian forces massing in Galicia, while General Zhilinskii's Northwestern Front (First and Second Armies) was charged with the task of clearing the Germans from their East Prussian stronghold and advancing on Berlin. Nominal control was exercised by Grand Duke Nikolai Nikolaevich, who as Supreme Commander-in-Chief had the thankless job of coordinating these scattered forces along a 1,400-kilometre front.

Commander-in-Chief Zhilinskii had only recently achieved the army's higher ranks after a career spent in various command and staff positions. In 1911, he had been suddenly elevated to the post of Army Chief of Staff, in which capacity he had made the irresponsible commitment to speed up the Russian mobilisation. He then served for a few months as Governor-General of Warsaw and Commander of the Warsaw Military District, before assuming command of the front. A coarse and bullying taskmaster, he was known in the general staff apparatus as 'the living corpse'.[4] A fellow officer later complained that Zhilinskii's abilities did not qualify him for the post of front commander – an estimation which was entirely confirmed by events.[5]

General P K von Rennenkampf commanded the First Army. A Baltic German by birth, he had spent a good deal of time in the Far East, where he had helped to suppress the Boxer Rebellion in China. He afterwards commanded a cavalry division and an army corps during the Russo-Japanese War, during which his alleged enmity with Samsonov is supposed to have begun.[6] In 1907, Rennenkampf was appointed Governor-General of Vilna (Vilnius) and commander of the Vilna Military District, and served there until the beginning of the war. A cavalry commander who served under him praised Rennenkampf as 'a soldier of exceptional energy, determination, courage and military capability', while at the same time hinting darkly that his 'moral reputation was considerably damaged'.[7]

Acting on instructions from *Stavka*, on 13 August Zhilinskii set forth his ideas for the front's advance into East Prussia. The First Army was to move from its assembly area along the middle Neman River into German territory north of the Masurian Lakes in order to turn the German left flank in the Insterburg area and isolate it from the fortress of Konigsberg. Samsonov's Second Army was to advance simultaneously northward from the middle Narew River to the west of the lakes, in the general direction of Rudczany-Rastenburg. It was assumed that once the Germans were sufficiently engaged with Rennenkampf, Samsonov would strike them in the rear and flank and cut off their retreat across the lower Vistula. The Russians would have a total of 19 infantry and 8½ cavalry divisions for the operation, backed by 1,194 guns, of which only 12, however, were of the heavy type. Facing them was the Eighth German Army, numbering 13 infantry and one cavalry divisions and 1,044 guns, of which 39 were heavy.[8]

Upon closer examination, however, the Russian advantage becomes more apparent than real. For example, while nearly all the German soldiers were literate and technically proficient to some degree, the mass of Russian recruits was still drawn from an illiterate peasantry with almost no technical skills. This created obvious problems for an army which sought to wage a modern war. Also, Russian units tended to be somewhat 'lighter' than their German counterparts, with a two-division Russian corps having only 108 guns, including 12 howitzers, while the same German formation could muster 160 guns, including 52 howitzers.[9] Moreover, in spite of the Russian soldier's reputation for endurance, it was calculated that a Russian corps could march only about 15–20 kilometres a day – and that with some difficulty, while a German corps could cover up to 30 kilometres per day for several days at a time.[10] The combination of these factors meant that in a war in which modern means of communication, firepower and the ability to manoeuvre rapidly were at a premium, the Russians would be at a distinct disadvantage.

Still, on the face of it, the Russian plan for the invasion of East Prussia was logically sound, given the configuration of the frontier and the Russians' quantitative superiority. However, there were a number of difficulties which rendered the success of such a move highly problematical.

Among the most serious were the numerous dislocations caused by the hurried Russian mobilisation. According to Plan 'A', First Army would only reach 50 per cent of its authorised strength by the 15th day of mobilisation, and Second Army 75 per cent by the same date; neither army was scheduled to reach full strength until the 36th and 40th days respectively.[11] The haste with which these armies were thrown into the offensive inevitably affected the ability of their supply and communications services to maintain an advance. As will be seen, the consequences of this fateful move were not long in revealing themselves.

The Russians would also be advancing into a hostile country to which the Germans had done everything they could to make it more defensible. Even the terrain seemed to conspire against an invader and created a number of natural obstacles to an advance. Chief among these was the line of the Masurian Lakes, stretching nearly 70 kilometres from Angerburg to Johannisburg. The few defiles between the lakes could easily be blocked by small forces based on such fortified towns as Lötzen. Even more important from the defender's point of view, the lake system had the effect of dividing any advance into East Prussia from the east and south into non-supporting halves, which enabled the defender to engage each attacker in detail.

Furthermore, whereas earlier Russian fears of a German advance on Warsaw had caused them to neglect their rail communications in northern Poland deliberately, the Germans had spent years developing their trans-Vistula rail system to meet just the sort of Russian offensive now being undertaken. Their east–west rail net was especially well-developed and allowed the Germans to shift forces rapidly from one front to another, as the situation demanded.

The Germans were well aware of the advantages which their interior lines gave them and had spent years preparing for just such an eventuality; they had been conducting war games in East Prussia, based on the assumption of a two-pronged Russian invasion. In three of these exercises (1905, 1907, 1913), the Germans elected to fight a holding action against the Russian 'Neman' (First) Army, while throwing up to 4/5 of their forces against the 'Narew' (Second) Army. In all three exercises the 'Narew' Army was surrounded and destroyed. The results of these exercises eventually became known to the Russians in prophetic detail, although the responsible commanders did nothing to prepare for such an eventuality.[12]

Finally, Samsonov also had the immense burden of being new to the job and unfamiliar with the Russian plan and the forces under his command. Zhilinskii had only made matters worse by taking the best officers with him when he left Warsaw for front headquarters, leaving Samsonov with mediocrities like General P I Postovskii as his Chief of Staff.[13]

The Russian invasion of East Prussia began on 12 August when the First Army's leading cavalry units crossed the frontier. These were followed by the main body on the 17th in the general direction of Insterburg. Rennenkampf was opposed by General von Prittwitz's Eighth Army, numbering three corps and other units, while another corps remained at Ortelsburg to watch for the arrival of the Second Army. The latter, meanwhile, was struggling to reach the frontier along a broad front stretching from Augustow to Novogeorgievsk. Some of Samsonov's scattered units (I, II, VI, XIII, XV and XXIII corps, three cavalry divisions and an infantry brigade) had to advance more than 100 kilometres to reach the border.

The army's march was fraught with every kind of difficulty imaginable. The rear services were in a state of chaos from the very beginning, because the army had moved out before it was fully concentrated. In many cases field kitchens failed to arrive and some divisions lacked organic transport. The supply situation of XXIII Corps was so bad that it could only be maintained through the other corps' rear services, which in turn increased further the strain on them. Communications were no better, and everywhere there was a lack of trained personnel and equipment.

The march to the front was conducted in stifling heat over sandy roads, which quickly exhausted men and animals alike. The virtual collapse of the army's supply service meant that many units did not eat for days at a time. These conditions would have sorely tried the best troops, but were particularly onerous for the reservists who had only recently arrived from their peacetime occupations. General-Lieutenant N A Kliuev claimed that 60 per cent of his XIII Corps consisted of newly-arrived reservists and that company officers were in short supply. He saw that time was needed to turn these 'dressed-up peasants' into real soldiers, and tried to convince Samsonov of the necessity of conducting an 'unhurried offensive', which would allow the army to put its supply situation in order.[14]

As much as Samsonov might have wished this, he had no choice but to adhere to Zhilinskii's rigorous timetable for the advance. Second Army was already behind schedule, even though its corps were making forced marches over the terrible roads of over 20 kilometres per day.[15] However, these efforts did little to satisfy the front commander, who remained blind to his subordinate's difficulties. He chided Samsonov in an 18 August telegram, charging that the latter's delay was putting First Army in a 'difficult position'. Samsonov replied that he could go no faster, and promised to cross the frontier on the 20th.[16]

The two Generals were also at loggerheads over the direction of the army's advance. Zhilinskii's original orders had directed the army almost due north for a speedy junction with Rennenkampf. However, Samsonov reoriented the axis of the army's advance significantly to the north-west, in the direction of Osterode and Allenstein. He evidently believed that a flanking movement by Second Army through Rastenburg would be too shallow to cut off the Germans' retreat, which explains his preference for a deeper and more westerly advance. In this regard, he was undoubtedly right, as Zhilinskii's cautious approach had little chance of cutting off the Germans. Unfortunately, Samsonov's otherwise intelligent decision had the effect of spreading his army along too broad a front and increasing the distance between the Russian armies, which gave the Germans more time and space to operate against one or the other. Samsonov's show of independence was also the beginning of a protracted wrangle with Zhilinskii over which direction the army should take, and only served to deepen their mutual distrust at a time when close coordination and understanding were essential.

Meanwhile, the Germans were preparing to meet Rennenkampf's advance. Von Prittwitz had deployed his army along the Angerapp River in expectation of fighting the battle there; but General von Francois, the independent-minded commander of the German I Corps, moved forward on the 17th and engaged the Russians at Stalluponen. The battle was indecisive, however, and the Germans soon broke off the action. The fighting resumed around Gumbinnen on the 20th, and at first all went well for the Germans. Their I Corps and von Below's I Reserve Corps made good progress against the Russians' flanks north and south of the town, but frontal attacks by von Mackensen's XVII Corps quickly broke down and the German centre was thrown back with heavy casualties. Despite this setback, the Russians had been roughly handled and the Germans looked with confidence to renewing the battle the next day.

That very evening, however, von Prittwitz received a message from General von Scholtz, commanding the German XX Corps at Ortelsburg, that Second Army had begun crossing the frontier near Soldau. Although he had daily expected news of Samsonov's arrival, the Russians' appearance in strength so far west so completely unnerved the German commander that he immediately gave orders to retire *behind* the Vistula, to avoid being cut off. He soon countermanded the move at the urging of his staff and instead ordered part of his army to concentrate against Samsonov's left flank. Von Scholtz was accordingly ordered to take up position in the Hohenstein area to delay the Russian advance, while von Francois' I Corps and an infantry division were to entrain immediately for the south-west. It should be noted that at this stage there is no evidence of a plan to encircle the Russian Second Army, as the additional forces necessary for such a manoeuvre – I Reserve and XVII corps – were not included in the planned movement. For the time being, these formations were merely ordered to fall back as part of a general withdrawal, with their future employment contingent on Rennenkampf's movements.

For von Prittwitz, his momentary loss of nerve spelled the end of his tenure as Army Commander. No sooner did General von Moltke, the German Chief of Staff, learn of von Prittwitz's intention to abandon the sacred soil of East Prussia to the invader than he relieved both the Army Commander and his Chief of Staff. General Paul von Hindenburg was called out of retirement to take command of the Eighth Army, and Major-General Erich Ludendorff, the hero of Liège, was brought from the west as his Chief of Staff. Even before his arrival, the energetic Ludendorff set about issuing orders for the army's redeployment, which were identical to the ones already issued by the outgoing army command.

Meanwhile, the Russian Second Army continued its stumbling progress across the frontier, an exhausted and hungry mass, hardly worthy of the name. By the end of 21 August its VI Corps was approaching Ortelsburg, while most of the remainder of the army was still south of the frontier, as Samsonov obstinately continued to push his army to the north-west. The Russians had thus far encountered almost no resistance, and the German observation aircraft which shadowed the army's advance were almost the only indication of the enemy. Second Army's intelligence of the Germans' whereabouts, however, was in as poor a state as the rest of its services. The army's corps lacked organic cavalry for reconnaissance and the vaunted Cossacks were completely useless as gatherers of information.

The first serious fighting between the two armies took place on the 23rd, when the Russian XV Corps (General N N Martos) collided with the left flank of the German XX Corps in the Orlau-Frankenau area. The Russian corps suffered heavy casualties and had to call on XIII Corps for assistance.

This had the effect of pulling the latter sharply to the west and opening a gap between it and General A A Blagoveshchenskii's VI Corps near Ortelsburg. The additional pressure did, however, cause the Germans to pull back that evening to a more defensible position to await the arrival of reinforcements. These were only just beginning to trickle in, as the first elements of I Corps began to take up position west of Usdau. Both I Reserve and XVII German Corps meanwhile had been able to break contact with First Army and set out by forced marches towards the Seeburg-Bischoftein area on the morning of the 25th. For the time being, however, XX Corps would have to bear the weight of the Russian attack alone.

The Germans' redeployment was immensely aided by Rennenkampf's dilatory actions following the battle of Gumbinnen. The Germans were astounded by his failure to follow up, and in fact, First Army did not move significantly until the 23rd. Rennenkampf's sluggish response to the changing situation gave the defenders the opportunity they needed to turn the bulk of their forces against Samsonov without worrying unduly about being attacked from the rear. One German staff officer attributed Rennenkampf's slowness to the latter's alleged dislike of Samsonov, dating back to their service in Manchuria. 'I cannot rid myself of the impression', he wrote, 'that I mentioned to General Ludendorff at the time, that General Rennenkampf did not want to help General Samsonoff', although he refused to believe that Rennenkampf knowingly sought the latter's destruction.[17] Whatever the truth behind the story, it certainly seemed to have influenced the Germans' actions during these critical days and to have given their command the confidence necessary to carry out its risky manoeuvre.

Samsonov did not learn of the fighting around Orlau until late on the morning of the 24th, due to the poor communications between the corps and Army Headquarters. The minor German withdrawal at the close of the action made a strong impression, however, and seemed to confirm intelligence reports from Front Headquarters regarding the small forces facing him. Samsonov accordingly issued orders for a continuation of the advance to the northwest, this time with Zhilinskii's reluctant approval. XIII and XV Corps would advance on Allenstein and Osterode, while General L K Artamonov's I Corps, subordinated directly to Zhilinskii, would remain in the Soldau area to guard the army's left flank. General K A Kondratovich's XXIII Corps (a single infantry division) would cover I Corps on the right, while VI Corps was to advance to the Bischofsburg-Sensburg area. This unfortunate compromise between Samsonov's and Zhilinskii's conflicting plans merely served to widen the existing gap between VI and XIII Corps to a distance of nearly 40 kilometres, effectively cutting off the former from the army's main body.

The order was sent out over the wireless in the clear and was immediately intercepted by the Germans, and was made known to Army Headquarters

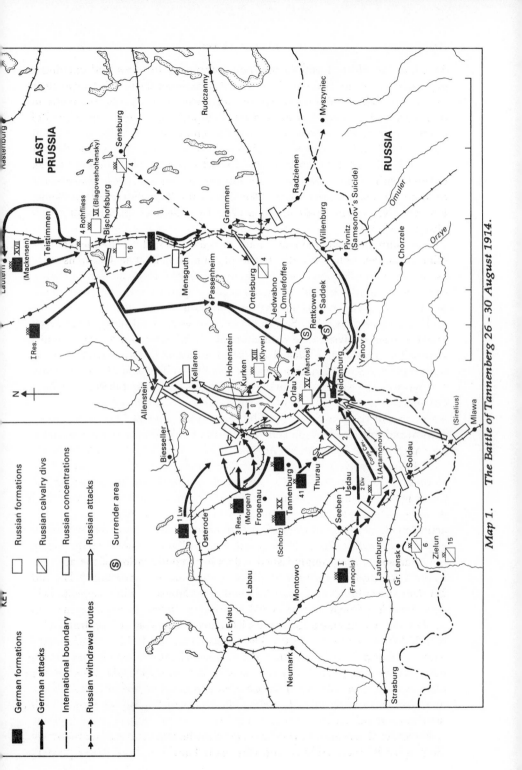

Map 1.   The Battle of Tannenberg 26 - 30 August 1914.

KEY

German formations

□ Russian formations

German attacks

⬚ Russian cavalry divs

International boundary

⬚ Russian concentrations

Russian withdrawal routes

⬚ Russian attacks

Ⓢ Surrender area

EAST PRUSSIA

RUSSIA

N

Kastenburg

Sensburg

Rudczanny

Myszyniec

Radzienen

Grammen

Willenburg

Pivnitz (Samsonov's Suicide)

Chorzele

Omuler

Orzye

4 Rothfliess

Teistimmen

XVII (Mackensen)

Lauern

Bischofsburg

VI (Blagoveshohensky)

16

Mensguth

Passenheim

Ortelsburg

4

Jedwabno

L. Omulefoffen

Rettkowen

Saddek

Willenburg

Yanov

Neidenburg

XV (Martos)

Orlau

XI

Kellaren

Hohenstein

Kurken

XIII (Klyver)

Allenstein

Bieseller

I Res.

Usdau

Thurau

41

Tannenberg

XX (Scholtz)

Frogenau

3 Res. (Morgen)

Osterode

1 Lw

Labau

Montowo

Seeben

Corps Cav.

2 Div

1 (Artamonov)

Soldau

Lautenburg

Gr. Lensk

Zielun

6

15

Mlawa

(Sirelius)

Dr. Eylau

Neumark

Strasburg

the next day. This was just one of many valuable messages which the Germans picked up during the operation. Rennenkampf was also broadcasting his limited intentions, which confirmed the Germans' previous estimation of him and must have eased their anxieties considerably.

Samsonov's knowledge was far less concrete. By the evening of the 25th, however, disturbing news was beginning to filter into Army Headquarters regarding the concentration of large German forces in the Lautenburg area (I Corps) and the passage of significant enemy forces through Rastenburg (VI Corps) the previous day. Samsonov was sufficiently disturbed by these reports to dispatch his Quartermaster-General to Front Headquarters to explain his misgivings about continuing the advance. However, Zhilinskii is reported to have cut the envoy short, saying, 'Tell General Samsonov that he is imagining the enemy where there is none. Let General Samsonov show a little more courage, and everything will be alright.'[18] In the face of such a peremptory and insulting reply, Samsonov had no choice but to order a continuation of the advance along the lines already laid down.

The German counter-offensive began on the 26th, although it did not develop as smoothly as the army command had hoped. Their I Corps' effort against the Russian left flank developed slowly due to von Francois' reluctance to begin a major attack until he was ready. The attack was therefore not pushed vigorously and made only slight progress. Further north, a German assault caught the Russians by surprise near Thurau, and the defenders fell back on some disorder. However, General Martos remained unaware of this threat to his left flank and his XV Corps continued northwards, capturing Hohenstein later that day.

The day's heaviest fighting took place far to the north-east, where the German I Reserve and XVII Corps collided with the unsuspecting VI Corps near Bischofsburg. What started as a small engagement, quickly grew in size as the Germans committed increasing numbers of troops; the attackers themselves were close to exhaustion, having marched up to 50 kilometres since the previous day. Towards afternoon, the Russians began to give way, and by evening were in full retreat south towards Ortelsburg. General Blagoveshchenskii himself was caught up in the collapse and did not even notify Samsonov of the disaster until late that same evening. This message, like so many others, failed to arrive in time.

If the German attack against the Russian left on the 26th had been an half-hearted affair, the renewed assault at dawn on the 27th was pushed with deadly earnest. The massed bombardment of the Russian trenches by heavy artillery was particularly effective, so that there was little for the infantry to do but advance through the gaps made in the enemy defence. The Germans took Usdau at midday as the Russian I Corps began to fall apart as much from panic and hunger as from fighting. The bulk of the corps fell back on Soldau, leaving only a thin cavalry screen to contest a German advance on Neidenburg, deep in Second Army's rear.

The German attack in this sector was greatly aided by Artamonov's execrable handling of his I Corps. His notion of command consisted of touring the front in an automobile to make his 'presence' felt, thus ensuring that he saw the battle not as a single entity, but as a series of isolated and disjointed incidents. This probably explains his report to Samsonov that the corps was holding 'like a rock', only an hour before abandoning Usdau.[19] Artamonov also failed to inform Samsonov that his corps had been routed, so that the army commander remained ignorant of the magnitude of the disaster until later in the day. For this singular piece of incompetence, Samsonov relieved Artamonov of his command and replaced him with General-Lieutenant A A Dushkevich.

Both sides undertook to attack the other further north, although neither achieved any noteworthy success. XV Corps's attack against von Scholtz's left made some initial progress, but stiffening German resistance soon brought it to a halt. A projected German attack to turn XV Corps's exposed left flank was called off at the last minute, due to a false report of a Russian breakthrough further north.

VI Corps continued to fall back on the right, although the German pressure on this flank was not so severe. Indeed, so certain was the German Eighth Army command of success in this area that I Reserve Corps was ordered westward to Allenstein, which the Russians had occupied that afternoon. Meanwhile, XVII Corps continued to pursue the disorganised Russians southward. However, the danger of Rennenkampf suddenly debouching in the rear of the German left wing was increasing by the hour and caused their command no end of worry. Units of the Russian First Army had already reached Rastenburg, and cavalry was probing as far west as Heilsburg, although neither Rennenkampf or Zhilinskii seemed aware of the opportunities or the danger.[20]

27 August was the decisive day, when the elements of the eventual Russian defeat finally fell into place. For Samsonov it had been an unrelieved series of catastrophes, the full extent of which he was unaware due to the poor state of his communications and the incompetence of the corps commanders on his flanks. His orders issued late that evening for the following day are evidence of his fatal misunderstanding of the changing situation. Instead of ordering a withdrawal and extricating his troops from the closing trap, or at least halting the advance until the situation on his flanks became clearer, he obstinately persisted in his plans to attack. Kliuev was ordered to march his entire corps westward and, in conjunction with XV Corps, to attack towards Lautenburg in order to destroy von Scholtz's corps and relieve the German pressure on the army's left wing. I and XXIII Corps would continued to hold their positions 'at all costs', and VI Corps was to cover the army's flank in the Passenheim area.[21] By issuing these orders Samsonov effectively sealed the fate of his army.

He needlessly compounded his error the next morning by leaving his headquarters in Neidenburg to take charge of the desperate attack against the German centre. In his last message to Zhilinskii, Samsonov informed the front commander that he was temporarily breaking off communication. Shortly afterwards, he received the news of VI Corps's rout and admitted to the British attaché that the situation was now 'very critical'.[22]

Even this belated piece of enlightenment did not deter Samsonov from his idea of retrieving the situation by attacking the German centre, even though it was by now obvious that the threat lay on the flanks. It would appear that Samsonov, utterly at sea in a rapidly changing situation, adopted this reckless course out of sheer stubborn despair, when the proper action would have been immediately to order the army's withdrawal. Now revealed as unsuited for the position of army commander, Samsonov reverted to the role he understood best – that of the Cossack cavalry commander at the head of his men.

At Front Headquarters in Bialystok, the scales had suddenly fallen from Zhilinskii's eyes as well, and he began to act with unaccustomed energy. He immediately dispatched an order to Samsonov to pull his forces back to the line Ortelsburg–Mlawa, but Samsonov was already out of reach and never received the message. Zhilinskii also ordered Rennenkampf to 'render assistance' to Second Army by advancing his left flank to Bischofsburg,[23] although by now these measures were a case of too little, too late.

All along the front, the Germans were moving in for the kill. That same morning, part of von Francois's corps ejected the feeble Russian rearguard from Soldau and these quickly fell back to join the rest of Dushkevich's I Corps streaming towards Mlawa. The main body of Germans pressed on towards Neidenburg and routed the defenders after a brief fight. General Kondratovich (XXIII Corps) became separated from his men during the battle and was only located the next day south of Mlawa, for which he too was relieved of his command. By the end of the day, the Germans were well in the Russian rear at Muschaken.

Samsonov's cherished attack against the German centre never really got under way, and by the time he reached Martos's headquarters at Nadrau the Russians themselves were being hard pressed by the German XX Corps. At first, the Russians held their ground, inflicting heavy losses on the attackers and taking a number of prisoners; but by late afternoon, the defenders began to give way under the weight of the German assault, which included a newly-arrived division from northern Germany. Only towards evening did Samsonov give in to Martos's entreaties to order a withdrawal, although he had rejected the idea only a few hours before. Unfortunately, Samsonov specified that XV Corps should retreat through Neidenburg, unaware that the Germans had captured it earlier in the day.

I Reserve and XVII German corps were also moving to close the trap to the east, although a communications breakdown hindered their full coordination with each other and the army's western wing. Klieuv's XIII Corps had left Allenstein early on the 28th to link up with Martos in the area of Hohenstein for the attack on the German centre. The Germans arrived soon afterwards and quickly overwhelmed the small rearguard. They then set out in pursuit, but faulty march orders and spirited Russian resistance prevented von Below from bringing his full force to bear on the Russian rear. Nevertheless, Kliuev's position here was critical, and by the time he received Samsonov's withdrawal order around midnight, his XIII Corps was hemmed in on three sides, with only the Schwederich defile to the south remaining open. To the east, following a confused day of marching and countermarching, the main body of von Mackensen's corps had occupied the Passenheim gap deep in the Russian rear. Smaller detachments watched the Russians near Ortelsburg, although VI Corps remained disorganised and made no effort to attack.

From this point, the story of Second Army's final collapse is quickly told. A retreat under the circumstances described would have been exceedingly difficult in any event, but was certainly beyond the strength of men who were already disoriented by exhaustion, hunger and defeat. XV Corps began falling back on the evening of the 28th. Unfortunately, General Martos quickly became separated from the main body and was taken prisoner, depriving the Russians of their best commander at a critical moment. The retreat continued without him and became increasingly confused as units and their supply columns became entangled on the narrow forest roads. Fighting even broke out accidentally between units of XV and XIII Corps as they passed through Kummusin on the night of 29–30 August. XV Corps pressed on until it collided with the German screen north of Muschaken and was halted. Unable to break through, the main body, it turned east until it was hemmed in and forced to surrender near Rettkowen on the 30th.

XIII Corps at first had an easier time of it, although it had a good deal further to march. The troops successfully negotiated the passage between the lakes and by the evening of the 29th had reached Jablonken. After the accidental encounter with XV Corps, Kliuev divided what remained of his corps into three columns and continued south. These attempted to break out of the Kaltenborn forest, but were repeatedly halted by German machine gun detachments guarding the exits from the woods. By the afternoon of the 30th, the Russians could do no more, and one by one the columns surrendered. By the close of the following day, most of the other units remaining in the pocket had been rounded up as well.

In all, 2½ corps (1st, 2nd, 6th, 8th and 36th infantry divisions), or about half of Samsonov's army, were killed, wounded or captured in the pocket. One German source puts the number of prisoners as high as 92,000.[24] As many as 10,500 officers and men did succeed in breaking through the German ring and rejoining their units.[25]

Even more might have escaped had the belated efforts at relief by I and

VI corps been better coordinated and more vigorously pursued. A relief
column under General-Lieutenant L O Sirelius set out from Mlawa for
Neidenburg on the evening of the 29th. I Corps's unexpected burst of
activity took the small German garrison there by surprise and the Russians
succeeded in recapturing the town on the afternoon of the 30th. This small
victory ultimately came to naught, however, as Zhilinskii ordered Sirelius to
pull his forces back to Mlawa the next day. The situation was much the
same in VI Corps, which remained inactive south-east of Ortelsburg in
spite of Samsonov's instructions to proceed to Passenheim. Blagoveshchenskii did not move until he received an order from Front Headquarters
on the morning of the 30th, which instructed him to advance on Willenburg
and make contact with Samsonov. That day the corps advanced as far as
Radzienen, before receiving Zhilinskii's order that evening to break off the
action and fall back across the frontier. This ineffectual sortie was a fitting
end to the Russian conduct of the battle.

What remained of the Russian Second Army retreated across the border
to the line of the Narew River, where General S M Sheideman took over
from the distraught Postovskii. The army was now so demoralised and
reduced in strength that when the Germans turned against Rennenkampf in
early September, it could only stand by and watch impotently as another
Russian army was defeated.

As the Russian corps within the pocket entered upon their final agony,
one tragedy still remained to be played out – Samsonov's. After leaving
Martos's headquarters on the evening of the 28th, Samsonov and his staff
set off on horseback in search of VI Corps. An officer who encountered him
the next morning describes a man already on the verge of physical and
moral collapse. The general's condition was such that he had to be helped
on and off his horse, and at times his mind wandered.[26] The party remained
at Orlau until midday before pressing on to the south. However, movement
was becoming increasingly difficult because of the German patrols roaming
throughout the shrinking pocket. At one point Samsonov's group tried to
break through the enemy cordon, but was turned back. After this incident,
his Cossack guards gradually slipped away, leaving the general and his staff
to fend for themselves. Samsonov was by this time an utterly broken man
and was only dissuaded from committing suicide by the strenuous objections of the other officers. With the coming of night, the party had to
proceed on foot, as their mounts could no longer negotiate the narrow and
marshy forest paths. The exertion only aggravated the general's asthmatic
condition, and the group had to halt repeatedly to let him catch his breath.
Sometime after midnight on the 30th, Samsonov managed to slip away from
his men and shot himself southeast of Willenburg. His companions were
unable to locate his body in the darkness and eventually decided to push on
and managed to reach their own lines later that day.

The Germans later found Samsonov's body and buried it near the same site. The general's widow was later allowed to travel to the area, where she identified her husband's body from his personal effects. The body was then returned and interred in the family vault in the village of Akimovka, in southern Ukraine.

The subsequent fate of many of those involved in the Tannenberg debacle was also an unhappy one. Martos and Kliuev spent the remainder of the war in German captivity. Postovskii later received a command assignment and suffered a nervous breakdown. Generals Artamonov, Blagoveschenskii and Kondratovich were all relieved of their commands, and the latter two were dismissed from the service entirely. General-Lieutenant V A Oranovskii, Chief of Staff for the Northwestern Front, received a field command and was murdered by mutinous troops in 1917. Zhilinskii was sacked for his poor handling of the operation and was later dispatched to France as the Russian representative to the Allied Supreme Council. He later joined the White fores at the beginning of the civil war in Russia and died there in 1918. Rennenkampf was also blamed for the East Prussian defeat and was removed from his command in November 1914 because of his poor performance in the Lodz operation. He was arrested by Soviet authorities in southern Russia in late 1917 and executed the following year.

Conversely, Tannenberg elevated Hindenburg and Ludendorff to the status of folk heroes. Within two years they had reached the pinnacle of command and achieved a fame which would outlast the war. Much of their popularity at the time and since was due to the Germans' strenuous attempts to depict Tannenberg as the triumph of Teutonic quality over Slavic quantity. Even the battle's name reflects the propagandist's skilful touch, as the fighting never even reached the village of that name. The German command gave the battle the name of Tannenberg almost as an afterthought, in order to expunge the memory of the Teutonic Knights' defeat by a Polish-Lithuanian force in 1410 near the same site.[27]

Most Western and Soviet accounts of the East Prussian operation tend to portray Samsonov as the innocent victim of events entirely beyond his control and absolve him of much of the blame for the disaster which befell his army. In turn, they hold Zhilinskii and Rennenkampf chiefly responsible for the debacle, while at the same time pointing to the Russian army's myriad systemic defects. There is certainly *some* truth in this charge. Zhilinskii's baleful influence is felt throughout; from his irresponsible pledge to speed up the Russian mobilisation, to his belated and ineffectual efforts to rescue Second Army when it was already too late. His bullying treatment of Samsonov stung the latter's pride and no doubt impelled him to take risks he might otherwise have avoided. The case against Rennenkampf is less clear. Although the pace of his army's advance after 20 August was unforgivably slow, treasonable motives cannot be adduced from this circumstance alone.

However, the serious professional and systemic shortcomings examined here should not blind the reader to Samsonov's grave faults as a commander, however appealing his personal qualities. Three mistakes in particular stand out. The first was Samsonov's blatant disregard of Zhilinskii's instructions prescribing the direction of the army's advance. While it is true that the front commander's plan was too cautious to yield a decisive result, had Samsonov obeyed orders he probably would have saved his army. Disagreeing as he did with Zhilinskii's orders, Samsonov should have had the courage to resign. As it was, his duplicity in pursuing his own course did him no honour and his army untold harm. The second mistake was his 27 August order to his central corps to continue the attack. And while much of the general's previous conduct of the battle may be forgiven due to the army's communications breakdown, Samsonov issued these orders even after the extent of I Corps's rout had become known. Nor did he change his mind the next morning upon learning of the collapse of VI Corps on his right flank, when he could no longer have been in any doubt as to his peril. 27 August was the last day Samsonov could have hoped to extricate his army from the trap, but his perverse insistence on continuing the attack against the German centre doomed it to defeat. Finally, Samsonov's decision on the 28th to leave his command post was irresponsible in the extreme and effectively removed him from contact with front headquarters and his corps at a crucial moment. From this point his already tenuous control of the army collapsed completely, and his individual corps commanders – with the exception of Martos, by no means a brilliant lot – were left to their own devices. While Samsonov's fatalistic ride into oblivion[28] may be understood from an individual point of view, it was a grossly irresponsible act on the part of an army commander charged with the lives of his men.

These actions sealed the fate of Second Army more than any single piece of incompetence by Rennenkampf or Zhilinskii. If Samsonov was ill-served by superiors and subordinates, he ultimately proved himself no better a general than the others. Thus far from being an unwitting victim, Samsonov's downfall can be traced largely to his own serious shortcomings as a commander.

Chapter Notes

1. A. Knox, *With the Russian Army 1914–1917*, Vol. I, p. 60. (Hutchinson & Co., London) (1921).
2. Quoted in P N Bogdanovich, *Vtorzhenie v Vostochnuiu Prussiiu v Avguste 1914 Goda*, p. 41. (Buenos Aires) (1964).
3. According to Plan 'A', the armies on the German and Austro-Hungarian fronts were not scheduled to reach full strength until between the 33rd and 45th days of mobilisation. See A M Zaionchkovskii, *Podgotovka Rossii k Imperialisticheskoi Voine*, pp. 398–99. (Gosudarstvennoe Voennoe Izdatel'stvo, Moscow) (1926).
4. A I Verkhovskii, *Na Trudnom Perevale*, p. 26. (Voennoe Izdatel'stvo, Moscow) (1959).
5. B Gourko, *Memories & Impressions of War and Revolution in Russia 1914–1917*, p. 10. (John Murray, London) (1918).
6. The alleged Rennenkampf-Samsonov feud remains one of the battle's great mysteries, and it seems impossible to determine its validity. Colonel Max Hoffman, First General Staff Officer of the German Eighth Army, tells of a 'venomous interview' between the two at the Mukden rail station, after Samsonov accused Rennenkampf of not coming to his aid during the battle of Liaoyang. However, Hoffman did not actually witness the alleged altercation, and only heard about it later, although it certainly influenced his appreciation of Russian behaviour in August 1914. See his *War Diaries and Other Papers*, Vol. II, p. 41. (Martin Secker, London) (1929). According to a contemporary Russian source, Rennenkampf's dislike of Samsonov was no secret. See Verkhovovskii, p. 27. However, another source states that Rennenkampf was wounded before Liaoyang and did not return to his command until two weeks after the battle, although this account does not exclude the possibility of a later clash between the two men. See J Savant, *Epopée Russe*, p. 263. (Colman-Levy, Paris) (1945). A British historian has recently claimed that Rennenkampf's altercation was actually with another officer, who was probably the cavalry general P I Mischenko. See N Stone, *The Eastern Front 1914–1917*, p. 310, note 19. (Hodder and Stoughton, London) (1975).
7. Gourko, p. 10. By contrast, Samsonov is described as 'morally irreproachable' (p. 11).
8. A M Zaionchkovskii, *Mirovaia Voina 1914–1918*, 2nd ed., pp. 75–76. (Gosudarstvennoe Voennoe Izdatel'stvo, Moscow) (1931). A later Soviet source makes out

the overall Russian advantage to be somewhat less: 250,000 men against 200,000, with the latter having an even greater advantage in heavy artillery. See I I Rostunov, ed; *Istoriia Pervoi Mirovoi Voiny 1914–1918*, vol. I, pp. 250, 252. (Izdatel'stvo 'Nauka', Moscow) (1975).

9. A M Zaionchkovskii, *Mirovaia Voina, Manevrennyi Period 1914–1915 Godov na Russkom (Evropeiskom) Teatre*, p. 21. (Gosudarstvennoe Izdatel'stvo, Moscow-Leningrad) (1929).

10. *Ibid*, p. 24.

11. N N Golovin, *Iz Istorii Kampanii 1914 Goda na Russkom Fronte, Nachalo Voiny i Operatsii v Vostochnoi Prussii*, p. 76. (Izdatel'stvo 'Plamia', Prague) (1926). Hereafter referred to as *Nachalo Voiny*.

12. The story of the German war games and the Russians' prior knowledge of their outcome is confirmed by several Russian sources. See Bogdanovich, pp. 27, 29; also N N Golovin, *Iz Istorii Kampanii 1914 Goda na Russkom Fronte. Plan Voiny*, p. 92 (Paris) (1936). Hoffman (II, p. 23) does not refer to any war games prior to 1914, although he states that the Germans were prepared to throw the bulk of their forces against either Russian army, depending on the situation. General Erich Ludendorff, Eighth Army Chief of Staff during the battle, states that it was not fought according to a preconceived plan, although he was probably referring to the battle itself and not to the overall German approach to the defence of East Prussia. See his *War Memories 1914–1918*, vol. I, p. 47. (Hutchinson & Co., London) (1919).

13. According to Knox (I, p. 69), Postovskii was highly-strung and known in the army as 'the mad Mullah'.

14. A R-P, Prichiny Neudach II Armii Generala Samsonova v Vostochnoi Prussii v Avguste 1914 g. (Po Zapiske Generala Kliueva)'. *Voennyi Sbornik*, Book IV, p. 156. (Belgrade) (1923).

15. Bogdanovich, p. 59.

16. *Sbornik Dokumentov Mirovoi Imperialisticheskoi Voiny na Russkom Fronte (1914–1917 gg.)*. *Vostochno-Prusskaia Operatsiia*, p. 251. (Gosudarstvennoe Voennoe Izdatel'stvo, Moscow) (1939). Samsonov kept his word and crossed the frontier on the evening of the 20th, a day behind schedule.

17. Hoffman, II, pp. 313–14. A later Soviet source supports this thesis, adding that even Zhilinskii could not force Rennenkampf to advance more quickly because of the latter's close ties with the Tsar's mother, Maria Fedorovna. See Verkhovskii, pp. 27–28. However, an emigré source discounts this and blames Rennenkampf's failure to move more quickly on the same supply problems which plagued Samsonov. See Golovin, *Nachalo Voiny*, pp. 164–70.

18. Bogdanovich, p. 105; Verkhovskii, p. 27.

19. Golovin, *Nachalo Voiny*, p. 239. Samsonov's aide at I Corps headquarters had earlier described Artamonov as a liar and his Chief of Staff as 'some kind of cretin'. See *Sbornik Dokumentov*, p. 260.

20. Such was the air of unreality which pervaded Russian headquarters at this time that the battle for East Prussia was considered all but won. In a 26 August memorandum, General-Lieutenant Yu N Danilov, Quartermaster-General of the General Staff, was already thinking in terms of pressing the offensive beyond the Vistula with new armies and making Samsonov Governor-General of occupied East Prussia! See *Sbornik Dokumentov*, pp. 281–82.

21. *Ibid*, p. 296.
22. Knox, I, pp. 73–74.
23. *Sbornik Dokumentov*, p. 302.
24. Hoffman, II, p. 328. An emigré source agrees with this figure, but claims that only 25,000 of those taken prisoner were unwounded. See Golovin, *Nachalo Voiny*, p. 337.
25. Ya K Tsikhovich, ed., *Strategicheskii Ocherk Voiny 1914–1918 gg. Chast' I*, p. 97. (Vysshii Voennyi Redaktsionnyi Sovet, Moscow) (1922).
26. Bogdanovich, pp. 219–22.
27. See Hoffman, (II, p. 312) and Ludendorff (I, p. 57) for their accounts of their decision to name the battle.
28. See Knox (I, p. 74) for Samsonov's attitude on the morning of the 28th.

2

Sir Ian Hamilton
and the Dardanelles, 1915

John Lee

'The poor old chap looked to me very haggard – almost broken up; so were some of the staff . . . I am honestly very sorry to see Hamilton go. He is a gentleman, and has always been courteous and considerate to us. The British Army has never believed in him, but he is a good friend to civilians, and has breadth of mind which the army does not in general possess[1].'

Thus did C E W Bean, the official historian attached to Australia's forces, mark in his personal diary the passing of Lieutenant General Sir Ian Hamilton as Commander-in-Chief, Mediterranean Expeditionary Force in October 1915. Writing in his journal in London, Viscount Esher exclaimed, 'Ian Hamilton has been made the scapegoat in Gallipoli . . . The Government cannot deprive him of the honour of having carried out the most difficult and splendid landing operation ever planned. But they can deprive him of everything else, and they evidently mean to do so[2].'

Hamilton certainly had to carry a great deal of blame at the time for the failure of the Gallipoli campaign, seen by most of his professional contemporaries as an infamous waste of resources. As criticism of the conduct of the fighting on the Western Front mounted between the wars, Hamilton's reputation was briefly enhanced as his effort was seen as the alternative strategy that could have shortened the war by some years. But today he figures largely as an archetypal British bungler in a number of ill-considered and badly written books on 'great military failures' which invariably cite the only book consulted on the campaign, Robert Rhodes James' 1965 publication, *Gallipoli*.

James' problem, in a well-researched and well-written book, is that he belongs to that school of thought that finds the whole campaign pointless to the extent that even if Hamilton had succeeded, he accepts none of the advantages that might have accrued to the Allied cause. While paying respect to Hamilton's experience and professional skills, and commiserating with his difficulties and his sheer bad luck, not least in some of the subordinates foisted upon him, James still makes a harsh judgement on what he calls 'the mystery of his personal failure'. He considers that Hamilton had his chances for success and missed them due to his failure to act properly as a Commander-in-Chief. In the worst excess of criticism he implies that any skilful aspect of planning, either in April or August 1915, were all the work of excellent staff officers to which Hamilton can lay no claim. This simply fails to understand the relationship between a commanding general and his staff in the planning of military operations.

Truly, once a writer has a knife into Sir Ian Hamilton it glides in up to the hilt! A more considerate look at the campaign, and in particular setting its extraordinary origins in the wider context of the war in 1915, will suggest that Hamilton was given an almost impossible task in the first instance, and was subsequently asked to achieve decisive results with wholly inadequate resources at every stage in the proceedings.

In March 1915, Hamilton had been the senior lieutenant general on the Army List and was GOC Home Forces, charged with the defence of the United Kingdom against possible German invasion. He almost certainly hoped for, and might have expected, a more active command after a long and distinguished military career.

This son of a colonel of the Gordon Highlanders had entered the Army just as the purchase of commissions was abolished. He was commissioned into an infantry regiment in 1873 and the following year joined the Gordons in India to begin nearly twenty five years of service life based there. As a particularly intelligent young man, he endured the monotony of the subaltern's life but was soon showing signs of unorthodox tactical thinking and a special interest in rifle shooting, especially after winning an 'extra first' placing at the School of Musketry, Hythe, Kent in 1877. His homeward bound battalion was retained in South Africa in 1881 and he was caught up in the heavy defeat inflicted upon the British by the Boers at Majuba Hill, sustaining a shattering wound to the left wrist from which he never fully recovered.

In 1882 came one of those career moves that have long echoes down the years. Having passed the entrance requirements for the Staff College, Camberley, Hamilton gave up his place to accept an invitation from General Sir Frederick Roberts to rejoin him in India as one of his aides-de-camp. Thus he was drawn into the 'Roberts Ring', the 'Indians', which in the late Victorian and Edwardian Army, where so much still depended on patronage, would open some doors to advancement but see others close quite firmly.

Hamilton continued to combine a wealth of practical experience (he even managed to participate in the 1884–5 Nile expedition, when he should have been on home leave.) with a questing mind and search for improvement in military efficiency. As a captain he wrote a spirited attack on 'army bull' in favour of more practical training in an 1884 publication, 'The Fighting of the Future'. This led to Roberts asking him to initiate the training of the entire Indian Army in improved musketry, which he did with spectacular success. This work was to be consummated when Hamilton was made Commandant of the School of Musketry, Hythe in 1898 and introduced his training to the whole of the British Army. If the infantry of the BEF were made famous in 1914 for handling their rifles like so many machine-guns, the roots of that skill lay in Hamilton's teaching.

In 1890, Hamilton was the youngest colonel in the Army (but only promoted along with the 'Indian' officers, Nicholson and Beresford, after a political row that had to be settled in Cabinet.) To give some idea of his intellectual horizons, he was, as a published poet, giving much helpful advice to Rudyard Kipling, then a new writer looking for a publisher.

His posting at Hythe meant that he was well placed to take command of an infantry brigade in the South African war. He gave distinguished service at Elandslaagte and Ladysmith, and, when his old mentor, Lord 'Bobs', took command he was given an all-arms force to cover the flank of the advance to Pretoria. He would have achieved renown anyway but was made especially popular by the despatches of Winston Spencer Churchill, soon published as 'Ian Hamilton's March'. In his memoirs, Horace Smith-Dorrien leaves us this picture of a general at his very best:

> 'He was a delightful leader to follow, always definite and clear in his instructions, always ready to listen and willing to adopt suggestions, and, what is more important, always ready to go for the enemy and extremely quick at seizing a tactical advantage, and, with it all, always in a good temper[3].'

Hamilton returned from South Africa a lieutenant general, at the side of Lord Kitchener, whose able Chief of Staff he had been. The Elgin Commission was formed to investigate the conduct of the late war, particularly in its more unfortunate early aspects. Hamilton, now Quarter Master General of the British Army, gave full vent to his opinions on the poor showing of sections of the Army and its leadership. In particular, he denounced shock cavalry as an anachronism, and the sword and lance as mere medieval toys. Deep enmities were formed in this period and W G Nicholson, soon to be the first holder of the new post of Chief of the Imperial General Staff, declared that Hamilton 'had a tile loose'.

Despite holding a succession of very important posts in the years up to 1914, including GOC Southern Command and Adjutant General, there remains a sense that Hamilton's career had taken a wrong turn somewhere. He was increasingly shut out of that group of senior commanders forming around Nicholson and French, and providing the leadership of the nascent British Expeditionary Force. It should be noted that twice during this period he turned down opportunities to be the next Commander-in-Chief, India, so he was clearly hoping for a more central role in the Army's future.

His celebrated tour as an observer with the Japanese army during the 1904–05 war in Manchuria saw the production of his two volume *Staff Officer's Scrapbook*, which enhanced his reputation as a deep thinker about the nature of modern way and the problem of getting the infantry across the 'killing zone', though the book also betrays his tendency to yearn for a more chivalric approach to war. It also produced an unfortunate contretemps with King George V, who took grave exception to some typically irreverent remarks Hamilton made about a Japanese aristocrat[4]! It should, perhaps, be pointed out that in that era of a highly conservative military élite, Hamilton was always known as moving in high Liberal circles; one more reason for the hierarchy to keep him at a distance, and, perhaps, this fear of offending the main tendency in the Army prevented a strong Liberal government from advancing 'their man' as far as they might have.

During the period 1910 to 1914, Hamilton was GOC Mediterranean and Inspector General of Overseas Forces, a post created for and refused by Lord Kitchener, who feared it as a backwater. Hamilton used the time to develop his thoughts on war and only the outbreak of the real thing prevented his publication of a remarkable treatise on the nature of armies, which advocated great use of air power, mechanisation, night attacks and many such advanced and innovatory ideas.

He was back in England at the end of July 1914, expecting to succeed to the new and powerful position of Inspector General of all the Forces, home and overseas, through which he would have been able to mould the training and equipment of the Empire's army in its entirety. But even this was to be denied him, as the appointment was switched, with only three days to go, to Sir John French.

The outbreak of war was to change all that. Sir John got the command of the BEF. Hamilton offered to serve under him in any capacity, but was instead appointed to command the Home Defence Force. He asked for the command of II Corps on the sudden death of its commander, Lieutenant General Sir James Grierson, but that went to Sir Horace Smith-Dorrien. Hamilton resigned himself to the task of overseeing the mobilisation and rapid expansion of the Territorial Army, and of preparing the country for defence.

The war that most professionals thought would be violent and short became stalemated, and new and unexpected difficulties had to be overcome. The Western Allies were aware of the great sacrifices made by Tsarist Russia in her efforts to assist the common struggle against the Central Powers in 1914. So, when a plea for help came from the Grand Duke Nicholas, for an allied effort to distract powerful Turkish forces operating against Russia's flank in the Caucasus, there was the strongest sense of moral obligation to spring to Russia's aid.

The Secretary of State for War, Lord Kitchener, was strongly moved by the appeal of 2nd January, 1915, but had no troops available at that time or place. He therefore gave strong backing to the offer by Churchill for a naval demonstration against the Dardanelles, with its implied threat to Constantinople. But this First Lord of the Admiralty, with the world's largest fleet in his hands and military stalemate all around, had other and more ambitious plans. He had proposed immediate action against Turkey back in November 1914 and now, with particularly sanguine hopes about the effect of huge naval guns on the forts protecting the Dardanelles, he asked Vice Admiral Carden, commanding the squadron blockading Turkey, to make his suggestions for passing a fleet into the Sea of Marmora for an attack on Constantinople.

Carden's hypothetical plan for a slow and methodical reduction of the outer and inner forts, and the vital clearing of the minefields, was carried by Churchill to the War Council meeting of 13 January and presented as a low-cost, low-risk method of breaking the deadlock in Europe. That the plan was pushed through so easily, without the real nature of its innumerable problems being aired, illustrates how utterly defective was the higher direction of the war by Britain and her allies at this stage.

There were several naval experts, British and French, predicting that the task was impossible for ships alone. The major General Staff study of the Dardanelles as a military problem, carried out in 1906, had already concluded that an attack by ships alone would be quite useless and that a combined operation would be so hazardous that they were not prepared to recommend it. One of the authors of that report, Sir Charles Callwell, was Director of Military Operations in 1914/15 and still viewed the affair with the greatest degree of scepticism. The point is that none of this expert opinion was received by the politicians charged with conducting the war through the War Council. They heard only the impressive voices of Lord Kitchener, willing enough to let the Navy try it so long as it cost him no troops, and of Churchill, who was desperate for action and whose fertile brain saw huge strategic possibilities.

These possibilities soon began to impress themselves on all the participants. It was hoped that the appearance of a powerful fleet off the Golden Horn would precipitate a political crisis that would take Turkey out of the war. It would secure the intervention of Italy on the side of the Allies and galvanise the whole of the Balkans into a coalition against the Central Powers. It would open a supply line to Russia, releasing her grain to the West in return for badly needed munitions. The tragedy of 1917 makes this Russian aspect of the campaign more poignant. However severe the critics of the Dardanelles campaign, there are few, if any, who deny that if it had been properly conceived and prepared, with resources truly adequate to the task, it was an operation full of prospects and worthy of an attempt.

But instead, what began as a naval demonstration to relieve Russia (rendered unnecessary, as it happened, by the complete defeat of the Turks in the Caucasus), became an order for a naval expedition to bombard and take the Gallipoli peninsula, with Constantinople for an objective. Only then was thought given to whether any troops might be needed to occupy the conquered territory! It was precisely in this mood that the War Council decided in mid-February that some troops would be needed to consolidate the expected success.

The two divisions of the Australia and New Zealand Army Corps (ANZAC) completing their training in Egypt were made available, as was the Royal Naval Division by the Admiralty. Only with extreme reluctance, and more than one change of mind, did Kitchener release from Britain the regulars of the 29th Division, but all these troops were provided only with the proviso that they were auxiliary to the main effort by the Anglo-French fleet.

The greatest single mistake of the campaign was made at this point. 'No one suggested the advisability, now that troops were to be sent, of avoiding the risk of piecemeal attack, and of waiting for a combined operation with all the advantages of surprise. Even the question of ordering the General Staff to work out preliminary plans for the employment of the troops was not discussed. In these omissions lay the root cause of failure'[5].   Instead, the naval attack was begun on 19 February and the outer forts were thoroughly knocked about. Parties of marines and ratings were able to land at Sedd el Bahr and destroy some damaged guns there. The attack would have passed into the Narrows but bad weather delayed further progress. The net result of the attack in that inclement season was to announce our serious interest in the area to the enemy with the greatest clarity.

As Kitchener continued to express his reluctance to commit his troops, Churchill was then arguing that they were absolutely vital to the success of the operation, which they had to see through to a decisive conclusion. This coincided with a reconnaissance report by General Birdwood, the ANZAC commander and Kitchener's preferred choice for chief of the expeditionary force as it was then constituted. Birdwood had accepted the Royal Navy's argument for attacking at Cape Helles, having originally preferred to try cutting the peninsula at the narrow Bulair Isthmus. On 4 March he reported firmly that ships alone would never secure the Narrows and that troops would need to attack and seize the dominant heights at Khilid Bahr.

Kitchener was being drawn inexorably into ever greater commitments against his will. As an added complication, the French hastily assembled a colonial division in North Africa and offered it for service in the Eastern Mediterranean. They appointed the very senior d'Amade to command it (indeed, he expected supreme command for himself) and Birdwood was too junior to lead such an enlarged force. Under these inauspicious circumstances Ian Hamilton was thrust onto centre stage.

Although we know from the society gossip of people like Venetia Stanley and Lady Gwendoline Churchill that Hamilton was expecting this important command from around 4 March, which tells us much about security of

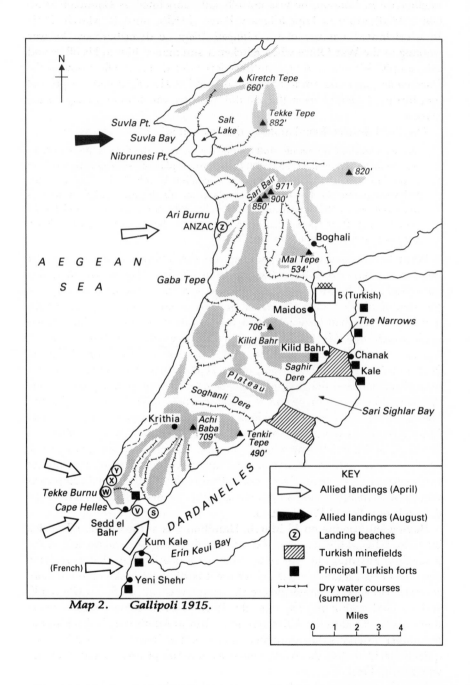

Map 2.   Gallipoli 1915.

N

Kiretch Tepe
660'

Suvla Pt.
Suvla Bay
Nibrunesi Pt.

Salt
Lake

Tekke Tepe
882'

▲ 820'

Sari Bair 971'
         900'
850'

Ari Burnu
ANZAC Ⓩ

Boghali

Mal Tepe
534'

A E G E A N

S E A

Gaba Tepe

XXXX
5 (Turkish)

Maidos

The Narrows

706' ▲

Kilid Bahr

Kilid Bahr

Chanak
Kale

Saghir
Dere

Sari Sighlar Bay

Plateau

Soghanli Dere

Krithia

Achi
Baba
709'

Tenkir
Tepe
490'

Ⓨ
Ⓧ
Ⓦ

Tekke Burnu

Cape Helles

Ⓥ Ⓢ

Sedd el
Bahr

Kum Kale
Erin Keui Bay

(French)

Yeni Shehr

DARDANELLES

KEY

Allied landings (April)

Allied landings (August)

Ⓩ Landing beaches

Turkish minefields

Principal Turkish forts

Dry water courses
(summer)

Miles
0   1   2   3   4

intelligence in London, he was not officially appointed as Commander-in-Chief, Mediterranean Expeditionary Force (MEF), until 12 March, 1915. In a celebrated passage of his *Gallipoli Diary* he describes how he was working at the War Office when Kitchener summoned him to his office and said simply,'We are sending a military force to support the fleet now at the Dardanelles, and you are to have command[6].' If Hamilton had not pressed him further, it would seem that he did not have much more to say on the matter!

The Field Service Regulations of the day stated:

> 'As soon as the Commander-in-Chief of the forces in the field is appointed, he will be furnished by the CIGS with the approved plan of campaign, and with an appreciation of the military situation, including detailed information on the following points: 1) The forces to be placed at his disposal and their state of mobilisation; 2) the armed forces and military resources of allied and hostile powers, with their special characteristics; 3) the theatre of war; 4) any information that may be of use to him[7].'

What he got was a 1912 handbook on the Turkish Army, a woefully inaccurate map and a bare description of his force during which it was impressed upon him that the 29th Division was on temporary loan only. He was denied his own choice of Chief of Staff (what a difference that might have made) and had General Braithwaite thrust upon him. During a briefing in which the DMO, Callwell, referred to Greek plans of attack requiring 150,000 men, Kitchener insisted that half that number would suffice. Hamilton had some 80,000 men; about 50,000 rifles. Kitchener stressed a number of points – that he did not expect large scale military operations; that any attack was to be made with the whole force or not at all; that Hamilton was absolutely forbidden to spread the operations into Asia Minor. With this paucity of information, Hamilton and the nine officers of his General Staff left immediately for the Eastern Mediterranean. The administrative staff would not be fully appointed and in place for another two weeks. It was a style of war reminiscent of the small colonial campaigns that these British officers had grown up with; it was hardly adequate to the demands of a World War in 1915.

Having left London on 13 March, Hamilton was at the island of Tenedos by 17 March and the very next day witnessed the major naval assault on the inner forts guarding the Narrows. What a traumatic event that must have been for British soldiers to see. Three great battleships sunk and three more severely damaged by mines before the attack was called off. To Churchill, and to bold young participants like Roger Keyes, these losses were as nothing compared to the Allied resources. But to Admiral de Robeck and to the soldier observers they were more than could be borne, and together they quickly decided that the Army would assault the peninsula and clear the way for the Fleet.

Now the problems of such an ill-prepared expedition came home to roost.

With no orders as to the exact nature of the task, troopships had been loaded to economise on space and arrived in the theatre of war with units spread over several vessels. The harbour at Mudros had a magnificent natural anchorage but was utterly devoid of port facilities, and the island of Lemnos was deficient in accommodation and water for large numbers of troops. Hamilton and his staff had only been in post for a few days, with no time to study their own resources, let alone those of the enemy.

The one really great advantage of the amphibious power, the ability to descend upon the enemy coast as a shock force, was denied to Hamilton. His force had to steam away to Alexandria to be completely re-organised for action and the Turkish 5th Army, under its new German commander, Liman von Sanders, was left in leisure to prepare itself fully for the obviously impending attack.

Consider the problem facing Sir Ian Hamilton. It should first be stressed that never in human history had his task – an assault landing in the face of an enemy who was prepared and armed with rapid-firing weapons – been attempted. The planning staff had only the 1913 *Manual of Combined Naval and Military Operations* to guide them, which, of course, presumed a very high degree of advanced planning, intelligence gathering and secrecy for this, the ultimate in hazardous operations of war. This lack of secrecy and advanced preparation led such a sober and careful analyst as Colonel Maurice Hankey, Secretary to the War Council, to conclude in a memorandum of 16th March that 'it is conceivable that a serious disaster may occur[8].'

The naval and military planning staffs had to learn their task as they went. The lack of administrative and quartermaster staffs from the very start meant that the headquarters staff did much of their original work for them, not always satisfactorily, as the medical officers discovered when they finally arrived, and this unfortunate division within the staff became a prevalent and increasingly problematic aspect of the campaign. It must be surmised that British generals, so used to improvising in their colonial wars, were not entirely averse to operating with a small personal staff; Hamilton certainly displayed this tendency.

As the force was re-organised in Egypt, many shortcomings were revealed. All the formations were new and largely untried; even the 29th Division was an unrehearsed assembly of overseas garrisons, filled up with reservists, and was denied the usual ten per cent reinforcement allowed divisions proceeding on active service. From the outset there were serious shortages of ammunition, with no reserves for sustained battle. There were shortages of engineers, signals and supplies and materials of every sort.

As the problem of the assault was studied, it became clear that the margin for success was very slim indeed. Although never certain of the enemy strength, Hamilton's staff did identify the six divisions that Liman von Sanders had to defend the coast from Bulair in the north to Besika Bay in Asia Minor. An attack on the narrow Bulair isthmus, much favoured by some of Hamilton's severest critics, was ruled out by the Royal Navy as being too far from their real objective – the forcing of the Narrows – and by the Army because of the strength of the position. We know that von Sanders hoped to receive the attack there and had two divisions in place.

Since Asia Minor was specifically excluded by Kitchener's orders, this left only the Gallipoli peninsula itself, with its extremely restricted number of landing places. Hamilton was determined, again under Kitchener's guide-lines,to throw his whole force ashore as quickly as possible, three divisions in attack and the other two as reinforcement after feinting operations at Bulair, Kum Kale and Besika Bay.

The two ANZAC divisions were to go ashore just north of Gaba Tepe, on a stretch of open beach that led quite quickly to fairly open country. They were to establish themselves across the peninsula and cut off the Khilid Bahr plateau from the north. The 29th Division was given the most difficult task of assaulting the Cape Helles positions, hoping that the powerful guns of the Fleet would allow them to secure a footing on the three narrow beaches available to them.

Despite the problems and the risks, confidence was very high; the Turk was not greatly respected as an opponent; the first day objectives were as ambitious as anything seen on the Western Front. But the outwardly-ebullient Hamilton knew that, with such large enemy forces gathered around Constantinople, the task was far from easy and that more troops would be needed to exploit the expected early success. His diary reveals his acute anxiety at asking for any additional resources at all; every request for men or material was tentative in the extreme. His original instructions from Kitchener had virtually forbidden any such requests; he knew that the 29th Division was 'on loan' and had seen Kitchener take away troops in South Africa from officers who asked for more; lastly, there was an extraordinarily damaging breakdown in communication whereby Hamilton was never informed that Sir John Maxwell, the commander in Egypt, had been ordered to make many more troops available to Hamilton should he need them.

Given the paucity of their resources and the difficulties of organising such a major and novel operation at such short notice, it is customary to give high praise to the planning of the attack. With the wisdom of hindsight, it is very easy to criticise the plan for being too rigid to cope with the extraordi-nary events of 25 and 26 April. Perhaps Sir Ian Hamilton should have refused to attempt such a doomed operation. That was asking too much of a professional officer of the British Empire, called upon in the hour of his country's greatest need to accomplish what could have been a decisive task in the war. As the hour for the attack drew near, all thoughts of failure had to be put aside and the fate of the battle entrusted to the splendid fighting men of the expeditionary force, backed by the most powerful navy in the world.

As it happened, the assault landings on 25 April came as close to complete failure as anyone might have feared, through a combination of bad luck, overconfidence in naval gunnery, some failures in leadership, and a superb performance by the Turkish defenders. In some respects it could have been even worse. The feints built into the overall plan, especially by the Royal Naval Division at Bulair and by the French in Besika Bay, paralysed Liman von Sanders for nearly forty-eight hours, tying down four of his six divisions before he felt able to commit them to the main battle. Given the glare of publicity surrounding the attack, that really was a brilliant achievement.

The first landing, made by the Australian division at dawn, was put ashore nearly a mile further north than it should have been. War is made up of such uncertainties; there is little point in searching for scapegoats to explain such an error. The defences at Gaba Tepe proved to be so powerful that the attackers may have fortuitously avoided a terrible massacre. Instead they were deposited in a thinly-held but utterly unfamiliar area, now famous as Anzac Cove – or more briefly Anzac. Troops landed rapidly in great numbers (15,000 men in twelve hours) and, obedient to their orders, pushed inland as vigorously as they could. The wildly confusing terrain swallowed them up; command and control disintegrated as resistance stiffened and losses, especially amongst battalion officers, mounted. If the wrong landing place was the first piece of bad luck, then the second was that the commander of the 19th Turkish Division had chosen that day to exercise his troops in the vicinity. He was Mustafa Kemal, a commander of genius, who ended the day putting in counter-attacks with slightly more than one division, contained the two attacking divisions within a tight perimeter, forcing them to cling desperately to positions which would change but little for the next three months. In a real crisis of confidence, the Anzac generals discussed whether to evacuate that evening, so badly had things gone wrong. They sought the advice of their Commander-in-Chief. It will always be a matter of conjecture whether they had talked themselves through their crisis before an inspirational message from Sir Ian Hamilton impressed upon them the need to 'dig, dig, dig, until you are safe'.

Such a crisis did not develop at Cape Helles but things went far from well there either. This was the most obvious of all the points of attack and the Turks had prepared their defences very well. The landings were in broad daylight at the insistence of the Royal Navy and, given the failure of the ships' guns to suppress the defenders, the results were nearly disastrous. The point to stress is that the attackers thought something like a full Turkish division was deployed at this end of the peninsula. This helps to explain the reluctance of several bodies of troops to push forward as vigorously as they might have done. Certainly a good opportunity to exploit a highly-successful landing at 'X' beach was not developed; at 'W' beach the 1st Battalion, Lancashire Fusiliers performed incredible feats of gallantry to storm a heavily-wired beach; at 'V' beach the main attack by more than two battalions, with a bold attempt to use the *River Clyde* as an early assault landing ship, was comprehensively defeated with very heavy losses.

The British Army displayed all its magnificent courage and the rigid, inflexibility of its hierarchy that day.

The fiasco at 'Y' beach points up some of the difficulties. It was a brilliant stroke by Hamilton to devise this idea to put two battalions ashore behind the main defences and at an improbably-difficult landing place. These troops got ashore completely unopposed and could, if properly directed, have penetrated to Krithia village or have taken the Cape Helles defences in the rear. But there was an embarrasing confusion over which of the two colonels was in command locally, and the final orders from General Hunter-Weston, GOC 29th Division, implied that the force was only there to prevent Turks moving south until the remainder of the division got ashore and joined them later that day. The force dug in and repelled Turkish counter-attacks but accomplished nothing further. Early next day, the local commander evacuated the position! During the first day, with things going badly elsewhere, Roger Keyes had offered to put more troops ashore at 'Y' beach; Hamilton would have agreed but he had no reserves to hand, and left the decision to the executive commander, Hunter-Weston, who took the advice of Admiral Wemyss against trying to alter the battle plan after it had begun.

This was not a wholly unreasonable consideration for soldiers and sailors operating in such difficult circumstances, in those days before radio communication existed between commanders isolated on great warships and the troops struggling ashore in open boats. It was the military orthodoxy of the day that higher commanders should not interfere with the conduct of battle once joined. Hamilton made the point quite clearly himself: 'A soldier might as well try to correct the aim of his bullet after he has pulled the trigger as a general to handle his attackers once they are "over the top" '[9].

What was Hamilton to do after these early setbacks? He was under instruction from Kitchener to see the business through once it had begun. During 26 April, enemy resistance began to slacken and his forces were better established ashore, especially in the Helles sector. If he had had the ten per cent reinforcement to which 29th Division was entitled, or if he had known that four brigades of infantry in Egypt (42nd Division and 29th Indian Brigade) were earmarked for his use, then possibilities were still great. What he knew for certain was that delay would see large Turkish reinforcements moving into the area now that the plan was exposed in its entirety. The battered and exhausted 29th Division made a hopeless attack on Krithia on 28 April, was easily checked by the Turks, and the trench deadlock set in quickly on all fronts.

Kitchener's worst fears were being realised. From originally agreeing to assist the Navy to occupy Constantinople, he was now committed to major land operations, with all the danger to Britain's eastern empire in the event of a humiliating defeat at the hands of a Moslem foe, and with the united opposition of the rest of the Army committed to fighting the main enemy (Germany) on the main front (France and Flanders).

Adhering to the original objectives of the campaign, the forcing of the Dardanelles by the Fleet, Hamilton made his main effort to secure what was thought to be, erroneously, the key to the Khilid Bahr plateau – the hill of Achi Baba. With hopes raised by the comprehensive defeat of heavy Turkish counter-attacks, he pulled in reinforcements from ANZAC and Egypt, and ordered Hunter-Weston to attack again at Krithia on 6 May. The battle was fought by men who were either exhausted from ten days of uninterrupted effort since the landings or who had been barely twenty four hours on the peninsula; commanded by a general singularly lacking in imagination, who would attack frontally and in broad daylight to avoid the perils of night operations; with an artillery so starved of ammunition as to make its bombardments a mockery; and against an enemy being reinforced steadily, and outnumbering the attackers at every stage of the fighting from start to finish. Three days of attacks ended in complete failure; 6,500 casualties for barely six hundred yards of No Man's Land.

The situation could not continue in this way and Hamilton made it clear to Kitchener that no further progress could be expected with the troops to hand. In one of those rare expressions of outright anger, he expressed his frustration at the disappointed hopes of the expedition:

> 'The chief puzzle of the problem is that nothing turns out as we were told it would turn out. The landing had been made but the Balkans fold their arms, the Italians show no interest, the Russians do not move an inch to get across the Black Sea.'[10]

In response to questions from Kitchener, Hamilton asked for reinforcements of at least two divisions and preferably four. He heard that the grossly understrength 52nd (Lowland) Division was to be sent. He then had to endure a prolonged silence from London as the government entered into a severe political crisis brought on by the 'shells scandal' in France and the creation of the first coalition government of the war. Instead of adequate reinforcement, Hamilton received a cable from Kitchener urging him to continue to seek an early decision. How that goad must have stung! If critics wonder why Hamilton, through his British and French corps commanders at Helles, kept up a steady series of attacks on the Turkish entrenchments, the reason was there in Kitchener's orders.

It was during this hiatus in the higher direction of the campaign, in mid-May, that Birdwood first proposed a breakout to the left of Anzac, which coincided exactly with Hamilton's desire to try and force a decision in the north, especially as the Navy showed no interest in renewing its attack by sea. As so often in this ill-fated campaign, if the troops had been ready for the attempt immediately, great things might have been achieved. Instead procrastination gave the enemy time to reinforce and entrench still further.

The new Dardanelles Committee decided to make a major effort to break the deadlock and Hamilton was informed that he would receive three divisions of the New Army by mid-July, with a further two Territorial divisions by early August. There would have been even more territorials but for the restricted availability of shipping. From being starved of men, Hamilton had now to refuse new formations because of the physical impossibility of accommodating them. It was transport difficulties which severely delayed the arrival of these reinforcements, so that only the 13th Division was on time and got some combat experience at Helles (and performed notably well at Anzac as a result), whereas the 10th and 11th Divisions had not enough time to acclimatise themselves, let alone see any action, before they were committed to battle. Once again delays in decision-making and implementation at the highest levels made the task on the peninsula more difficult than it might have been. For the planned night operation, only the moonless 6–7 August would suit, and the troops had to be used then or delayed for a further month, with all the attendant problems of enemy awareness, submarine menace and worsening weather. This tight schedule also made it impossible for Hamilton to let these new troops hold the static Helles front to release the veteran units for the August effort.

The plan for the August offensive was a desperate one. Birdwood thought he could accomplish the aim of seizing the commanding heights of the Sari Bair ridge with an extra three or four brigades of infantry. Hamilton gave him five (three of 13th Division, one of 10th Division, and Cox's 29th Indian Brigade). Two covering columns and two main assault columns were to be launched at dead of night into the wildest, most difficult country of the whole peninsula. The problems were fully understood but, if the troops would simply thrust onward and upward into this lightly-held enemy territory, the element of surprise in the whole scheme was expected to bring success by dawn. The preparation for this part of the battle included a quite brilliant feat by the much-maligned staff officers of the MEF, namely the 'smuggling in' of 37,000 reinforcements over four nights into prepared accommodation in the cliffs of the Anzac beachhead in total secrecy.

The additional divisions available meant that the offensive could be extended to include Suvla Bay, to secure a good anchorage and base area, to clear away the suspected Turkish artillery in the plain and generally to secure Anzac's flank and assist the main attack. The task, a relatively straightforward one, was given to the new troops of IX Corps under the command of Lieutenant General Sir Frederick Stopford.

The question of who should command the new corps illustrates what a low level of priority was given to Hamilton's requests when so very much was expected of him. He originally asked for Bruce Hamilton (no relation), a real fighting soldier of great drive and determination. Kitchener refused.

Sir Ian then asked for energetic, younger commanders like Byng or Rawlinson, currently doing well in Flanders. Kitchener refused. Instead he offered Sir Bryan Mahon, who had raised the 10th (Irish) Division, but Hamilton had found him rather temperamental in the past (he was to prove to be so again later in the August fighting) and he would not accept him. Kitchener reverted to the seniority rankings in the Army List and, discounting one candidate on grounds of physical fitness, Hamilton was given Stopford, an elderly, if well-educated, general who had never commanded troops in battle in his life.

Stopford originally grasped the plan quite well; understood the need to cross Suvla plain quickly and seize the line of the Tekke Tepe ridge to secure the whole area. He had this drummed into him by Birdwood and by Aspinall (the future official historian) of GHQ. In his written appreciations, Stopford often referred to the importance of seizing the ridge, though he increasingly complained of the difficulties he faced. Under the influence of his deeply-pessimistic Chief of Staff, Reed, he began to demand regular siege operations as if he faced the conditions of warfare prevalent on the Western Front, instead of a handful of covering troops (which the staff had predicted accurately) on a great empty plain. There were many warning signs in IX Corps orders of a lack of urgency, of objectives being lowered, of the ominous phrase 'if possible' being introduced very often.

Despite the keenness of the New Army troops, the level of generalship in this corps was universally abysmal; the staff work execrable; the field and junior officers devoid of experience. But a self-inflicted difficulty was to make things even worse. Appalled at the way the April effort had been compromised by the lack of secrecy, Hamilton went to extraordinary lengths to see that the August offensive achieved the necessary surprise effect upon the enemy. Orders and maps were only released to attacking units as they headed for the beaches; these new troops went ashore hardly knowing where they were or what they were supposed to do. A vigorous leadership would have shown them the way. A Montgomery-like officers' conference would have helped to make sure that the local commanders could have played their part correctly. But these units arrived direct from England and were scattered over several islands for the few days they had to prepare for the attack. Once again the delays complicated an already difficult task.

The great August offensive, in which boldness of conception and execution was to overcome numerous violations of the Field Service Regulations concerning night operations, ran into trouble within hours of its start. The four attacking columns moved off into the dark led by officers of the New Zealand Mounted Rifles and local guides who knew the area as well as anyone might, and there were some brilliant early successes for the covering forces of New Zealanders and New Army troops. The two main columns were then defeated by the terrain, exacerbated by the darkness and the physical exhaustion of otherwise excellent troops, and by a series of personal failures by some otherwise first-rate officers. Some, attempting so-called short cuts, instead of longer, less-complicated paths, plunged units into chaos; others made good advances and then inexplicably sat their men down to rest when a small extra effort would have secured a vital, if not decisive, grip on key positions.

The exasperation is captured in the measured words of the official historian:

> 'This, however, is no uncommon phenomenon. In many a hard-fought battle, when the issue trembles in the balance, a tiny mischance will tip the scales from overwhelming victory to irretrievable defeat. A slight error of judgement by a subordinate, the mistake of a guide, or the failure of an order to reach its destination, may prove the deciding factor; and many a well-laid plan will be classed as an illegitimate gamble which, in the hands of a luckier general, would have led to resounding success and be acclaimed as a mark of his genius[11].'

Daybreak on 7 August found the attackers short of their objectives everywhere and the enemy alerted. The next few days saw desperate fighting as the attack was kept up, seeing some momentary possibilities of great success if fresh troops had been available and seeing, increasingly, the impressive figure of Mustafa Kemal imposing his will on the battlefield as his reinforcements poured in and he directed crushing counter-attacks which ended all chances of success.

Hamilton's whole attention was taken up with this, the major aspect of the battle. Not until 8 August did two of his staff officers, Aspinall and Dawnay, visit Suvla Bay and alert him to the tragic wasted opportunity there. The opposed landing on the night of 6–7 August had been a very trying shock to the men of the 10th and 11th Divisions, but it had been made catastrophic by the absolute chaos created by the corps and divisional staffs. It literally took days to get the jumbled units into anything resembling an attacking force. When Hamilton made his only direct interference in an operational plan, to try and get a brigade of 11th Division to seize the crest of the Tekke Tepe ridge ahead of a general assault, the wretched staff recalled two battalions which had gamely pushed forward and thus was the vital Scimitar Hill position abandoned at the moment Turkish reinforcements arrived from the Bulair lines. Early on 9 August the attack was completely defeated; much blood was to be shed in vain efforts to re-take Scimitar Hill.

Despite further reinforcements at Suvla, all attacks there were poorly delivered, and stoutly resisted by growing Turkish forces. On 15 August, Hamilton finally dismissed the wholly unrepentant Stopford and brought in de Lisle, Hunter-Weston's successor in command of 29th Division, to command IX corps (causing Mahon to resign his command because he would not serve under an officer junior to him in the Army List). It is one of the supreme ironies of the whole campaign that, now the surprise was lost and the enemy was firmly in control, Kitchener saw the error of his ways and sent out Byng, Fanshawe and Maude – those vigorous, young commanders requested by Hamilton – to oversee the new stalemate that they would have never have permitted to occur had they been in place just a few weeks earlier.

A new crisis arose which spelled the end of the Gallipoli venture. Bulgaria joined the Central Powers and a concerted attack on Serbia saw the Allies embroiled in a new campaign, every bit as ill-conceived and executed as the Dardanelles, to support her through the Greek port of Salonika. Serious consideration was given to evacuating all or part of the peninsula to provide troops for the new theatre. Hamilton was asked to estimate what losses might be entailed. His deeply pessimistic reply (shared by all his contemporaries – the eventual brilliant success of the evacuation was predicted by no one) coincided with a ferocious attack on him in London by the journalists, Murdoch and Ashmead-Bartlett, and he was peremptorily recalled on 15 October, 1915. His successor, Sir Charles Monro, was a Western Front commander who could not wait to wind up this resource-consuming sideshow.

Hamilton was never again employed in the command of troops, though many of his contemporaries were anxious that his enormous talent be put to proper use in such demanding times. His political masters were not prepared to inflame the controversy over the failure by giving him important duties. He spent the remainder of the war gathering and presenting material to the Dardanelles Commission investigating the whole operation. Even here his bad luck dogged him; much of the evidence he accumulated would have been damning against Lord Kitchener. He was personally loath to use this but the sudden death of the national hero at sea in June 1916 made it impossible. General Callwell studied the documents for the War Office and saw the case mounting against Kitchener but wrote to Hamilton on 5 July 1916, 'The tragedy of the "Hampshire" simply precludes publication at present'[12].

Instead the Commission, which included the jealous and vengeful Field-Marshal Nicholson, became an exercise in obfuscation. The interim report of February, 1917 revealed the ill-prepared drift into the campaign but the government refused to publish the full report while the war was in progress. Thus Hamilton was kept under the cloud of failure from which his reputation can be said to have never recovered. When a truncated report was finally published in 1919, the worst criticism levelled at him was that he was over-optimistic and should have made his difficulties known more clearly at the time. He was found 'guilty' of obedience to his Secretary of State for War.

'No British general has ever been given a more difficult task than that which confronted Sir Ian Hamilton from the outset of the operation'.[13]

Few people doubt the ability of Ian Hamilton as a soldier and a thinker; none doubt his courage and loyalty. The Australian official historian especially praises his imaginative approach to a series of very difficult problems, and the daring with which he used his persistently inadequate resources.

But all commentators, from his firmest friends like Roger Keyes, Liddell Hart and Aspinall-Oglander, to the harshest of his many critics, find fault in his lack of ruthlessness as a commander. This man of such obvious, proven talent failed to impose his will upon his generals at a number of important points in the campaign. He could have insisted that troops be put in at 'Y' beach on 25 April; subsequently he could have insisted that Hunter-Weston made better use of night to cover the inevitably frontal attacks in the Helles sector; and, while the Anzac generals understood their task in August (but still failed), he should certainly have acted more firmly to galvanise the Suvla generals into earlier action. Fellow soldiers who admired his fighting record despaired of the way in which he seemed to abdicate command responsibility. Commenting on the handing over to Hunter-Weston of the conduct of the second battle of Krithia in May, Aspinall-Oglander said that 'all that was left to him of the high office of Commander-in-Chief was its load of responsibility'[14].

To set against this failure, more a defect of character than of professional expertise, one should remember that the British Army of 1915 had firm doctrinal views on the relations between a Commander-in-Chief and his generals, and one of the keenest exponents of this doctrine was the erstwhile Staff College tutor and Hamilton's Chief of Staff, General W P Braithwaite. Some commentators, C E W Bean chief amongst them, think that Braithwaite carried this doctrine of non-interference in the executive command to extreme lengths and positively isolated Hamilton from effective control of the campaign. Others, including J F C Fuller and Liddell Hart, saw it rather as the British Army hastily adopting the trappings of the Moltke system of the German Army without instituting any of the necessary reforms down to the battalion and company level. We were trying to replicate a flexible military system, using one that was notoriously rigid in this general sense of deference to seniority; a failing both of the Army and, of course, of the society that produced that army.

Having reverently created a General Staff on the German model, which certainly did some good work in the years before the outbreak of war in 1914, that same General Staff was shattered to pieces when it was needed most, as its qualified members rushed to take field commands in the BEF before the 'quick war' was over. The complete lack of a guiding hand in the decision-making process early in 1915 meant that Britain and France drifted into a major land operation in the Eastern Mediterranean with no careful thought as to the means necessary to carry through such important work to a victorious conclusion. Hamilton is innocent of the bizarre origins of the campaign in which the ultimate failure is so firmly rooted.

Instead he was given a near-impossible task of invading the enemy heartland with inadequate forces, after the enemy had been given more than two months' notice of the impending attack. He achieved a local tactical surprise to get over the most difficult task, the actual landing, and then the lack of reserves immediately to hand prevented further success. The original and continuing failure to make it properly clear, to both Maxwell and Hamilton, that Sir Ian could have drawn heavily on Egypt for reinforcement is one of the most serious charges to be laid at the door of Kitchener and his impotent General Staff.

The more general problems of coalition warfare, with a major ally to be accommodated and with heavy demands on still scarce resources of men and munitions, then impinged on the whole campaign. Again, this failure to decide where the main effort should be, and to see that the resources expended to no avail on the Western Front could have had decisive effects at almost any time at Gallipoli, are further charges to be laid at levels more senior than Ian Hamilton. What reinforcements were sent, and this includes the last big effort in August, were either too few, too ill-prepared or too late.

A soldier of Hamilton's calibre, with a properly prepared task force, or with more consistent support once the battle had been joined, could have achieved great success. We have evidence of his German and Turkish adversaries that he was repeatedly on the brink of local victory but was never able to thrust home the advantage. If British politicians finally became exasperated with this general who was always 'nearly successful', they should have examined why they demanded so much from a commander while denying him the timely resources he needed. Instead, Hamilton was called home, effectively in disgrace, and very much the victim of a badly-conceived enterprise.

Hamilton's fertile brain kept working and he continued to produce innovative ideas on war and society. Churchill had once said that he was capable of thinking in army corps and continents and it is worth conjecturing whether he might not have been better suited to the highest levels of the direction of war. In 1924, on the strength of his writings, Ramsay Macdonald offered him the post of Secretary of State for War in the first Labour government. He refused because he could never have served in a 'socialist' cabinet. Who can say what such an imaginative thinker and experienced practitioner, firm friend of mechanisation, air power, and a unified Ministry of Defence, might have been able to do for the future development of the British Army between the wars?

Chapter Notes

1. K Fewster (Ed.), *Gallipoli Correspondent: The Frontline Diary of C.E.W. Bean*, p. 169. (Allen & Unwin, Sydney) (1983)
2. M V Brett (Ed.) *Journals and Letters of Reginald, Viscount Esher*, Vol III p. 264, (Ivor Nicholson, London) (1934)
3. General Sir H. Smith Dorrien, *Memories of Forty-Eight Years' Service*, p. 182, (Murray, London) (1925)
4. Both the witticism and the offence are somewhat lost to our modern sensibilities. Hamilton had described how he was introduced to an aristocratic Japanese general while the latter was taking his bath and of his momentary difficulty in distinguishing between the smiling, pock-marked face of the general and the sponge floating in the water beside him. It loses something in the re-telling! But King George V was so outraged by the passage that he tried to have publication of the volume banned.
5. C F Aspinall-Oglander, *Official History: Military Operations: Gallipoli* Vol. 1, pp. 68–9, (Heinemann, London) (1929)
6. Lieutenant General Sir Ian Hamilton, *Gallipoli Diary*, Vol. 1, p. 2, (Arnold, London) (1920)
7. Aspinall-Oglander, *op. cit.* p. 90
8. Aspinall-Oglander, *op. cit.* pp. 101–102
9. J North, *Gallipoli: The Fading Vision*, p. 274, (Faber, London) (1936)
10. T A Gibson, 'Eyeless in Byzantium: The Tragedy of Ian Hamilton,' *Army Quarterly*, October, 1965
11. C F Aspinall-Oglander, *Official History: Military Operations: Gallipoli* Vol. II, p. 200, (Heinemann, London) (1932)
12. I Hamilton, *The Happy Warrior: A Life of General Sir Ian Hamilton*, p. 421, (Cassell, London) (1966)
13. Aspinall-Oglander, *op. cit.* Vol II, pp. 386–7
14. Aspinall-Oglander, *op. cit.* Vol 1, p. 332

3

Robert Nivelle and the French Spring Offensive of 1917

Anthony Clayton

When military command is disastrous, is it because of inadequate armament, or because of the personal shortcomings of particular leaders, or is it because the social and political order that gave the leader his command was itself deficient? The history of French commanders of the last one hundred and fifty years from Bazaine through to Gamelin, and on to the Algiers *putsch* generals of 1961 can richly fuel any debate. All three sets of causes appear in the career of General Robert Georges Nivelle, who, after a meteoric rise, was to prove one of the most disastrous generals of this century.

Nivelle's family, a military one, was on his father's side part-Italian. His mother was English, the daughter of one of Wellington's officers; he was born in 1856. He began his military career at the *École Polytechnique* and later became an artillery officer. He was an excellent horseman and had many of the attributes of a cavalryman. The outbreak of war in 1914 found him in command of an artillery regiment. He greatly distinguished himself at the Marne when he drove his regiment's guns through disintegrating French infantry to engage the Germans at point blank range, all with such efficiency that they were routed. Brigade command followed in October 1914, a divisional command early in 1915 and command of the III Corps by the end of that year. The III Corps was part of the French 2nd Army in the Verdun sector; its commander was Philippe Pétain.

The III Corps included the 5th Infantry Division whose commander was General Charles Mangin, one of two officers to have great influence upon Nivelle. Mangin came from the colonial infantry and had built a reputation in Africa as a tough fighting general. He had served in Marchand's dramatic march to Fashoda and been wounded three times in various colonial campaigns. Before the war he had campaigned vigorously for the creation of a *Force Noire*, a large Black African army, and the great expansion of the

Régiments de Tirailleurs Sénégalais owed much to him. But Mangin had another less heroic reputation; professionally able though he was, Mangin was a ruthless soldier, indifferent to casualties and death. He also held views that African, colonial or Maghreb, soldiers were less imaginative than metropolitan Frenchmen, and less physically sensitive; so, being able to bear pain and suffering the better, they made ideal troops for shock attacks. In 1916, Mangin had driven certain French reserve units too hard which had led them to break; his career might have come to an end had it not been for Nivelle, who intervened to exculpate him.

The second officer to have great influence upon Nivelle was even more sinister, his exceptionally able chief of staff, Colonel d'Alenson. D'Alenson was a tall, emaciated, gloomy man suffering from a terminal disease but burning with an inward fire to achieve what he believed was his life's mission, staff work for major victory, before death. Neither Mangin or d'Alenson were likely to counsel prudence, the latter was at times almost insane.

The Nivelle-Mangin-d'Alenson partnership first went into action on the eastern flank of the right bank of the Verdun sector in April 1916. In contrast to the tenacious but defensive style that Pétain had both prescribed for the left bank and preferred generally, Nivelle ordered his III Corps to mount a series of local attacks on the Germans, achieving, at some cost, a measure of success. The more important consequence, however, was the impression this apparent energy in command made on the French Commander-in-Chief, Joffre, who had for some time been irritated by both Pétain's caution and insistent demands for reinforcement. On 19 April Joffre ordered the elevation of Pétain to a more general supervisory command, that of the Centre Group of Armies, while Nivelle was given command of the 2nd Army.

Verdun had immense symbolic importance for France; this outweighed its real military significance but led to the hardest fighting of the war on the French sectors of the Western Front.[1] At this time the Germans had a wedge-shaped salient driven into the French system of forts surrounding Verdun. In the centre of this wedge, two miles away and clearly visible from Nivelle's headquarters, was the fortress of Douaumont. Douaumont, at a height of 1,200 feet, dominated the area and was the cornerstone of the whole Verdun defensive system. It had been built to be enormously strong with eight foot thick concrete walls, numerous gun and machine-gun turrets, all encircled by wire, railings and a moat. But it had nevertheless been captured by the Germans in February 1916, principally because of the negligence of the French command. Its loss was a heavy psychological blow to the French Army. Nivelle and Mangin, now commanding on the right bank, were determined on its recapture.

They had, however, to wait until the autumn for their opportunity. Until mid-July, the German Army commander, von Falkenhayn, maintained the pressure on the French with successive attacks, capturing Fort Vaux, the other important right bank fort in the first ring of Verdun's defences. Pétain, from his army group command, directed the overall defence, Nivelle tried to recapture Fort Vaux but his counter attack was beaten off with heavy casualties and Pétain forbade any repetition. In the last series of attacks, the Germans turned to the use of phosgene gas and were within an inch of breakthrough. Pétain was pessimistic. Nivelle remained the reverse, planning further counter attacks. Mangin mounted these, initially with success but suffering a bloody check on 11 July. But by early July, the Germans had decided to cease their attacks, probably because they realised that a policy of attrition was not going to succeed, that they were not going to be able to take the city, and the emphasis had moved to the Somme. The new German commanders, Hindenburg and Ludendorff who had succeeded von Falkenhayn, ordered a defensive strategy for Verdun.

Nivelle's prescription for success, fully backed by Mangin and d'Alenson, was a mix of psychology and artillery. He still held tenaciously to the military philosophy of the French Army at the outbreak of war: that an attack mounted with sufficient violence and brutality, with *élan* and *cran* (guts), body to body fighting and the will to triumph, must bring victory – a philosophy with its roots in Bergson and foreshadowing Hitler. Such an attack was to be preceded by a massive artillery bombardment, led in by a creeping barrage and, when successful, to break through and fan out. The lessons of the first two years of the war, in particular those of the Somme, were lost on him, but not on Pétain, who only allowed him to go ahead after very careful preparation. This, after a minor disaster with brave but untried West African troops, included mock attacks over ground prepared to resemble the approaches to Douaumont.

For his autumn attack, then, over 500 additional guns, including two huge new 400 mm railway guns, were provided to support the 2nd Army's own artillery – a gun to every fifteen yards, 15,000 tons of shells. Three days of bombardment, targeted on Douaumont and all known German forward gun positions and lines, began on 19 October. The effect, especially that of the 400 mm guns, which proved exceedingly accurate, and of gas shells, was devastating. Douaumont had virtually to be evacuated. The bombardment ended with a lengthening of range at 2 pm on the 22nd. French troops in their forward trenches cheered, as if assaulting. The Germans believed this was the moment for the infantry attack and batteries that had not been located opened fire – mostly to be destroyed.

The infantry assault opened on the 24th, in useful conditions of dense mist. The assault was supported by a new horror for the badly shaken Germans, massed mortar fire, which, together with the artillery, was coordinated into a creeping barrage controlled by a field telephone system with wires dug six feet deep into the mud. The field guns fired seventy yards, the heavy guns 150 yards ahead of the infantry who advanced at a speed of twenty-five yards per minute. Three divisions of Mangin's army pressed home the attack across the sticky mud and shell craters, a further three followed and at about four in the afternoon soldiers of one of France's finest regiments, the *Régiment d'Infanterie Coloniale du Maroc*, RICM, composed at the time of two battalions of élite *Coloniale* Infantry, a battalion of *Tirailleurs Sénégalais* from West Africa and two companies of Somalis from Djibouti, entered Douaumont, the tiny residual German garrison reduced by a final horror, flame-throwers.[2] This triumph was followed by the recapture of Fort Vaux on 2 November, and on 15 December Nivelle mounted a further eight-division attack on the Germans which regained three miles of territory and captured 9,000 prisoners.

These victories do, however, need to be set in context. The Germans were suffering from the attrition following their summer attacks. Crown Prince Rupert of Bavaria's troops were tired, cold and wet in a very severe early autumn; their trenches were collapsing from rain and frost and their guns were worn out. Morale was low, all offensive spirit had gone. But as a result of the victory, Germany lapsed into gloom while France rejoiced. Everyone spoke of Nivelle and forgot Pétain.

The victory came at a moment that was politically difficult.[3] The Briand *Union Sacrée* government was under increasing parliamentary pressure. The French High Command, in particular Joffre, was taking severe direct criticism for the failure of the Somme offensive and much indirect criticism over the extent of his powers. Briand had earlier decided to remove Joffre as soon as the Verdun battle was over. But the choice of a successor was complicated by political factors. Of the experienced commanders, Pétain had been openly hostile and contemptuous towards politicians. Foch had already been removed by Joffre and, unfairly, as he had been critical of the operation, was associated with the Somme failure; it was also put about that he was suffering from stress. Franchet d'Espérey, de Castelnau and Fayolle were all too staunchly Catholic to be judged reliable. What better successor then than this fresh-thinking General Nivelle, a Protestant of charm and tact with political figures? The laurels of Douaumont were thought to outweigh any lack of experience and Nivelle was offering what the politicians wanted, a new quick solution to the military stalemate. On 12 December, Nivelle, his real contempt for politicians carefully concealed, became Commander-in-Chief, an astonishing rise for a man who had been only an artillery regimental colonel two and a half years previously.

The promotion went to Nivelle's head, fuelled the ambitions of Mangin, and was seen by the stricken d'Alenson as his great and final opportunity. To Nivelle, Douaumont was the pattern, all that was needed to be done was to repeat the tactics; no thought was given to the particular conditions in which they succeeded. To use a modern term, he and his staff began to hype themselves up with their own confidence and talk of success to come; Nivelle saw himself inheriting the mantle of Condé and Napoleon. With no real study of the suitability of tactics that had secured a local level success for a major front level battle, with a refusal to listen to any counsel of caution, and with once again repetition of the virtues of *élan* and *cran*, speed and surprise, to rupture the enemy lines, plans for a spring offensive were initiated. The area chosen lay on the Aisne to the west of Verdun, where the Germans held the Chemin des Dames ridge to the north of the river.

The plan, as it evolved, provided for a curtain-raiser, designed to attract German reserves. It would take the form of a British ten division attack on both sides of Arras, to be launched on 9 April. There were to be also two similar subsidiary French attacks, one on the Somme and one in Champagne. The main French attack was planned for the 12th when the *Groupe des Armeés de Reserve* (Nivelle preferred *de Rupture*) would assault the Chemin des Dames ridge, on the right bank of the river Aisne. Twenty divisions were to attack in the first wave with fourteen more immediately behind, the whole supported by massive concentrations of artillery fire. 'Laon in twenty four hours and then break out' was Nivelle's forecast.

The twenty-five mile stretch of ground selected for the main weight of the attack was not at all well chosen. The Chemin des Dames ridge – which owed its named to a favourite riding ground for the daughters of King Louis XV – was a formidable defensive position even without the attentions of Hindenburg and Ludendorff. The French had a bridgehead on the right bank of the Aisne approximately fifteen miles in length opposite part of the Chemin des Dames. However, further west, first the right bank and then both banks were German held. The Aisne was some fifty yards wide, a canal ran parallel to it. On the right bank were either flat marshy ground dominated by the ridge, or the actual slopes of the ridge itself. The ridge was over 600 foot high with a flat plateau top, along which ran the Chemin road from Fort Malmaison to a small village named Craonne. At a slightly lower height, the ridge continued on to Fort Brimont. The slopes of the ridge, covered in coppices, were difficult for infantry and impossible for artillery.

From the start, French misgivings were expressed about the plan. A staff colonel, Renouard, took the plan to General Lyautey, the Minister for War in Briand's cabinet. Lyautey was horrified 'But, surely, Renouard, this is a plan for the army of the Grand Duchess of Gerolstein' he exclaimed.[4] Lyautey tried to oppose the plan and gave serious thought to the possibilities of dismissing Nivelle. But the political climate was hostile to any strong Minister for War. Politicians suspected military dictatorship aims and sought to impose greater political control on all military operations. In despair, Lyautey resigned in March 1917. The Briand government fell in consequence two days later, and was replaced by one headed by the octogenarian Ribot. In this administration the Minister for War and perhaps the most powerful man in the government was Painlevé. Painlevé had, as a Minister in Briand's government, opposed the appointment of Nivelle. He was himself a supporter of Pétain and opposed to large costly offensives, believing that the best France could offer was limited scale attacks for particular objectives. Although he was a very able man intellectually and politically, Painlevé nevertheless failed to grasp the nettle.

His first attempt to do so, on 22 March, was a plea to Nivelle to revise the plan on the grounds of the changing world situation, German withdrawals, the first Russian Revolution, and the likelihood of America's entry to the war. His pleas fell on deaf ears, Nivelle arguing that the German withdrawal was an asset freeing more French than German divisions, and that an extension of the French right would remedy the narrowing of the front. Moving ever further from reality, Nivelle even talked of an advance of thirty kilometres in three days.

In the next ten days, Painlevé received other weighty expressions of anxiety, among them from Pétain, Franchet d'Espérey and Micheler, the three Army group commanders. Ever more worried, Painlevé called a conference on 3 April attended by Ribot, other ministers, and Nivelle. Nivelle once again spoke in complete self-confidence of assured victory; he threatened resignation if he was not allowed to proceed. By this time, the interaction of the two men upon each other was actually worsening the situation, Nivelle becoming the more determined to plunge ahead while Painlevé was driven into a corner – if he accepted Nivelle's resignation or dismissed him, a major political crisis would follow, if he did not do so, a major military disaster might follow. The French political structure was not firm enough to enable him to act as he should have done and he gave way.

Nivelle was generally successful in securing the co-operation of the British. His personal charm, Protestant beliefs and command of English greatly impressed Lloyd George, the British Prime Minister, at their first meeting in January 1917. Lloyd George was as anxious for a quick solution as the French political leaders and, further, the plans of this persuasive and convincing French general put the major onus on the French. He invited Nivelle to London to a meeting of the War Cabinet later in the month, after which he was even more enthusiastic.

The British Commander-in-Chief, Sir Douglas Haig, agreed to co-operate as required. Six newly arrived divisions took over from the French, extending the British sector to the right as far as St Quentin. Thereafter, Haig began to have reservations and increasing doubts over Nivelle's plans. To make matters worse, at a secret meeting of the War Cabinet, from which the Army's Chief of the Imperial General Staff, Sir William Robertson, had been politely excluded, Lloyd George had decided that Haig should be subordinated to Nivelle. Haig reacted violently and, as a result, was allowed a right of appeal and told the direct subordination would last for the period of the offensive only. The relationship however was not a smooth one, Haig resenting Nivelle's authority, lack of experience and style in communication.

The difficulties of ground, severe enough in themselves, were compounded by the failure of Nivelle and his staff to understand the basic principles of military intelligence or military security; this failure was to be one of the main battlefield causes of the disaster.[5] The French press forecast the outline of the plan. Nivelle discussed it freely and set outlines of it with no regard to any 'need to know' principle. Far more serious and with results directly attributable, were the German capture of documents in trench raids and local attacks. Unnecessarily early, units – even companies – received written orders for their part in the forthcoming attack. One such, taken from a captured French sergeant during a raid on 3 March, provided the Germans with a clear statement that the forthcoming attack was a major one aiming at nothing less than breakthrough. Another document captured in a local attack on 6 April was in fact the order of attack of the entire French 5th Army. Crown Prince Rupprecht was delighted, at the time of the attack there was little that the Germans did not know.

French intelligence was aware that the Germans knew a great deal and warned Nivelle, advising some change of plan. The warning fell on deaf ears, Nivelle would allow of no postponement. To make matters worse, the Germans acquired a local air superiority over the area, assisting their own reconnaissance and gunsiting, and at the same time precluding much French activity.

The German commanders, Hindenburg and Ludendorff at the top, Crown Prince Rupprecht and the immediate 7th Army sector commander, General von Boehn, turned their intelligence to good use. They thinned out their units on the immediate front, concentrating their main body of troops and reinforcements on the ridge. In the areas they vacated, everything was either destroyed, booby trapped or in the case of water wells, poisoned. Nine divisions had occupied the line at the turn of the year; the number had increased to forty by early April. They occupied a complex matrix of barbed wire, artillery positions and machine-gun posts, linked together in an excellently planned and effective system of defence in depth. This system, known to the Germans as the *Siegfried Stellung* and to the British as the Hindenburg Line, could use to the full all the advantages offered by the terrain. Depth was provided by a lightly held first line, a second line held with some measure of fortification and a third very strong line. An easy success over the first line led to a killing ground where attackers could be mown down by the machine-gunners in the second and third lines. Divisions were doubled, the second in a pair being given an intervention or counter-attack role.

The German system was later described in the *Times* by one war correspondent as no longer either one of definite strategic points or any elaborate trench system.[6] Instead there were 'innumerable minor scraps of trenches' and machine-gun positions. These latter the Germans called '*Mebu*' (*Maschinen Eisen Betun Unterstand*) and a number were built upon pre-war quarries or in caves. They were essentially subterranean reinforced concrete structures, generally a group of three pits connected in a chamber below from which steps led up a concrete shaft to the machine-gun position. The roof of each pit was circular, raised a few inches only above the ground with apertures for the gun and for observation. The *Times* correspondent noted that the target which each pit offered was equivalent to a London pavement cellar opening with the lid propped open a few inches – a target which only a direct hit would knock out.

The British supporting attack on the left, in the Arras sector, began in wind and sleet but on time, on 9 April. Three armies were involved. Horne's 1st Army was to take the strongly protected Vimy Ridge, so covering Allenby's Third Army which was to attack the Hindenburg Line. Gough's 5th Army was to attack further south. The attack achieved a general initial success. The German front line trenches were cleared, the Vimy ridge taken by Byng's Canadian Corps, and a considerable dent, six kilometres at its greatest, was punched in the German line. It was, however, unwisely pursued, after the initial success, at a time when the Germans had reorganised their defence, in particular with the usual Western front combination of wire and machine-guns. Little further progress was made, with the Australian 4th Division, part of the 5th Army, taking heavy casualties. The pressure was maintained out of loyalty to the French, Nivelle having twice postponed the start of this main *Groupe des Armée de Reserve* assault in view of heavy rain.

This assault finally began on 16 April after a very heavy artillery preparation. The preparation unfortunately served as the last and conclusive intelligence indicator to the Germans of the direction of the attacks. It had been intended that the bombardment would last five days; the postponement extended it. The Germans grasped its significance and replaced guns and repaired breaches in the crucial sectors. On the left, was Mangin's eighteen division strong 6th Army on a ten mile front which included most of the Chemin des Dames; eight divisions were to make the initial attack. On the right, was Mazel's seventeen division strong 5th Army whose sector included Craonne and extended to Brimont. The 10th Army was the immediate reserve, ready to exploit the anticipated successes.

At 0600, in conditions of driving rain, tens of thousands of young Frenchmen from country and town, inadequately clad peasants from the savannah lands of Senegal and French Soudan, Kabyles from the Nementcha and Aurès of Algeria, and *djellaba*-wearing Berber mountain men from the Rif and the High Atlas of Morocco, poured out from the comparative security of their trenches into the attack. Immediately, undetected and undestroyed, German field artillery and machine-guns opened up and the carnage began. Further back, the German *mebus*, and other works dug deep into the chalk hills, had survived the fire of the French 75 mm field guns. Now they added their support. Of the French heavier guns, the long barrelled pieces had a flat trajectory and the only weapon really suitable for the terrain, the 155 mm Schneider howitzers, were insufficient in number; only some 420 were available; at least twice that number were

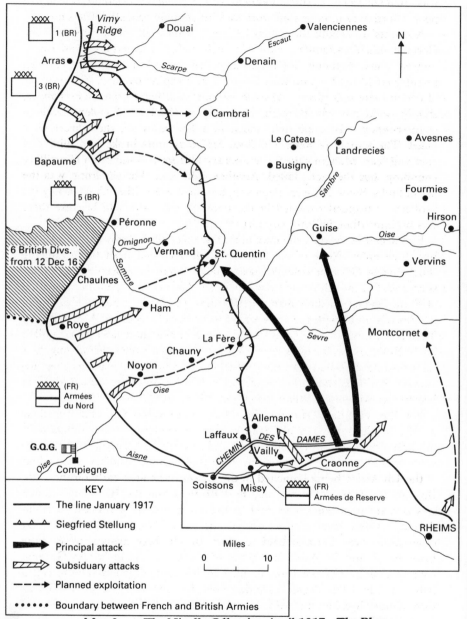

Map 3. *The Nivelle Offensive April 1917 - The Plan.*

needed. Ammunition supplies, too, were inadequate and artillery support was often lacking at a critical moment. Other French shortcomings included poor co-ordination, poor staff work and inadequate casualty clearance.

Accounts from both the forward French armies tell the same story. The German machine-gunners, either in their *mebus* or emerging from caves, mowed down battalion after battalion. In these conditions the French infantry could not keep up with the artillery creeping barrage. *Elan* and *cran* of which there was plenty, down to bayonet and hand grenade exchanges, simply could not win through, especially in the face of violent German counter-attacks. In some units most, in a few cases all, the officers were killed. The morale of some *Tirailleurs Sénégalais* units broke in a misery of cold and fear. Mangin called a temporary halt for a resumption of artillery pounding, but the tactic failed. Another failure, on Mazel's front, was the use of tanks. Some 130 were deployed, but most were either blown up by the artillery or trapped stranded in the midst of the battlefield because there was no immediate infantry support.

By the end of the day, the maximum advance, a 5th Army gain, had been but three miles. None of the first day objectives had been taken and the third line of German defences was intact. There had been a few minor successes. On the 6th Army front, the young Captain Juin, a future Marshal of France, stood on the Chemin des Dames, the furthest advance of any of the Army's units, with the survivors of three battalions of the *1er Régiment des Tirailleurs Marocains*.[7] Over extended, the regiment had later to be pulled back. But the 'swallows of death' as the Germans called them from their dark flowing *djellabas*, chanting and shouting religious slogans as they advanced, had displayed the redoubtable fighting qualities which were to become world famous twenty-seven years later at Cassino.

For the next day, Mangin and Mazel both wanted to continue their attacks on the same axis of advance. Nivelle, evidently aware things were not proceeding according to plan, ordered Mazel's 5th Army to strike north-eastwards in the hope of linking up with the second subsidiary attack, that of the 4th Army, being launched in the Champagne area early on the 17th. But the 5th Army could not take Fort Brimont and the 4th Army's attack was contained, at enormous cost to the attackers, by a resolute German defence. A few local gains, notably one near Vailly that secured good observation over German held territory by all three armies, were made between 17 and 20 April, but some of these were soon lost to German counter-attacks. On the 19th, Painlevé, on a visit, urged Nivelle to call a halt, in vain. He began agitating for the appointment of Pétain as Commander-in-Chief, but Ribot was afraid of the political consequences of what would amount to an admission of failure.

By the evening of the 20th, however, the French were exhausted and had to pause. Nivelle wished to resume the offensive on the 23rd. He made plans to commit his reserve army, the 10th Army, on the 5th Army front and he

requested further British diversionary attacks. But the casualties his armies
had already suffered, magnified in political circles by rumour, the slump in
morale following the failure of those attacks, and shortages of ammunition
forced limited objectives upon him and postponement until early May. And
in Nivelle's case, delay and limited objectives meant failure.

The size of the failure is best measured by the losses. The French Army
had by this time, 25 April, lost approximately 30,000 killed, 100,000
wounded and 4,000 taken prisoner; most of those killed lost their lives on
the 16th. Neither the meagre territorial gains nor the capture of 16,000
Germans, together with modest quantities of field and machine-guns could
redress the balance.

Nivelle's spell was broken. On 23 April, President Poincaré very firmly
forbade further attacks on the Chemin des Dames; this moratorium was
followed a few days later by another order forbidding further attacks on
Brimont. Nivelle protested, but in vain; he also tried to lay the blame on
Mangin.[8] The sands of time were running out on him. On 29 April, Pétain
had been appointed Chief of Staff of the French Army, as a political
compromise; any hope Nivelle might still have entertained of a major
offensive was thereby ended. Early in May, limited operations in the
Soissons area failed, though Craonne was occupied and more of the Chemin
des Dames was cleared, leaving an uneasy stalemate on the ridge. The cost
was further heavy casualties for which Ribot and Painlevé must bear at least
part of the blame.

Resignation was urged on Nivelle; at first he seemed willing but then he
refused to go. On 15 May, Pétain was appointed Commander-in-Chief, but
it was only after undignified scenes of shouting and recriminations that
Nivelle finally made way for him on the 19th.

Professor Ralph Stogdill, the American authority on leadership, notes
'predictive accuracy' as an important attribute of a leader.[9] Nivelle certainly
illustrates most clearly what happens in the reverse situation. Nivelle had
made such exaggerated claims, with such apparent authority, that his failure not only ruined himself but also seriously undermined French soldiers'
confidence in their command. Before Nivelle's offensive, Pétain had assessed
the tired French Army was capable of one more offensive, but only one, and
that must be a success. Nivelle had brought failure, not as bloody as Joffre's
offensives had been but more serious in the context of the attrition of the
French Army and the hopes that had been dashed. Mutiny was the result,
with a number of regiments refusing to enter the trenches, displaying red
flags, and electing soldiers' councils. Thousands of soldiers deserted, some
regiments marched to Paris to demand a negotiated peace, and there were a
number of cases of serious sabotage.

Only the hero of Verdun, Pétain, could restore order and discipline so
rendering his country his second great service as *Le Médecin de l'Armée*. And
in 1945, de Gaulle was to take care not to deprive the disgraced head of the

Vichy regime of his *maréchalat*.

Of the trio who took Douaumont but failed on the Chemin des Dames, d'Alenson died, a disappointed man, a few weeks after the battle. Mangin, who was removed by Nivelle on 6 May, had to face a Court of Inquiry. This exonerated him but he had to wait until 1918 before he was again given a command, in which he was very successful.

The theories in N F Dixon's *The Psychology of Military Incompetence* are amply born out in the case of Nivelle.[10] The undoubted virtues he had shown before 1917 turned to touchy, rigid, and over-controlled behaviour when under the stress of Supreme Command, with consequent errors of judgement, rejection of unpalatable information, stereotyping of outgroups, an authoritarianism based on a wish for showy assertion and when failure became evident, scape-goating. But fortune was kinder to him than thousands of his soldiers. He was exonerated from any serious misconduct by an enquiry in October 1917, and was appointed to a command in North Africa. Later he received one or two sinecure military appointments in France. In 1920 he was given the privilege of representing France at the tercentenary celebrations marking the arrival of the *Mayflower* in the USA, and in 1924 he died.

Nivelle has found no real defenders. At the time, the British Chief of the Imperial General Staff, General Sir William Robertson, recorded that he felt that Nivelle 'had been cruelly handicapped by having doubt thrown upon his plan by his government'.[11] Robertson had, however, earlier expressed strong reservations on Nivelle's plans. Nivelle himself wrote nothing. A few French military historians have developed Robertson's theme, General Weygand for example writing:

> He was fighting an enemy forewarned whose dispositions and forward defences, 6–7 kilometres in depth provided an effective resistance. He was constrained by unfavourable weather hampering air observation. Above all he suffered from a fundamental error in his conception and in his execution, from political intervention.[12]

But this is only a limited defence. Perhaps the relatively merciful treatment given to Nivelle between 1917 and his death was an indication of the wider failures, both political and military; neither side could fully admit the magnitude.

Chapter Notes

1. The fighting at Verdun is fully described in Alistair Horne, *The Price of Glory*, (London, Macmillan), (1962).
2. The RICM, with the 3rd Regiment of the Foreign Legion the most decorated regiments in the French Army, survives today under a new title of *Regiment d'Infanterie-Chars de Marine*.
3. The political circumstances of Nivelle's appointment are fully set out in Winston S. Churchill, *The World Crisis, 1916–1918, Part 1*, (London, Butterworth) (1927), xi, 'The Nivelle Experiment'.
4. André Maurois, *Marshal Lyautey*, (London, Bodley Head) (1931), pp. 237–238.
5. Churchill, *World Crisis*, pp. 272–273 describes the security failures.
6. *The Times*, 8 May 1917, provides this interesting description of the works.
7. Maréchal Juin, *Je Suis Soldat*, (Paris, Conquistador) (1960), pp. 43–45.
8. Jean de Pierrefeu, *French Headquarters*, (London, Geoffrey Bles, n.d.) pp. 155–156 notes this scapegoating.
9. Bernard M. Bass, *Stogdill's Handbook of Leadership, A Survey of Theory and Research*, (New York, Free Press), (1981), p. 363.
10. Norman F. Dixon, *On the Psychology of Military Incompetence*, London, (Jonathan Cape, 1975). A useful summary written by Dr Dixon appears in *The British Army Review*, 56, August 1976, pp. 21–22.
11. Robertson to Haig, 17 April 1917. The text of this letter appears in David R. Woodward (Editor), *The Military Correspondence of Field Marshal Sir William Robertson*, (London, Army Records Society), (1989), p. 175.
12. Général Weygand, *Histoire de l'Armée Française*, (Paris, Flammarion), (1938), p. 368. The translation is that of the author of this chapter.

4

Sir Hubert Gough and the German Breakthrough, 1918

Anthony Farrar-Hockley

In the days when sons followed their fathers' professions, the British Army numbered whole families amongst its officers; three generations might be serving simultaneously. Such a family were the Goughs. From Colonel George Gough and his wife, Elizabeth, parents in the late eighteenth century, there followed in direct line over the next one hundred and fifty years a field-marshal, four generals, a brigadier-general, and five other regular officers, to say nothing of those who served in the Army for the duration of various wars. Among these were two brothers, Hubert and John, sons of General Sir Charles Gough. They were born respectively in 1870 and '71.

The Goughs were by then an Irish family, principally Protestant, though there had been some intermarriage with Catholics. The brothers were not pressed by their father to enter the Army, but their pride in his accomplishments in India and the military games he played with them no doubt influenced their decision to join it. Moreover, once each boy had made the decision, he advanced from indolence at Eton to working hard at the Royal Military College at Sandhurst. There, both were judged intelligent, lively, and enterprising. They were naturally good at ball games. Unusually, among their contemporaries, they read avidly and widely. John Gough developed his talents in sketching and water colour painting. The quick witted, quick tempered Hubert took up steeplechasing with considerable success. During the last decade of the nineteenth century, the brothers joined the measured pace of professional military life at home and abroad.

Hubert Gough had been gazetted to a cavalry regiment, the 16th Lancers, John to the Rifle Brigade. In garrison, an officer was rarely required for more than four hours a day, though during manoeuvres he would be confined to the field. Junior officers might then be given mildly exciting tasks such as reconnaissance, otherwise practice for war was deliberate and infrequent.

After eight years in India, Hubert Gough was due for a year's leave at home, but while he was making plans for this in the previous year, 1897, one of the periodic insurrections on the North West Frontier afforded him a first staff post as an assistant commissariat officer, responsible for keeping a brigade supplied with its daily needs by pack animals. In the mountainous approaches to the Tirah *maidan*, he learned some important and hard lessons about logistics in the field, as much from his own errors and omissions as those he observed among the professional members of the notoriously slack Department of Supply and Transport whom he had been sent to supplement. In notepads and, more often, in his diary, he wrote down these lessons and did not hesitate to add further notes where his own judgements of people and events proved wrong or unduly severe.

Hubert Gough did not return to India after his leave, having secured a place by competitive examination at the Staff College, Camberley. While there, the Boer War began. He at once volunteered for 'special service' in South Africa, fell into despair as he saw other officers departing for the Cape, but soon found he was among those required. He sailed from Southampton on 28 October, 1899.

The war in South Africa progressively drew in a considerable part of the British Army and thus many junior and middle ranking officers who would hold senior appointments in the Great War of 1914–18; for example, in the cavalry, French, Haig and Allenby. Hubert Gough's first task was to act as adviser to a group of South Africa irregulars, settler volunteers. He was quick to see that what they lacked in formal military training was to an extent outweighed by the skills they had acquired as horsemen, in marksmanship with their rifles, and an eye for ground from the hazards of life on the veldt. But he was soon posted to the headquarters of Lord Dundonald's brigade, the more welcome as this formation was a part of the force advancing to relieve Ladysmith, among whose besieged garrison was John Gough.

During the early months of operations in South Africa, the chief weakness of the British forces was a want of decision by the senior commanders, a weakness which become increasingly clear to their subordinates. Nowhere was this more true than in the corps under Sir Redvers Buller attempting to cross the Tugela river to relieve Ladysmith. Buller was renowned for courage under fire but he was daunted by high responsibility. He was deeply shaken by the casualties incurred whenever he advanced, even when the numbers were moderate and inevitable in the furtherance of operations. Drawn into intelligence work, chiefly scouting, Hubert Gough was appalled at the muddle due to orders given late, often followed quickly by counter orders, by gains thrown away due to precipitate withdrawal, and a want of boldness. The standards of staff work were also low, due partly to the lack of clear responsibility between one branch and another – the British Army had no general staff at that time.

Three months after his arrival in South Africa, he was given command of a composite regiment of colonial cavalry and mounted infantry*, which he led towards Ladysmith on 28 February, 1900. In the early evening, Gough received orders from Lord Dundonald to stop; it was 'too dangerous' to continue. Confident that the Boers were departing, he disobeyed the instruction and thus led in the first relief party to a cheering garrison.

During the next eighteen months, following the overall defeat of the Boer standing forces, Gough's regiment was involved in small-scale mobile counter-guerrilla operations. He made a name for himself as a commander to be relied upon, an officer who did not send back to higher authority to endorse his plans. He was promoted to brevet lieutenant-colonel. He grew confident, perhaps overconfident. Tracking a force of two hundred Boers along the Blood river in mid-September, 1901, he made a dashing plan to capture them. What he had not considered was that his prey was a detachment of a much larger force which, as his own encirclement developed, was immediately approaching. His open flank was suddenly fired upon by riflemen in ambush; five hundred Boer horsemen directly ahead began to charge. Gough's regiment was broken and scattered and he barely escaped capture. Returning downcast to his base, he wrote a full description of the action, making no attempt to disguise his error of judgement. To his great relief, his seniors, wishing to encourage bold enterprise, decided that he had made a fair judgement for which he should not be blamed. Thus encouraged, he pursued a Boer raiding party in the following November and, in a spirited action, was wounded but triumphant.

Two years after his arrival in South Africa, with much experience of open warfare and a high reputation in the Army, he was sent home to recuperate. But in regimental seniority, he was not much more than young 'Goughie'; for under the system of promotion, he reverted to the rank of captain in the 16th Lancers to await a vacancy for a majority, when his brevet would be reactivated. But though he volunteered to return to South Africa while the war continued, and John remained there, it soon ended. The staff then beckoned; in a staff appointment, his brevet was effective. He was posted first to be a brigade major at Aldershot, principal staff officer to a commander of the old school. The two men quarrelled a good deal of the time, not least because Brevet Lieutenant-Colonel Gough 'has a tedious habit of questioning the regulations . . .', as his brigadier reported. Gough was glad to be transferred to teach at the Staff College in 1904. In that establishment there was a new professional climate encouraged by Henry Rawlinson, the commandant, in which the lessons of operations in South Africa were being drawn upon for changes in organisation, equipment and training. John Gough, just awarded a Victoria Cross, was sent home to be a student. The brothers worked hard in their respective activities. Both were clearly

---

* Because there were insufficient cavalry for mobile operations, selected battalions of infantry were mounted but went into action principally on foot.

marked for early promotion.

In 1906, Hubert was appointed to command his regiment in Aldershot. At the same time, the Inspector-General of Cavalry, Douglas Haig, instructed him, quite irregularly, to act as his chief staff officer, principally in the conduct of staff rides for officers and cavalry exercises, an arrangement which continued when Edmund Allenby succeeded Haig as Inspector-General. Gough's life was thus very full but rewarding. He was able to develop ideas about adaptation of the old traditional cavalry formations to ground, and to introduce ideas concerning regimental operations by night. He won the confidence of both Inspectors-General but preferred working with Haig whom he found full of original ideas. To the envy of many of his contemporaries, he was appointed in 1910, at the age of 40, to command a brigade at the Curragh, some thirty miles to the south of Dublin.

Ireland was again approaching a critical phase in its political relationship with the British Government. Home Rule was demanded by the Irish Nationalists, a term that did not mean severance of ties with the parliament in London, but the transfer of powers 'of a glorified county council' to a legislature in Dublin. The Liberal Party under Asquith were minded to give in to them, despite the determination of the Protestant majority in Ulster to deny it. The latter were descendants of the Protestant settlers who had struggled successfully to deny Catholic rule in Ireland. Now, organised as the Unionists under the leadership of Sir Edward Carson, they were not going to see that victory set aside. The Conservative Party in Great Britain supported the Ulster Unionists, condoning, encouraging even, the illegal arming and drilling of Ulstermen with the intention of resisting Home Rule if necessary by insurrection. It was an issue which might bring down the Liberal government and bring the Conservatives to power. The Liberal Prime Minister, Mr Asquith, believed he could ride out the difficulties, though he advised King George V that when political powers were transferred to Dublin there would be 'tumult and riot, and more than the possibility of bloodshed in Ulster.' On 22 September, 1912, the King asked his Prime Minister,

> . . . 'Do you propose to employ the Army to suppress such disorders? This is, to my mind, one of the most serious questions which the Government will have to decide. In doing so you will, I am sure, bear in mind that ours is a voluntary Army; and Soldiers are none the less Citizens; by birth, religion and environment they may have strong feelings on the Irish question . . . Will it be wise, will it be fair to the Sovereign as head of the Army, to subject the discipline, and indeed the loyalty of his troops, to such a strain?'

It was rumoured that 'military opinion' was against the Home Rule policy, but it was largely the opinion of a number of retired officers in Ireland; only a very small number of serving officers and men had openly expressed disagreement. One senior officer, Major-General Henry Wilson, Director of Military Operations in the War Office, exacerbated difficulties by supplying the leader of the Conservatives, Bonar Law, with details of government policy and military plans for Ireland. Even so, due to the ineptitude of the Secretary-of-State for War, the Chief of the Imperial General Staff, and the Army commander in Ireland, a critical difficulty arose on 20 March, 1914. By this time, Asquith had offered the Unionists temporary exclusion from Home Rule; those counties with a Protestant majority in the province should remain within the system of government employed in Great Britain for sufficient time to permit a new government in London to review their position. Dissatisfied with the concession, it was believed that Carson's armed civil volunteers were preparing for action. The Army and Navy were alerted to be ready to maintain internal security, and to avoid straining loyalties, any officer or other rank who had 'direct family connections in the disturbed area of Ulster' and wish to be left out of operations would be permitted to do so. Otherwise, they must obey orders or resign. But at a conference on 20 March, 1914, the Army commander in Dublin narrowed this exemption to those whose families were domiciled in Ulster. When Hubert Gough, present among the senior officers, asked whether this applied to those who, like himself, had close connections there, he was told that it did not. Moreover, he was then openly singled out as a potential dissident.

Hubert Gough's hot temper now clouded his judgement. He decided to resign, but managed to put the issue without partiality to the officers of his units. Sixty officers then said they wished to resign in addition to the brigadier. A further five claimed exemption under the provision for domicile. When this was reported to Whitehall, there was great alarm. Asquith belied that by exempting officers with direct 'connections' with Ulster, his original provision, the difficulty would be settled. Further muddles in the War Office and intriguing by Henry Wilson, maintained the crisis. The King intervened, cooling heads in the War Office. Lord Roberts and Douglas Haig advised members of the Army Council to withdraw the ultimatum. John Gough met Hubert when the latter was ordered to London.

After a difficult passage within the War Office, Gough was given an assurance, written at his request and authorised by the Cabinet, that the incident leading to the resignations had been based on a 'misunderstanding'. The ultimatum was withdrawn.* The Army was not to be used to enforce the implementation of the Home Rule Bill.

Gough returned to the Curragh to find to his embarrassment that he was regarded by many as a hero. A minority of officers in the Army considered that he had behaved 'badly' or 'precipitately', but these views soon faded.

---

* An outcome of Gough's passage of arms with the War Office was the resignation of French as CIGS and Seely as Secretary of State for War, both having been criticised for coming to an accommodation with Gough over a matter which was outside their powers.

In Whitehall, however, among members of the Liberal Party, and within the middle and upper ranks of the civil service, a sense of outrage persisted. An Army officer had, it was believed, deliberately set out to thwart a policy of the elected government, and had succeeded with impunity.

The 'mutiny at the Curragh', as some described it, was soon forgotten; within a few months, the world was at war. The Gough brothers were sent immediately to the Continent, Hubert with his brigade, John as Chief of Staff to the corps commanded by Douglas Haig. In the summer withdrawal, and the autumn advance into Flanders, Hubert Gough enhanced his reputation as a decisive, practical cavalry commander, ever ready to exploit an opportunity. These capabilities were again in demand in the mighty clash of the meeting engagement in October and the German onslaught round Ypres in November.

A trench line was established from the Channel to the Swiss border. The British Army prepared to break it open in the New Year, 1915, and while making preparations for this, John Gough was mortally wounded during a visit to his regiment. His death threw Hubert into 'a bitter period of anguish', relieved only by the demands of a critical defensive action. The close relationship between the brothers had been enhanced by their common profession. For example, John had poured out his criticism to Hubert of command weaknesses during the siege of Ladysmith and been dissuaded from making formal representations about them. Hubert had consulted John closely during the Curragh incident. John's death left him with an abiding sense of loneliness which was never entirely relieved, despite enjoyment of a happy life with his wife and daughters.

In April, 1915, he was transferred to command an infantry division, the 7th, in Haig's First Army. Almost at once, he was involved in a major operation and won the confidence of his command by taking the decision not to proceed with a relief and attack at Aubers Ridge as ordered because it was impractical. It was unusual for divisional commanders to take such a responsibility and was to become increasingly so. He continued his practice of visiting the forward trenches regularly, of reconnoitering personally ground to be attacked, and listening to the views of local subordinate commanders. He maintained a close relationship with his artillery commander. He talked regularly and 'spoke very easily with the soldiers', a practice which many of his peers found difficult or failed to employ. In July, 1915, he was promoted to lieutenant-general to command I Corps. Within a month, he took issue with the visiting Lord Kitchener, Secretary-of-State for War, pressing the need for abandonment of the policy of voluntary service and the adoption of conscription as a means of raising the huge numbers of soldiers essential for victory. Gough's extrovert personality did not at all offend Haig, his Army commander; rather he was fascinated by, perhaps envied, his subordinate's outspoken nature which contrasted so markedly with his own reserve.

In the autumn of 1915, Haig's First Army was ordered to attack between La Bassée and Loos, principally to engage German forces during French offensives in Artois and the Champagne.

The British objective was a mining area. The German defences were dug in among pitheads and slag heaps, among which they counter-attacked fiercely to regain losses of ground. The struggle swayed to and fro; a fresh impetus was needed. Haig had been promised the General Headquarters reserve but the Commander-in-Chief, Sir John French, fatally delayed its release. The British operation subsided, though it had, at great cost, provided the promised diversion for the French. The latter's offensives had failed with a huge bill of casualties.

Gough instituted an enquiry into why I Corps had failed to break open the enemy line at Loos, when they had been close to success. The basis of this was not accusatory to his divisions but specifically on the basis of 'What errors did we make, what did we fail to foresee?' Many useful lessons were drawn but neither in his own corps nor in the Army as a whole was the problem of command and control resolved. The fundamental difficulty was maintaining communications between those engaged in fighting and those behind in the command chain who had the means of relieving their difficulties. The principal signalling equipments relied on wire and even cable buried deep tended to be broken by bombardment.

It remained unsolved to the summer of the following year, 1916, when the Fourth Army under Sir Henry Rawlinson was launched into an offensive north of the Somme river. Haig, who had succeeded French as Commander-in-Chief, believed that they had a fair chance of breaking open the German line in this sector in which the countryside was largely unbroken and from which German troops had been taken for the protracted battle at Verdun. To exploit Rawlinson's anticipated breach, he formed a Reserve Army, mostly of cavalry, under Gough. When the first strike in July failed to open the enemy defences, this command was diversified to include the two left flank corps in the offensive line with the aim of remounting operations which had failed at almost every point. For while the Germans were certainly short of manpower on the Somme, they had not failed to develop strong and deep defences in the sector. The 'Reserve' Army soon became the Fifth, a new command in the British Expeditionary Force.

From July, then, to mid-November, Gough and Rawlinson continued the offensive, sometimes together, sometimes separately. Despite the physical difficulties of getting into the forward trenches, Gough continued to visit them frequently. He was not wounded, though three of his ADCs in succession became casualties while accompanying him. His aim was continually to inform himself of conditions; as much as anything, he wished to minimise the mounting of attacks which had no potential for success. When the Germans withdrew to shorten their line in February, his presence forward enabled the Fifth Army as a body to follow rapidly. By the opening of 1917, Lloyd George had succeeded Asquith as Prime Minister. He was altogether dissatisfied with the Haig's conduct of operations in France and Flanders. Though unaware of it, Gough was one of those considered to replace him, though not by Lloyd George. Realising that the replacement of Haig would be politically and militarily contentious, he left him in the post, but subordinated him to his French counterpart, General Robert Nivelle (See Chapter 3). The latter had impressed him with a dynamic briefing in which he promised to overcome the Germans using tactics employed successfully at Verdun. But by the end of April, these had proved inadequate and the exhausted French Army mutinied to the extent that its soldiers would no longer undertake offensive operations. Nivelle was replaced by Pétain. The task of diverting the Germans from attacking the French line thus fell to the British. Haig chose to attack in Flanders.

The campaign opened prematurely with the explosion of three huge mines under the Messines-Wytschaete ridge in June. General Plumer, commanding the Second Army in this sector, was deliberate and cautious. Surprised by the success of this blow, he was unable to exploit it. Haig did not press him, preferring to wait for Gough to assume the principal role.

The strength of the German positions, many constructed in ferro-concrete bunkers on this front, and their possession of the higher ground posed formidable difficulties. Seasonal rain was imminent. Gough was determined that they should make every preparation possible, drawing on past lessons; and was frustrated that he could not see the ground for himself. The British positions were under close German observation by day. Though Gough did not share Haig's optimism that a thorough bombardment would open a way into these defences, he was opposed to the concept of a gradual advance, favoured by Haig's staff, which would give the Germans the opportunity to construct new defences behind those they lost. After a thorough appreciation of his task, he decided to drive deep from the outset to gain the higher ground and remove the British positions in the Ypres salient from enemy observation. The French on his left flank delayed the opening until 31 July, when nine British divisions advanced. Though they had some success and casualties were less than a third of those on the first day of the Somme offensive, Gough apprehended that they were in for a long and bloody slogging match. By 16 August, when the battle area was saturated with rain, losses were becoming severe, gains fractional. He told the Commander-in-Chief that operations should be cancelled.

Haig did not agree: the Russian armies were collapsing, the French unreliable. The war effort depended upon the British Expeditionary Force effort until the United States, which had joined the Allies, could raise and bring to France a mass of fresh troops. So Fifth Army maintained the offensive and became notorious as the formation which drove on irrespective of conditions. Units dreaded posting to its ranks.

Believing still that the Germans were close to collapse, ignorant of the terrible conditions in Flanders, and seized with the idea that success simply depended upon organisation, Haig and his General Headquarters staff were content to leave the blame for failure with Gough. Plumer reluctantly took up a partnership in the offensive but was no more successful. He joined Gough on 7 October in proposing an end to operations. They were refused. They concluded finally on 11 November, with the capture of Passchendaele, an objective in the first week of August.

Haig's standing in public esteem, with many of his political colleagues, and in the Army continued to dissuade Lloyd George from dismissal of the Commander-in-Chief, but he was determined to deny him the resources for further offensives in 1918. Having already added to the burdens of the British Expeditionary Force by agreeing that they should take over forty miles of the French line, he also declined to provide the manpower to make up their losses. To bind Haig still more, he took the initiative in the formation of a Supreme War Council in Paris, which would take responsibility for future strategy which meant, in effect, that they would wait until the Americans arrived in 1919. But this assumed that the Germans would also conveniently remain on the defensive. General Sir William Robertson, Chief of the Imperial General Staff, warned the Cabinet that,

> . . . if it would pay us to wait for the Americans and to defer our main effort until 1919, it would equally pay the enemy to deprive us of the opportunity and to try to get a decision in 1918 . . .

For Germany had now the prospect of drawing on the greater part of the eighty divisions on the Eastern Front to reinforce the West. The Bolsheviks had seized power in Russia in November, 1917, and it was believed, with good reason, that they would be unable to continue the war. But Lloyd George regarded Robertson as Haig's agent. He took no steps to guard against such a contingency. As we now know, on the very day that the 1917 offensive ended at Passchendaele, General Erich Ludendorff, *de facto* Chief of Staff of the Imperial German Army*, came to Mons to open planning with the army groups of Crown Prince Rupprecht of Bavaria and the imperial crown prince for a major offensive in 1918. Ludendorff recorded the essential points he made at the meeting.

> . . . The strength of the two sides will be approximately equal. About thirty five divisions and one thousand heavy guns can be made available for an offensive. That will suffice for *one* offensive; a second great offensive, say as a diversion, will not be possible.
>
> Our general situation requires that we should strike at the earliest moment, if possible at the end of February or beginning of March, before the Americans can throw strong forces into the scale.

---

* Ludendorff's post was First Quartermasteer-General, subordinate to the Chief of the Great General Staff, von Hindenburg, but he functioned effectively as Chief of Staff to the German Army.

We must beat the British.
The operations must be based on these three conditions.

On 21 January, by which time the British line had been extended to the Oise, Ludendorff had decided that the principal thrust should be made between that river and the Scarpe. This was to be Operation 'Michael'. Other options, if 'Michael' faltered or failed, were to be:

George 1	– north of the River Lys	in April to
George 2	– south of the River Lys	to assist Michael
Mars	– round Arras	in the
Archangel	– south of the Oise	event of
Achilles/	– round	Michael
Hector	– Rheims	failing
Roland	– into the Champagne	

Ludendorff was now able to increase his flexibility because the reduction of commitments on the Eastern Front had increased his assault divisions to seventy-four in number. These troops were to be comprehensively trained for their task, indeed, retrained in certain aspects. Assaults would be led by storm battalions, specially equipped with a high proportion of light machine guns, mortars and flame throwers. The storm troops would not move forward in massed waves but in numerous small groups. Initially, these would be directed to capture key defensive points in the enemy line, but thereafter, as they were drawn into a *melée*, local commanders would select successive targets on their own initiative. Taking advantage of this method of weakening the British line, each division would then advance 'battle groups' comprising conventional infantry battalions augmented by heavy and medium machine guns, in company with field artillery and engineers. The new developed German tanks would assist the infantry on selected axes. By this means, the enemy defences would be progressively rolled back, denying the opportunity for deliberate counter-attack. For the first time, aircraft joined closely in the ground exercises, developing methods of identifying formation positions.

On 10 March, as training reached a final stage, the formal order was issued over Hindenburg's signature.

his Majesty commands.
1. The Michael attack will take place on the 21 March. Break into the hostile position at 9.40 a.m. . . . .

Three German armies were to be employed in the assault and exploitation. Von Below's Seventeenth and von der Marwitz's Second, both in the army group of the Bavarian Crown Prince, were to 'push forward to the line Arras-Albert to upset the balance of the British Army . . . ' Von Hutier's

Map 4.   *The German Breakthrough 1918.*

KEY

German attacks
21 March – 5 April

Subsequent attacks
9 April – 17 July

Line 21 March 1918

Line 17 July

Allies

Germans

Army boundaries

X X X   Allied boundaries

Eighteenth, from the army group of the Imperial Crown Prince, was to capture the crossings of the Crozat canal and hook round behind British forces resisting von der Marwitz's Second. Thereafter, the aim was to roll on, disorganising and destroying the British Expeditionary Force in conjunction with the contingency plans such as George 1 and 2. The frontage of attack was sixty miles, of which eighteen were defended by Julian Byng's Third Army, the remaining forty two by Gough's Fifth, moved south from Flanders to relieve the French between the Somme and the Oise . . .

Byng had fourteen divisions to hold his front – twenty eight miles in all. Gough had eleven infantry and three cavalry divisions, the latter counting as one of infantry. This disparity was explained by Haig as being due to the fact that the French had reserves available to assist Fifth Army in the event of a crisis. In view of the uncertain state of their Army, this was not altogether reassuring. Of immediate importance, twelve divisions on a frontage of forty two miles were not able to accomplish as much in the development of defences as fourteen covering twenty eight, of which only eighteen were expected to be in the critical sector . . . Much digging, bunker construction, wiring, revetting, road and rail making was required, huge quantities of ammunition and stores had to be moved. Specialist engineers undertook certain work, such as tunnelling and the laying of railways, pioneers and labour companies were employed in the rear areas, together with prisoners-of-war; but forward, in areas within enemy artillery range, the bulk of the preparatory defensive work fell to the Royal Engineers field companies and the men in infantry and cavalry divisions. Field Marshal Smuts, visiting the line at the end of January, made these remarks among others in a report to the War Cabinet.

> The burden falls in the main on the infantry. Consequently, divisions which have completed their term in the defensive line have, almost immediately, to be turned on to the construction of defence works. The result is that they suffer in regard both to rest and training . . . In addition, it must be borne in mind that the infantry are 100,000 men below strength until the new organisation has been completed. . . .

The 'new organisation' reduced the number of infantry battalions in a division from twelve to nine – three brigades each of three battalions. This simply produced nine battalions at full strength as distinct from twelve well below, but it did not put any more men into the line. Haig had asked for six hundred thousand to make good his casualties and had been given one hundred thousand.

By the end of January, having motored, flown, and walked over his frontage of forty miles, Gough accepted French advice that he was unlikely to be threatened in the southernmost sector along the Oise, where inundations had made the ground marshy. He was therefore able to concentrate his force in defence of about twenty eight miles. With some exceptions, there was agreement with GHQ that a withdrawal would become necessary to the line of the Crozat Canal and the River Somme, on which defences were to be constructed, but in the northern sector, Peronne and the line of the Tortille stream should be held, both to maintain north-south communications and the left flank of Byng's Third Army. Where there was disagreement was in the numbers of troops available to hold the positions, and the time, labour, and defence stores necessary for defence preparations.

The GHQ general staff reckoned that seven of Gough's twelve divisions could be put into the front positions leaving five in reserve. They were simply following a rule of thumb; this arrangement provided each corps with a division in reserve, and one for the army commander. It was the outcome of preparing for war solely by use of a map – not one of the senior general staff officers ever came to see Gough's front, though invited to do so on a number of occasions. Seven divisions on a frontage of twenty eight miles gave each division four, and assumed two brigades in the front line each with two of its battalions forward. A battalion per mile was inadequate for the density of firepower required to sustain a bombardment and hold off an enemy attacking with a superiority of numbers exceeding 4:1. Moreover, their ground was exceedingly broken; they were lying in that zone which had been devastated by the battle of the Somme and its extension and ruined by the Germans when they drew back to shorten their line in December, 1916. To avoid offering the enemy important areas of dead ground – ground which, due to its rise and fall, offered cover from fire – some locations required a high density of troops. Visiting Gough and touring his corps area, Haig realised that he was in difficulties and gave him an additional division, the 39th. Two GHQ reserve divisions were placed behind the Fifth Army but at a distance which precluded their use within twenty four hours of release. Gough asked if they might assist in the preparation of defences but this was refused.

Labour was short everywhere. The French forward positions were in many places well sited and developed but the corps rear areas had neither wire nor trenches. The Crozat-Somme-Tortille defences also had to be prepared, and the Peronne bridgehead strengthened. There were shortages of barbed wire and revetting material. Many bunker sites awaited the arrival of heavy timber. Yet the morale of the Fifth Army was high, not a little due to Gough's own frequent contact with and encouragement of his officers and soldiers in the divisions.

The Secretary-of-State for War, Lord Derby, was unaware of this. He wrote to Haig on 5 March,

> It looks now as if an attack might come within a very short time on your front, and on that part of the front of which Gough is in command. You know my feelings with regard to that particular officer. While personally I have no knowledge of his fighting capacity, still, it has been borne upon me from all sides, civil and military, that he does not have the confidence of the troops he commands, and that is a very serious feeling to exist with regard to a

Commander at such a critical time as the present. I believe the Prime Minister
has also spoken to you on the subject . . . if by any chance you yourself have
any doubts on the subject, I hope by this indefinite order . . . to give you a
loophole which would make your task easier if you desired to make a change
. . .

Gough's reputation as the commander who had persisted with the offensive in Flanders in 1917 had reached London through many sources, the
most influential being those officers whom he had removed from their
appointments. He had never, of course, made public his own repeated
representations to Haig to bring operations to an end in the summer, and
again in the autumn. There had long been also a number of brother officers
who had been jealous of Gough's rapid rise to command of a corps and then
an army. His detractors found support in Whitehall and Westminster, who
had not forgotten his part in the 'Curragh mutiny'. He was aware of such
feelings, though not of their extent, but they did not affect his confidence.

In the first three weeks of March, 1918, there was ample evidence that a
German offensive was imminent. Intelligence had long since suggested that
the area between the Oise and the Scarpe rivers was the most likely front of
attack. Air photographs and prisoners of war supplemented deeper sources
to show that General von Hutier's Eighteenth Army had come into the line
with completely fresh forces. The Fifth Army defence plans were far from
complete. Much of the Crozat Canal-Somme line had simply been traced
without a trench being dug. The same was true for the switch line due to be
developed between the Fifth and Third Armies. Third and Fifth Army
harrassing and counter-bombardment fire swelled during the third week of
March. In a ground mist on the night of the 20th–21st, one of Gough's
battalions gathered thirteen prisoners in a raid and several of these told
their interrogators that the British line was to be attacked at about 9.30 am,
preceded by a preliminary bombardment at 4.40. Warnings were issued
throughout the Army, the outpost line was fully manned, and batteries lying
silent moved to alternative sites, a series of measures frequently rehearsed.
As visibility grew worse after midnight, many divisional commanders
manned fully their positions throughout the corps battle zones.

At 4.40 am, eight thousand German guns, howitzers and trench mortars
opened fire, initially upon all targets identified over the weeks of preparation as headquarters or communications centres, artillery locations, and
bivouac areas of immediate reserves. After these had been drenched and
pounded, fire fell upon the outpost and main trench lines, pausing sometimes for as much as half an hour to encourage the inhabitants to surface
and to see whether an assault had begun before raking them through once
more. Finally, fire switched to those lines through which the storm troops
would pass.

This bombardment fell upon ten miles of Third Army front and among
the four corps of the Fifth, in line from the left VII, XIX, XVIII, and III.

Wakened by the noise, Gough learned that there was no movement forward by the enemy and so wisely returned to bed to rest for a while.

At 8.30 he asked GHQ to release the two reserve divisions so that they could begin to move. This was at once agreed. He sent one to Watts (XIX), the other to Maxse (XVIII). The 39th Division had already been passed to Congreve (VII).

Gough had now to contain his impatience for action. He knew that he would simply be a nuisance to the corps commanders in their areas as the assault broke over their outposts at 9.40, so he had to be content with the information coming in by telephone through the morning while making plans with his air commander, Brigadier-General L E O Charlton. There were no aircraft in the air just then because the ground mist persisted, but at 12.30 four were launched on reconnaissance sorties. Half an hour later, the commander of the French Third Army, General Humbert, arrived. It was known that his force has been positioned round Clermont by General Pétain as a contingency reserve; but he had had no instructions to reinforce the British and had simply come to discover what was happening. When he departed, Gough told his staff to inform all corps that they were to conduct a delaying operation across the whole front, falling back as necessary but, most importantly, maintaining 'an intact, though battered and thin line in the face of the German masses . . . ' By this means, he aimed to keep the Army from being progressively destroyed. It was not precisely what he had been ordered to do but now that the battle had begun, he fixed upon his own strategy for achieving the central aim: holding firm the right flank of the British Expeditionary Force and his connection with the French. He then spoke to each corps commander, telling him that he was en route to his headquarters, beginning with Butler (III).

III Corps had fourteen battalions forward which had been attacked by fifty three. Though some of the enemy had broken through their lines, the majority were held up by small groups fighting on in strong points. Butler did not think he could get these scattered parties out, even by a deliberate counter-attack. If he stayed too long, his remaining forces would be destroyed piecemeal. His left flank had been penetrated. Gough told him not to waste his resources on counter-attacking except locally to relieve acute crises. Otherwise, he had to leave to fight his way back to the Crozat Canal while maintaining his flanks with the French on the right and XVIII Corps (Maxse) on the left.

Maxse reported that he had lost four battalions; five were still fighting, isolated in his forward zone from which he had drawn the remainder back. He was concerned that his flanks were opening, and it was agreed that the restoration of the line with his neighbours was a matter of urgency.

At XIX Corps, the smallest of the four, Gough discovered that the greater part of the front was intact. As in the other corps, the flanks had been opened, but the 50th Division, from GHQ reserve, was en route. Given this reinforcement, General Watts was confident that he could keep his corps intact.

At Templeux la Fosse, Gough found Walter Congreve VC, the brave but frail commander of VII Corps. His line had been assaulted throughout the day to the point of being broken open. The Irish regiments of the 16th Division had restored it with three counter-attacks. They were continuing a dogged defence. He had sent the 39th Division to fill the gap opened between himself and Watts.

This tour covered a distance of about 140 miles. When he returned to his headquarters at Nesle, just west of the Somme, Gough believed that his soldiers were delaying the Germans to give sufficient time for the arrival of British reinforcements – Haig was drawing on divisions from Flanders, he knew – and, in greater strength, those of the French. General Humbert's visit had satisfied him that the French were on the point of releasing divisions. He was wrong. Pétain was fearful of a German attack and of the effect of an offensive upon his soldiers. He responded tardily and meanly to calls for the deployment of part of his reserve of fifty divisions. In appreciating the reaction of the Allies to his offensive, Ludendorff had correctly assumed that

> It is not to be anticipated that the French will run themselves off their legs and hurry at once to help their Entente comrades . . .

That evening, Gough spoke to Herbert Lawrence, Haig's chief of staff, reminding him that air reports showed clearly that the Germans were still bringing forward fresh divisions to Hutier's Eighteenth and Below's Second Armies. They must expect the offensive to continue for many days. He noted that

> Lawrence did not seem to grasp the seriousness of the situation; he though that 'the Germans would not come on again the next day . . . after the severe losses they had suffered', he though that they 'would be busy clearing the battlefield, collecting their wounded, reorganising and resting their tired troops.'

Though he did not speak to Haig, the latter took a more realistic view. Against the advice of his staff, he directed that the First and Second Divisions from Flanders should go to the Fifth rather than the Third Army. The latter was allocated one and the GHQ artillery reserve. But this good news did not reach Fifth Army headquarters until later. Meantime, Gough discussed the next phase of air operations with Charlton, targets for bombing and first light reconnaissance. He learned that the Royal Flying Corps were fighting a demanding battle to hold off the enemy fighter-interceptors.

The battle was suspended during part of the night, resuming uncertainly for Germans due to mist once more. Some direction was lost among their infantry until it cleared, when heavy fighting resumed. To restore the position on the Oise, the adjoining French commander had been given permission to take over a limited area in the III Corps sector.

Some doubt remained among the corps as to how far they might retire. This was clarified at 10.45 am in a signal from Nesle:

> In the event of serious hostile attack corps will fight rearguard actions back to forward line of Rear Zone, and if necessary to rear line of Rear Zone. Most important that corps should keep in close touch with each other and corps belonging to Armies on flanks.

Despite these clear terms, General Maxse mistook their meaning and withdrew his corps in daylight at some cost as far back as the Somme. Watts had to conform. In the south, the French failed to arrive and the enemy were only thrown back from the canal junction with the Oise by an epic battle fought by an ad hoc force of infantry and cavalry under Major St Aubyn of the 60th Rifles. Motoring back to a new headquarters site at Villers-Brettoneux, Gough stopped to talk to many small parties of troops along the Somme. They were cheerful and confident but very tired. Many men fell asleep as they halted. Two days of an intense struggle had taken a good deal out of them, but the underlying problem was that they had been engaged, as Field Marshal Smuts had noted, in heavy work for weeks without proper rest.

Haig was briefed at Villers-Brettoneux on the afternoon of Saturday, 23 March. There was agreement that forty five German divisions were engaged on Fifth Army Front – actually, there were forty seven – and that considerable losses had been inflicted upon them. Gough's own losses were becoming insupportable, however, though Haig did not bring him news of further reinforcement or relief. Judging from his diary entries, he did not believe all he heard. He was surprised to find Fifth Army back on the Crozat-Somme-Tortille line and apparently accepted that a number of divisions had not stood to fight – the 16th Division, he recorded, 'did very badly and gave way immediately the enemy showed.' This was the division which had mounted three valiant and successful counter-attacks on the 21st, restoring one of Congreve's flanks. It had withstood five assaults that day. This type of misconception arose from reports that the roads behind Fifth Army were choked with units moving back in undue haste. The whole Army and some of the Corps administrative echelons were retiring necessarily, some no doubt, lacking proper operational information, unduly alarmed. There were odd groups of men among them whose units had been largely destroyed, leaderless soldiers. But the important fact was that the Army was holding together, maintaining a defensive line against which the Germans had repeatedly to mount fresh attacks.

Meantime, other false impressions were growing. After the two commanders-in-chief met personally at Dury on 23 March, Pétain believed that Haig intended, if necessary, to withdraw the British Expeditionary Force independently to the north, that is to the Channel coast. Haig made no such proposal. Such a notion may have encouraged French agreement to bring General Fayolle's army into the line late on 24 March, relieving Fifth Army along the Somme to a point opposite Peronne.

This relief proceeded very slowly. The thin ranks of the Fifth Army were finding it increasingly difficult to maintain cohesion. None of the infantry identities remained; III Corps began to break up, because the French relief was not coordinated. Elsewhere ad hoc 'battalions' were mostly composed of a few dozen officers and men who had been thrown together. The same was true of batteries. Royal Engineers, pioneer entrenching battalions, units of the administrative services had all been drawn into the fighting line. The occasional arrival of divisions from Flanders, the first of which arrived on 24 March, provided brief opportunities for rest and replenishment. Stocks of food, weapons, ammunition and equipment were dumped forward to aid this process. Meeting Pétain again at Dury, Haig found him 'very much upset, almost unbalanced', more concerned to cover Paris than maintain Allied cohesion.

Seeking to arrest the enemy, Maxse arranged to counter-attack with the French on 25 March, Palm Sunday, but the French corps commander had to admit that it was beyond his capability. VII Corps was passed to Third Army. XVIII and XIX Corps continued to hold. As they were doing so, Pétain was accusing the Fifth Army of being 'broken'. He was addressing a meeting attended by the French President and Premier, General Foch, Lord Milner representing the British Government, and Robertson's replacement as CIGS, Henry Wilson. They had gathered at Haig's urging because he believed the Alliance was in danger of being sundered militarily by Pétain. It was fortunately accepted that General Foch should assume the appointment of Allied commander-in-chief. Haig and, most importantly, Pétain would be subject to his orders.

As Gough was directing the battle on 26 March, Foch arrived at his headquarters, demanding to know why he had been withdrawing and ordering him to hold the line hereafter 'at all costs'. Whilst this was not unusual behaviour among the French high command in crisis – it astonished the Fifth Army commander and his staff and occasioned a sympathetic response from Haig. But it was a sign of a run of events of which Gough had no inkling: political alarm in Lloyd George's War Cabinet; popular alarm in France and Britain that the war might be lost; and military intrigue on the part of Henry Wilson.

The struggle continued for a further two days. On the only occasion when he had to retire further, Gough telephoned General Foch personally to ask permission, which was granted. But when they reached a predetermined stop line to join the ad hoc 'Carey's Force', the German assaults were repulsed. Immediately, on Fifth Army front, Operation Michael had been brought to a halt.

On 27 March, Gough had been advised that he and his staff were to be rested. General Rawlinson and Fourth Army Headquarters were to take command of his sector. It was an unwelcome relief but there were plans to employ them in the preparation of defences from Amiens to the sea. Haig was hoping to shield Gough from dismissal. Lloyd George needed a scapegoat; for he was uncomfortably aware that the British Expeditionary Force had been imperilled by his own obstinacy in rejecting Robertson's advice and withholding reinforcements for France and Flanders. London was now full of stories that the whole of the Fifth Army had run away because they had no confidence in General Gough. On 4 April, Lord Derby ordered his relief from command. He was to return home. Haig promised that there would be an enquiry.

Lord Derby also promised an enquiry. None was ever held. Fighting to retain his tenure as Commander-in-Chief, Haig made no further efforts to press for a hearing. He did not even mention Gough's name in his despatches for the battle. Though employment for him was found immediately after the war in the rank of lieutenant-general, he was offered no further post after 1919, when he was put on half pay.

Yet truth will out. The officers and men of Fifth Army were understandably proud of their feat in denying the enemy's plan to break open their line. Even before they returned home, they began to demand recognition. If Gough's command had been hostile to him, they would not have included him in their movement for vindication; but reinstatement of his reputation was an important aspect of it.

In part due to this stimulus, the records began to be examined. In 1924, Haig sought Gough out to ask his forgiveness for not having taken up his case for any enquiry about the Fifth Army's operations. The two men resumed their friendship. In following years, Winston Churchill and Lord Birkenhead, in separate works, exposed the injustice Gough had suffered. The world, even Lloyd George, came to accept it. But prejudice in Whitehall, abiding there since the Curragh case, militated against restoration, at least to a general's pension. Still, he had friends who could circumvent this. In the Birthday Honours of 1937, he was awarded a GCB.

Chapter References

Unpublished sources and select bibliography

Unpublished Papers
Asquith Papers – Bodleian Library
Beddington Papers – Liddell Hart Centre for Military Archives, King's College, London
Esher Papers – Churchill College, Cambridge
Gough Papers – General Sir Charles Gough, Hubert Gough, John Gough – Gough family
Haig Papers – National Library of Scotland
Lloyd George Papers – House of Lords Records
Maze Papers – Maze family
Milner Papers – Bodleian Library
Piggot Papers – Copy held by Gough family
Cabinet Office records – Public Record Office: series 1913–14, 1917, 1918

Publications
Asquith, Roy Jenkins (London), (1964)
Churchill, Vol IV, Martin Gilbert (London), (1975)
George V, His life and reign, Harold Nicolson (London), (1952)
Goughie, Anthony Farrar-Hockley (London), (1975)
Haig, The Educated Soldier, John Terraine (London), (1961)
Private Papers of, Robert Blake (ed.) (London), (1952)
Lloyd George, *War Memoirs* (London), (1933–36)
Ludendorff, Colonel David Goodspeed (London), (1966)
—— *War Memories* (London), (1919)
(Pétain), *The Two Marshals*, Philip Guedalla (London), (1943)
(Robertson), *Soldier True*, Victor Bonham-Carter (London), (1963)
Armées française dans la Grand Guerre (Paris), (1923–4)
Army and the Curragh Incident, Ian F W Beckett (ed.) (London), (1986)
Artillerie beim Angriff am Stellenskrieg, Lieutenant-Colonel G. Bruchmuller (Charlottenburg), (1926)
Enstehen, Durchfuhrung und Zussamenbruch de Offensive von 1918, General H. von Kuhl (Berlin), (1923)
Fifth Army, General Sir Hubert Gough (London), (1931)

Fifth Army in March, 1918, W Shaw Sparrow (London), (1931)

First World War, Lieutenant-Colonel C. A'Court Repington (London), (1920)

French Army, P M de la Gorce (London), (1953)

Frenchman in Khaki, Paul Maze (London), (1934)

Military Operations, France and Belgium, 1918, Part 1, British Official History series, ed. Brigadier-General J.E. Edmonds

1918, The Last Act, Barrie Pitt (London), (1962)

Road to Passchendaele, John Terraine (London), (1977)

See How They Ran, (March, 1918), William Moore (London), (1970)

Turning Points of History, Lord Birkenhead (London), (1930)

World Crisis, Winston Churchill (London), (1927)

5

Sir Percy Hobart: Eclipse and Revival of an Armoured Commander 1939–45

J Paul Harris

Major General Sir Percy Hobart (known to his friends as 'Hobo' or 'Patrick') is widely regarded as one of the British Army's most distinguished soldiers of the 1930s and 1940s. Assessing his career and reputation fairly, however, presents peculiar problems. Between 1938 and 1945 he successively commanded three different armoured divisions but he led no formation into battle[1]. Thus, while there are no defeats to be explained away, he cannot be given the principal credit for any victory. He is usually considered an intellectual soldier and was certainly in the vanguard of British military thought on armoured warfare. Yet he left us with no treatise of military theory, indeed no military book of any kind. He had positive achievements to his credit, particularly as a trainer of armoured formations, but to a large extent his reputation rests on what his friends and admirers[2] thought him capable of accomplishing rather than on what he actually achieved.

Hobart's reputation has benefitted from the attention of a number of able and prolific writers[3] who have helped secure his place in British military history. Basil Liddell Hart, the military correspondent of *The Times* during the late 1930s, seems to have had a greater respect for Hobart than for virtually any other British soldier of his acquaintance. He and Hobart maintained an intermittent but ultimately voluminous correspondence over about eighteen years. In two influential books: *The Tanks*[4] and *Memoirs*[5], Liddell Hart helped establish Hobart's image as one of the most dynamic and intelligent soldiers of his generation. A substantial biography by Kenneth Macksey[6], once an officer of the Royal Tank Regiment and subsequently a historian of armoured warfare, is perhaps the principal monument to Hobart's career.

It is in this biography and particularly in Liddell Hart's foreword to it, that the case for Hobart is made most forcefully. Hobart, it is claimed, was Britain's Guderian and also her Rommel[7]. A tank pioneer between the wars, he had a prophetic vision of what tanks could achieve in the next European conflict. As Britain's foremost trainer of armoured forces, he showed great potential as a battlefield commander. It is consequently seen as a damning indictment of the system he served that he was never given the chance to lead British armour into action. His fall from favour in 1939 is presented as resulting from the myopia of his superiors coupled with the bluntness and lack of tact which, as with his contemporary, Guderian, were natural failings in a military radical[8]. The messiah of British armoured might was so despised and rejected by his superiors that, in the summer of 1940, with Britain under threat of invasion, he was unemployed by the Regular Army and reduced to commanding part-time soldiers of the Local Defence Volunteers. While he recovered to some extent from this nadir of fortune he never achieved all of which he was capable in this country's service.

What might be called the Hobart 'legend', as summarised above, is by no means entirely false and there is no intention in this essay to disparage a soldier who undoubtedly combined character, brains and professional zeal in unusual degree. Hobart's military concepts will, however, be given a more critical appraisal than they have generally received from historians. For only when his basic ideas and opinions have been carefully sifted can we assess his true position in the history of armoured warfare, whether as the British Guderian or otherwise.

*   *   *

Percy Hobart was born in India on 14 June 1885, third son of Robert Hobart, a member of the Indian Civil Service, and of his wife Janetta. Both parents came from County Tyrone, Ireland. Shortly after Percy's birth, the family returned to England, settling initially in Hampshire. In 1899 he won a classical scholarship to Clifton College. He served in the Cadet Corps there, developed an interest in military engineering and, in 1902, passed into the Royal Military Academy at Woolwich. Hobart thoroughly enjoyed Woolwich, being successful both in class and at games. At Chatham, the School of Military Engineering, he continued to do well, gaining an excellent final report. From there he went, in 1906, at the age of twenty-one, to India. Here he joined the 1st Bengal Sappers and Miners, generally considered a very fine unit.

Life for an officer in the Indian Army at that period appears strange by modern standards. Hobart's regiment had a code of bachelorhood and officers were expected to resign their commissions if they became engaged to be married. Polo, pigsticking and shooting big game were the customary off-duty activities. Hobart participated in these with enthusiasm while at the same time being given a good deal of military responsibility, on which he also thrived. His first campaign was the 1908 expedition to suppress the Mohmand tribesmen but, though he heard shots fired in anger at a distance, he was not personally involved in any fighting.

In 1911 he was appointed, as a staff captain, to assist with the preparations being made at Delhi for the Indian coronation. A fire-fighting organisation which he had created proved very effective when a tent caught fire not far from the King and Queen. He received the personal thanks of his sovereign for this service and the official thanks of the Government of India.[9]

How did Hobart's personality develop in the years of his early manhood, before the First World War? His most obvious characteristics appear to have been intelligence, energy and a general enthusiasm for both the physical and the intellectual aspects of life. While his liking for violent sports was regarded as normal and commendable, his literary tastes attracted less favourable comment. A remark deprecating his addiction to poetry was allegedly the only adverse comment one reporting officer made about him. He was sociable and talkative in good company. Even at this period, however, his manners appear to have left something to be desired. His vivacity and loquacity, coupled with a ready wit, appear to have made him somewhat overbearing. It is probably an early indication of a tendency not to suffer fools gladly that whereas his brother Charles, who was in the Indian Civil Service, was known as Hobart the Civil, he was known as Hobart the Uncivil.[10]

His temperament certainly did not improve with the passage of time. On the contrary a tendency to impatience and intolerance became more exaggerated as his career progressed. This may have been largely due to increasing self-confidence and authority but there is also some evidence of psychological problems. In his twenties he became subject to a type of extreme depression perhaps of the sort that his contemporary, Winston Churchill, called 'Black Dog'. A particularly severe mood of this type overcame him when left on his own during a hunting trip in 1913. Kenneth Macksey's biography quotes Hobart's own description of his emotional state

'. . . the blackness of the pit descended on my soul. God knows why. I've never been so bad before: without hope: the horror of utter darkness upon me . . .'[11]

When Britain entered the First World War on 4 August 1914 Hobart was in England on leave. Like so many of his countrymen, he was desperate to get to the Front before the chance for glory passed. As Adjutant of the 1st Bengal Sappers and Miners, however, he was ordered to return to India to play his part in preparing his own regiment for war. Fearing it would be all over before he saw action, he was plunged into a particularly severe depression after which he made a series of increasingly frantic but fruitless attempts to get the order countermanded. Having rejoined his regiment in

India, however, he was in France by New Year's Day 1915 and was with the Indian Corps in time for the attack on Neuve Chapelle on 10 March 1915 in which he was awarded the Military Cross.

A campaign against the Turks in Mesopotamia had been initiated as early as 5 November 1914 when 5,000 Indian troops landed at the head of the Persian Gulf. The 3rd (Lahore) Division, with which Hobart was serving as a GSO3, was transferred to that theatre from France, Hobart himself landing there on 5 January 1916. Until March 1917, when the division was moved to Palestine, he was to serve in the Mesopotamian campaign as a divisional staff officer and, for a time, as Brigade Major with the 8th Brigade. He developed a particular interest in aerial reconnaissance and made many flights, piloted by a friendly officer in the Royal Flying Corps.[12] The end of the war, by which time he had received six mentions in dispatches and the DSO, found him in Egypt.[13]

After the war, Hobart attended a short course at the Staff College Camberley and then went to the War Office as a GSO2. At the end of 1920, he was posted once more to India and, on 5 April 1921, joined the Wana Column which was charged with the suppression of warring tribesmen on the North-West Frontier. Distinguishing himself in these operations, he gained promotion from major to brevet lieutenant colonel and was again mentioned in dispatches. In 1922 he was posted as a staff officer to the hill station of Naini Tal. Here he applied for a transfer from the Sappers to the Tank Corps, a decision which he appears to have been contemplating for some time. He joined the Corps in April 1923, shortly before taking up duties as an instructor at the Indian Staff College at Quetta.[14]

Several of those who were to be the leading lights of the Royal Tank Corps were new recruits to it at this stage. One of these was Colonel George Lindsay, who became the Chief Instructor at the Tank Corps Central School at Bovington. While he was still in India, Hobart entered into correspondence with Lindsay. At this stage it was George Lindsay, with assistance and encouragement from Fuller, who was the intellectual leader of the RTC.[15] Hobart, in India, was in something of a backwater as far as advanced military thought was concerned and was apparently little more than an intelligent and enthusiastic disciple.

The dominant idea which Hobart absorbed during the mid-twenties was that the decisive striking forces in a future war would be 'Mobile Forces' or 'Mechanical Forces' consisting primarily of tanks, but getting support from 'The Royal Tank Artillery' (specialist tanks or self-propelled guns) and also co-operating with tactical airpower. The functions of such Mobile Forces would be to 'go for the nerve centres' i.e. the enemy's centres of command, communication and supply. The functions of infantry would be largely to occupy and hold ground the tanks had captured.[16]

This basic set of concepts became, in the 1920s, the common credo of an avant garde of British tank enthusiasts which included RTC officers like

Lindsay, Hobart, Charles Broad and Frederick Pile as well as J F C 'Boney' Fuller and Basil Liddell Hart. They sometimes referred to it rather grandiloquently as 'The Armoured Idea'.[17] It was to find its most radical expression in Fuller's book *Lectures on FSR III* (1932)[18] which dealt with future warfare between armies possessing well-developed armoured forces. It had a somewhat more tentative and cautious exposition in two War Office manuals written by Charles Broad: *Mechanized and Armoured Formations* (1929) and *Modern Formations* (1931).[19]

In his post-war writings, Liddell Hart tended to portray this *avant garde* as an under-privileged minority suffering under a generally repressive War Office apparatus. The reality was that, in the late twenties and early thirties, while Field Marshal Sir George Milne was Chief of the Imperial Staff (CIGS), the RTC radicals had a major influence in the War Office, out of all proportion to their numbers or to the size of their corps. When he became CIGS in 1926, Milne, in order to keep himself up to date with the most innovative ideas circulating in the Army, appointed J F C Fuller as his Military Assistant. Fuller quickly revived a proposal which Lindsay had put forward as early as 1924 for the formation of an Experimental Mechanical Force of about brigade strength consisting of armoured fighting vehicles, motorised machine gunners, artillery and engineers, the whole to be trained to work in conjunction with tactical airpower.

Fuller himself was appointed to command the force but threw away the opportunity to do so as a result of a dispute over a relatively minor administrative point. As a result, it was actually commanded by an infantry officer, Brigadier Collins, with whom the RTC radicals and Liddell Hart expressed some dissatisfaction. Nevertheless, its exercises, held on Salisbury Plain in 1927 and 1928, attracted worldwide attention and gave the RTC great prestige[20], so much indeed that conservative officers like Lieutenant-General Sir Archibald A Montgomery-Massingberd feared for the morale of the older arms.[21]

The termination of the Experimental Mechanical Force at the end of the 1928 training season certainly owed something to these conservative fears and was portrayed by Liddell Hart as a triumph for reactionary forces. In fact it may be doubted whether much more could have been learned from continuing experiments with roughly the same collection of units and the same equipment. The General Staff did proceed with other important mechanisation experiments. Broad's doctrinal pamphlets, embracing the lessons of the Experiment Mechanical Force as the RTC radicals saw them, appeared in 1929 and 1931 and the first Tank Brigade was set up in the latter year under Broad's command.[22]

Until 1931 Hobart was on the sidelines of British experimentation with mechanised forces but he was very much an interested observer. Though he had been Lieutenant Colonel in the RTC for four years, he had returned to England in 1927 still largely ignorant of the technical side of tanks. He consequently attended the Tank Corps Centre at Bovington before going on to become second-in-command of 4th Battalion Royal Tank Corps at Catterick.

When he arrived at Catterick, Hobart, who had never been blind to the attractions of the opposite sex, was involved in a passionate but socially awkward love affair. This was with Dorothea Chater (née Field) the wife of a sapper major. Hobart had known Dorothea's husband since 1912. His postings and Chater's had frequently coincided and so he and Dorothea were often in each other's company. Hobart's biographer rather coyly informs us that by the beginning of 1927, 'their emotions had practically overcome the resistance of conscience'. Dorothea was divorced in mid-1928 and she and Hobart were married in November of that year. Hobart was forty-three. This, his first and only marriage, appears to have been a successful one.[23]

It would be pleasant to record that, having at last found his life's partner, Hobart's temperament improved. Unfortunately there is little evidence of this. While he was with 4th RTC he had some ugly rows with his Commanding Officer, M C Festing. From the beginning of 1928, he actually outranked this officer, becoming a brevet Colonel while the CO was still a Lieutenant Colonel. This would have been a tricky situation for any two individuals but for Festing and Hobart it seems to have been particularly fraught. Festing seems to have had a somewhat fiery temperament while Hobart's maniacal drive and obsessive pursuit of his own ideas of efficiency were already becoming famous. On one occasion Hobart tried completely to reorganise the unit in Festing's temporary absence! Fortunately neither officer's career seems to have suffered lasting damage as a result of this friction.[24]

After 4th RTC, Hobart's next posting was to India where, early in 1930, he took command of the Southern Armoured Car Group. It was one of the few command appointments suitable for an RTC officer of his rank. Yet, because it removed him from the mainstream of armoured force development and because it separated him from his wife (who was pregnant and whom he did not want to submit to the ordeal of a long journey) he resented it bitterly. This Indian posting proved short-lived, however, and he was back in England by the spring of 1931 to command 2nd Battalion RTC. On his return he met, for the first time, his six month daughter Grizell, who was to be his only child.[25]

At last Hobart found himself at the centre of experimentation with armoured forces. In the training season of 1931, 2nd RTC joined the trial 1st Brigade RTC, commanded by Charles Broad. Even for a commander considered one of Britain's leading experts on armoured warfare, Hobart again proved a somewhat difficult subordinate. Kenneth Macksey records that, 'Both Broad and his brigade major, Ralph Cooney, remember some lively tussles to persuade Hobart to bend in their direction and the need to get their way by demonstrating that a radio trial, for instance, would benefit 2nd Battalion RTC as much as 1st Brigade RTC'[26].

The first Tank Brigade only worked together as a formation for a single fortnight on Salisbury Plain in 1931, yet in one exercise in particular it gave a performance of great significance. One of Broad's strongest convictions (which was, in fact, shared by Hobart) was that human voice over the radio was the only really satisfactory means of exercising control over an armoured formation during operations. On one occasion, while the Army Council was watching, the Tank Brigade made a lengthy approach march through a thick fog and then, controlled by Broad's voice on the radio, executed a manoeuvre in perfect order to come to a halt a short distance from the observation stands – a most impressive display. There were further exercises the following year and, in November 1933, the Brigade was established as a permanent formation with Hobart as its commander.[27]

It is important to assess the fundamental ideas held, at this critical period, by the RTC *avant garde* to which Hobart belonged. Because of the influence of Liddell Hart, their friend and champion, these tank enthusiasts have often been regarded by historians as the intellectual heroes of the British Army between the wars and higher military authority has often been censured for failing to give them their head. But their concepts, which seem to have become, in a rather extreme form, very deeply rooted in Hobart's mind, need a more critical appraisal than they have generally received.

It was one of their basic assumptions that the mechanisation of ground forces, coupled with the increasing effectiveness of airpower, would somehow result in a marked decrease in the size of armies. Little evidence was ever put forward in favour of this proposition but it became an article of their faith that mass armies of the type seen in the First World War were redundant.[28] An intellectual problem which may have been reinforced by this assumption was the tendency (typical of the British Army in peacetime) to think small. Broad's doctrinal pamphlets of 1929 and 1931 did not consider in detail mechanised formations larger than a single division. Consequently, though operations against the enemy's flanks and in his rear were discussed, these were little more than raids. The concepts of large-scale breakthrough and envelopment, so vital to the German approach to the use of mechanised forces, were missing from these pamphlets. Another problem was that the armoured brigades, the main striking forces discussed in Broad's tracts, lacked integral infantry or field artillery. One of the criticisms which the RTC radicals had of the Experimental Mechanical Force of 1927–28 was that it included too many different types of vehicle, each with different mobility characteristics. They wanted greater homogeneity and they got it in the first Tank Brigade which consisted solely of 180 tanks. In the early thirties, the RTC radicals were thus developing tendencies to operate tanks totally independently of other arms and to exaggerate what tanks could achieve on their own.[29]

His biographer argues that Hobart never had an 'all-tank' but rather an 'all-armoured' concept.[30] In other words he accepted the value of having armoured cars, armoured self-propelled guns, even infantry mounted in armoured carriers, attached (though not very closely attached) to a tank force. But he did not want unarmoured vehicles. For the long-term future of armoured warfare, the all-armoured concept was, up to a point, correct. Today, though armoured divisions still have many unarmoured supply vehicles, their artillery is armoured, tracked and self-propelled and their infantry is mounted in armoured personnel carriers or infantry fighting vehicles. But such a concept was simply not realistic in the short run. No army of the thirties or forties had the resources to mount all of the infantry of its armoured divisions in armoured personnel carriers or to make all their artillery self-propelled. The German panzer divisions were neither all – tank nor all – armoured. Most German *Schützen* (the infantry integral to panzer divisions) were carried in lorries and, in the early years of the war panzer division artillery consisted very largely of towed guns.[30] Yet experience would show that, within an armoured formation, co-operation between tanks and artillery and tanks and infantry, sometimes very intimate co-operation, was a vital necessity. However difficult it was to achieve, the effort had to be made. Hobart's dogmatic insistence that only armoured vehicles should be attached to tank formations was no help to the British Army and nor did it assist his own career.

Another aspect of tactics which the RTC collectively and Hobart in particular got wrong was tank gunnery. During the 1920s it became a shibboleth of the RTC's gunnery school at Lulworth that tanks must combine firepower and mobility in the most literal way – that they must not halt to fire, but fire on the move.[32] This doctrine was dominant in the Royal Tank Corps and its successor, the Royal Armoured Corps, right up to the Second World War and into the desert campaign. On some occasions firing on the move may have been worthwhile but in tank-to-tank combat it was generally a pointless waste of ammunition. Even today, when tanks are fitted with stabilisation devices, most tank officers believe their gunners stand little chance of hitting a moving tank at any considerable range while themselves in motion. Hobart, however, was inflexible on this point of RTC doctrine.[33] As he wrote to Liddell Hart in September 1939,

> 'I hear the new D.M.T. (Director of Military Training) thinks tanks ought to halt to shoot! God! I though we had killed and disproved that heresy ten years ago. I suppose that the elder generation are still amateur soldiers at heart, still unconsciously look on soldiering as a part-time occupation for a land-owning gentleman and are therefore happy to accept inferiority to the professional standards of even a conscript army. Cromwell said, "I must have men who make some conscience of their work".'[34]

This is Hobart at his worst: laying down corps doctrine with a quasi-religious dogmatism, not really backing up his points with reasoned argument, and, on balance, wrong.

Hobart's views on armoured warfare were to become of particular importance because, in 1933, he became the Inspector RTC – the head of his corps. Moreover, when, in November of that year the new CIGS, Sir Archibald Montgomery-Massingberd, took the decision to establish the Tank Brigade as a permanent formation, Hobart was appointed, as we have seen, its commander. In the same month, Hobart wrote to George Lindsay who was commanding 7th (Motorised) Infantry Brigade, proposing cooperation during the training season of 1934 and outlining his beliefs about the significance of armoured forces in the opening stages of a European war:

> 'My own feeling is that Air and Gas will play so large a part that concentration of troops or any plan involving deployments à la von Schlieffen, with every road full of marching echelons will be quite impossible.
>
> All this implies that large armies and mass deployments are out of date. That only forces can move dispersed and be controlled, dispersed will have much effect.'[35]

The classic force of this kind was the Tank Brigade.

Like both Fuller and Liddell Hart, Hobart thought infantry had only very subordinate roles to play in armoured warfare. But he believed that the Tank Brigade by have 'a Secure Base of operations. And this must be mobile.' Motorised infantry could help form and protect such a base. An attached infantry unit (not an integral part of the Brigade) might also be useful to the Tank Brigade for tasks such as:

> 'Collection of prisoners etc. Holding a defile by which Tank Brigade require (sic) to return. Securing a town or other centre.'[36]

These were hardly starring roles which Hobart was offering to Lindsay!

In reply Lindsay suggested that, 'having gone as far as we have in the development of the Tank Brigade and the Motorised Infantry Brigade, we must now take a step forward and organise, and experiment with a Mobile Division.' He wanted this to consist of a mechanised cavalry brigade, supporting troops and aircraft. While Lindsay still envisaged the Tank Brigade as a decisive striking force, his thinking on mechanised warfare was becoming considerably more sophisticated than Hobart's.[37]

Despite not seeing exactly eye-to-eye with Lindsay (with whom he was not obliged to co-operate until the closing stages of the training season) Hobart's mood in the summer of 1934 appears to have been essentially buoyant. At the start of the collective training period of the Tank Brigade, in July, he explained to Liddell Hart that 'this year we are concentrating on the role indicated in Army Training Memorandum No 10, para 3(i), viz 'The strategic or semi-independent role of not less than a tank brigade against, some rearward enemy objective . . . ' He was particularly encouraged by the attitude of the CIGS, Montgomery-Massingberd:

> 'Most of the Great Ones scoff of course, but we are lucky indeed in at least having so far-seeing, resolute and open-minded a CIGS, who is giving us a chance to try and is so remarkably understanding.'[38]

Towards the end of the training season, however, the Tank Brigade was incorporated into a 'Mobile Force' which also included two armoured car squadrons, 7th Motorised Infantry Brigade, a field artillery brigade, an anti-aircraft battery and a motorised engineer company. Commanded by George Lindsay, this force was to exercise against 1st Infantry Division, under Major General J C Kennedy, which had two armoured car squadrons and a cavalry brigade attached. The exercise which was directed by General Sir John Burnett-Stuart, the General Office Commanding-in-Chief Southern Command, is probably the most controversial ever conducted by the British Army in peacetime, more ink having been spilt over it than over some battles. A great deal of the attention it has received is also certainly misplaced – its influence having been massively overstated by Liddell Hart who claimed that it broke the wave of progress on whose crest the advocates of armoured mobility was riding up to September 1934.[39]

There are several accounts of this exercise already in print[40] and space does not permit a detailed narrative here. Suffice it to say that Burnett-Stuart set George Lindsay a very demanding and perhaps time-constrained task and that the umpiring of the exercise was unfair to the Mobile Force – the majority of the umpires being from the older arms and anxious to see the RTC discomfited. Yet it is by no means clear that (as Liddell Hart implied) Burnett-Stuart, who was broadly sympathetic to the idea of mechanised mobility, programmed the Mobile Force to fail. As with most unfortunate events in peacetime armies, muddle was more in evidence than conspiracy. Lindsay made three successive plans for his conduct of the exercise. The first of these was fiercely opposed by Hobart and abandoned for that reason. Another was submitted in advance to Burnett-Stuart and dropped in deference to his advice. The plan the Mobile Force actually attempted to implement failed, at least in part, because Hobart 'felt the whole exercise had become a farce and refused to co-operate.'[41]

Evidence that the outcome of this exercise caused the General Staff to go slow on the development of armoured forces is hard to find. Montgomery-Massingberd took the decision to form the British Army's first Mobile Division that autumn and, when in February 1936, the Cabinet at last permitted a serious rearmament effort, the War Office formulated rather an ambitious programme of tank procurement. Hobart did not himself believe that the Mobile Force exercise had done any real harm. In a letter to Liddell Hart in October 1934, while expressing the view that it had been a 'frame up' to raise the morale of the infantry and cavalry, he also indicated that a revival of the spirits of these arms was badly needed. He believed that

' . . . the Powers were confident that the morale of the Tank Brigade would be unbroken whatever they did. And I think they were justified in that confidence.'[42]

Hobart personally suffered no damage to his status in the Army. In 1936, when he was coming to the end of his term as Inspector RTC, Montgomery-Massingberd commented glowingly upon him.[43]

If there was a casualty of the Mobile Force exercise it was George Lindsay's reputation. He had little role in the development of British armoured forces beyond this point. He retired in 1939 and, though he was recalled to service during the war and promoted, did not lead troops in battle or have much impact on doctrine. His decline was particularly unfortunate in that, in the mid-thirties, he had been the most sophisticated thinker on armoured forces the RTC possessed, certainly in advance of Hobart. He may be accused of lack of 'grip' in allowing Hobart to over-ride one plan and fail to participate fully in attempts to implement another, and this may be an indication of the wrong sort of temperament for field command. It does not, however, reflect on his value as a military thinker. The RTC, in the late thirties, might have profited from his relatively balanced approach to mechanised warfare had he not been sent to serve for four years as a District Commander in India[44]. The Mobile Force exercise highlighted an aspect of Hobart's personality on which contemporaries were frequently to comment. For subordinates Hobart could sometimes be a nightmare to work with[45]. For immediate superiors his temperamental behaviour was frequently exasperating and occasionally dangerous.

In March 1937, after commanding the Tank Brigade for nearly three and a half years, Hobart went to the War Office as Deputy Director of Staff Duties (Armoured Fighting Vehicles) a post which he held only briefly before becoming Director of Military Training. It seems clear that Hobart disliked the War Office, being temperamentally unsuited to administrative work in an environment he could not dominate. There were certainly reasons for an RTC officer to feel frustration in the War Office at this period. The arrival of new equipment was slow, (though that was not entirely the War Office's fault), the cavalry was being mechanised rather than the RTC expanded, and Hobart had the impression that the Adjutant-General, Lieutenant General Harry Knox, was extremely hostile to his Corps[46]. He also believed, with some reason, that the organisation which was being proposed in the War Office for the new Mobile Division was faulty. With the benefit of hindsight, however, we can see that Hobart's counter-proposals on the structure of future British mechanised formations were themselves seriously flawed.

Hobart's pride and joy was the Tank Brigade about which he could wax lyrical. Writing to Liddell Hart about it he once quoted Cromwell, 'I have a lovely company. If you could see it you would love it too.'[47] He was still uncomfortable with the concept of a full-sized mechanised division of all arms and thought the Tank Brigade, an all-tank formation, should form the basis of a slimmed-down, easily manoeuvrable Mobile Division or 'Tank Striking Force', as he preferred to call it. 'I am convinced,' he wrote in a paper of February 1937, 'that the faster a formation moves, the smaller it must be if control is to be properly exercised.' He consequently felt that, 'we should avoid adding anything to the Force beyond the minimum necessary to its protection at rest, for temporarily holding the enemy's attention and forming a pivot for manoeuvre and for holding an obstacle for a short time.' He wanted only one infantry battalion in the 'Tank Striking Force' together with one tank brigade and a reconnaissance element consisting of armoured cars and light tanks.[48]

In a slightly later paper he explained that the artillery of the type of 'Tank Striking Force' or 'Tank Division' which he was recommending 'must be reduced to a minimum in view of the weight of ammunition and numbers of vehicles' and recommended only eight 75 pdr gun howitzers.[49] Similarly, he did not wish to encumber the formation with any large number of engineers and wanted just enough to conduct hasty, improvised repairs of a minor character and to carry out minor demolitions. While water crossings might occasionally be necessary, ad hoc attachments of engineering person-nel and bridging equipment would have to suffice for this.[50]

Liddell Hart who seems to have approved of it, reckoned that the struc-ture Hobart was proposing for an armoured division in 1937 would contain about 400 tanks and only about 4,000 men.[51] The experience of the Second World War would seem to indicate that this was vastly too tank-heavy. A mere eight guns, even if these were medium artillery rather than field pieces, could not possibly provide enough firepower. The provision of infantry he recommended was equally inadequate for many kinds of operation. That Hobart should have intended a division with so many tanks to have no integral bridging capability is truly amazing and mine clearance is a prob-lem he does not seem to have considered at all. Hobart nevertheless retained this basic conception of an armoured division until at least 1941.[52]

In September 1938, after ten not very happy months as Director of Military Training, Hobart was sent to Egypt to command a Mobile Division being formed there. This embryonic formation consisted of a Mechanised Cavalry Brigade comprising 7th Hussars mounted in light tanks, 8th Hussars in trucks (later replaced by light tanks), and 11th Hussars in armoured cars, a Tank Group of two RTC battalions in light and obsolete medium tanks and the Pivot Group consisting of 3rd Regiment Royal Horse Artillery and a single infantry battalion. Hobart set to work immediately and with great energy to weld the division into a formidable team. He had considerable success, gaining by his enthusiasm and determi-nation the lasting devotion of some of his subordinates and imprinting his personality upon the division to such a degree that the imprint long out-lasted his command.[53]

But almost as soon as he arrived in Egypt, serious friction arose between Hobart's divisional headquarters and Headquarters British Troops in Egypt (BTE), under Lieutenant-General Sir Robert Gordon-Finlayson. Kenneth Macksey attributes the friction to Hobart's determination to supply the material requirements of his own division, to his irritation at the complacency existing at HQ BTE and to Gordon-Finlayson's mental slowness[54]. All of this is quite likely – up to a point. But Hobart almost always thought organisations he did not control complacent and inefficient. And a pattern of disputes with immediate superiors was now so well established in his career that to heap blame for this one onto Gordon-Finlayson's shoulders scarcely seems reasonable.

Shortly before returning to England to become Adjutant-General, Gordon-Finlayson had to make out a confidential report on Hobart which, as was normal practice, was shown to its subject before being sent on to the War Office. We do not have a copy of the report itself but Hobart took detailed notes on it which are quoted by his biographer:

> 'Difficult to serve with or understand. Active in mind and body. Very hard worker. Brain quick and full of ideas. Considerable drive. Impetuous in judgements . . . Wide technical knowledge Royal Armoured Corps. Unduly optimistic about its capacities. Marked reluctance to listen to others' opinions and is too impatient with staff officers, too jealous with regard to his own formation. Gives impression not placing much value on other arms . . . does not get the willing best from his subordinates and has not welded them into a happy and contented body.'[55]

The punch line was that Gordon-Finlayson did not believe that Hobart would make a good field commander and considered that he was not suitable for promotion. His forté was judged to be as a technical adviser on armoured fighting vehicles.

Given that the author of this report was going to be the next Adjutant-General, its consequences for Hobart's future were likely to be serious. But to what extent was it unfair? Hobart's impatience with the views of others when they conflicted with his own is undeniable. That he did not place much value on anything except tanks in mechanised warfare is a fact we have already documented. Whilst some officers of Hobart's division were devoted to him, it is by no means unlikely that his methods and attitudes were causing resentment among others – particularly in the cavalry units of whom he had a generally low professional opinion. It is probable that strong methods were necessary to convert some units from the habits appropriate to peace to those suitable for war and Gordon-Finlayson may be considered to have been in a weak position to write this report as he had not visited Hobart's division in the field. Yet it seems likely that Gordon-Finlayson's comments had a basis in reality and, with the available evidence, the extent to which some may have been unfair is, at this distance of time, extremely difficult to gauge.

In April 1939 Gordon-Finlayson was replaced as commander BTE by Lieutenant-General Henry Maitland-Wilson, known as 'Jumbo' because of his considerable girth. Initially relations between Maitland-Wilson and Hobart appear to have been quite good. But there was considerable acrimony over a large signals exercise held in the desert that October. Again the available evidence simply does not allow us to make a judgement as to rights and wrongs of the affair. Hobart did not claim that his division was faultless but resented the rather public nature of 'Jumbo's' rebuke and its tone, which he thought 'querulous'. In a letter to his wife on 27 October 1939 he wrote

> 'We had a conference on our exercise today. C-in-C found a lot of faults; almost all small matters of detail (or stupidity on the part of individuals) . . . It seems that he was bent on finding something wrong.'

On 10 November 1939 'Jumbo' wrote to General Wavell, the C-in-C Middle East, asking for Hobart's removal. Hobart, he indicated, was an excellent trainer of an armoured formation with regard to technical detail and the work of small units but

> 'His tactical ideas are based on the invincibility and invulnerability of the tank to the exclusion of the employment of other arms in correct proportion. These ideas combined with the excessive centralisation of his command under his own hands are in my opinion unsound and are already beginning to reflect themselves in the training of units.'

Maitland-Wilson considered Hobart too self-opinionated and lacking in stability to be able to adapt himself to his superior's wishes.[56]

Perhaps partly because of his physical unfitness, 'Jumbo' was given relatively little opportunity for field command in the Second World War and there has been a tendency to portray him as a Blimp. Yet little evidence on which to base such a judgement has been produced. Maitland-Wilson was a close friend of Wavell's and it is difficult to imagine Wavell associating voluntarily with a fool. Whatever the reason for Maitland-Wilson's wish to get rid of Hobart, his assessment that Hobart's tactical ideas were based on tanks 'to the exclusion of the employment of other arms in correct proportion' was accurate.

Hobart in November 1939 was truly a 'fallen star'. He was retired from the Army with effect from 9 March 1940 and became unemployed, except by the Local Defence Volunteers of the South Midlands. The restoration of his fortunes owed something to the journalism of Liddell Hart and to the advocacy of Lieutenant-General Frederick Pile, a former RTC colleague, who was now commanding Britain's anti-aircraft defences. Certainly he was brought to the attention of the new Prime Minister, Winston Churchill, who became very much an admirer, perhaps seeing something of himself in Hobart's drive, strong sense of mission and obstreperousness. Hobart had made an appeal to the King to get his dismissal in Egypt over-turned, but while that move did not succeed, the Prime Minister's influence was probably crucial in getting him other job offers. He turned down the newly created post of Commander Royal Armoured Corps because he thought it carried too little real power. He later accepted command of the newly established 11th Armoured Division, a post which he held for two years before going on to fulfil his most important mission of the war.[57]

In March 1943 he accepted command of the 79th Armoured Division, eventually nicknamed 'Hobo's Funnies'. This 'division' was really an organisation to develop equipment for, and to train units of, specialist tanks – amphibious, minesweeping, obstacle-clearing and night-fighting – for the assault on Fortress Europe. Hobart excelled at the work and won general acclaim. On 8 June 1944 he followed the 'Funnies' to the Continent to assess their performance up to that point and to make suggestions for their continuing employment. He still did not really have a combat command – the 'Funnies' did not fight as a division but were allocated to normal infantry and armoured divisions according to their needs. But at least he was on active service in the field and was to remain so until the end of the European war.[58]

Hobart had been made a Knight of the British Empire in 1943. He retired from the Army in 1946. He served as lieutenant governor of the Royal Hospital Chelsea (1948–57) and become Colonel Commandant of the Royal Tank Regiment. He died of cancer at Farnham, Surrey on 19 February 1957.[59]

*   *   *

Hobart generated controversy for much of his military career and no assessment of him can be definitive. On the whole he has been favourably treated by historians. Inspired by Liddell Hart, some have tried to find the intellectual heroes of the British Army between the wars in the messes of the RTC. Hobart may seem an obvious candidate to be acclaimed in this way. He undoubtedly had many cardinal virtues: physical and moral courage, intelligence, enthusiasm, honesty and a driving ambition to achieve military excellence in his country's service. But was he Britain's lost Guderian – the man who, had he been given his way, could have made British armoured forces the equal of their German opponents?

This may be doubted. Guderian appreciated as early as the 1920's that a combined arms approach was the essence of success in mechanised warfare. As late as 1941, Hobart had still not adequately grasped that point. Hobart's 1937 view that an armoured division should have only one infantry battalion, eight howitzers and a mere handful of sappers was shown by the experience of the Second World War to be very wide of the mark. Liddell Hart began the process of mythologising Hobart (and by implication himself) quite early in the Second World War. In May 1940 he wrote to Hobart in the following terms

'My Dear Hobo,

if there be any silver lining to the clouds hanging over our infantry masses in France it is the marvellous vindication that the last week or so has brought to the methods you developed with the Tank Brigade in 1934 and subsequently. I have just been reading through my comments on these exercises – the least they could do if they had any sense, would be to give you the opportunity of trying to counter the German application of the ideas which were originated and first practised in this country'.[60]

This was nonsense. Though the Germans were inspired by the successful British use of tanks in the First World War, by early British experimentation with mechanised formations and by some British military writing, the dominant trend in German thinking on mechanised warfare had deviated radically from Hobart's ideas by the end of the 1920s. The Meuse crossing operation of 12–13 May 1940, without which the panzer divisions could not have spearheaded the envelopment of 1st French Army Group, had depended on an assault by the substantial amount of infantry integral to the panzer divisions followed by rapid bridging by their integral engineer units.[61] But both infantry and sappers continued, well into the Second World War, to receive far too little emphasis in Hobart's conception of armoured warfare.[62]

We can never know how Hobart would have performed commanding an armoured division on active service in the desert. When Hobart left Egypt his fellow Major-General, Richard O'Connor, commented on the excellence of Hobart's training of 7th Armoured Division. But as Lord Carver has pointed out, up to Beda Fomm, when the Italians were already badly demoralized and in full retreat, 7th Armoured Division actually did little fighting in O'Connor's subsequent, celebrated campaign. Carver is implicitly critical of the impact of Hobart's military ideas on the performance of 7th Armoured Division against the Germans later on.[63] It does seem likely that Hobart's teaching was at least partly responsible for the excessive emphasis on dispersal which bedeviled British armour in the early stages of the desert war.[64] And, as several writers, have noted, tanks *per se* were not the be all and end all of armoured warfare in the wastes of North Africa.[65] Artillery and anti-tank guns, in particular, had a degree of importance in mobile warfare which Hobart, as late as 1941, gave little indication of having perceived.

A letter Hobart wrote to Liddell Hart in August 1942 showed that he was puzzled as to the correct response to Rommel's tactic of using tanks and anti-tank guns in close conjunction – often employing his tanks as bait to lure British tanks onto his anti-tank guns.[66] What British tanks actually needed when up against a German anti-tank screen was prompt and substantial artillery support, sometimes coupled with the assistance of infantry. But such a solution would not have been feasible with the very tank-heavy, tank-centred armoured divisions which Hobart continued vociferously to advocate in the early years of the war – against the better judgement of his military superiors. Hobart's success with specialist armour should not obscure the fact that his ideas on the structure and tactics of more conventional armoured divisions were seriously flawed.

Together with the many excellent qualities which we have already enumerated, significant flaws may be detected in Hobart's personality as well as in his military thought. Generally he displayed a ruthless, driving determination to succeed, but occasionally he was overtaken by fits of very severe depression and he had a persistent tendency to extreme irritability.[67] He was frequently very hard on subordinates[68] and he clashed with several immediate superiors before his dismissal by Maitland-Wilson.

Thus Hobart's fall in November 1939 was a tragedy in the classic sense, caused by defects in the hero's character and the narrowness of his vision. But, unlike most of the other 'Fallen Stars' in this volume, Hobart was again to perform in a rôle eminently suited to his abilities and to make a significant contribution to eventual victory.

Chapter Notes

1. This statement may seem surprising to readers who associate Hobart's name with leadership of the celebrated 79th Armoured Division of specialised armour. But the division never fought as a single formation. Its brigades and units were placed in support of the corps or divisions to whom they were allocated for specific operations but remained under Hobart's command. Thus his head-quarters had the demanding task of ensuring that specialist armour was fit, trained and available as the battle situation demanded. In addition, Hobart was heavily involved in the preparation of advice for forthcoming operations includ-ing the evolution of new doctrine – as he was for the Rhine Crossing, for example. Changing situations throughout the campaign in North-West Europe demanded changes in equipment and the retraining of units to use it, all of which was done under Hobart's close personal supervision. His duties took him to every corner of the battle front. Thus, although never, strictly speaking, a battlefield commander, he was never far from the scene of the action, satisfying himself that all was done as it should be. From Montgomery downwards, the higher commanders were unstinting in their praise of the work of the division and of Hobart's role as its commander. The sadness and bitterness of the past were at last obliterated by the overwhelming success of his last and greatest venture. See Nigel Duncan, *79th Armoured Division: Hobo's Funnies* (Profile, 1972) passim.
2. One of his greatest admirers was the wartime Prime Minister, Winston Churchill. In 1942 Churchill wrote that Hobart was 'a man of quite exceptional mental attainments with great strength of character' and believed 'that if . . . I had . . . insisted upon his controlling the whole of tank developments, with a seat on the Army Council, many of the grievous errors from which we have suffered would not have been committed.' Quoted in Hobart's *Dictionary of National Biography* entry (DNB 1951–60) by M R Roberts.
3. As well as by writers mentioned below, Hobart is given very favourable treat-ment in many parts of Brian Bond's standard work, *British Military Policy Between the Two World Wars* (Clarendon) 1980.
4. Basil Liddell Hart, *The Tanks* Vols I & II (Cassell) 1959.
5. Basil Liddell Hart, *Memoirs* Vols I & II (Cassell) 1965.
6. Kenneth Macksey, *Armoured Crusader* (Hutchison) 1967.
7. ibid, p. IX.

8. ibid, pp. 171–178. On p. 178 Macksey attributes Hobart's relegation to the retired list in 1940 to 'the shortcomings of a myopic bureaucracy'.

9. The above paragraphs on Hobart's early life are taken partly from Macksey, op. cit., pp. 3–18 and partly from the DNB (1951–60).

10. Macksey, op. cit., pp. 10–14.

11. ibid, pp. 16–17.

12. ibid, pp. 19–61.

13. D.N.B. (1951–60).

14. Macksey, op. cit, pp. 70–79.

15. See for example Lindsay's ambitious and far-ranging staff papers, '*The Organisation and Employment of a Mechanical Force*', a memorandum from Lieutenant Colonel G Lindsay to HQ RTC Centre, 25 April 1924, 15/12/1/2 Liddell Hart Papers, LHCMA and '*Suggestions Regarding The Best Means of Rending The Royal Tank Corps In Particular And The Army In General More Suited To The Probable Requirements Of Future Warfare*', 15 May 1926, 15/12/4, Liddell Hart Papers, Liddell Hart Centre for Military Archives, King's College London. Lindsay's thought in the twenties is discussed at some length in J P Harris, 'British Armour 1918–40: Doctrine and Development', Chapter 2 of Harris and Toase, *Armoured Warfare* (Batsford) 1990.

16. Macksey, op. cit, pp. 80–86.

17. See, for example, Hobart to Liddell Hart, 6 December 1940, 1/376/116, Liddell Hart Papers, LHCMA and Macksey, op. cit, p. 96.

18. J.F.C. Fuller, *Lectures on FSR III* (Sifton Praed) 1932, passim.

19. Copies of these doctrinal tracts are held at the Tank Museum Library at Bovington. Their contents are discussed in some detail in J P Harris, op. cit, pp. 37–40.

20. The Experimental Mechanical Force and Fuller's dispute with the War Office over it are discussed in several books. For a recent view by the present writer see J P Harris, op. cit, pp. 35–37. For a much more pro-Fuller account see Liddell Hart, *The Tanks*, Vol. I, pp. 241–246.

21. See Montgomery-Massingberd's unpublished *Autobiography of a Gunner*, p. 53, Montgomery-Massingberd Papers, LHCMA.

22. J P Harris, op. cit, pp. 37–40.

23. Macksey, op. cit, pp. 87–89 and D.N.B. 1951–60.

24. Macksey, op. cit, p. 91.

25. ibid. p. 97.

26. ibid, p. 103.

27. Macksey, *The Tank Pioneers* (Jane's) 1981, pp. 86–88.

28. Modern Formations, section 5, Size and organization of armies, pp. 12–13 and section 6, 'The effect of the aeroplane,' pp 13–14, Tank Museum Library.

29. J P Harris, op. cit, pp. 35–40.

30. Macksey, *Armoured Crusader*, p. 166.

31. Eric Grove, *German Armour 1939–40*, (1976) p. 21.

32. Liddell Hart, *The Tanks*, Vol I, pp. 228–229.

33. See Hobart's December 1936 memorandum on '*Tank Gunnery*', 15/11/4, Liddell Hart Papers, LHCMA.

34. Hobart to Liddell Hart, 21 September 1936, para. 4, 1/376/35(a)b, Liddell Hart Papers, LHCMA.

35. Hobart to Liddell Hart, 10 November 1933, 1/376/5, Liddell Hart Papers, LHCMA.

36. *Use of Armoured And Mechanised Forces In The Early Stages Of A European War, November 1933*, 1/376/5, Liddell Hart Papers, LHCMA.

37. Harold Winton, *To Change An Army* (Brassey's) 1987, pp. 177–178.

38. Hobart to Liddell Hart, 24 July 1934, 1/376/8, Liddell Hart Papers, LHCMA.

39. Liddell Hart, *The Tanks* Vol I, p. 332.

40. A good and relatively recent account is to be found in Brian Bond, op. cit, pp. 165–170.

41. Winton, op. cit, pp. 179–183.

42. Hobart to Liddell Hart, 7 October 1934, 1/376/9, Liddell Hart Papers, LHCMA.

43. Macksey, *Armoured Crusader*, pp. 127–129.

44. Bond, op. cit, p. 184 and Winton, op. cit, p. 222.

45. Duncan, op. cit, p. 391.

46. Hobart to Liddell Hart, 12 September 1936, 1/376/35(a)b, Liddell Hart Papers, LHCMA.

47. Hobart to Liddell Hart, 21 September 1936, 1/376/35(a)b, LCMHA.

48. *Organisations Of Higher Mobile Formations*, 3 February 1937, 15/11/6, Liddell Hart Papers.

49. *Organisation of Units and Formations In The Regular Field Force Using Armoured Fighting Vehicles*, pp. 18–19.

50. ibid, pp. 15 and 19.

51. Liddell Hart to Hobart, 2 January 1941, 1/376/121, Liddell Hart Papers, LHCMA.

52. Hobart to Liddell Hart, 12 January 1941, 1/376/122, Liddell Hart Papers.

53. Macksey, *Armoured Crusader*, pp. 157 and 174.

54. ibid, pp. 157–158.

55. ibid, pp. 162–163.

56. ibid, pp. 165–173.

57. ibid, pp. 177–242.

58. ibid, pp. 242–321, Duncan, op. cit, passim.

59. DNB 1951–60.

60. Liddell Hart to Hobart, 24 May 1940, 1/376/86.

61. For a recent concise account of the rise of the German panzer forces up to and including the 1940 campaign see W Heinemann, 'The Development of German Armoured Forces 1918–40' in Harris and Toase, op. cit, pp. 51–69.

62. Just how far both Hobart and Liddell Hart were, in 1940 and the first half of 1941, from a true appreciation of the German organization for and conduct of armoured warfare is well illustrated in their correspondence. On 2 January 1941 Liddell Hart commented to Hobart on the structure on the contempory British armoured division. 'It is rather appalling to think of an armoured division with 17,000 men. Whatever is the number of vehicles?' (1/376/121, Liddell Hart Papers) Hobart replied on 12 January, 'My dear Basil – yes, of course, an Armoured Division of 17,000 with several thousand vehicles, mostly unarmoured is a monstrosity. Like the WO which conceived it, it must be paralysed by its own obesity.' (1/376/122 Liddell Hart Papers.) But in fact German panzer divisions at this period were themselves around 17,000 men strong and had

mostly unarmoured vehicles. The armoured divisions which Hobart advocated were truly monstrous – monstrously tank-heavy. On 1 May 1941 Hobart again wrote to Liddell Hart on armoured division composition, 'I am still as I have always been in favour of tank bdes being wholly armoured – I would like 3 armd bdes, each of 3 tank regts only – plus a small 4th Bde of infantry + guns and a big recce unit.' (1/376/131 Liddell Hart Papers) Hobart seems to have been advocating a ratio of tank regiments to infantry battalions of perhaps 9:1, something far more ridiculous than anything his War Office superiors conceived. All the documents quoted above are in the LHCMA.

63. For O'Connor's comment on Hobart's training of 7th Armoured Division see Macksey, *Armoured Crusader*, p. 173. For Carver on 7th Armoured Division see Michael Carver, *Dilemmas Of The Desert War* (Batsford) 1986, pp. 13–13.

64. The perniciousness of this tendency is strongly emphasised in Carver, op. cit, p. 16. Hobart's obsession with dispersal emerged as early as 1934. See Hobart to Lindsay, 10 November 1933, 1/376/5, Liddell Hart Papers, LHCMA.

65. F W von Mellenthin, *Panzer Battles* (Oklahoma) 1956, pp. 15–17 and Turner and Hamilton, *The Sidi Rezegh Battles* (OUP) 1957, p. 53.

66. Hobart to Liddell Hart, 25 August 1942, 1/376/171, Liddell Hart Papers, LHCMA.

67. Macksey, *Armoured Crusader*, pp. 16–17 and 103.

68. This is pointed out even by those who respected and liked him. Horace Birks is quoted on his treatment by Hobart in Macksey's *Armoured Crusader*, p. 109 and the same phenomenon is discussed by Nigel Duncan, op. cit, p. 1.

6

Maurice Gamelin and
the Defeat of France, 1939–1940

Martin S Alexander

Few officers have suffered the ignominy reserved for General Maurice-Gustave Gamelin. Since June 1940 he has been largely an object of scorn – 'the man who lost the Battle of France'. According to one contemporary, the journalist André Géraud ('Pertinax'), 'No-one wished to know him; people avoided him as though he had contracted the plague.' In 1947 A J P Taylor reviewed Gamelin's memoirs, *Servir*, in an article with the cruel title 'General Gamelin: Or How to Lose'. He described Gamelin as a 'political soldier [. . .] standing by in philosophical detachment' whilst France hurtled down a road to military disaster. Quite justifiably, the Canadian scholar John Cairns remarked in 1974 that: 'To date, for Gamelin, it has been something like thirty years of open season.' Hounded by normally dispassionate academic studies as well as by predictably partisan memoirs, the general had 'almost been reduced to caricature: diminutive, softhanded, puffy faced [. . .]; an endlessly dilatory political soldier, a finally disastrous generalissimo.' As late as 1982, the influential French historian Jean-Baptiste Duroselle sneered that Gamelin was 'a man [. . .] who fostered an illusion', a man of straw.[1]

Recent years have, however, seen various currents of revisionism in the historiography of the later Third Republic. The drift in some of these has been towards refurbishing Gamelin's long-maligned reputation. Douglas Porch, exploring the general's relations with French Intelligence from 1930 to 1940, has suggested that Gamelin 'does not appear to have been the weak and characterless man of legend. On the contrary, he bent his energies towards keeping a [politically and doctrinally] restive army [. . .] in line'.[2] This chapter seeks to extend this line of argument. It endeavours to respond to Cairns' injunction 'to consider Gamelin as fairly as it considers every commander on whom finally the sun did not shine.'[3]

In the case of Gamelin, the first task of any revisionism must be to recapture a sense of the reputation he enjoyed before his fall from grace. In the spring of 1940, the very eve of the Battle of France, he bestrode the stage of Allied grand strategy. His voice carried weight in Paris; his views were valued in London. He counted many of France's leading politicians among his friends. In Britain, to which he had paid visits in May and September 1937, September 1938 and June 1939, he was accorded an affection rarely shown to any foreigner. The British respected his qualities as a 'thinking man's general' and referred to him – in an expression coined by Leslie Hore-Belisha, Neville Chamberlain's Secretary of State for War – as *'notre Gamelin'*.[4]

Even the description of Gamelin as a 'fallen star' is echoed in contemporary appraisals. Colonel Jacques Minart, part of Gamelin's personal *cabinet* from September 1939 to May 1940, wrote that the general was 'blessed with an extra-ordinary intelligence and flexibility of mind'.[5] Gamelin was, by this time, not only polished but vastly experienced. His career had advanced effortlessly. As chief of the General Staff from 1931 to 1935 he had learned how to accommodate the vicissitudes of politics.[6]

At that time, and after his promotion to the vice-presidency of the *Conseil Supérieur de la Guerre* (CSG) in 1935, Gamelin had avoided falling foul of the often-ephemeral administrations of the Third Republic. As Minart aptly remarked, 'neither the changes of government nor the passage of successive ministers of war through the Rue Saint-Dominique had exercised any harmful influence over his personal destiny.' On the contrary, Gamelin had developed a consummate skill for exploiting his contacts in the corridors of power. 'An ever-present, thanks to the head start given him by his promotion to general at the age of forty-five, as the teams around him fell apart he retained a profound belief in his own star.'[7]

Celestial imagery of this sort inspired another senior collaborator of Gamelin during the phoney war, General Jules Armengaud of *L'Armée de l'Air*. Head of French air liaison to Poland in September-October 1939, Armengaud commanded the air defences of Paris in 1940. Worried by the speed with which the Wehrmacht had overcome the Poles, Armengaud preached caution among the Franco-British political and military leadership – a leadership which 'wore the contented smiles of men who [thought they] knew the value of our [high] command, the virtues of the French soldier and who, remembering our victory on the Marne, had faith in the lucky star of France.'[8]

The supposedly 'lucky' Gamelin had been born in Paris in 1872. Though tutored by Jesuits, Gamelin grew up a broad-minded liberal. He acquired a lifelong passion during adolescence for painting, philosophy and history. More than of most modern commanders, it could justifiably be claimed that Gamelin was an 'educated soldier'.[9]

Tactful and intelligent, Gamelin was the antithesis of the military philistine. Observers who expected all soldiers to be rough and ready could be misled by this sophistication. Augusta Léon-Jouhaux, the wife of a leading French trade unionist, scrutinised Gamelin during their imprisonment together at Schloss Itter, in Austria, from 1943 to 1945. 'I asked myself [notes her diary] if he would not have been more suited to a career as a scholar or ecclesiastic'. France's Prime Minister from March to June 1940, Paul Reynaud, criticised Gamelin for having the manner of a bishop or a prefect.[10] But Reynaud's censorious tone was to be expected. He and Gamelin had been at loggerheads since 1934, when he had antagonised the high command by lobbying for the scheme of then-Major Charles de Gaulle to reorganize the French army into an all-professional *armée de métier*. Reynaud's support of de Gaulle had, in Gamelin's sight, been politically provocative and professionally distracting – fanning parliament's suspicions of military praetorianism and distracting the government from the rearmament and mechanisation on his own agenda.[11]

This pre-war dispute ensured that de Gaulle and Reynaud sought opportunities to censure Gamelin. Indeed, in his war memoirs, de Gaulle described how he visited Gamelin in March 1940 at the latter's wartime headquarters in the Château de Vincennes. He condemned Gamelin for an excessive intellectualism – 'reminiscent of a military research scientist, locked up in his laboratory, experimenting in search of a magic formula for victory'.[12]

These, however, were retrospective critiques. They were not voiced *before* the fall of France. Rather, they were calibrated to enhance the subsequent reputation of their authors for clairvoyance.[13] De Gaulle, for example, conscious of his dubious political legitimacy not just in June 1940 but also at the time of his comeback in May 1958, had a particular need to denigrate former mainstays of the Third Republic.

Gamelin was not a narrow military technician. From first to last, he strove to ensure amicable civil-military relations. The issue was one of understandable importance to him. When he graduated from the *École de Guerre*, in 1899, the Dreyfus Affair was at its height. When, in 1906, he joined the staff of an earlier rising star of the French army, General Joseph Joffre, the dust had hardly settled from the *affaire des fiches* – the Radical party's attempt to republicanise the officer corps and purge diehard monarchists and Bonapartists.

The First World War reinforced Gamelin's convictions about the proper intersection between political and military authority. In 1914 he served as chief of operations to Joffre, by then the French Commander-in-Chief. According to legend, he conceived the French counterattack on the Marne: his stock rose as he was credited with helping to save Paris.[14]

Joffre's dismissal in December 1916, however, scarred Gamelin deeply. Certain lessons forcibly impressed themselves: most enduringly, that a general needed a cross-bench alliance of supporters in parliament and the press. Gamelin therefore consciously ingratiated himself with senators, deputies and journalists, placing premiums with a syndicate of political insurers. Among his friends were Albert and Maurice Sarraut, Radical party barons from Toulouse; Joseph Paul-Boncour, a neo-socialist senator; and the *Alliance Démocratique* conservatives, Jean Fabry and André Tardieu.

It was Tardieu, then prime minister, who appointed Gamelin Deputy Chief of the General Staff in 1930. The republican Gamelin was intended to counterbalance General Maxime Weygand, then newly-appointed Chief of the General Staff. Weygand had risen on the coat tails of Foch, the Allied Supreme Commander, in 1918. Irascible and impetuous, Weygand tolerated the *Troisième République* but could not bring himself to love it. Indeed, to secure appointment in 1930, he was obliged to compose a disclaimer of anti-republican designs – a disclaimer which the War Minister, André Maginot, had to read aloud in parliament.[16]

It was, then, through choppy waters that Gamelin navigated towards high command in his own right. The latter became his in January 1935, when Weygand retired. Gamelin was named Chief of the General Staff and Commander-in-Chief Designate for time of war. The last holder of the combined posts had been his own mentor, Joffre. Gamelin understood perfectly what was required of him: to mediate, to construct and conserve a consensus between the Army and the Republic.

Yet Gamelin was no mere figurehead. He had an impressive blend of staff and command experience. In 1917–18 he had led the 9th Infantry Division and an ad hoc corps. From 1919 to 1925 he honed his skills as a diplomat, heading the French military mission to the Brazilian Army. Between 1925 and 1927, he pacified the Druze rebellion in French-mandated Syria. As the historian Paul-Marie de La Gorce has commented, Gamelin's record stood in marked contrast to that of Weygand, the staff officer *par excellence*. Gamelin had directed difficult operations at the front. He 'could not be accused [. . .] of being but the shadow of a great commander'. All the same, Gamelin ascended the military hierarchy in the late 1930s not least because – as Germany's military attaché in Paris remarked in 1937 – he was 'the exceptional French soldier who [. . .] did not [. . .] arouse the belief that he was making himself too powerful'.[17] Widely admired and trusted, Gamelin was the French high command's master impresario of bureaucratic politics.

Down to 1939, Gamelin's main mission was to rearm France against the possibility of renewed conflict with Germany. In June 1936 the *Front Populaire*, led by Léon Blum, took office. Its minister for war was the Radical deputy from the Vaucluse, Edouard Daladier (who was also charged with 'co-ordinating' national defence). This is not the place for a full reappraisal of Daladier's achievements in charge of French war preparation in 1936–40 (when, from April 1938 to March 1940, he also served as prime minister). Nevertheless, the qualities he displayed in masterminding France's rearmament from 1936 to 1939 require acknowledgement. In Vivian Rowe's words, the 'urgency with which an often maligned Daladier expanded the armed forces, developed new weapons and prepared for a war that he [. . .] looked upon with loathing [. . .] has seldom been recognised'. As Jeffery Gunsburg has added, there is 'much to admire in the way Gamelin built a smaller and industrially weaker France into a powerful military machine to oppose Germany.[18]

In short, Daladier and Gamelin not only identified the threat from Nazi Germany; they responded to it robustly, via their four-year rearmament scheme of 7 September 1936. This programme dwarfed the defence effort of previous conservative governments – including that of 1934 in which the war minister had been Marshal Philippe Pétain, who, from 1940 to 1945, headed the collaborationist Vichy regime. Despite being elected to advance social reform, Blum and Daladier did far more for guns than for butter. They personified the Left's tradition of Jacobin patriotism. Through his co-operation with them, Gamelin was a key member of a triumvirate which laid the basis for France's ability to resist Germany in September 1939.[19]

On the war's outbreak, Gamelin was concerned with the difficulty posed by Belgian neutrality. The French frontier with Belgium lacked heavy fortification of the Maginot Line type. From 1920 to 1936, France had enjoyed a military convention with Belgium. After the convention's abrogation, Gamelin had pinned his hopes on covert collaboration with his Belgian counterpart, General Edouard Van den Bergen. Employing the French military attaché in Brussels, Colonel Edmond Laurent, as a go-between, Gamelin sought to obviate the absence of a formal Franco-Belgian alliance.[20] But the Belgians clung to their neutrality in 1939–40, seeing in it the only means of avoiding internal political turmoil and conflict between Flemings and Walloons. Indeed, in Judith Hughes's words, 'the Belgians viewed France's failure to construct concrete bastions in the north as primarily a danger to themselves; the unfortified frontier constituted an invitation to the Germans to repeat their strategy of 1914.[21] Having exaggerated the political leverage of francophile Belgian army officers, Gamelin found that his hopes of reviving the 1914–18 Anglo-Franco-Belgian alliance were misplaced.

Consequently, in September 1939 the Allies faced unpleasant choices over the means of defending Northern France. They could stand pat along the border with Belgium. This was quickly ruled out: the region's high water-table rendered it unsuitable for an emergency programme of heavy defence works. Moreover, the Pas-de-Calais and the Nord contained key French industries. Shielding the coal mines, steel works and engineering factories of Lille, Douai and Valenciennes demanded a strategy of forward defence. Thus the debate turned around two alternatives: an advance of the Allied left flank to the River Scheldt (or Escaut), known as Plan E; or a bolder intervention, termed Plan D, to the River Dyle, a waterway east of Brussels.

Neither manoeuvre could be initiated, however, until Belgium requested Allied assistance or Germany violated Belgian neutrality.[22] During

September and October 1939, the Allied commanders settled on Plan E. General Sir Edmund Ironside, Chief of the British Imperial General Staff, voiced his dislike of the plan. He feared for the BEF's supply lines which, in Plan E, would have run parallel to the coast, between the Scheldt and the Channel. For the sake of Anglo-French unity, however, Ironside's reservations were not sustained.[23]

Plan E resulted, in part, from Gamelin's seniority and his stature in the sight of the British War Cabinet. (The latter had agreed in staff talks during July and August 1939 to subordinate the BEF to his authority).[24] Because of the modest size of British ground forces, it was accepted in London, and at BEF headquarters in France, that the French would call the tune in land strategy.[25] Plan E's adoption stemmed, also, from the compelling logic of a forward defence. The strategy was doubly attractive to the Allies. First, it promised to protect the output of vital French war industries. Secondly, it offered to accomplish an old French wish to displace any fighting from French soil onto Belgian.

In November 1939, however, the Allies switched from Plan E to the more ambitious Plan D. Gamelin has been castigated for this change – one which, in May 1940, diverted some of the best Allied units into northern Belgium, away from the German breakthrough on the Meuse. The formations which executed Plan D included nine all-motorised divisions of the BEF, and General Henri Giraud's French VIIth Army (which contained the 1st Light Mechanised Division and two motorised infantry divisions, the 9th and 25th). The decision to shift from Plan E to Plan D – though it led to the expression of concern on the part of his senior subordinate, General Alphonse Georges – was indeed strongly favoured by Gamelin.

But the decision was far from being Gamelin's alone. Taken at an inter-allied command meeting at Vincennes on 14 November 1939, the modified plan had the support of Britain's military leaders. The latter included Ironside and the Chief of the Air Staff, Air Chief Marshal Sir Cyril Newall. It is not surprising that the revised manoeuvre won such broad assent. It greatly increased the likelihood of incorporating the Belgian Army – a mobilised force of twenty-two divisions – into Allied dispositions.[26]

The change of plan was detailed in Gamelin's *Instruction Personnelle et Secrète* (IPS) Number 8, of 15 November. It was ratified by the Franco-British governments on 17 November, in London, at the third meeting of the SWC (the inter-allied Supreme War Council). There were opportunities at several levels in the Allied high command to turn down Plan D. Instead, at the time, there was general acquiescence. Many who scarcely quibbled with the Dyle manoeuvre when it was adopted were, with hindsight, to censure it after the *débâcle* of May–June 1940. Then, Allied politicians and military chiefs alike sought to lay responsibility for the defeat at each other's door. As the individual whose signature was attached to Plan D, through IPS No. 8, Gamelin served as a convenient scapegoat.[27]

A second controversy surrounds the affair of *les plans tombés du ciel* at Mechelen-sur-Meuse, in January 1940. The facts may be briefly summarised. Two German staff officers carrying plans of the Wehrmacht's western offensive piloted their aircraft too close to the German-Belgian border and were forced down. The failure of the Germans to burn their papers before Belgian soldiers captured them provided Allied intelligence with a fortuitous insight into Wehrmacht planning. Why, critics ask, did the incident not lead to a radical re-thinking of Allied strategy?

The documents showed that the main German attack would fall through the Low Countries. This confirmed French and British intelligence appreciations. Commentators have suggested it must have been apparent to the Allies that the Germans would revise their strategy in the light of this accidental disclosure of their original intentions.

The affair was not, however, altogether an open-and-shut case. It occurred to the French that they might be facing a German deception – a ruse to plant misleading plans on the Allies. The circumstances appeared suspicious: the slipshod navigation by the aircraft, the half-hearted attempt to destroy the documents. The German secret services had already outwitted their British counterparts once (over the Venlo affair of November 1939, when two SIS operatives were captured on the Dutch-German frontier as they sought contacts with supposed anti-Nazi figures from the German opposition).[28] Venlo left Colonel Maurice Gauché, head of the French 2e Bureau and Colonel Louis Rivet, chief of the SR (*Service de Renseignements*), doubly wary of being duped by the Mechelen incident.[29]

French intelligence had identified large Wehrmacht deployments of tanks and motorised units east of Holland and Belgium since the return of German forces from Poland in October 1939. Major German mobile forces remained in northern Westphalia and the Rhineland in the early months of 1940.[30] Indeed, in attending to the dramas at Sedan and Monthermé during the battle for the Meuse crossings from 12–15 May 1940, it is easy to overlook the fact that the Germans *also* deployed massed armour in the north during their May 1940 offensive. In *Fall Gelb*, or the so-called 'Manstein Plan', adopted in February 1940, 9th Panzer Division, as well as two SS motorised divisions, were launched into Holland, whilst the XVIth Panzer Corps of General Hoepner, with 3rd and 4th Panzer Divisions, was directed into the Gembloux Gap in Belgium. Admittedly, French headquarters also over-estimated the barrier represented by the Ardennes and the Meuse. This led to overconfidence. It caused neglect of tactical intelligence and air reconnaissance which, at the eleventh hour, on 10 and 11 May 1940, reported German armoured columns advancing on Sedan and Dinant.[31] But some senior German commanders were themselves slow to endorse the bold strategy of *Fall Gelb*. Doubts persisted on the German side over the *Sichelschnitt* manoeuvre entrusted to the XVth, XLIst and XIXth Panzer Corps of Generals Hoth, Reinhardt and Guderian – and whether it could knock France right out of the war.[32]

After the criticisms that Gamelin mismanaged the defence of Northern France and Belgium and, secondly, that he misunderstood the plans which so adventitiously came the Allies' way at Mechelen, a third charge is sometimes levelled against Gamelin's conduct in May 1940. It is said that he remained too aloof and delegated too much responsibility to his principal operational subordinate, General Georges, Commander-in-Chief of the North-Eastern Theatre. It is alleged that he treated the campaign of May 1940 as 'Georges's battle'. Yet this, too, is an accusation which close scrutiny calls into question.

First, it has to be noted that Gamelin's responsibility was not just for co-ordinating all three French armed services and for overseeing the British forces in France; he also had to co-ordinate operational theatres outside North-West Europe. His task demanded vision. It required him to retain a broad strategic perspective on the Allied war effort as a whole. His role was not that of an Army or even an Army Group Commander. Rather, it foreshadowed the part played later in the Second World War by grand strategists such as General George C Marshall and Field Marshal Lord Alanbrooke. Gamelin can, indeed, be labelled a 'political general' in a distinctly complimentary sense. For he showed awareness of how the skills of the military manager had superseded boots-and-spurs generalship as the key factor in high command. He was, perhaps, the first senior military leader of 1939–45 to re-learn how the conduct of war at the summit was a business straddling the frontiers of grand strategy and politics. As the novelist Jules Romains acknowledged, after visiting Vincennes in December 1939:

> 'those who tell you that Gamelin has made his successful career thanks to the politicians [. . .] forget that high-ranking military men always have to reckon with politicians.'[33]

Though necessarily sensitive to politics, Gamelin also saw more of the Franco-British forces than might have been expected in view of his burdens as inter-Allied commander. For all the calls made on him by meetings of the SWC and the French *Comité de Guerre*, Gamelin was no invisible troglodyte. Quite the reverse: he tried three times in the war's first two months to acquaint himself with conditions at the front. On 27 September 1939, with the commander of Army Group No. 2, General Gaston Prételat, he visited the French Vth Army in Alsace. At its headquarters in Saverne, he conferred with the Army Commander, General Victor Bourret, the latter's Chief of Staff, General Jean de Lattre de Tassigny, General Aubert Frère of 13th Corps and General Georges Bloch of 5th Corps. Later that day, Gamelin travelled to Lorraine. There, he spoke with the commanders of the 20th Corps and 9th Corps, Generals Hubert and Laure, in the presence of General Edouard Requin, the commander of their parent formation, the

IVth Army. Completing this inspection, Gamelin visited the 5th North African Division and 26th Infantry Divisions, units of IIIrd Army, and talked to that Army's Commander, General Charles Condé and Chief of Staff, Colonel Tessier.[34]

Gamelin again visited the front on 7 October and 15–16 October 1939. On the former occasion, he toured the IInd Army of General Charles Huntziger, bordering Luxembourg, and the IXth Army of General André Corap, west of the Ardennes. On the latter, he inspected the formations on the Belgian frontier. He conferred with General Georges Blanchard, commander of French 1st Army, General Jules Prioux, commanding the French armoured cavalry corps, General Lord Gort and Lieutenant General Sir Henry Pownall, Commander and Chief of Staff of the BEF. Finally, he visited General Fagalde of French 16th Corps, on the Channel coast.[35]

On 8 January 1940 Gamelin returned to the BEF, to invest Gort and Ironside with the Grand Cross of the Légion d'Honneur. But such ceremonial did not blind him to the serious business of war. With the medals distributed, he took Ironside on a two-day inspection to Alsace, and conferences with Bourret of Vth Army, and with General Henri Dentz, who had been Deputy Chief of the French General Staff in 1938–39 and was now commanding 12th Corps. Still accompanied by Ironside, Gamelin proceeded to Fort Hoche in the Maginot Line and then to meetings with Generals Prételat, of Army Group No. 2, Requin, of IVth Army, and Condé, of IIIrd Army.[36]

Gamelin made a further tour of front-line units on 8–9 March 1940. This time he returned to units on the Channel flank, and to those defending the Franco-Belgian border. He conferred with General Gaston Billotte, directing Army Group No. 1, Generals Giraud, Blanchard and Corap, of VIIth, Ist and IXth Armies, as well as with Gort and Pownall, and the British corps commanders, Sir John Dill and Sir Alan Brooke. The units Gamelin saw included the 68th Infantry Division of General Beaufrère on the coast, 9th Infantry Division under General Henri Didelet, 53rd Infantry Division under General Etcheberrigaray and 21st Infantry Division under General Lanquetot (all of Giraud's army); 2nd North African Division under General Dame and 82nd Infantry Division under General Armingeat (both in Blanchard's Ist army); 18th Infantry Division under General Duffet, 61st Infantry Division under General Vauthier and 101st Fortress Division under General Portzert (all in Corap's IXth Army).[37]

On 22 and 23 March, Gamelin made a final front-line inspection. As on his January mission, he was accompanied by Ironside. This ultimate tour took Gamelin back to Huntziger's IInd Army. It also included a return to Condé's IIIrd Army in Lorraine, where he visited the Maginot fort of Rochonvillers and conferred with General Freydenberg, commanding the colonial infantry corps, as well as with the staffs of the 20th, 56th and 2nd Infantry Divisions.[38]

Such activity indicates that Gamelin maintained a commendable level of contact with the front for a higher commander of his rank and responsibilities. It is not the case that Gamelin was personally out of touch. What appears to have happened, to judge by the performance of French formations in May 1940, is that his bidding was too often done badly – and, in some instances, not done at all.

The operational 'lessons' of the German campaign in Poland impressed Gamelin from the very outset. He saw that Wehrmacht methods were closely and accurately monitored by French intelligence.[39] Even more detailed appraisals reached Gamelin once French air force and army missions to Polish headquarters had filed their reports.[40] As early as 13 September 1939, Gamelin expressed concern to his staff about the 'tremendous moral and material effectiveness' of low-level air attack on the Poles. 'We'll have to teach them a lesson they'll not forget [he added], whenever they attempt low-altitude sweeps [here].'[41] Beginning the next day, 14 September, Gamelin ordered his *cabinet* to communicate to the higher staffs of the North Eastern theatre his anxiety about German tank-aviation tactics.

Periodic command conferences were also called that autumn, to brief Generals Georges, Prételat, Bineau and Doumenc. Besides these gatherings, Gamelin charged the inspector of infantry, General Joseph Dufieux, with responsibility for intensive training to deal with air and armoured attack. Dufieux was dispatched to the frontiers in this capacity as early as 14 September 1939, to 'see for himself that precautions against enemy aviation and the anti-aircraft battle were really receiving priority attention among front-line units'. As Gamelin reflected in October, the 'vital thing' was that 'troops like ours, which aren't yet battle-hardened, be capable of withstanding a German onrush made in maximum strength.' Palpably unjustified was an allegation in June 1940 by the US Ambassador in Paris, William C Bullitt, that neither 'Gamelin [. . .] nor any of his subordinates [. . .] drew any lessons whatsoever from the German invasion of Poland [. . .] No training whatsoever was given to the French troops in methods of resisting combined attack by airplanes and tanks'.[42]

The shock of the French collapse lured Bullitt into hyperbole. Yet he was correct in sensing that something had gone awry. Gamelin, for all his inspections and injunctions, failed to eradicate the inertia which prevailed in *some* Allied headquarters in 1939–40. Minart, a member of Gamelin's *cabinet*, lamented that field commanders too rarely acted upon the general's 'wise suggestions'. Subordinates, 'more often than not too old, lived on memories of the victory of 1918 and failed to show evidence of the activity we desired.' The most glaring examples – though not the only ones – were found in the IXth and IInd Armies on the Meuse. There, in one commentator's words: 'Neither Corap nor Huntziger had got a grip on all their troops.'[43]

Nonetheless, it has to be reiterated that Gamelin lacked clear evidence of dereliction or incompetence among his field commanders before May 1940. Without such evidence, however, he could not implement a wholesale house-clearance or *Limogeage* of subordinates.[44]

For another reason, too, Gamelin had to tread carefully: he knew that many of these subordinates had their own political *parrains*, or 'godfathers', in parliament – supporters whose influence could be applied on the irresolute Daladier, should Gamelin threaten to dismiss them. When the failures of nerve and the bungled counterattacks west of the Meuse from 13 to 18 May 1940 at last gave grounds to wield a new broom, Gamelin was himself dismissed by Reynaud before he could ring any changes. He was left to ponder ruefully what might have occurred in 1914 had his own mentor, Joffre, been sacked after the Battle of the Frontiers, without being given time to regroup and win the Battle of the Marne.[45]

The phoney war disguised deficiencies at many levels of the Allied forces. These would become clear only under the stress of combat. Senior Allied generals recognised that active operations would expose shortcomings which had previously resisted identification – and, therefore, rectification. It was of limited use to know from experience that *some* would prove unequal to their tasks. No crystal ball could reveal precisely *who* they would be. As Ironside mused in his diary, in January 1940:

> 'We shall not know until the first clash comes. In 1914 there were many officers and men who failed, but old Joffre handled the situation with great firmness. Will the *Blitzkrieg*, when it comes, allow us to rectify things if they are the same? I must say I don't know.'

Prior to that baptism of fire, Gamelin was forced to acknowledge, as he put it, that at 'certain levels of responsibility, it is no longer a matter of giving orders but of persuading'.[46]

Over and above the untried quality of Allied generalship, Gamelin had to keep at least one eye on the political 'front' behind him. The nerves of many politicians in Paris were fraying long before the military position of the Allies began to collapse. Gamelin's headquarters' diary on 18 September 1939 noted a warning he gave his staff that: 'When the war really begins [in the west], it will come as a very rude awakening.' A week later, in similar vein, Gamelin complained that 'the military operations are nothing – it's the government, the politicians and their cliques that are difficult to bear.'

There was, on occasion, an Alice-in-Wonderland quality to the concerns of the Allied governments. When, in December 1939, the French cabinet solemnly discussed divorce provision in family law, even Anatole de Monzie, the Minister of Public Works – certainly no warmonger – confessed that he would be embarrassed to admit how the government spent its time. The Minister for the Colonies, Georges Mandel, once the *Chef de Cabinet* to France's indefatigable First World War leader, Georges Clemenceau, sneered that he 'couldn't imagine such a debate taking place in front of

Clemenceau in 1918.' 'Another time!' jotted de Monzie in his diary; 'Another war!'[47]

Episodes such as this underlay Gamelin's anxiety about the Home Front. The respite in the winter of 1939–40 benefited the Allies in several ways: it enabled them to increase their munitions' production, form seventeen new French divisions under the 'Five Month Plan' of November 1939, and strengthen the BEF from four divisions in October 1939 to ten divisions by May 1940.

The stalemate, however, had negative effects too. It was quickly dubbed 'the bore war' and, in the words of Neville Chamberlain's assistant private secretary, John Colville, boredom bred discontent.[48] The trouble was that few in high places saw cause for alarm. As A J Liebling, *The New Yorker*'s Paris correspondent, shrewdly noted:

> 'They knew that so long as Daladier headed the government there would be no effectual war – that eventually the war would die of dry rot, *which was what ninety percent of the French politicians [. . .] wanted*.[49]

Gamelin had a better grasp than most of the dangers that lurked in a false sense of security. His respect for the Wehrmacht's combat experience in Poland meant, in practice, that he would be the last person to throw French troops into a hasty attack on Germany. On the other hand, he was aware that the military balance on the front line was not the only factor to consider when judging how far time might favour the Allies rather than the Germans. It would be welcome, Gamelin prudently rejoined to Reynaud in October 1939, 'to gain time to continue the material preparation of the country and the units [of the Army]'; but 'there was the Home Front to be held too – requiring high and undivided morale'.[50]

As time passed, so Gamelin's unease mounted. On five occasions during the winter he believed the German offensive in the west to be imminent: on 2 October 1939; from 10 to 15 October; on 12 November, when French intelligence detected German concentrations east of Belgium and Holland; from 15 to 17 January 1940, when the German plans fell into Allied hands at Mechelen-sur-Meuse (though, in that instance, he did not wholly share the alarm of the Belgian General Staff); and in early April 1940.[51] During the fourth alert, on 17 January 1940, he lamented to Edouard Herriot (the President of the Chamber of Deputies), that the 'most serious thing at the present time is that lots of people believe we can wage and win this war without fighting a battle'.[52] Many French politicians indeed preferred to think that a rapid decision on land was impossible. The memoirs of General Armengaud – an airman who, it will be remembered, had witnessed the Wehrmacht's success in Poland – corroborate Gamelin's concern about government complacency.

> 'I saw these men [he noted] state as a certainty that the Battle of France would be a long war of time and attrition.'[53]

Gamelin, in contrast, did not consider that Hitler had any reason to postpone the clash of arms. In the autumn of 1939 he judged that the Germans would attack France before the winter because 'Germany had an army at the ready; [and] she had, he considered, every advantage in seeking the decision before Allied armaments attained their maximum level.'[54]

In fact the Germans did not attack until May 1940. But then the politicians cracked in a matter of days: witness the panic that swept Paris on 16 May at the rumours of panzers roaming near Soissons and Chantilly. Though Gamelin had foreseen the dangers and warned about them, politicians such as Reynaud still jumped at the chance to make him a scapegoat for the defeat. As André Géraud noted perceptively, soon after the *débâcle*:

> 'It is certainly true that those in power in 1940 were not by a long chalk the equals of those of 1914, Poincaré and Millerand. With hindsight, too, the dispositions ordered by Gamelin do perhaps seem preferable to those adopted by his successor [Weygand].'[55]

Since Gamelin's role was that of a grand strategist and inter-Allied co-ordinator, a subordinate had to have more specific responsibility for the Allied forces on the North Eastern Front. Before the Battle of France began, the logical choice for this position was General Georges. In 1939–40 he was widely admired. Only the stern test of battle revealed that, as Gamelin put it later, Georges 'had the soul of a chief of staff, not that of a wartime commander'.[56]

Interestingly, prior to 10 May 1940, Gamelin and Georges were *both* regarded as natural wartime commanders. In the *Journal of the Royal United Services Institute*, in 1938, Gamelin was described as 'a born leader' by a well-informed British commentator, Brigadier T G G Heywood (who had served in Paris from 1933 to 1936 as military attaché).[57] Similarly, the editor of the newspaper *L'Époque* thought, in July 1939, that Gamelin 'would, in war, more than fulfil the high expectations the nation had of him'. This observer felt that 'if anything his military virtues were more those of a wartime leader than a peacetime trainer'. Gamelin's sang-froid served him well in the pandemonium that followed the German attack in 1940. In contrast, as Jeffery Gunsberg has noted, 'Georges collapsed under the strain on 14 May'.[58]

Much criticism has been directed at the French command arrangements for the higher direction of the war in 1939–40. Mobilisation in September 1939 activated the structures provided under the Law for the Organisation of the Nation in Time of War, of 11 July 1938. This legislation prescribed that the overall conduct of the war was the government's task. Ministers convened in a *Comité de Guerre*, chaired by the President of the Republic, to determine grand strategy. Representatives of the government, together with the chiefs of the Air Force and Navy, and Gamelin as Chief of Staff for National Defence, co-ordinated the war effort with the British via the meetings of the SWC – the senior forum for the making of Franco-British grand strategy.[59]

Except for a *co-ordinating* function in national defence, invested in him since January 1938, Gamelin never obtained any executive power whatsoever over the Air Force or Navy. The former's Chief of Staff, General Joseph Vuillemin, moved out of Paris to a war headquarters in the village of Saint-Jean-les-Deux-Jumeaux. The Chief of the Naval Staff, Admiral François Darlan, established his command post in the Château de Maintenon near Rambouillet.

Gamelin remained – in form if not necessarily in substance – the government's principal strategic advisor. At the same time, however, mobilisation placed on him an additional responsibility as Commander-in-Chief of French Land Forces. On 1 September 1939, he transferred to his war headquarters at the Château de Vincennes, in eastern Paris. There, he expanded his small peacetime *cabinet militaire* into a personal staff directed by his long-serving *Chef de Cabinet*, Colonel Jean Petibon. The latter was a 'hard-driving officer whose arrival at a colonelcy at the age of forty-five was considered precocious in the French Army'.[60] Gamelin's staff was reorganised in three sections: one, under Lieutenant Colonel Henri Simon, dealt with national defence; the second, headed by Lieutenant Colonel François Guillaut, had charge of French ground forces; the third, led by Lieutenant Colonel Olivier Poydenot, handled inter-Allied liaison.[61]

Metropolitan France itself was divided into two vast sectors: the 'Zone of the Interior' and the 'Zone of the Armies'. The former was directed by General Louis Colson. It was concerned with the mobilisation of reservists, regimental depots and training camps. The 'Zone of the Armies' signified the expected front-line. It was sub-divided into 'fronts' or theatres: one on the Pyrennees, another facing Italy and the principal front, the northeast, facing Germany and Belgium. For quartermastering, transport, reliefs and communications, the North-Eastern Front came under the *Major-Général des Armées*. This was, at first, General Henri Bineau, a former commandant of the *Centre des Hautes Études Militaires*. In December 1939, Bineau was replaced by the Army's expert in motorisation, General Joseph Doumenc, who had won his spurs organising supply convoys to Verdun in 1916. Their headquarters was located at the Château de Montry, in the Marne valley, mid-way between Vincennes and Georges's command post, the GQG (the *Grand Quartier Général*). The latter was installed at Les Bondons, a château near the small town of La Ferté-sous-Jouarre, some sixty kilometres east of Vincennes.

With France and Germany at war, the northeast inevitably became the principal theatre. As Franco-British mobilisation progressed, three army groups were formed: No. 1 commanded by General Billotte, along the border with Belgium; No. 2 under General Prételat, behind the Maginot Line; and No. 3 led by General Garchéry, in Alsace and Franche Comté. A fourth group, under General Olry, garrisoned Provence and the Alpes Maritimes, keeping watch over Italy.

These three army groups of the northeast came under the authority of Georges. In September 1939, Georges had the formal title of *adjoint*, or assistant, to Gamelin. This created difficulties for subordinates. The British Government had, on the eve of war, agreed to place its forces in France within the French chain of command. Chamberlain and the British Chiefs of Staff wished to avoid the poor liaison that had bedevilled the Allied armies in 1914–18. Yet the French arrangements in the autumn of 1939 left Gort and Pownall, the Commander and Chief of Staff of the BEF, unsure whether they reported to Georges, or directly to Gamelin.[62]

A clearer definition of responsibilities was required. As early as 20 September 1939, Gamelin's *cabinet*, was 'conscious of the need to put an end to the ambiguity created by the presence of the GQG alongside Georges.' But Petibon, Gamelin's Chief of Staff, at this point 'did not yet entirely share this opinion'. In late September, his mind was changed by André Pironneau, director of the newspaper *L'Époque*. The journalist warned 'that the general was the target of a cabal, some people even going so far as to claim there was bad blood between Gamelin and Georges and concluding: "Georges is the man we should have".' To investigate this gossip, Lieutenant Colonel Guillaut visited Les Bondons on 1 October. He returned to Vincennes with a disturbing report that 'certain officers at GQG were wondering aloud: "Who is in command?" '.[63]

This left Petibon and Gamelin in no doubt that the 'question of the command needed to be re-thought'. They considered re-attaching GQG to Gamelin's headquarters. However, when the high command was finally reorganised in January 1940, it confirmed the authority of Georges over the North-East, removing his designation as Gamelin's *adjoint*. When the Battle of France began, Georges, though still answerable to Gamelin in the same manner as the theatre commanders for the southeast and Pyrennees, had direct authority for the armies facing Germany.[64]

With hindsight, Petibon concluded that his chief had made a great mistake by failing to grasp the nettle and remove Georges altogether during the phoney war. Petibon thought Gamelin should have shown greater ruthlessness once Georges's listlessness became evident. He felt Gamelin should have emulated the purge of sub-standard generals that Joffre carried out in August 1914.[65]

More than one observer wondered if Georges was sufficiently robust for his job in 1939–40. Britain's military attaché in Paris, Colonel William Fraser, judged in June 1939 that Georges was 'not a fit man and that the weight of the responsibility which would be his in war might be too much for him'. Everyone knew that Georges had been grievously wounded at Marseille in 1934. (He was in a protocol party at the side of the visiting King Alexander of Yugoslavia and was hit by four bullets fired by Croat assassins engaged in killing the monarch.) Georges' injuries proved a troublesome legacy. They would – Gamelin subsequently confessed – have provided a pretext to retire him on health grounds before 1940.[66]

Another means of removing Georges presented itself in an idea from Daladier, broached in late 1938, to rejuvenate the high command by cutting the retirement age from sixty-five to sixty-three. In January 1939 it was proposed that, as a first step, the letters of service of generals who would reach sixty five that year should not be renewed. Had this measure been adopted, Georges would have faced mandatory retirement on 1 January 1940. But the reform was abandoned when Daladier would not allow his trusted Gamelin to set an example by retiring himself. Georges had allies in parliament and the press, especially on the right. Furthermore, he was popular with a number of British personalities whose influence increased markedly after the war's outbreak. These individuals included Major General Louis Spears, an MP prominent in the Anglo-French Parliamentary Association and Winston Churchill's personal envoy to Paul Reynaud during the Battle of France. Churchill himself was a friend of Georges: they toured French defences in Alsace together in August 1939.[67]

This inseparability of political from military considerations had at least one curious result for the historical record: opponents of Gamelin sometimes advanced arguments that were at best inconsistent, when not downright contradictory. This was particularly the case with those who censured him for his 'political' qualities. For example, a hostile Belgian diplomat, who had known Gamelin during the general's posting to Brazil in the 1920s said, in June 1940, '*that Gamelin was a politician*, appointed to the head of the French forces by Daladier' – yet finished by concluding '*that his appointment to a command of this magnitude and importance was not only a stupidly costly blunder but another crime chargeable to the politicians.*' With critics wrapping themselves in tangles such as this, it is relevant to recall the judgement of Vivian Rowe that this 'extraordinary system of command' is precisely what 'relieves General Gamelin of much of the responsibility for France's disasters.'[68]

Once the Battle of France was underway, both Daladier and Gamelin had reason to regret their earlier deference towards Georges and his backers. It was not long before Vincennes grasped that Georges was not, after all, equal to his task. He appeared to be too inert – to be observing the battle instead of seeking to control it. Without further ado, Gamelin and his staff acted to assert their own influence over the direction of the campaign. This is a point which may cause surprise. But it can only do so because critics have been predisposed to view Gamelin as a desk-bound bureaucrat, out-of-touch, complacent and superannuated. The record of Gamelin's exertions in May 1940 does not, however, sustain such a charge.

As has been shown, Gamelin regularly held command conferences during the phoney war, chiefly with Georges, Bineau, Billotte, Prételat and Dufieux. He had repeatedly toured army, corps, and divisional head-

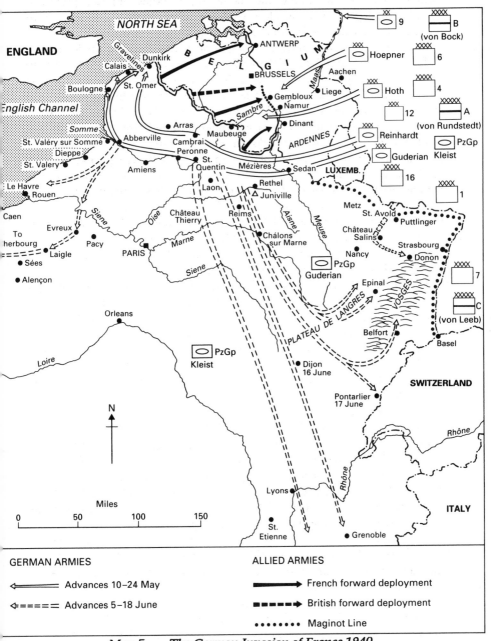

Map 5.   The German Invasion of France 1940.

GERMAN ARMIES

⟸══════ Advances 10–24 May

⟸════ Advances 5–18 June

ALLIED ARMIES

➡ French forward deployment

■■■➡ British forward deployment

•••••• Maginot Line

quarters at the front. Likewise, the record of Gamelin's conduct, from 10 May 1940 until Reynaud dismissed him nine days later, reveals not just his energy but also his coolness under pressure. He first visited Les Bondons, to see Georges, as early as 2.15 in the afternoon of 11 May – the second day of the German offensive.[69] Two days later, at 9 am on the 13th, accompanied by Doumenc, (the *major-général*), General Louis Koeltz (Deputy Chief of the Army Staff responsible for intelligence), and Vuillemin (head of *L'Armée de l'Air*), Gamelin went back to GQG to see Georges again.

On the 14th, Gamelin's concern for the conduct of the battle emerged unequivocally. At 8.30 am his staff contacted Georges, Doumenc and Vuillemin to convene them for 9.45 at Les Bondons; fifteen minutes later Gamelin's adjutant, Major Christian de l'Hermite, took a telephone call summoning the general to a meeting of the *Comité de Guerre* in central Paris at 9.30 that same morning. Gamelin, his war diary records, 'protested and got the meeting put back till the afternoon'. At 9.15 Gamelin set off for Georges's headquarters, where he remained until 1.15 pm before returning to Vincennes. That afternoon, at 3.30, Gamelin went to Les Bondons again – the second time he visited Georges that day. Meanwhile, Gamelin secured permission from Daladier – who was still defence minister – to miss the simultaneous meeting of the *Comité de Guerre*. Plainly Gamelin subordinated political considerations to his need to be at the main army headquarters, alongside the shaken Georges.

The next day, 15 May, at 7.45 am, Gamelin received the overnight situation reports. He learnt of the disintegration of Corap's IXth army, under attack between Rocroi and Dinant by German mechanized forces that included General Erwin Rommel's 7th Panzer Division. At 9 o'clock Gamelin dispatched Lieutenant Colonel Guillaut, a section chief in his personal *cabinet*, to ascertain at first hand the IXth Army's condition. Meanwhile, Gamelin himself left Vincennes to visit GQG once more, this time lunching at Les Bondons and staying with Georges for over five hours. It was 4 pm when Gamelin finally returned to Vincennes.

Late that day, he was warned by telephone of a 'very strong [German] motorised column advancing in the direction of Moncornet, with nothing much remaining between Paris and the panzer divisions'. The evening was an anxious time. Talk turned to evacuating the headquarters. Essential documents were packed in readiness for a move. The collapse appeared most calamitous on the IXth Army's front.

> 'This Army', one contemporary military report put it, 'was [. . .] poorly trained and poorly led and was holding a sector much longer than normal so that it was very over-extended.'[70]

Having visited Corap for an on-the-spot assessment, Colonel Guillaut at this juncture reappeared at Vincennes. He confirmed to Gamelin the

> 'lamentable state in which he had found the IXth Army headquarters – like a

lifeless corpse [*sans vie et sans réactions*] – entirely ignorant of the situation of the army's divisions'. Fortified works were said to be 'unoccupied [. . .] the whereabouts of their keys unknown'. The troops were reportedly in disorder, 'devoid of any taste for the fight'. The 'most serious thing', concluded Guillaut, was that 'from the moment the Germans appeared, everyone had run away.'[71]

The next day, 16 May, saw Paris gripped by panic. An overwrought Reynaud had telephoned London to tell Churchill that a French collapse was imminent. Still discounting so desperate an eventuality, the British Prime Minister flew to Paris to put heart into his allies.

That afternoon, amid scenes graphically described in his own memoirs, Churchill conferred at the Quai d'Orsay with Reynaud and Gamelin. From the windows he could see bonfires on the lawn, into which officials were tipping barrow-loads of diplomatic documents. Like a crew preparing to scuttle their ship, the French were burning their archives. Turning to Gamelin – who was describing the course of operations on a giant wall map – Churchill broke into his execrable French to growl: '*Mais où est la masse de manoeuvre?*' In what was surely the nadir of his career, Gamelin could only shrug and confess that, in this crisis, the Breda manoeuvre had left him no strategic reserve.[72]

On 17 May, Gamelin spent part of the morning at the War Ministry in Paris, conferring with Daladier. At 2 pm he travelled again to Les Bondons – a trip he repeated the next morning, 18 May, at 9.15, returning to Vincennes at 1.15. In mid-afternoon that day, Vincennes received a call from Georges to say that Reynaud and Pétain – newly appointed Deputy Prime Minister – were en route to Georges' headquarters to assess the situation for themselves.

Late on 18 May, the tension at Vincennes eased somewhat. The German threat to Paris appeared to have diminished for the time being. Fresh intelligence had accurately reported that the German mechanised columns were turning towards Calais – 'a direction that was also extremely dangerous [noted Gamelin's war diary], but towards a more distant objective'. The Germans, it was remarked, seemed 'intoxicated by the ease of their advance and their deployments, [and] by getting stretched out were becoming more vulnerable'.

Because of the politicians' faintheartedness, Gamelin opposed any precipitate withdrawal from Vincennes. A move to the Loire chateaux would take him 'too far away from Paris. He needed to remain close to the government; "otherwise [he said] there's a risk that everything will fall apart [*sans cela tout risque de craquer*]".' Rejecting panic measures, Gamelin proposed to order Georges to abandon Les Bondons and install himself and his staff alongside Doumenc at Montry. In this way, Gamelin planned to tighten the central direction of the battle, by combining the staffs of the *major-général* and GQG. 'General Doumenc', said Gamelin, 'is proving magnificent, eliciting everybody's admiration – but he is overburdened; [the reorganisation] would avoid him wasting his valuable time on to-ings and fro-ings'.

19 May 1940 proved to be Gamelin's final day in command. It began with 'bad news of the overnight situation and no news at all of Giraud [commanding the VIIth Army in southern Holland]'. At 7.45, accompanied by his adjutant, de l'Hermite, and two of his staff, Simon and Guillaut, Gamelin set off yet again to visit Georges at GQG. Gamelin's party was shocked to find Georges no longer master of himself, still less of the military situation. Gamelin reached for an order pad, sat down and, in his own hand, drafted a directive for the commanders of Army Groups Nos. 1 and 2, Generals Billotte and Prételat, and for the Chief of the Air Staff, Vuillemin.[73] Known as *Instruction Personnelle et Secrète* No. 12, this directive has been criticised for retaining a courteous, almost diplomatic, style. (It opened: 'Without wishing to interfere in the conduct of the battle . . .'). However, the *Instruction* neither minced words nor lacked urgency. It outlined the only practicable option for an Allied counterstroke. Gamelin intended that a pincer attack by mobile forces, organised by Billotte from the north and by General Robert Touchon with the VIth (Reserve) Army from the south, should cut the panzer corridor. The latter was still stretched thinly westwards from the Ardennes towards Abbeville. More than this, IPS No. 12 signalled the start of what Gamelin intended to become an energetic personal direction of the campaign. 'Everything's now a question of hours', it concluded.[74]

Reynaud, however, had other ideas. At 1 pm one of Gamelin's ordnance officers, Major Lorenchet de Montjamont, telephoned Weygand. The latter's aeroplane had just landed in Paris after his arrival from Beirut, at the behest of Reynaud. As far as Gamelin was concerned, this was the reappearance of an unwelcome ghost from the past. Gamelin now regretted his generosity in August 1939, when he had brought Weygand out of retirement to command French forces in Syria and Lebanon.

From the outset, Weygand had proved meddlesome. He visited Paris in December 1939, volunteering his own schemes for a bolder prosecution of the war. This endeared him to a kindred spirit, Reynaud, who was at that time Minister of Finance. Once Reynaud had succeeded Daladier as Prime Minister, on 21 March 1940, Weygand was given further opportunity to present himself as a rival grand strategist. On 3 April 1940, Gamelin was disconcerted, and Daladier 'furious', on hearing that Reynaud had secretly invited Weygand home to address the French War Cabinet.[75]

On 9 May, the very eve of the German attack, Reynaud opened a civil-military crisis by summoning a cabinet meeting to discuss 'the state of the command'.[76] In an hour-long monologue, Reynaud directed a torrent of abuse at Gamelin. Stirring up their six-year-old feud, Reynaud spiced his dislike of Gamelin with an indictment the general's opposition to the recent and unsuccessful Allied expedition to Norway. The latter operation had been championed by Reynaud, who wished to carry the war to the Germans. However, 'Gamelin's eyes [were]', as Ironside had noted months earlier, 'glued on the north-east frontier.' Reynaud and his entourage, impatient with the Allied strategy of blockade, wished to open new fronts on Europe's peripheries. Gamelin was unimpressed. He preferred to husband his forces in France. Of Reynaud's plan to 'push the war more determinedly', Ironside noted sceptically on 24 March 1940: 'I don't think that Gamelin has much faith in that idea. He said that if they want to do something they must form an assault brigade from the deputies and start it off themselves.' By the cabinet meeting of 9 May, the Allies were in headlong retreat from Norway. Angry and vulnerable as a result of the misadventure, Reynaud censured Gamelin in scenes which one minister likened to 'witnessing an execution'.[77] By the end of the first day of the Battle of France (10 May), Gamelin was confiding to his staff 'how he had learnt that, in Reynaud's view, there were only two capable generals: "Weygand and Giraud – as for Georges, he's as worthless as Gamelin".'[78]

On 19 May, therefore, Gamelin understood that Reynaud planned to replace him with Weygand. De Montjamont informed Weygand that Gamelin was awaiting him, with Georges, at Les Bondons. An hour later, at 2 pm, de l'Hermite telephoned from GQG to tell de Montjamont that the situation was 'deteriorating'. Weygand was redirected to Vincennes. At 2.45 Gamelin left La Ferté for the last time. In his staff car he spoke bluntly to de l'Hermite: 'Georges [he said] is finished. I drafted a communiqué for him this morning at 9 o'clock. We agreed it. At 10 o'clock it still hadn't been issued.' Gamelin added that Georges had ceased to exercise command through his corps commanders and was trying to issue orders directly to his divisional generals.[79] Subsequently Gamelin reflected how Georges's

'character showed itself not to be up to the high standard of his intelligence [. . .] Right from the start of the crisis, he was overwhelmed. He did not know how to organise his work, became submerged in details and exhausted himself to no avail'.[80]

At 3.15 that afternoon Weygand arrived at Vincennes, to a frosty greeting from Petibon. When Gamelin returned, the two generals withdrew to confer behind closed doors. Gamelin explained how the campaign had unfolded. That evening Vincennes received a call from Weygand's adjutant, Colonel Roger Gasser. The latter wanted another meeting between his chief and Gamelin for 9 o'clock the following morning, 20 May.[81]

Gamelin realised that the fruits of Weygand's intrigues and Reynaud's erratic judgement had finally ripened. He knew that, for him, it meant the end. Thirty minutes later, at 8.45 that evening, an officer from Reynaud's staff arrived at Vincennes bearing a personal letter from the Prime Minister to Gamelin. 'Well', said the latter, in a tone that was both resigned and understandably bitter, 'I hope General Weygand is more successful than me'.

The next morning, 20 May, Gamelin cleared his desk. Weygand, relishing his sudden elevation, observed the barest civilities. He dismissed Gamelin's offer to update him on the overnight cables and intelligence reports. Ushering Gamelin to the door he tapped a folder that he carried under one arm, saying: 'I have the secrets of Foch'. 'I retorted', recalled Gamelin, 'that *I* had had those of Joffre and they had not sufficed'.[82]

Was Gamelin incompetent or ill-treated? In the context of the wider tragedy of the French defeat, the question may not seem of central importance. Yet, in Gamelin's case, the historian cannot but ponder the consequences of contingent factors, politics and plain bad luck. As Gamelin was later wont to reflect, Joffre had often been asked who deserved the credit for winning the Battle of the Marne; the old Marshal had always replied that he was not sure, but that he knew who would have been blamed had the battle been lost.

This chapter has closely documented Gamelin's movements and meetings in the critical ten days in May – 'General Gamelin's real war', as they have been described.[83] Such minute attention to the chronology perhaps conveys a sense of the hectic pace of those days. It also indicates the vigour and the imperturbable self-control which Gamelin displayed as the plans of the Allies went swiftly and catastrophically awry.

For as soon as Gamelin had grasped the extent of Georges' inadequacies, he sought to remedy the situation by first-hand initiatives. The steps he took included eight visits to GQG at Les Bondons – two of them on 14 May – over the course of the ten days from 10 to 19 May. He also acted to enhance the authority of the better French commanders. For instance, he widened the responsibilities of General Billotte. The latter was a tactically-progressive officer who, in the autumn of 1939, had championed the constitution of armoured divisions, before assuming command of Army Group No. 1 in Belgium. It was to Billotte that Gamelin turned over the direction of the critical battle in Northern France and Belgium. Billotte began by conferring with Gort and Pownall of the BEF, and with King Léopold of the Belgians, to weigh up the options for a counter-attack. But on 21 May, Billotte's staff car crashed as it hurried through the blackout. Billotte died of his injuries two days later. The fatality removed 'a general of great character' and – as an officer on the French central staff commented – 'deprived us of the one man capable of bringing off the difficult manoeuvre on which so much depended. From that day on, our Armies in the north [. . .] were at sixes and sevens'.[84] Billotte's elimination disrupted the efforts of the northern Allied armies to regroup before the Germans consolidated their breakthrough. It was a blow Gamelin could not have foreseen.

Just as unfortunate, and equally unpredictable, was the carelessness of another leader of whom much was expected, General Henri Giraud. Commanding the powerful French VIIth Army in Southern Holland,

Giraud enjoyed the confidence of both the rank-and-file and the higher headquarters ('our most dashing leader', in the words of Captain André Beaufre, a member of Doumenc's staff at Montry). Deployed on Giraud's right, the BEF, too, was well disposed to co-operate with him in a counter-stroke. He had 'impressed [. . .] very much indeed as a great "thruster" and a most determined commander', according to Gort's Deputy Chief of Staff.[85] In general reserve, prior to the Breda plan's adoption, VIIth Army included two motorised infantry divisions and a mechanised division whose high-performance Somua medium tanks outclassed German Panzer Mark Is, IIs and IIIs. Yet before he could withdraw these units from Breda to counterattack the panzer corridor, Giraud, too, was eliminated. In a misfortune uncannily like that of Britain's General Sir Richard O'Connor at the hands of the Afrika Korps in 1941, Giraud blundered into a German patrol on 18 May and was captured.[86]

Gamelin then turned to a third alternative, General Huntziger – commanding IInd Army at Sedan. But all decisions about a successor to Georges were then taken out of Gamelin's hands with Weygand's appointment in his own stead. As the crisis reached its climax, the government acted entirely in character and 'lost its cool', in the words of the commander of the Paris air defences. In the eye of the storm, when nerves of steel were needed, the politicians decided, instead, to drop the pilot. They threw overboard 'the one figure in a position to gauge and master the adverse elements. Yet it was the moment when they should have built up his self-confidence, by showing their own confidence in him.'[87]

Writing in 1956, one French historian termed the Battle of France 'the war of lost opportunities'.[88] Perhaps armies make their own luck; yet the fortunes of war do seem to have favoured the Germans in 1940. Gamelin could not legislate for accidents which removed his most able subordinates. At Montcornet, on 17 May 1940, de Gaulle's hastily-constituted 4th DCR (*Division Cuirassée de Réserve*), counter-attacked the 1st and 10th Panzer Divisions of XIXth Panzer Corps. Some of de Gaulle's tanks came in sight of Guderian's mobile command vehicle. The boldest of the panzer generals himself almost became a French prisoner. On 20 May, Rommel was surrounded for some hours by French units. He, too, barely avoided capture. Had either episode ended differently, a brake might have been applied to the German dash to the sea – a dash which, later on 20 May, reached the coast and drove a fatal wedge between the Allied armies.

Ill-fated or ill-treated, Gamelin had an endearing line in self-deprecation. When his staff showed him a biography of himself by Maurice Percheron, newly-published in October 1939 in a series entitled 'Great Figures of Our Time', Gamelin barely gave the book so much as a glance. For the same reason as he had rejected an offer by Daladier in 1938 to promote him Marshal of France, Gamelin turned dismissively on his heels. 'Leave it [he retorted]; let them at least wait till I've won some battles.'[89]

Gamelin was denied the laurels of victory of subsequent Allied generalis-
simos. Nor did he share the glory won during the Liberation by a new
generation of French commanders – Pierre Koenig; de Lattre de Tassigny,
who liberated Strasbourg in 1945; Alphonse Juin, commander of the French
corps in Italy from 1943 to 1945; and, most revered of all, Philippe Leclerc,
with his young lions such as Jacques Massu, in the legendary *2eme Division
Blindée*.

Yet, before his disgrace, Gamelin had demonstrated that he understood
the task which faced those Allied supreme commanders called upon to
direct the struggle to overthrow Hitler. This task was, of course, in the first
place to manage the human and material warlike resources of a multi-
national coalition. In the second place it was to harness political régimes as
diverse as those of Britain, the United States, the Soviet Union and France,
getting them to unite in pursuit of a common goal. As a grand strategist,
Gamelin had correctly discerned what would be required to overthrow Nazi
Germany.

Having exhorted his subordinates to attend to training and morale,
Gamelin was aghast at the French Army's failure to withstand the *Blitzkrieg*.
He showed some awareness that a danger lurked within the Allied camp.
But he had not been able to put his finger on its source. As one of his staff
reflected, in 1939–40 Gamelin 'had all too accurate a vision of things',
having 'from the outset formed an unfavourable impression of the worse-
than-mediocre attitude of our troops towards combat'.[90]

Yet Gamelin received no complaints to guide him to specific locations of
any malaise, or to allow him to gauge its extent. 'In my rapid but frequent
inspections [he wrote later], I never encountered a general or a troop
commander who said to me that he had no confidence in his men.'[91]
Strikingly similar conclusions were reached by Ironside, when he accompanied Gamelin to inspect the French IIIrd and IVth armies in January
1940. All the generals treated Gamelin with respect, 'though they laughed
and joked with him. They were certainly not overawed by him and I
thought their relations with him very happy indeed.'

> I tried in my mind [Ironside concluded] to sum up the state of the French Army
> and its fighting value. I must say that I saw nothing amiss with it on the
> surface. The Generals are all tried men, if a bit old from our view-point. None of
> them showed any lack of confidence. None of the [BEF] liaison officers say that
> they have seen any lack of morale.[92]

In the context of perceptions like this, the military failure, when it came,
was an affront to Gamelin's sense of professionalism. He harboured no
illusions as to the damage this failure did him, the French Army and France
herself. And, to be sure, the sight of the French collapse dismayed a watching world. 'I was bitterly disappointed', wrote a senior official in the United
States State Department on 27 May 1940, 'when General Gamelin proved

inadequate'. For his part, Gamelin might have agreed with another American, A J Liebling, who reflected that the disappearance of the French Army

'had altered the position of every nation on the Continent [. . .]; it reminded me of the death of the uninsured breadwinner of a large and helpless family.'[93]

Another witness to Gamelin's fall from grace was the American Ambassador, Bullitt. He advised Washington that the general was a 'crushed and broken man'. Not only this: in late May, the press corps in Paris buzzed with rumours that Gamelin had shot himself.[94]

In fact, Gamelin was not inclined to a suicide à la Samsonov. In June 1940, he still sought to work for the Allied cause. Like de Gaulle – if not so eloquently – Gamelin realised that in her defeat in 1940 France had lost a battle, not the war. He wrote to Weygand, offering to serve in any capacity in which he could be of use to France. The offer elicited no response. Gamelin was left in his Avenue Foch apartment, to await the German entry into Paris.[95] Only later, when time hung heavily in prison from 1942 to 1945, did he seem to become 'haunted by thoughts of the defeat'.[96] The incarceration must certainly have tried his composure – for, with an irony probably lost on their German gaolers, the other captives at Itter included both Reynaud and Weygand.

Throughout the war, Gamelin stood aloof from the public recriminations over the Fall of France. Instead, he wrote his memoirs. The task afforded him a source of intellectual distraction during his wartime confinement. It also enabled him to make a case in his own defence – for he had refused to speak out in 1942, when Pétain brought him and five other luminaries of the Third Republic before a show trial at Riom on charges of neglecting France's war preparation.

In the late 1940s Gamelin testified to the French parliamentary inquiry into events between 1933 and 1945. But, unlike Weygand, he shunned publicity and steered clear of politics. By the early 1950s, he was a semi-recluse, occasionally sought out for interview by historians of a new generation which viewed the drama of 1940 as a subject for scholarly research rather than scurrilous polemic.[97] At the end, Gamelin was admitted to Val-de-Grâce military hospital. There he died on 18 April 1958, aged eighty five. Few noticed his passing: all eyes in France were fixed on the crisis of the Fourth Republic in Algeria and the manoeuvres to engineer the return to power of a more successful 'political general' of 1940 – Charles de Gaulle.

In his twilight years, Gamelin recognised full well that he had paid the price for an Allied defeat. The short note sent to Vincennes late on 19 May 1940, from Reynaud's *cabinet*, informed Gamelin of his replacement and, almost mockingly, added the 'government's thanks for the services you have rendered the country in the course of a long and brilliant career'. Attached to the note were copies of decrees naming Weygand as Commander-in-Chief of all theatres of operations. The double irony in this remained with Gamelin till the end of his life. For Weygand gained a true generalissimo's authority – something that Gamelin had never possessed.[98] Secondly, and tragically, Weygand used that authority not to continue the fight from the French Empire but to browbeat the politicians at Bordeaux into an armistice and bring about a national humiliation from which, fully fifty years later, France had not wholly recovered.[99] It was Gamelin's destiny to be regarded as the man who lost the Battle of France; but it was Weygand's and Pétain's decision to sully the honour of the French officer corps and stain the good name of France.

Chapter Notes

* I am grateful to my University of Southampton colleagues, Dr Tony Kushner and Dr George Bernard, for suggesting improvements to an earlier draft of this essay.

1. Pertinax [pseud. of André Géraud], *Les Fossoyeurs. Défaite militaire de la France. Armistice. Contre-Révolution* (New York: Maison Française), [2 vols.] (1943), I, p. 97; A J P Taylor, *Europe: Grandeur and Decline* (London: Penguin) (1977), pp. 289–94; J C Cairns, 'Some Recent Historians and the "Strange Defeat" of 1940', *Journal of Modern History*, Vol. 46, No. 1 (Mar. 1974), pp. 60–85 (quotations: p. 81); J -B Duroselle, *Politique Etrangère de la France. L'Abîme, 1939–1945* (Paris: Imprimerie Nationale), (1982), p. 55.

2. D Porch, 'French Intelligence and the Fall of France, 1930–40', *Intelligence and National Security*, Vol. 4, No. 1 (Jan. 1989), pp. 28–58 (quotations: pp. 45, 52).

3. Cairns, 'Some Recent Historians', p. 81. Continuing reluctance to rehabilitate the general's reputation is apparent in the remark that 'As for General Gamelin, he bears a crushing responsibility', in Jean Doise and Maurice Vaïsse, *Politique Etrangère de la France: Diplomatie et Outil Militaire* (Paris: Imprimerie Nationale, 1987), p. 341.

4. Quoted in François Bédarida, *La stratégie secrète de la drôle de guerre. Le Conseil Suprême Interallié, septembre 1939-avril 1940* (Paris: Fondation Nationale des Sciences Politiques), (1979), p. 60. On the pre-war visits to Britain see Gen. M -G Gamelin, *Servir*, (Paris: Plon) [3 vols.] (1946–7), II (*Le Prologue du Drame. 1930-août 1939*), pp. 276–7, 281–2, 350–3, 440–1.

5. J Minart, *P C Vincennes. Secteur 4* (Paris: Berger-Levrault), [2 vols.] (1945), I, p. 74.

6. See Maurice Vaïsse, *Sécurité d'Abord. La politique française en matière de désarmement, décembre 1930-avril 1934* (Paris: Pedone), (1981). Cf. the general's own recollections of this work: Gamelin, *Servir*, II, pp. 56–65, 72–8.

7. Minart, *P C Vincennes*, I, p. 74.

8. J Armengaud, *Batailles politiques et militaires sur l'Europe. Témoignages, 1932–1940* (Paris: Editions du Myrte), (1948), p. 200.

9. On Gamelin's early life see Pierre Le Goyet, *Le Mystère Gamelin* (Paris: Presses de la Cité), (1976), pp. 13–21.

10. A Léon-Jouhaux, *Prison pour Hommes d'État* (Paris: Denoel Gonthier), (1973), pp. 52–3; Reynaud's formula in the diary for 9 Apr. 1940 of the Secretary to the

French War Cabinet, Paul Baudouin: *Neuf Mois au Gouvernement. Avril–Décembre 1940* (Paris: La Table Ronde), (1948), p. 24. Cf. the description on 19 Mar. 1940 of Gamelin as ' *"un grand préfet – pas plus"* ' in the diary of the President of the French Senate, Jules Jeanneney: *Journal Politique. Septembre 1939–Juillet 1942* (Paris: Colin), (1972), p. 35.

11. See Brian Bond and Martin S Alexander, 'Liddell Hart and de Gaulle: the Doctrines of Limited Liability and Mobile Defense', in Peter Paret (ed.), *Makers of Modern Strategy: From Machiavelli to the Nuclear Age* (Princeton NJ: Princeton University Press), (1986), pp. 598–623; Robert A Doughty, 'De Gaulle's Concept of a Mobile, Professional Army: Genesis of French Defeat?', in Lloyd J Matthews and Dale E Brown (eds.), *The Parameters of War: Military History from the Journal of the US Army War College* (London: Pergamon-Brassey's), (1987), pp. 243–56.

12. Charles de Gaulle, *Mémoires de Guerre* (Paris: Plon) [3 vols.], (1954), I (*L'Appel, 1940–1942*), *Livre de poche* edn., pp. 38–9. Cf. Gamelin, *Servir*, III (*La Guerre. septembre 1939–19 mai 1940*), pp. 289–90.

13. Cf. favourable contemporary assessments of Gamelin in the diary for 23 Sept. 1939 of Senator Jacques Bardoux: *Journal d'un Témoin de la Troisième. 1 septembre 1939–15 juillet 1940* (Paris: Fayard), (1957), pp. 96–7; also 'The Life of General Gamelin', *Picture Post*, Vol. 4, No. 13, 30 Sept. 1939, pp. 32–7, published without attribution but written by the *Manchester Guardian's* Paris correspondent, Alexander Werth, who reflected on 22 May 1940 that he felt 'ashamed of having spoken highly of Gamelin without really knowing a damn thing about him. Glad I didn't sign that article in *Picture Post* last September.' (A Werth, *The Last Days of Paris* [London: Hamish Hamilton, 1940] p. 72.)

14. Le Goyet, *Mystère Gamelin*, pp. 22–36; R -G Nobécourt, 'Gamelin et la bataille de la Marne (Septembre 1914)', *Bulletin de la Société d'Histoire de Rouen*, 10 Nov. 1973, pp. 181–7.

15. See R -G Nobécourt, 'La disgrâce du général Joffre en décembre 1916', *Bulletin de la Société d'Histoire de Rouen*, 15 May 1976, pp. 99–114; Gamelin, *Servir*, II, pp. v–vi, xx–xxxii, 37–40, 55–6, 59–65; Minart, *P C Vincennes*, I, p. 69.

16. See Philip C F Bankwitz, *Maxime Weygand and Civil-Military Relations in Modern France* (Cambridge, MA: Harvard University Press), (1967), pp. 35–40; Bernard Destremau, *Weygand* (Paris: Perrin), (1989), pp. 198–204.

17. P -M de La Gorce, *The French Army: A Military-Political History* [trans. Kenneth Douglas] (New York: George Braziller), (1963), p. 293; Col. Kuhlenthal to Col. F G Beaumont-Nesbitt, (British Military Attaché, Paris), 11 Mar. 1937, in F[oreign] O[ffice] General Correspondence, 371, 20693, C2085/122/17, P[ublic] R[ecord] O[ffice], London.

18. V Rowe, *The Great Wall of France: The Triumph of the Maginot Line* (London: Putnam), (1959), p. 94; J A Gunsburg, 'General Maurice-Gustave Gamelin, 1872–1958', in Patrick Hutton (ed.), *Historical Dictionary of the Third Republic* (Westport CT: Greenwood Press), [2 vols.] (1986), I, pp. 412–13.

19. R Frank[enstein], *Le Prix du Réarmement Français* (Paris: Publications de la Sorbonne), (1982); idem, 'Le Front Populaire a-t-il perdu la guerre?' *L'Histoire*, No. 58 (July-Aug. 1983), pp. 58–66. Pertinax, *Les Fossoyeurs*, I, pp. 113–18; Cf. Duroselle, *L'Abîme*, pp. 46–51; Anthony P Adamthwaite, *France and the Coming of the Second World War* (London: Cass), (1977), pp. 95–8, 106–9.

20. See Pierre Le Goyet, *Missions de Liaison* (Paris: Presses de la Cité), (1978), pp. 261–300.

21. J M Hughes, *To the Maginot Line: The Politics of French Military Preparation in the 1920s* (Cambridge MA: Harvard University Press), (1971), p. 223.

22. Gamelin's assessment of the strategic problem posed by Belgian neutrality on the war's outbreak in his note to Daladier, D. no. 4/Cab. F.T., 1 Sept. 1939, in *Documents Diplomatiques Français, 1932–1939* (Paris: Imprimerie Nationale) [two series] (1963 et seq.), 2nd ser., Vol. XIX, Doc. No. 353, pp. 357–8; cf. J R Colville, *Man of Valour: The Life of Field Marshal the Viscount Gort VC* (London: Collins), (1972), p. 152; Le Goyet, *Mystère Gamelin*, pp. 229–30. For Plans E and D see Donald W Alexander, 'Repercussions of the Breda Variant', *French Historical Studies*, VIII, No. 3 (Spring 1974), pp. 459–88; Brian Bond, *Britain, France and Belgium, 1939–1940* (London & Oxford: Brassey's), (1990), pp. 27–33.

23. Gen. Albert Lelong, French Military Attaché, London, to Gamelin (reporting a talk with Ironside and Major Gen. Sir Richard Howard-Vyse, head of British liaison at Vincennes, about BEF deployment in France), 19 Sept. 1939, Carton 7N 2817 (*État-Major de l'Armée: 2e Bureau/Grande-Bretagne*, [July-Oct. 1939]) S[ervice] H[istorique de l'] A[rmée] de T[erre], Vincennes: also Col. R[oderick] MacLeod and Denis Kelly (eds.), *The Ironside Diaries, 1937–1940* (London: Constable), (1962) [hereafter: *Ironside Diaries*]), pp. 108, 112–13; Brian Bond (ed.), *Chief of Staff: The Diaries of Lieutenant General Sir Henry Pownall* (London: Leo Cooper) [2 vols.], (1973), I, pp. 233–43.

24. Colville, *Man of Valour*, pp. 125–6; *Ironside Diaries*, p. 77; 'Report on Anglo-French Staff conversations, Stage Three', 28–31 Aug. 1939, in '*France and the Low Countries: Planning and Operations, 1 February 1939-18 June 1940*', W[ar] O[ffice] 32/11424. PRO.

25. Sir Ronald I Campbell (British Minister-Counsellor, Paris Embassy, 1938–9), letter to the author, 3 Dec. 1977; the British liaison officer to Belgian GHQ in May 1940 has confirmed this point, testifying that the BEF's smallness in 1939–40 meant 'French army officers of all ranks enjoyed a superiority complex' and, in a friendly fashion, 'treated us as learners in the military arts'. (Brig. G M O Davy, unpublished memoirs, Chapt. 12, p. 9.)

26. Colville, *Man of Valour*, pp. 152–4; D W Alexander, 'Repercussions of the Breda Variant', pp. 477–86.

27. Gamelin, *Servir*, III, pp. 138–52; Colville, *Man of Valour*, pp. 150–1; Ironside, letter to Gamelin (re: possible responses to German invasion of Holland), 5 Nov. 1939, Fonds Gamelin 1K 224, Carton 7, Dossier labelled '*Correspondence avec les britanniques*', sub-dossier III 'novembre 1939', SHAT; *Ironside Diaries*, pp. 148–57. Also Bédarida, *La stratégie secrète*, pp. 149–81; Duroselle, *L'Abîme*, pp. 78–81; Bond, *Britain, France and Belgium*, pp. 26–31.

28. Gamelin's defence of the Dyle-Breda Plan in his retrospective note, '*Les Causes de nos revers en 1940*', pp. 4–5, (dated by internal evidence to 1956–7), Fonds Gamelin, 1 K 224, Carton 7, Dossier labelled '*Les Causes de nos revers en 1940*', SHAT. On Venlo see Christopher M Andrew, *Secret Service: The Making of the British Intelligence Community* (London: Heinemann), (1985), pp. 433–9. On the Mechelen episode: US Naval Attaché (Brussels), report no. C-9-c/2233-D to Intelligence Division, Office of Chief of Naval Operations, Washington DC, 16 Jan. 1940, President's Secretary's File, Box 196, Folder: 'Estimates of Potential

Military Strength', Vol. 1, No. 10, Franklin D Roosevelt Presidential Library, Hyde Park, New York [hereafter: FDRL]; Minart, *P C Vincennes*, I, pp. 119–38; analysis in Jean Vanwelkenhuyzen, *La "drôle de guerre" en Belgique – les plans tombés du ciel* (Paris: Plon, '*L'Histoire de notre temps – Toute la vérité*', No. 2, (1967), pp. 149–81; idem, *Les avertissements qui venaient de Berlin. 9 octobre 1939–10 mai 1940* (Paris & Gembloux: Duculot), (1982), pp. 64–123; Jeffery A Gunsburg, *Divided and Conquered: The French High Command and the Defeat of the West, 1940* (Westport CT: Greenwood Press), (1979), pp. 136–8; Bond, *Britain, France and Belgium*, pp. 35–45.

29. Gen. André Beaufre, *1940: The Fall of France* (London: Cassell), (1967); (New York: Alfred A. Knopf), (1968), p. 168 (American edn.); Gen. Maurice-Henri Gauché, *Le Deuxième Bureau au Travail, 1935–1940* (Paris: Amiot-Dumont), (1953), pp. 192–200; Paul Paillole, *Notre Espion chez Hitler* (Paris: Laffont), (1985), pp. 170–3.

30. Gauché, *Le Deuxième Bureau*, pp. 178–86; Gamelin, *Servir*, III, pp. 82, 94–5, 115–6.

31. See Martin S Alexander, 'Prophet without Honour? The French High Command and Pierre Taittinger's Report on the Ardennes Defences, March 1940', *War and Society*, Vol. 4, No. 1 (May 1986), pp. 52–77; Paul Paillole, *Services Spéciaux, 1935–1945* (Paris: Laffont), (1975), pp. 185–6; outpost and aerial reconnaissance reports of 10 and 11 May 1940 in FN IX-1, Cabinet Georges, 10 mai, pp. 1, 3, 5–6, 8, 15, 17; FN Cabinet Georges, 11 mai, pp. 3, 5, 11, SHAT.

32. See Harold C Deutsch, *The Conspiracy against Hitler in the Twilight War* (Minneapolis MN: Minnesota University Press), (1968). The gradual conversion to the *Sichelschnitt* plan of most senior German generals (except Field Marshal Fedor von Bock, commander of Army Group B), is subtly explicated in John J Mearsheimer, *Conventional Deterrence* (Ithaca NY and London: Cornell University Press), (1983), pp. 101–33.

33. J Romains, *Sept Mystères du Destin de L'Europe* (New York: Maison Française), (1940), pp. 99–100; cf. criticism that 'he [Gamelin] considered that the battle in progress was "General Georges' battle" ' in Gen. Maxime Weygand, *Recalled to Service* (trans. E W Dickes, London: Heinemann), (1952), p. 49; Gamelin's later reflections on the charge that he delegated excessively to Georges, in *Servir*, III, pp. 404–5.

34. Cabinet du Général Gamelin – Journal de marche, entries for 27–8 Sept. 1939, Fonds Gamelin 1K 224, Carton 9, SHAT (hereafter: Gamelin – Journal).

35. Ibid., 7 Oct. 1939, 15–16 Oct. 1939. Cf. Bond, *Chief of Staff*, I, pp. 242–6; Gamelin, *Servir*, III, pp. 116–7, 387; *Ironside Diaries*, pp. 116–24.

36. *Ironside Diaries*, pp. 198–204.

37. Gamelin – Journal, 8–9 March 1940.

38. Ibid., 22–3 March 1940; Gamelin, *Servir*, III, p. 292; *Ironside Diaries*, pp. 231–3.

39. See Gauché, *Le Deuxième Bureau*, pp. 164–77; Gamelin, *Servir*, III, pp. 61, 87–91, 101–5, 487–92.

40. From Gen. Louis Faury (French Army) and Gen. Jules Armengaud (French Air Force), reproduced in Gamelin, *Servir*, III, pp. 492–5; Le Goyet, *Mystère Gamelin*, pp. 235–9; Armengaud, *Batailles politiques et militaires*, pp. 95–8, 135–40, 304–16.

41. Gamelin – Journal, 13 Sept. 1939.

42. Ibid., 14 Sept. 1939, 14 Oct. 1939; W C Bullitt, letter to Judge R Walton Moore

(Asst. Secretary of State), Washington DC., 7 June 1940, R Walton Moore Papers, Group 55, Box 3, FDRL. The historian D W Alexander has acknowledged Gamelin's understanding of the German methods used to defeat Poland, and his strenuous efforts in the 1939–40 winter to improve French training accordingly ('Repercussions of the Breda Variant', pp. 473–5).

43. Minart, *P C Vincennes*, I, p. 77; Pertinax, *Les Fossoyeurs*, I, pp. 88–9.

44. The verb *limoger* entered the French vocabulary in August 1914 when, after the failures in the Battle of the Frontiers, Joffre removed scores of generals from front-line commands and reassigned them to interior duties ('sending them to Limoges'). Over 140 officers of brigadier-general rank and higher were purged, including 38 of the 82 divisional generals, nine corps commanders and two out of the five army commanders. See Pierre Rocolle, *L'Hécatomb des Généraux* (Paris: Plon), (1985).

45. Gamelin, *Servir*, I (*Les Armées Françaises de 1940*), pp. 15–16; III, pp. 405, 414–9, 427–33; Minart, *P C Vincennes*, II, pp. 176–7, 189–92; Pertinax, *Fossoyeurs*, I, pp. 57, 96–7.

46. *Ironside Diaries*, p. 204 (10 Jan. 1940); Maurice Percheron, *Gamelin* (Paris: Editions Documentales Françaises), (1939), p. 27.

47. Gamelin -- Journal, 18 Sept., 24 Sept. 1939; A. de Monzie, *Ci-devant* (Paris: Flammarion), (1941), p. 189.

48. Sir John R Colville, *The Fringes of Power: Downing Street Diaries, 1939–1955* (London: Hodder and Stoughton), (1985), pp. 25, 28, 48. On the Five Month Plan and the Allied material build-up, see Fonds Gamelin 1K 224 Carton 7, dossier labelled 'Le Problème des Effectifs, 1939–40', sub-dossier III 'Le Plan de Cinq Mois', SHAT; R H S. Stolfi, 'Equipment for Victory in France in 1940', *History*, 55 (Feb. 1970), pp. 1–20.

49. A J Liebling, 'Paris Postscript', in *The New Yorker Book of War Pieces: London 1939 to Hiroshima 1945* (New York: Schocken, [reprint of 1947 original] 1988), pp. 39–53 (quotation: p. 49).

50. Gamelin – Journal, 9 Oct. 1939.

51. Ibid. (dates indicated). Cf. Gamelin, *Servir*, III, pp. 155–63; Colville, *Fringes of Power*, pp. 38–40, 50–1, 70–1; John Harvey (ed.), *The Diplomatic Diaries of Oliver Harvey, 1937–1940* (New York: St. Martin's press), (1970), pp. 328–9, 354; *Ironside Diaries*, pp. 204–8.

52. Gamelin, *Servir*, III, p. 125.

53. Armengaud, *Batailles politiques et militaires*, p. 198.

54. Minart, *P C Vincennes*, I, p. 45.

55. Pertinax, *Les Fossoyeurs*, I, p. 97. Cf. remarks in D W Brogan, *French Personalities and Problems* (London: Hamish Hamilton), (1946), pp. 151–2, 154–5, 175. On the *grande peur du 16 mai 1940* see Pertinax, *Les Fossoyeurs*, I, pp. 93–5; de Monzie, *Ci-devant*, pp. 220–7; the account of the Paris Prefect of Police, Roger Langeron, *Paris, juin 1940* (Paris: Flammarion), (1946), pp. 19–20; the diary of one of the Quai d'Orsay diplomats, Hervé Alphand: *L'étonnement d'être: Journal, 1939–1973* (Paris: Fayard), (1977), pp. 41–2; Minart, *P C Vincennes*, II, pp. 151–63; Armengaud, *Batailles politiques et militaires*, pp. 215–6; Bankwitz, *Maxime Weygand and Civil-Military Relations*, pp. 295, 303, 319 (esp. sources listed at fn. 83).

56. 'Note sur le général Georges', 9 Dec. 1943, Fonds Gamelin, 1K 224, Carton 7, SHAT.

57. Brig. T G G Heywood, 'General Gamelin: Chief of the French General Staff of National Defence', *Journal of the Royal United Services Institute*, (Aug. 1938), pp. 607–13. I am grateful to Prof. Brian Bond for bringing this article to my notice.

58. Maj. C A de Linde, Despatch No. 1089, July 1939, reporting Pironneau's assessments of leading French generals, FO 371, 22917, C10869/130/17, PRO; Gunsburg, 'Gamelin', in Hutton, *Historical Dictionary*, I, pp. 412–13.

59. See Gamelin, *Servir*, III, pp. 222–4; on the SWC, Bédarida, *La stratégie secrète*; also *idem*, 'La rupture franco-britannique de 1940. Le Conseil Suprême Interallié, de l'invasion à la défaite de la France', *Vingtième Siècle*, No. 25 (Jan.-Mar. 1990), pp. 37–48.

60. A J Liebling, *The Road back to Paris* (New York: Paragon House), (1989), pp. 31–2.

61. Interview with Gen. Olivier Poydenot, Versailles, 27 July 1982; letters to the author from Gen. Poydenot, 3 Aug. 1982, 3 Apr. 1983, 11 Jan. 1985; Minart, *P C Vincennes*, I, pp. 70–4.

62. Bond, *Chief of Staff*, I, pp. 286–7; Colville, *Man of Valour*, pp. 129–30, 133–4, 169–70; *Ironside Diaries*, pp. 100–5, 116–7, 172.

63. Gamelin – Journal, 20 Sept., 26 Sept., 1 Oct. 1939.

64. Ibid., 1 Oct. 1939; Beaufre, *1940: The Fall of France*, pp. 163–4 (American edn.); Gamelin, *Servir*, I, pp. 44–77; Le Goyet, *Mystère Gamelin*, pp. 241–2, 246–50; Duroselle, *L'Abîme*, pp. 53–5.

65. Gen. Poydenot, interview with the author, Versailles, 27 July 1982.

66. Col. W Fraser, despatches, 16 June, 30 June 1939, FO 371, 22917, C8681/130/17 and C9363//130/17, PRO; Gamelin, *Servir*, III, pp. 49–50, 76–7, 98–99, 105, 256–70, 399–401, 432–3, 456–7.

67. *Ironside Diaries*, p. 90; Major-Gen. Sir Edward L. Spears, *Assignment to Catastrophe* (London: Heinemann), (1956), pp. 13–21; Winston S. Churchill, *The Second World War* (London: Cassell), (1948), I (*The Gathering Storm*), pp. 342–4, 357.

68. Rowe, *The Great Wall of France*, p. 106; the (unidentified) Belgian's remarks are found in Col. Martin F Scanlon (acting US Military Attaché, London), Report No. 41228, 4 June 1940, (emphasis added), Intelligence Division Despatch Lists, No. 2060–1130/176, Record Group 165, US National Archives, Washington DC. I am indebted to Dr. Alex Danchev, University of Keele, for drawing my attention to this reference, Cf. de Villelume, *Journal d'une Défaite*, pp. 135–6.

69. Gamelin – Journal, 11 May 1940. Unless otherwise stated, this journal is the source of the following account of Gamelin's movements and meetings from 10–20 May 1940. For his first visit to Georges after the Blitzkrieg had begun, on 11 May, cf. Gamelin, *Servir*, I, pp. 318–20; III, p. 395; Minart, *P C Vincennes*, II, pp. 109–20.

70. Col. M F Scanlon, report no. 41228, 4 June 1940, cited above (fn. 68).

71. Gamelin – Journal, 15 May 1940. Cf. version of Guillaut's report in English translation in Spears, *Assignment*, p. 148; also Gamelin, *Servir*, III, pp. 396–411; Minart, *P C Vincennes*, II, pp. 99–163; perceptive insights on IXth Army's shortcomings noticed in Nov. 1939 by Alan Brooke, in Sir Arthur Bryant, *The Turn of the Tide, 1939–1943. A Study based on the Diaries and Autobiographical Notes of Field Marshal The Viscount Alanbrooke* (London: Reprint Society), (1958), pp. 62–3.

72. Eye-witness accounts in Churchill, *The Second World War*, II, p. 42; de Villelume,

Journal d'une défaite, pp. 337–8; Harvey, *Diplomatic Diaries*, pp. 358–9; Alphand, *L'étonnement d'être*, pp. 41–2. Cf. Martin Gilbert, *Winston S Churchill: Finest Hour, 1939–1941* (London: Heinemann), (1983), pp. 349–51; Spears, *Assignment*, pp. 149–50.

73. Gamelin – Journal (entries for dates cited). Cf. idem, *Servir*, III, pp. 411–31; Minart, *P C Vincennes*, II, pp. 164–93.

74. Text reproduced in Le Goyet, *Mystère Gamelin*, p. 339; also Gamelin, *Servir*, I, pp. 3–4, Cf. Gamelin's defence of IPS No. 12 and the thinking behind it, in *Servir*, I, pp. 4–5, 10–21; critical discussion in Gunsburg, *Divided and Conquered*, pp. 241–4; Duroselle, *L'Abîme*, pp. 143–6.

75. Gamelin – Journal, 3 Apr. 1940. On Weygand's visits to Paris in Dec. 1939 and Apr. 1940, see de Villelume, *Journal d'une Défaite*, pp. 129–30, 135, 258–9; *Ironside Diaries*, pp. 169–71; Weygand, *Recalled to Service*, pp. 24–7, 34–41; Destremau, *Weygand*, pp. 379–82, 385, 396.

76. De Monzie, *Ci-devant*, p. 218.

77. *Ironside Diaries*, pp. 191, 233–4 (30 Dec. 1939; 24 Mar. 1940); de Monzie, *Ci-devant*, pp. 218–9. Cf. Jeanneney, *Journal Politique*, pp. 45–6; de Villelume, *Journal d'une Défaite*, pp. 328–9. On the Reynaud-Gamelin dispute over intervention in Norway in Apr. 1940 see Minart, *P C Vincennes*, I, pp. 183–231 (esp. pp. 225, 229); Armengaud, *Batailles politiques et militaires*, pp. 201, 205; François Kersaudy, *Norway 1940* (London: Collins, 1990), pp. 30–1, 52–6, 84, 151–4, 175–6; Vanwelkenhuyzen, *Les avertissements*, pp. 134–77.

78. Gamelin – Journal, 10 May 1940. Cf. idem, *Servir*, III, p. 337.

79. Gamelin – Journal, 19 May 1940; idem, *Servir*, I, pp. 20–1.

80. 'Note sur le général Georges', 9 Dec. 1943, Fonds Gamelin 1K 224, Carton 7, SHAT. Cf. Gamelin, *Servir*, III, pp. 432–3, 456–7.

81. Interview with Col. Roger Gasser, Paris, 1 May 1978.

82. Gamelin – Journal, 19 May, 20 May 1940; idem, *Servir*, I, pp. 7–8, 11–12; III, pp. 432–7. Cf. de Villelume, *Journal d'une Défaite*, pp. 340–3; Minart, *P C Vincennes*, II, pp. 196–8; Weygand, *Recalled to Service*, pp. 47–52.

83. Le Goyet, *Mystère Gamelin*, p. 298.

84. Beaufre, *1940: The Fall of France*, p. 191 (American edn.); on the disorganisation Billotte's death occasioned: Gunsburg, *Divided and Conquered*, pp. 248–9, 257–8, 272–4. For Billotte's progressive views on large tank formations, see his '*Étude sur l'emploi des chars*' [copies sent to Gamelin and Georges], no. 3748 S/3, 6 Dec. 1939, Archives Edouard Daladier, 4 DA 7, Dossier 1, sub-dossier a, Fondation Nationale des Sciences Politiques, Paris; and Gamelin, *Servir* III, pp. 275–81; criticism of Billotte's performance under pressure in May 1940 in *Ironside Diaries*, pp. 321–2.

85. Beaufre, *1940: The Fall of France*, p. 186 (American edn.); Lt. Gen. Sir Philip Neame VC, *Playing with Strife: The Autobiography of a Soldier* (London: Harrap), (1947), p. 249. Cf., however, Alan Brooke's doubts about Giraud (Bryant, *Turn of the Tide*, p. 61.)

86. Cf. Minart, *P C Vincennes*, II, pp. 196–7; Bankwitz, *Maxime Weygand and Civil-Military Relations*, pp. 301–3, 312 (esp. n. 58). For evidence that, in April-May 1940, Reynaud more than once considered promoting Giraud supreme commander in place of Gamelin, see Liebling, *The Road Back to Paris*, p. 96; also Gen. V Bourret, *La Tragédie de L'Armée Française* (Paris: La Table Ronde), (1947), p. 83.

87. Armengaud, *Batailles politiques et militaires*, pp. 215–6.

88. Col. Adolphe Goutard, *1940: La guerre des occasions perdues* (Paris: Hachette), (1956).

89. Gamelin – Journal, 1 Oct. 1939.

90. Minart, *P C Vincennes*, I, pp. 75–6.

91. Gamelin, *Servir*, III, p. 387.

92. *Ironside Diaries*, pp. 203–4.

93. R Walton Moore (Asst. Secretary of State), letter to W C Bullitt, 27 May 1940, R Walton Moore Papers, Group 55, Box 3, FDRL; Liebling, *The Road Back to Paris*, p. 106.

94. W C Bullitt, letter to R Walton Moore, 7 June 1940, R Walton Moore Papers, Group 55, Box 3, FDRL; Pertinax, *Les Fossoyeurs*, I, p. 96; Werth, *The Last Days of Paris*, p. 71.

95. This letter to Weygand, of 3 June 1940, is reproduced in Gamelin, *Servir*, III, p. 438. Cf. Le Goyet, *Mystère Gamelin*, pp. 349–50.

96. Léon-Jouhaux, *Prison pour Hommes d'État*, p. 53.

97. These included John Cairns, Philip Bankwitz and Jean Vanwelkenhuyzen (conversations between the author and these historians).

98. For Reynaud's note and the decrees see Gamelin, *Servir*, I, pp. 7–8, 77–9; also Col. Robert Villatte, 'Le changement de commandement de mai 1940', *Revue d'Histoire de la 2e Guerre Mondiale*, II, 5 (Jan. 1952), pp. 27–36; André Reussner, 'La réorganisation du Haut Commandement au mois de mai 1940', ibid., III, 10–11 (June 1953), pp. 49–59.

99. Bankwitz, *Maxime Weygand and Civil-Military Relations*, pp. 290–316; idem, 'Maxime Weygand and the Fall of France: A Study in Civil-Military Relations', *Journal of Modern History*, 31 (Sept. 1959), pp. 225–42. On 1940's legacy, cf. Martin S Alexander, 'After 50 Years: the spectre that still haunts France', *The Times*, 2 June 1990, p. 12; Jean-Pierre Azéma, *1940: L'Année Terrible* (Paris: Editions du Seuil), (1990); Henry Rousso, *Le Syndrome de Vichy, 1944–198 . . .* (Paris: Editions du Seuil), (1987).

7

Sir Edmund Ironside:
The Fate of Churchill's First General
1939–40

Wesley K Wark

In the photograph, General Sir Edmund Ironside pounds down some Whitehall pavement in full 1939 regalia: helmet and gas mask clutched in his right hand, a tangle of papers and a map tucked under his left arm. The photographer has caught him with his eyes closed, the face craggy and set, pipe clenched in his teeth, hat tipped slightly back from his forehead. Ironside's famous physical 'presence' hovers; the 6'4" body, still solid at age 59, appears barely contained by his General's uniform; the right sleeve of the tunic is a mass of creases suggesting, like some piece of gothic religious statuary, great energy. It is a photograph entirely appropriate to its text, for Ferdinand Touhy had set out in *Twelve Lances for Liberty* to eulogise the Allied war leaders; Ironside, the British Chief of the Imperial General Staff (CIGS), was already a familiar and favourite study of his. In a chapter devoted to 'Ironside of Ironside,' Tuohy developed a comparison between Ironside and Kitchener as wartime CIGS', in favour of the former. The text surrounding the photograph extolls Ironside's military experience, strategic judgement, linguistic abilities and forthright language, boldness and physique.[1] Yet beneath the caption of the photograph, an anonymous previous owner of my copy of *Twelve Lances* has added a more brutal and brief encomium; 'Proved unequal to the job.'

The startling juxtaposition of text, photograph and comment illustrates well the extreme interpretations put upon Ironside's career and abilities in his days of fame. The trajectory of Ironside's progress from stardom to oblivion was especially steep. It begins, essentially, in September 1939 when he is appointed to the post of CIGS, to everyone's surprise, including his own. The ascent lasts until the early Spring of 1940, when Ironside's conduct of the campaign in Norway brings him under severe pressure and criticism, and plummets downwards in May, June and July as the war turns against Britain. Ironside is forced to resign as CIGS at the end of May 1940 and lasts but two further months in the role of Commander-in-Chief, Home Forces. Then, at the age of 60, he goes into retirement, retreats to the 'fastness' of his farm in East Anglia and, although made a Field Marshal and elevated to the peerage, vanishes from the public mind. Ironside features but once more in the history of the Second World War, as a codename for one of the myriad of deception plans mounted to confuse the Germans about the details of the Normandy landings in 1944.[2] This once famous soldier was quickly reduced to a phantom.

The graph of Ironside's rise and fall contains some essential clues to his fortunes in war. The surprise nature of his appointment as Chief of the Imperial General Staff was itself the product of political calculations and of personal influences. The net effect was to leave Ironside with a weak power base. Norway came at the apex of his career. Yet the campaign he was forced to direct in Norway bore little resemblance to the broader Scandinavian strategy that he had envisaged and embraced with such enthusiasm. Ironside's backing for a Scandinavian thrust to end the 'bore war' was enough to mark him out as a leading candidate for scapegoat when the British Army suffered its series of humiliating defeats, withdrawals and evacuations during April and May 1940. His end as CIGS came with the defeat of the Allied armies in France and as British grand strategy for the prosecution of the war unravelled. In the midst of a ravenous 'Colonel Blimp' campaign, which sought to place the blame for the events of 1940 on the men in power in the 1930s, Ironside did not last long as C-in-C Home Forces.[3] He was replaced by General Alan Brooke in July 1940, on the grounds that a younger commander with direct experience of the blitzkrieg and 'total war' in France was needed.[4] In short, Ironside became CIGS for the wrong reasons, was forced to fight a wrong war in Norway, and was wrongly identified as one of the 'old gang' in the summer of 1940. A continuous thread is provided by the fact that Ironside, who was Winston Churchill's choice as Britain's first wartime CIGS, collaborated and disputed with Churchill over Norway, and finally fell out with his friend and political master during the summer of 1940 over strategy for the defence of Britain against invasion.[5] Against the changing fortunes of war have to be traced the exigencies of a personal friendship and alliance of martial spirits that existed between the Army's Chief and the most forceful and warlike politician of the day.

The story of the British conduct of the war in 1939–40 has been well and thoroughly told; that of Ironside's part in the making of British strategy has been, until recently, almost entirely neglected. To retrieve careers and stories from oblivion is not easy, even where official documentation exists in profusion, as it does for the 1939–40 period, long available for research use in the Public Record Office. There is no biography of Ironside, and his memoir of this period of his career was left unfinished at his death in 1959. Fortunately, an extremely comprehensive personal diary, which Ironside kept continuously and compulsively from 1918 until his death, has survived. Yet the true value of this diary, perhaps the largest private military diary in the English language, has been masked by the appearance of a heavily edited and censored version covering the years 1937 to 1940. This volume was the work of Ironside's loyal military assistant, Colonel Roderick MacLeod, who became in the post-war years the chief, and often only, defender of Ironside's reputation and fame.[6] With the aid of the original, unpublished version of the diary, it is now possible to reconstruct Ironside's role and strategic thinking during his tenure as CIGS. His claims to strategic genius and his undeniable flaws appear very much in keeping with the times. Seeing the conduct of the Phoney War through the very individual lens of the diary may not lead to any profound revision of our overall understanding of the British war effort, but such an approach allows us a new glimpse of the personal struggles and ideas that underpinned the first, calamitous months of the war and offers a chance to penetrate the collective mentality, hopes and illusions of the British high command.

One imaginative effort to return Ironside to the forefront of events during the Phoney War can be found in François Kersaudy's work on the Norway campaign. Kersaudy rightly understands Ironside as one of the principal supporters of military action in Scandinavia, but portrays the CIGS as having pursued his own private and grandiose strategy for operations in the region, as being frequently at odds with Winston Churchill over the scale and nature of action to be taken in the north, and as something of a pawn in a complex manoeuvre staged by Neville Chamberlain to ensure that no military action whatsoever was taken.[7] Stripped of its context, the military planning engaged in by the War Office under Ironside's direction is made to seem ridiculous – Kersaudy calls it 'tragi-comic.'[8] Even the physical portrait of Ironside is a caricature. According to Kersaudy, Ironside was a 'dapper seven-footer in his early sixties, with a square jaw and drooping eyelids . . .'[9] Height and age are wrong, and the slightly simian features accorded to Ironside do not match any of the photographs, drawings or descriptions of Ironside that I have seen. But such are the difficulties in drawing a lost and complex figure back into the historical record.

The Norway campaign is the key to understanding Ironside's fall from power. Yet to fathom what went wrong for him, one must understand the gulf that opened up between his imagined Scandinavian campaign and the operations in Norway that eventually occurred; to understand how Ironside was tempted by Scandinavia as a theatre of war, one must understand something of Ironside's strategic outlook; to understand how it was that a single failure in a relatively small theatre could so profoundly influence his fortunes, one must know the history of Ironside's appointment, and especially of his relations with Churchill, whose star rose as Ironside's fell.

Ironside becomes CIGS

Summoned to the War Office on the afternoon of 3 September, 1939, Ironside fully expected to have his appointment as Commander-in-Chief of the British Expeditionary Force confirmed by the Secretary of State, Leslie Hore-Belisha. Ironside had seen 40 years of military service and was the senior officer on the active list in the Army. His military career was varied and colourful. He had served in the Boer War, in India, on the Western Front during the First World War, commanded the Allied intervention forces against the Bolsheviks at Archangel, performed in the Middle East and Balkans during the troubled years of the early 1920s, and in the interwar years held senior appointments in India, Britain and the Middle East. Ironside did not hesitate to boast, when the Second World War broke out, that he was the only officer left in the British Army who had experience of high command in war. He regarded himself as indisputably the right man to command the British Expeditionary Force, and had been led to believe (and convinced himself) that his being brought back to Britain from Gibraltar in the spring of 1939 as Inspector General of Overseas Forces was but a prelude to the C-in-C post.[10]

Instead, Ironside found himself being asked to serve as Chief of the Imperial General Staff; the job he so coveted was to go to Lord Gort, the incumbent CIGS. Ironside's long diary entry for this day is most illuminating. He notes the shock of the news, Hore-Belisha's initial flattery (telling Ironside that he took a 'broader view of the war than anyone else') and then his anger at Hore-Belisha's ill-judged revelation about how his appointment had been secured. The Secretary of State for War confessed to his future CIGS that he had had to fight hard in the Cabinet for the appointment and had only won because of Winston Churchill's backing. Then, as Ironside recorded the conversation, 'it had been said that I talked too much and was unreliable' and that 'the report was that the Chiefs of Staff Conferences would be completely upset if I were in them.'[11] The rest of the interview was, in Ironside's recording, stormy. Ironside accepted the post only after Hore-Belisha indicated that he didn't believe these accusations. But it was scarcely a good start for this duo. Hore-Belisha's own diary, as filtered through the telling of his editor, R.J. Minney, downplays Ironside's reactions and puts Hore-Belisha's action in a better light:

> I saw Ironside and told him of his appointment as CIGS. At first I think he was a little disappointed, as he had expectations of being C-in-C, but he warmed to it during our talk. I said I was going to be quite frank about what his critics had said. When he spoke up for himelf, I told him that he need not put up any defence. The decision had been made and I would stand by him. I urged him to be frank with me always, and that, if he had any criticism to make, to say it to me and not outside.[12]

Whatever the precise truth about the interview, Ironside took on the job of

CIGS with a heavy heart, knowing that he would have to win the war not from a supreme field command, but from a desk in Whitehall, and that, in addition, he would have to win over a Cabinet who mistrusted him. The kernel of bad feeling between Ironside and Hore-Belisha had been planted. The narrowness of his political support was revealed, and Ironside was made aware of the uncomfortable truth that his fortunes lay to some extent in the hands of Winston Churchill, the newly appointed First Lord of the Admiralty. Their relationship went a long way back, to common service in the Boer War, but Ironside, while admiring the sweep of Churchill's strategic imagination, had reservations about its application. Winston Churchill's only reference to the background to Ironside's appointment tells of a three day long conclave between the two men in late August 1939, following Ironside's return from a mission to Poland, during which they, like seers, shared an effort 'to measure the unknowable.'[13] Churchill's biographer, Martin Gilbert, relies on the Hore-Belisha account and adds in a footnote that 'Before the outbreak of war, Churchill had been much impressed by Ironside's energy and ability.'[14]

Ironside had now to convince a sceptical Cabinet of his value and show that he was his own master, and not simply a catspaw of Churchill in the strategic realm. He had to work under a Cabinet Minister (Hore-Belisha) whom he quickly came to loathe for his lack of application and military judgement.[15] But the fact of his position, and his own sympathy for Churchill's restless search for offensive military opportunities would ultimately place Ironside firmly in Churchill's camp yet impose on him a difficult duty to resist such an identification and to translate the First Lord's projects into justifiable military operations, with an independent, War Office, rationale.

From this perspective, it is possible to begin to understand how Scandinavia acted as a temptation on a grand scale to Ironside. It was a temptation in the first instance because it was an imaginative project mooted by his principal backer, the First Lord. It developed into a more complex temptation, as Ironside struggled with his own doubts about the strategic wisdom of aspects of the Churchillian project and sought, ultimately, his own rationale for the operation. The individual cast of Ironside's progress into temptation brought few benefits in the end. He could not avoid serious friction with the powerful Churchill, nor could he hold on to the scepticism and caution which had initially informed his judgement on Scandinavian plans.

Temptation Rebuffed

When Ironside became CIGS, Britain's prewar grand strategy had already been dealt one serious blow. In the aftermath of the Munich crisis in 1938, and as the hopes that had been placed in that settlement proved hollow, British policy swung from appeasement to deterrence.[16] The new deterrent strategy was founded on the construction of an Eastern Front, in order to face Hitler with the dangers of a two-front war. Guarantees to Poland, Roumania, Greece and Turkey in the spring and summer of 1939, designed to bring their forces into the balance of power, provided some of the architecture of this Eastern Front.[17] The French Army and Maginot Line, in company with the Royal Navy and the RAF, would provide the military component in the West. Yet the smaller states in Eastern Europe and the Balkans were seen as but the first line of a deeper and more ambitious Eastern Front, which would incorporate the Soviet Union in either an active military role, or at the least as a menacing presence for Hitler and a supplier of war materials to the front-line states. The signing of the Nazi-Soviet pact in late August 1939 came as a shock to Western strategists, especially as it gravely undermined the two-front strategy. The quick and ruthless military conquest of Poland by Germany and the Soviet Union in September 1939, effectively completed the destruction of Britain's plans for an Eastern Front against the Third Reich.

At the very outset of his time as CIGS, Ironside was thus forced to watch the attack on Poland and the collapse of British grand strategy from the sidelines. Britain had no forces which she could bring to bear to alter the outcome in Poland, and the French were determined to avoid unnecessary offensives on land. The watching was painful for Ironside, not only because he had developed an association with the Polish Army during the Archangel campaign and during visits to exercises in the 1920s, but also because he had reported enthusiastically on their prospects shortly before the outbreak of war.[18] There is a hint of the disappointment and frustration that Ironside felt about the outcome in an exchange between the head of the British Military Mission to Poland, General Carton de Wiart, and Ironside upon de Wiart's somewhat miraculous escape to England. Upon arrival at the War Office, de Wiart recalls that he was greeted by Ironside with the remark: 'Well! Your Poles haven't done much.' I felt that the remark was premature and replied: 'Let us see what the others will do, sir.'[19] Ironside may have taken this rejoinder to heart. In any case, the fall of Poland left the CIGS with only a skeleton war strategy, with only embryonic forces to deploy, with a powerful lesson about relying on theatres of war where Britain could not influence the outcome, and with victorious German armed forces potentially free to concentrate for their next blow wherever they wished. The military initiative was clearly with the Third Reich, or indeed as many believed with the military combination of the Third Reich and its new ally, the Soviet Union.

What remained of British grand strategy as an inheritance from the past was a reliance on a long war strategy, with an emphasis on the attrition of German military capabilities through the application of a blockade, followed by air attacks and eventually by a combined Anglo-French offensive on land against a weakened and straightened foe.[20] As a strategy it looked to a distant and, in the circumstances of 1939, almost unimaginable future. It had little precise application to the tasks at hand, and offered little scope for action to the CIGS.

For Ironside, the early months of the war were taken up with myriad efforts to secure the British Expeditionary Force in France and establish its role, to agree on Anglo-French defensive strategy, to train a new conscript army at home, to establish a programme for the wartime expansion of the army and to secure industrial supply – and, not least, to learn the ways of being a senior staff officer in Whitehall and of the conduct of war 'by committee.' There were battles enough on the bureaucratic front. Ironside had to struggle hard to win approval for his programme for a 55 division army.[21] He fought a losing battle with the Air Ministry over the creation of a tactical air force under Army control to provide close-support for the ground forces. In the midst of these struggles and with the lessons of Poland and the quick collapse of the Eastern front fresh in his mind, it is scarcely surprising that Ironside should resist the temptation of a new campaign in a new theatre of war when this was first presented to him.

The possibility of operations in Northern Europe existed at first only as a gleam in the eye of Navy strategists and the First Lord, Winston Churchill. Indeed, Churchill had taken up his Cabinet post in September 1939 with one such offensive plan already in mind. It was to be code-named 'Operation Catherine' and called for an attack by heavily armoured and protected units of the British Fleet into the Baltic in order to wrest control of that sea from the Germans, separate the Third Reich from its Soviet ally, and create a menacing diversion on one of Hitler's unprotected flanks. When 'Catherine' found little favour in the Admiralty, despite Churchill's insistence that it should be studied intensively and preparations be made, it was relatively easy for the First Lord to shift his attention northward to the Scandinavian peninsula.[22]

The peninsula, and especially Norway, assumed importance in the first instance for two reasons. One was that Norwegian neutrality and the long shipping channel down the territorial waters of the Norwegian 'Leads' punched a worrying hole in the British naval blockade of Germany; another was the knowledge that Germany was heavily dependent on imports of high-grade iron ore from Sweden, much of which passed through the ice-free port of Narvik in Northern Norway during the winter months.[23] The imperatives of Britain's long-war strategy seemed to determine that Britain should do something to plug the hole in the blockade and deny the German war machine a vital resource. As early as 19 September 1939, Winston Churchill was urging that the Royal Navy should go into action to block the Norwegian shipping channel and cut off the flow of imported iron ore to Germany.[24] He believed (wrongly) that there was a precedent for such action in the First World War. However, he failed to convince the Cabinet in the face of objections about the violation of neutral rights and the likely impact on Britain's relations with other maritime powers, above all the United States; concerns about maintaining good relations with Norway in order to secure use of the large Norwegian merchant marine; and some confusion about the precise extent of German ore imports via Narvik. What was decided in the autumn of 1939 was that there should be a military study made of a British incursion into Scandinavia.[25]

Ironside's first exposure to the temptation of Norway came with the completion of a report by the Joint Planning Committee (JPC) in mid-November 1939. The Joint Planners had been instructed to assess the prospects for British intervention in Norway in the event of a Russian invasion: an eventuality that seemed likely in the context of the Soviet occupation of the Baltic states and the diplomatic pressure then being put on Finland. The JPC study aroused all the cautionary instincts in Ironside's strategic thinking. He described the operation in his diary as a sideshow, without political or military benefit for Britain, and one that was likely to grow in its appetite for men and material. It reminded him, he remarked, too much of the Archangel expedition which he had commanded in 1918–1919. The diary entry ends 'I would have none of it.'[26] Despite these staunch words, Ironside was to begin to feel the pull of real temptation towards a Scandinavian operation in a little over a month.

Churchill's Big Ideas

On 17 December, Ironside again penned a fervent strategic promise in his diary: 'I will have no sideshows.'[27] The very next day, he was to begin to change his mind: a first step on the road to his wholehearted commitment to British intervention in Norway. Temptation came to Ironside in the guise of one of Churchill's 'big ideas.' On 18 December, Ironside sketched out in his diary the nature of Churchill's plan. It called for British intervention at Narvik in Norway to block the supply of Swedish iron ore to Germany, and an effort to control the coastline of the country.[28] While Churchill had been pressing this plan on his Cabinet colleagues for some time, this was Ironside's first exposure to the scheme. It lodged, perhaps in part because of Ironside's admiration for Churchill's vision and his degree of dependence on the First Lord. But exposure to the Norway plan also came at a ripe moment in the evolution of Ironside's own strategic thinking. On 30 November, the Soviet Union launched a military assault on Finland. Ironside's sympathies were very much with the Finns and his diary makes clear the degree to which he hated having to watch passively as the Soviets eventually ground down the impressive Finnish defences.[29] More immediately pertinent to Ironside's receptivity to Churchill's Norwegian scheme was the fact that he had begun to feel anxious about French planning and the French strategic outlook, and was especially concerned about French projects for opening a second front in the Balkans or Middle East.[30] Yet he shared the view of the French high command that Hitler was faced with the necessity for action in order to sustain his political position and was casting wildly about for some opening.[31] The three elements of a new strategic picture were background influences on Ironside: the opening of the Russo-Finnish Winter War helped turn his attention to Northern Europe; he naturally sought some escape from unrealistic (and French-controlled) plans for a new Second Front; and he accepted the view of Hitler as an irresolute but dangerous gambler. Ironside would soon find ways to turn these, and other aspects of the military situation into positive arguments for the Norway venture.

Once exposed to Churchill's project for Scandinavia, Ironside was to work closely with the First Lord. Their joint struggle to fashion the plan into an acceptable military operation brought these two men into their greatest period of intimacy. As early as 28 December, Churchill was appealing to Ironside for his aid in constructing a full-blown plan. The CIGS was called back to London by the First Lord, from a brief shooting holiday. As he wryly put it 'the war is more important than pheasants.'[32]

Ironside brought the same enthusiasm and desire for action to bear on the plan as did Churchill. Sceptics in the Cabinet and in military circles could scarcely distinguish between the two. They became, to such minds, 'the crazy gang.' Yet Ironside, as his diary reveals, was to push his exploration of the potential benefits and dangers of the Scandinavian plan well beyond Churchill's thinking. It is in this exploration that one can best measure both the strategic wisdom and misjudgements of the CIGS.

From Churchillian Temptation to Self-Conviction

Ironside became obsessed with the Scandinavian project from the moment that it was revealed to him. His diary entries for the last two weeks of December 1939 show that he engaged in a period of feverish thought and planning about the Northern theatre, perhaps impelled by the imminent timetable for action that Winston Churchill wished to impose, and a feeling that great strategic opportunities beckoned.[33] In this two week period, Ironside constructed a remarkable grid of ideas about the uses and value of British action in Scandinavia. In the process, Churchill's plan for naval action was translated by Ironside's vigorous imagination into a war-winning strategy. Some of Ironside's notions of advantage and incentive were based strictly on a perception of enemy power; others had almost nothing to do with Germany. Some of Ironside's concepts were a product of the available intelligence, others were largely intuitive.

The very first element of advantage that commended the Scandinavian operation to Ironside's mind concerned the strength of the blow that a stoppage of Scandinavian iron ore would allegedly deal to the German war economy. Ironside was particularly impressed by a report circulated to the Service departments by MEW (the Ministry of Economic Warfare), authored by the German emigré industrialist Fritz Theissen, which drew a lurid picture of the damage that would be inflicted on German armaments production by interdiction of Scandinavian ore.[34]

But the economic dimension of Scandinavian strategy did not remain uppermost in Ironside's mind for long. The CIGS quickly shifted his attention to the direct and indirect military advantages that might accrue to Britain. Ironside had from the outset to confront the problem that Scandinavia might be seen as just the sort of sideshow that he had been decrying for months. He responded by labelling it as a 'legitimate' sideshow, one that involved operations in a remote theatre of war, where the scope of involvement could be limited, and where defensive positions, once acquired, would be difficult to overthrow. It would be a small war, featuring specialist troops.[35] Ironside's early planning imagined the operation as limited to two brigades, specially equipped for Arctic conditions and manned by ski troops. This definition of 'legitimacy' would quickly become blurred, as Ironside's thinking about the required scope of operations and the size of forces to be employed grew, and as the justification for the operations shifted to the broader canvas of its impact on the German war machine.

By 29 December, 1939, Ironside was far enough along in his thinking to provide an outline to his military colleagues on the Chiefs of Staff Committee. In a draft paper on 'Our Strategy,' Ironside argued that British operations in Scandinavia would bring four benefits: they would upset German calculations; cause dispersion; confuse Germany's 'curious leader'; and allow Britain to escape from her passive and purely defensive military posture.[36] When General Pownall, the Chief of Staff of the BEF, first heard Ironside's ideas on the Scandinavian campaign, and in particular its disruptive impact on Germany, he could only express his bewilderment and dismay. Pownall's own diary records these feelings: quoting Ironside to the effect that a Scandinavian action would 'upset the even tenor of their [the Germans'] development,' Pownall wrote to himself, 'Oh God what does that mean?'[37] It was a legitimate question, even though it came from a pen determinedly hostile to Ironside.

The answer was hidden from Pownall for two reasons. One was that the ideas and intelligence assessments that underpinned Ironside's enthusiasm for the Scandinavian operation were very much individually generated. The second was that some part of Ironside's fervour for opening up the Northern Front was based on his desire to deflect military operations, and even British strength, away from the Western Front, a policy adamantly opposed, naturally enough, by Pownall and his chief, Lord Gort.[38]

What did Ironside mean by his references to the impact of operations in Scandinavia on Germany? The answer rests very considerably in an understanding of the CIGS's outlook on the Third Reich. Any success in upsetting German calculations would not only damage what Ironside conceived to be the excessively rigid nature of German staff planning, but would strike a psychological blow against Hitler and perhaps even bedevil the poor state of relations that Ironside believed existed between the German General Staff and the *Führer*. All these ideas were important to Ironside's measure of the possibility of a successful outcome to British action in Scandinavia. He was convinced that the German General Staff in the current conflict was a poor shadow of the enemy that he had known, and written about, during the First World War.[39] In particular, Ironside was convinced that the German General Staff of the Hitler era lacked the flexibility and spirit so essential to the improvisation of military commands in a crisis.[40] If the Nazified General Staff could be thrown off their stride by a surprise British initiative in Scandinavia, and be forced to react to it because of their economic stake in the region, then Ironside hoped that some part of the fibre of the German military machine would be damaged and that subsequent German operations would be clumsy. It may have been that the current David and Goliath conflict between Finland and Russia suggested analogies to his mind. It was widely believed that the Soviet Union had been caught unprepared by the resistance that Finland had put up; if little Finland could force a great power to bungle, why could Britain not do the same to Germany?

Even Ironside might have acknowledged that the idea of causing an 'upset' to Hitler and the German General Staff was a bit woolly. But the second component of Ironside's enthusiasm for the Scandinavian intervention seemed to draw its strength from more concrete elements. The diversionary potential of a Northern Front appeared to be considerable.[41] If Germany could be drawn into military operations in Scandinavia, not only would she be at a disadvantage in terms of Britain's ability to deny the sea routes to German forces, but any such operation would, it was believed, tie up a minimum of 20 divisions. In the British calculation of the German order of battle, whose expansion was watched with alarm in the winter of 1939–40, this would leave the *Wehrmacht* with only 110 divisions on the Western Front.[42] Such a strength would be inadequate for the purposes of any German offensive against the 90-odd divisions that the French, British and Belgians might deploy. Ironside looked to secure even greater advantages from tying up German forces in Scandinavia. He believed that a German commitment in the north, in combination with the forces that the Third Reich must deploy on the Western Front, would rule out any German (or Russo-German combined) descent into the Balkans and Middle East.[43] Ironside was particularly, and in some ways presciently, sensitive to the vulnerability of the British position in the Middle East and looked on its defence with concern.[44] There may also have been an Allied calculation to Ironside's vision of the uses of a Northern Front. By December 1939, when the Scandinavian option was first considered, he had already been introduced to French interest in and pressure for a Balkan operation. In Ironside's mind, the French plan smacked of a replay of Salonika and was, in any case, heavily flavoured with French military politics, as it was the formidable General Weygand who was pushing the scheme from his headquarters in the Middle East.[45] It is not stretching the evidence of the Ironside diaries to surmise that the CIGS wished to tie down not only the Germans, but also his French allies to his own pet scheme for Scandinavia. It may also have been the case that the CIGS intended to use the opening of a Scandinavian campaign to divert British forces from the commitment to France. During the winter of 1939–40, Ironside grew to doubt whether the Germans would launch an offensive on the Western Front, and began to question the whole policy of pledging all British military resources for the inactive front lines of North West Europe. Ironside felt himself confronted with the vision of a lengthy stalemate on the Western Front and could not see any way to win the war from there.[46] Scandinavia offered a new strategic opening for an, until now, frustrated war effort.

Of all the elements of Ironside's personal calculation of the Scandinavian adventure, the most idiosyncratic was probably that which had to do with his reading of Adolf Hitler. As we have seen, Ironside talked of confusing Germany's 'curious leader'.[47] What Ironside meant was made clear in later diary entries. Ironside apparently believed that Hitler was a coward, and a being subject to nervousness and uncertainty over his direction of the German war effort. He made repeated comments of this sort in his diary, spoke of his ideas about Hitler in public without reservation and even turned a detailed reading of Rauschning's *Hitler Speaks* to account in the search for confirmation of his theories about the German dictator.[48] Ironside, whatever his attitude about the deficiencies of the new German staff officer, clearly believed that Hitler was both the controlling influence and the weak link in the German war effort. In promoting the Scandinavian adventure, Ironside was looking for a way to strike at Hitler directly. There were elements of a quaint romanticism in this vision of war between Britain and Germany as a form of personal combat with Hitler. Ironside had met the *Führer* once, briefly, during his visit to the German army manoeuvres in 1937. He came away unimpressed, and it may have been this single episode on which the edifice of Ironside's judgement about the German dictator rested.[49]

Yet another factor in Ironside's enthusiasm for the Scandinavian option was his belief that it was important to find a way for Britain to gain the initiative in the conduct of the war. He shared with Winston Churchill a powerful sense of frustration at being forced to act on the defensive and always in response to Hitlerian moves. It is clear that Ironside feared what he called the 'deadening' effect of operating on the defensive, although he had no precise evidence of any weakening of the home front or military morale during the winter of 1939–40.[50] But Ironside disliked the way the war was being run: the conduct of military operations was too tightly controlled by the politicians; Britain's military independence was cramped by French demands upon her; the public had no understanding of the real nature of war and the sacrifices that would be demanded. Ironside reserved a special blame for this state of affairs on the military punditry of B.H Liddell Hart, who had popularised the notion of the superiority of the defensive and whose recipe for winning the war, by exhausting Hitler in stalemate, Ironside found futile.[51] There is a revealing comment in the diary entry for 30 March, when Ironside writes: 'I am also sure that they [the Germans] are short of iron ore and stopping Narvik will upset them. If they react, we will soon come to a more warlike feeling.'[52]

Lastly, Ironside was desirous of keeping Finland in the war for as long as possible, for Finland was, in the new strategic context opened up by the Nazi-Soviet Pact and the Russian assault, a revived 'Eastern Front' in embryo. Ironside, in keeping with other British planners in this period, much feared the effect of a Soviet-German military combination, and wanted to pin down both powers wherever possible.[53] Support to Finland offered a chance to do this. Nor could Ironside entirely suppress his own feelings of sympathy for the Finns (strongly shared by British public opinion), especially as he was in communication with Marshal Mannerheim and the recipient of what he called some 'heartbreaking' demands for aid from the Finnish military commander.[54]

The pages of the Ironside diary dealing with planning for the British campaign in Scandinavia reveal that the CIGS developed a set of strategic rationales for the operation of such ultimately tempting strength and variety that all caution was put aside. These rationales were laid down in a burst of work and thought within the space of two weeks. Once fixed in his mind, Ironside, from the evidence of the diaries, was content with repeating and embellishing these ideas. Nothing new was added in the long period of indecision and inaction which gripped British strategy from January until March 1940. Indeed, the further the Scandinavian operation appeared from becoming reality, the more firmly did Ironside hold to his objectives. In Ironside's mind, the prospect of opening up a Northern Front had become the 'one great stroke' that might change the fortunes of the war.[55]

From Planning to War

At the same time that Ironside was constructing his arguments for the impact of Scandinavian operations, he was also busy sketching out what he saw as the necessary military plan. While much of the detailed military planning was to be done by the War Office staff, and the general scope of operations was to be a matter hammered out by the Chiefs of Staff Committee, Ironside's own early input was significant. It provides an insight into how Ironside thought the Northern Front could be fought successfully, a point that has often baffled later commentators. Here, Bernard Ash's summary may stand for the general indictment. He called Norway:

> a campaign . . . by the Allies conceived in folly, beset with delusions and conditioned by an apparently complete lack of appreciation of the kind of war they were going to have to fight.[56]

Fundamental to Ironside's planning for Scandinavia was the desire to go 'all out' to achieve the objectives of opening up a diversionary front for the Germans and strangling their iron ore supplies. Support for Finland was very much a peripheral aim. Ironside thought Churchill's more limited project for naval and mining operations in Norwegian waters, with ancillary military action, unlikely to be sufficient. Naturally enough, the CIGS wished to shift the effort to the land war, for only through a direct military occupation of the port of Narvik, the railway through Northern Sweden, the iron fields at Gallivare (Sweden) and the main Swedish iron ore port in the Baltic at Lulea, could Germany be properly damaged economically and threatened militarily. Ironside identified a number of major conditions that would have to be met, in order for the operation to be successful. These included the achievement of surprise, the success of diplomacy in ensuring the full co-operation of both Norway and Sweden, the availability of specialised and well-trained troops to provide the vanguard of a Scandinavian expeditionary force, the provision of a sufficient maritime supply-line, and the vital element of timing. Ironside decreed that the first echelon of his force must be established in their positions in the North no later than the end of March, in order to forestall potential German or Soviet moves.[57] In the event, none of these conditions were met and the original Scandinavian plan was finally shelved on 13 March, immediately following the capitulation of Finland.

The tone of weariness and regret that marks Ironside's reaction to what he assumed were the end of his plans was in striking contrast to the energy and elation of thinking displayed in December. The next day, Ironside wrote

> We must now settle down to thinking how we can do something to defeat the Germans in their steady progress for an attack. Our long-shot effort in Scandinavia has come to nothing, and for the life of me I cannot see any way by which to regain the initiative.[58]

The tone is scarcely lighter in the next day's entry:

> I put it behind me with all the anxious work it has meant. Few people believed that any such expedition could ever come off. We have certainly suffered a defeat. Lets try something else.[59]

The Phoney war was beginning to take its toll on Ironside. He began to consider seriously leaving the War Office to take the post of Commander-in-Chief in India.[60]

Yet something else was tried in early April 1940. Under pressure for action from a reshuffled French Cabinet, now headed by M. Reynaud, the British Government agreed at a Supreme War Council in London on 28 March to mine Norwegian territorial waters. The British also thought they had secured French approval for a complementary operation (another product of the imagination of Winston Churchill) to cut Rhine river traffic by aerial mining. In the event, Operation 'Royal Marine', as it was called, did not occur, but the British agreed, for the sake of alliance politics, and under the strong urging of Winston Churchill, to proceed with the naval action off Norway.[61] The Army's part in the operation was to make ready a small expeditionary force to conduct a protective occupation of Narvik and the other principal ports on the west coast of the country in the event of a German military reaction. The Royal Navy's operation 'Wilfred' (named unpromisingly after a small cartoon character) and the Army's 'Plan R4' were a far cry from the original operations envisaged by Ironside in Scandinavia. Moreover, the original forces for the Scandinavian operation had been dispersed after 15 March, and all that remained for 'R4' was one regular brigade and an undertrained and underequipped Territorial Division. The evidence from the Ironside diaries suggests that the CIGS did not take the same passionate interest in 'R4' as he had in the earlier plan, and doubted whether the Germans would react. Like the Royal Navy, and the rest of the British high command, Ironside was taken by surprise to find that British plans for minelaying followed by a protective occupation had been forestalled by a German invasion, whose planning had been in the works since mid-December 1939. In a diary entry for 8 April 1940, Ironside noted that reports had been received of German naval units moving against Norway. But he was sceptical and thought it probably connoted a German effort to break out into the North Atlantic. As he put it, 'Anyway, the mines are laid and we shall now see what the German reaction is to this violation of the neutrality of Norway. A hullabaloo probably.'[62]

Ironside and his COS colleagues were disabused early the following morning, with confirmation of the German landings in Norway.[63] What he now faced was neither his original Scandinavian project, nor the circumstances envisaged for 'R4' but instead the necessity of mounting a combined operation at very short notice and with inadequate forces to eject the German troops. Ironside also faced the new problem of trying to command offensive military operations from the War Office while having to respect the existing system of three-tiered committee decision-making.[64] Unlike Winston Churchill, Ironside was never enthusiastic about either prospect. In the event, British military operations in Norway during April and May 1940 were a record of dismal failure: of shifting military plans; a lack of

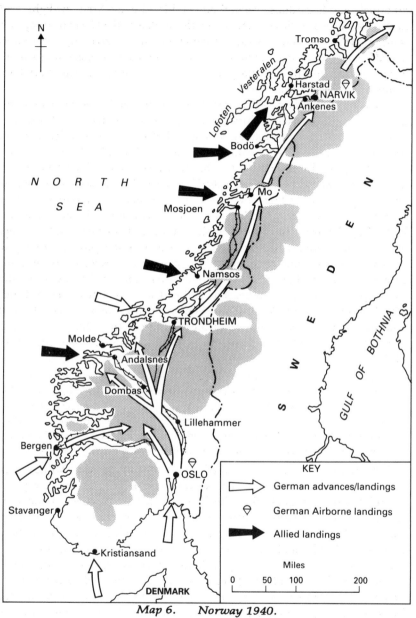

N

North Sea

S W E D E N

GULF OF BOTHNIA

Tromso

Vesteralen

Lofoten

Harstad
NARVIK
Ankenes

Bodö

Mo

Mosjoen

Namsos

TRONDHEIM

Molde

Andalsnes

Dombas

Lillehammer

Bergen

OSLO

Stavanger

Kristiansand

DENMARK

KEY

German advances/landings

German Airborne landings

Allied landings

Miles

0   50   100   200

Map 6.   Norway 1940.

coordinated command; improvised landings; constant retreat in the face of a German army pressing hard from the south; near complete vulnerability to air attack; and hazardous evacuations conducted in an Arctic twilight. Only at Narvik did Allied forces manage finally to defeat the German troops and re-occupy the city. But this success came too late to have any effect on the overall shape of the campaign and was, in any case, overshadowed by the grim news of impending military disaster on the Western Front. Narvik was captured only to be evacuated.

Ironside's fall began the moment that German forces launched their audacious plan to occupy Norway. The ground war that the British were now forced to fight in Norway was not the operation that Ironside had wanted. About the only advantage that he could imagine for it was that it would bring the British nation to what he called a more 'warlike feeling.'[65] Yet Ironside was inevitably identified, owing to his passionate support for another sort of Scandinavian plan, with the onset and outcome of the Norway campaign. His relations with Winston Churchill were tested and badly frayed during the course of that short and ill-starred affair. There were serious disputes between the two men over the proper strategy for Narvik and over the conduct of the operation designed to recapture Trondheim[66]. Ironside resented Churchill's tendency, as he saw it, to interfere in purely military matters. The Cabinet witnessed Ironside in dispute with Churchill and no doubt found him too combative and testy. Ironside also noticed this effect, without caring too much. In a diary entry for 13 April, he recounted the discussion at that afternoon's meeting of the Military Co-Ordination Committee.

> I wonder I kept my temper. I tried to get him [Churchill] to understand that what we wanted out of his committee was the political purpose for which military operations were required. It was not his business and impeded our work to have to submit military details to a civilian committee. Poor Sam Hoare was very shocked and became more and more polite. Oliver Stanley hardly said anything. The other civilian member, Burgin, said absolutely nothing.[67]

Deliberations became so heated and difficult in the Military Co-Ordination Committee once the Norway campaign was underway that Churchill had to request that the Prime Minister, Neville Chamberlain, take the chair.[68] Perhaps in response to the same problem, an initiative was taken in mid-April to create an additional set of military advisers to 'back-stop' the Chiefs of Staff. In the circumstances, it is not difficult to imagine that this initiative was aimed principally at Ironside, who found himself presented with General Sir John Dill, recalled hurriedly from a Corps Command in France, as his Vice Chief of the Imperial General Staff. Ironside was suspicious about the arrangement and feared being usurped or having to conduct a war with divided counsels.[69] Yet he accommodated himself to this change in the command structure for the space of a month until, under strong pressure from Winston Churchill, and in the midst of the retreat of the BEF in France to the Channel, Ironside vacated the post of CIGS and was replaced by Dill.[70]

The immediate effect of the Norway campaign was to touch Ironside with the stigma of defeat, to erode a precarious power base, and to undermine his previously close working relationship with Winston Churchill. Failure in Norway caused his strategic judgement to be discredited, perhaps unfairly. Many in the War Office and in the BEF came to doubt him, or to have their doubts confirmed, including the powerful Permanent Under-Secretary, P J Grigg, and the influential Chief of Staff to the BEF, General Sir Henry Pownall.[71] Nor was he too highly thought of in the Foreign Office, or among the staff at Number 10 Downing Street.[72] From early on in the Norway campaign, the trajectory of Ironside's fall takes on an aspect of inevitability.

From that time on, Ironside proved both too independent-minded and contentious, and too unsuccessful, to sustain the all-important support of Winston Churchill. Nor had Ironside's 'broader view of the war,' the other main ingredient in his original appointment, brought him any credit or advanced the British military cause. His ambitious plans for an operation in Scandinavia revealed the nature of his vision of the war. Even if Norway was not the campaign that he had wanted, and even if Ironside cannot be held directly accountable for the many reverses that were suffered in the fighting on land, the nature of the campaign in Norway clearly revealed that Ironside's strategic judgement, while genuinely broad and imaginative, was ill-suited to the military, political or diplomatic realities of the day. Alive as he was to the dangers of a passive military strategy, Ironside desired to pursue a forward policy in a difficult theatre of war at a time when Britain's military resources and political will were simply inadequate. Once fixed on the major project of operations in Scandinavia, Ironside allowed himself to be mesmerised by the fiction that he had created, showing an inflexibility of mind. When the original Scandinavian campaign was shelved, Ironside felt at a loss, and failed to give his full attention to subsequent planning for Norway. Perhaps most dangerous and inappropriate of all, was the contempt for the power of the German enemy that characterised Ironside's assessment of potential operations in Scandinavia. This took its most idiosyncratic form in Ironside's picture of the cowardly Adolf Hitler. Such contempt was a powerful solvent of strategic caution and could easily spill over into an arrogant confidence in his own planning. When two senior army officers voiced to him in February 1940 their concerns about the Scandinavian project, Ironside dismissed their protests as a product of 'terror' and lack of imagination. He thought these officers 'should be able to realise the vital show this all is.'[73] In the end, Ironside had not the strength of mind to be able to resist Churchillian temptation, or the self-reflexive understanding that much of what he invested in the Scandinavian plan was a product of a desire to build conviction as a bridge into the unknown.

Ironside as CIGS was not the empty-headed man of action depicted in some unsympathetic contemporary accounts. He was not simply the loyal and steadfast soldier portrayed in Winston Churchill's own account. Closer to the truth was the portrait of him during his tenure as Chief of the Imperial General Staff left by one of his staff officers, Major General Sir John Kennedy:

> I admired [Ironside] immensely. The post of CIGS was uncongenial to him, and he made no secret of the fact. But during those bogus months between September 1939 and May 1940 he had injected into our preparations for war a virility and imagination and forcefulness which would have been lacking but for his presence. 'His presence' may be the *mot juste*: he was powerful and impressive in physique, compelling in counsel, devastating in criticism. He had a more varied experience of the continental armies of Europe than his contemporaries; he had made full use of his great powers as a linguist.[74]

Finally, it might be added that while Ironside's tenure as CIGS encompassed such terrible setbacks as the defeat of Poland, the Norway campaign, and the collapse of France, it is unlikely that any other General would have been better able to cope with the need to prosecute a successful war effort with such inadequate resources and misplaced concepts of war as existed. Any CIGS of 3 September 1939 faced a fall.[75]

Chapter Notes

1. Ferdinand Tuohy, *Twelve Lances for Liberty* (London, 1940).
2. Michael Howard, *British Intelligence in the Second World War, vol. 5: Strategic Deception* (London, 1990), p. 125.
3. On the anti-Blimp campaign see Eric Homburger, 'Intellectuals, Englishness and the "Myths" of Dunkirk,' *Revue Francaise de Civilisation Brittanique*, IV, no. 1, pp. 82–100; and George Orwell, *The Lion and the Unicorn: Socialism and the English Genius* (London, 1941).
4. Ironside Diary, 19 July 1940. This and subsequent references are to the manuscript diary entries. Quoted with the permission of Lord Ironside, who retains the diary in his family's possession.
5. Martin Gilbert, *Finest Hour: Winston S. Churchill 1939–1941* (London, 1983), pp. 657, 675; Winston S. Churchill, *The Gathering Storm* (Boston, 1948), pp. 263–65. Both sources are circumspect regarding the dispute over counter-invasion strategy between Churchill and Ironside.
6. Colonel Roderick Macleod and Denis Kelly, eds., *The Ironside Diaries 1937–1940* (London, 1962); Macleod wrote Ironside's entry for the *Dictionary of National Biography*; Macleod's papers, held at the Liddell Hart Centre for Military Archives, King's College, London, reveal something of his activities in defence of Ironside.
7. François Kersaudy, *Norway 1940* (London, 1990), pp. 20–22.
8. *ibid.*, p. 26.
9. *ibid.*, pp. 20–21.
10. Ironside Diary, 7 May, 1939; letter by Ironside to Macleod, quoted in Macleod and Kelly, p. 75.
11. Ironside Diary, 3 Sept. 1939.
12. R.J. Minney, ed., *The Private Papers of Hore-Belisha* (London, 1962), p. 230.
13. Churchill, p. 401.
14. Gilbert, p. 3.
15. While Ironside had some respect for Hore-Belisha's abilities and 'drive' before he became CIGS, his diary entries show that he soon became very disenchanted with his Cabinet Minister, see for example, entry for 8 Sept. 1939, printed in Macleod and Kelly; Brian Bond, 'Leslie Hore-Belisha at the War Office,' in *Politicians and Defence: Studies in the Formulation of British Defence Policy 1845–1970*, eds. Ian Beckett and John Gooch (Manchester, 1981), offers an unusually

sympathetic portrait of Hore-Belisha.

16. D. Cameron Watt, *How War Came: The Immediate Origins of the Second World War, 1938–1939* (London, 1989) is the best study; for British defence policy in this period see N. H. Gibbs, *Grand Strategy, vol. 1: Rearmament Policy* (London, 1976); for one account of the political intelligence that supported the change in policy see Wesley K. Wark, 'Something Very Stern: British Political Intelligence, Moralism and Grand Strategy in 1939,' *Intelligence and National Security*, 5, no. 1 (Jan 1990), pp. 150–70.

17. A recent study by Anita Prazmowska, *Britain, Poland and the Eastern Front, 1939* (Cambridge, 1987) fails, in my estimation, to understand the strategic context.

18. F[oreign] O[ffice] 371, C10289/54/18, 20 July 1939, contains a record of two conversations between Ironside and the Polish army Commander-in-Chief, General Edward Smigly-Rydz.

19. Sir Adrian Carton de Wiart, *Happy Odyssey* (London, 1950), p. 160.

20. J.R.M. Butler, *Grand Strategy, vol. II: September 1939 – June 1941* (London, 1957), ch. 1.

21. *ibid.*, pp. 31–33.

22. Churchill *The Gathering Storm*, appendix B.

23. The real, and the perceived, value of Swedish iron ore imports to Germany has been the subject of much controversy. See Rolf Karlbom, 'Sweden's Iron Ore Exports to Germany, 1933–1944,' *Scandinavian Economic History Review*, no. 1 (1965); C.G. McKay, 'Iron Ore and Section D. The Oxelosund Operation,' *Historical Journal*, 29, no. 4 (1986), 975–78; and especially valuable, the account by Thomas Munch-Petersen, *The Strategy of Phoney War: Britain, Sweden and the Iron Ore Question, 1939–1940* (Stockholm, 1981).

24. Kersaudy, p. 15.

25. *ibid.*, pp. 15–20; Butler, ch. 5, for the official historian's account of the development of plans.

26. Ironside Diary, 16 Nov. 1939.

27. *ibid.*, 17 Dec. 1939.

28. *ibid.*, 18 Dec. 1939.

29. *ibid.*, 12 Jan. 1940; 12 Feb. 1940.

30. *ibid.*, 7 Sept. 1939; 3 Dec. 1939.

31. *ibid.*, 9 Nov. 1939.

32. *ibid.*, 28 Dec. 1939. The next day Churchill submitted a new plan of action to the Prime Minister, Neville Chamberlain, calling for naval operations to commence against German shipping in Norwegian territorial waters in early January.

33. see footnote 32; Kersaudy, pp. 22–24.

34. Ironside Diary, 20 Dec. 1939; Butler, pp. 99–100. The Theissen report was circulated to the Supreme War Council.

35. Ironside Diary, 21 Dec. 1939.

36. *ibid.*, 29 Dec. 1939; extracts from Ironside's draft paper are printed in Macleod and Kelly, pp. 174–76.

37. Brian Bond, ed., *Chief of Staff: The Diaries of Lieutenant General Sir Henry Pownall, vol. I, 1933–1940* (London, 1972), entry for 9 Feb. 1940.

38. Ironside Diary, 30 Dec. 1939.

39. *ibid.*, 5 Jan, 1 April 1940. Ironside interview with Frazier Hunt, *Daily Express*, 5 April 1940.

40. *ibid.*, 25 Dec. 1939; 5 and 6 April, 1940. Ironside gave an optimistic statement to the press about the progress of the war on the same day (5 April) that Chamberlain delivered his famous speech about Hitler having 'missed the bus.'
41. *ibid.*, 29, 30, 31 Dec. 1939.
42. *ibid.*, 29 Dec. 1939.
43. *ibid.*, 25 Dec. 1939.
44. *ibid.*, 7 Sept. 1939.
45. *ibid.*
46. A definite split existed on this issue between Ironside in London and the BEF staff in France, see Bond, *Pownall Diaries*, entries for 7 Mar. and 4 April 1940.
47. Ironside Diary, 30 Dec. 1939.
48. *ibid.*, 17, 24 Feb., 2 and 30 Mar. 1940.
49. *ibid.*, 26 Sept. 1937.
50. *ibid.*, 24, 26 and 30 Dec. 1939.
51. *ibid.*, 31 Dec. 1939; 14 Jan., 12 Feb. 1940.
52. *ibid.*, 30 Mar. 1940.
53. *ibid.*, 25 Dec. 1939.
54. *ibid.*, 12 Feb. 1940.
55. *ibid.*, 28 Dec. 1939. Ironside was still using similar language on 5 Feb. 1940.
56. Bernard Ash, *Norway 1940* (London, 1964), p. 6; also J.L. Moulton, *The Norwegian Campaign of 1940* (London, 1966), 45–46.
57. Ironside Diary, 29 Dec. 1939.
58. *ibid.*, 14 Mar. 1940.
59. *ibid.*, 15 Mar. 1940.
60. *ibid.*, 23 Mar. 1940.
61. Kersaudy, ch. 3; T.K. Derry, *The Campaign in Norway* (London, 1952), ch. 2.
62. Ironside Diary, 8 April 1940.
63. See the amusing story told by General Ismay about his being woken by a frantic and unintelligible duty officer attempting to spread the news without his false teeth in place, Hastings Lionel Ismay, *The Memoirs of General the Lord Ismay* (London, 1960), p. 118.
64. The CIGS consulted with his colleagues on the Chiefs of Staff Committee, who reported to the Military Co-Ordination Committee (a combined military-political body), which in turn reported to the War Cabinet, or full Cabinet as the situation required. Ironside, and many others, thought the system cumbersome and unworkable, Ironside Diary, 7 April 1940. See Ismay, ch. VIII for a description of 'Mr. Chamberlain's Machinery of War.'
65. Ironside Diary, 2 April 1940.
66. *ibid.*, 10 April, 12 April, 14 April 1940; at a midnight conclave on 11–12 April with Churchill, and the navy and air force chiefs, Ironside confessed 'I am afraid I lost my temper and banged the table,' quoted in Macleod and Kelly, p. 253.
67. *ibid.*, 13 April 1940.
68. Churchill, 586–88, who is not explicit about the problems he had in chairing the Military Co-Ordination Committee.
69. Ironside Diary, 13, 21, April 1940.
70. *ibid.*, 25 May 1940. According to Churchill, 'Ironside volunteered the proposal that he should cease to be CIGS, but declared himself quite willing to command the British Home Armies. Considering the unpromising task that such a com-

mand was at the time thought to involve, this was a spirited and selfless offer,' p. 73.

71. For a report of Grigg's views on Ironside, see John Colville, *The Fringes of Power, Downing Street Diaries 1939–1955* (London, 1985), entry for 12 April 1940, p. 102. Pownall had no good opinion of Ironside, even before Ironside became CIGS. On 13 June, 1938, Pownall wrote of him, 'there's always been more bluff and brawn than brain.' Entries for 10 and 30 April 1940 indicate that Pownall was fervently hoping that Ironside would be fired, Bond, *Pownall Diaries*, pp. 150, 298, 304.

72. The Permanent Under-Secretary of the Foreign Office, Sir Alexander Cadogan, was a bitter critic of Ironside; see, for example, his diary entry for 17 May 1940 in David Dilks, ed., *The Diaries of Sir Alexander Cadogan 1938–1945* (London, 1971); a young private secretary at No. 10, John Colville, noted the prevailing opinion of Ironside among the Downing Street staff in his diary, Colville, *op. cit.*

73. Ironside Diary, 8 Feb. 1940.

74. Sir John Kennedy, *The Business of War* (London, 1957), p. 52.

75. A similar conclusion has been reached independently by Brian Bond in his essay on 'Ironside' in John Keegan, ed., *Churchill's Generals* (London, 1991).

Biography of Field Marshal Lord Ironside (1880–1959)

— Born, Edinburgh 6 May 1880
— Commissioned Royal Artillery, 1899
— Service in South African War, 1899–1902
— Intelligence mission in German South West Africa, 1903
— Staff College, 1913
— Service in France, 1914–18
— G.S.O.1, 4th Canadian Division, 1916–1917
— Commandant of Machine Gun Corps School, Camiers, 1918
— Command of 99th Infantry Brigade, 2nd Division, 1918
— Commander in Chief, Allied expeditionary force, Archangel, USSR, 1918–19
— Command of British North Persian Force, 1920
— Commandant of Staff College, Camberley, 1922–26
— Commander of 2nd Division, Aldershot, 1926–28
— Commander of Meerut District, India, 1928–31
— Lieutenant of the Tower of London, 1931–33
— Quarter-Master General, India, 1933–36
— General Officer Commanding, Eastern Command, 1936–38
— Governor of Gibraltar, 1938–39
— Inspector General of Overseas Forces, 1939
— Chief of the Imperial General Staff, 1939–40
— Commander-in-Chief, Home Forces, May–July 1940
— Promoted Field Marshal, 1940
— Made Baron Ironside, 1941
— Died 1959.

8

Douglas MacArthur and the Fall of the Philippines, 1941–1942

Duncan Anderson

Promotion to a Far East or Pacific command in 1941 was the worst fate to befall any rising 'star' of the American or British officer corps. The débâcle at Pearl Harbor destroyed Admiral Husband E Kimmel, Commander-in-Chief of the Pacific fleet, and General Short, commander of United States Army forces in Hawaii: both were immediately relieved of command and never again employed on active service. Two months later in Burma, the British generals Lieutenant General Hutton and Major General John Smyth met the same fate. Languishing in Japanese POW camps, Major General Christopher Maltby, British commander in Hong Kong and Lieutenant General Arthur Perceval, British commander in Malaya, had ample time to ruminate on their ruined careers. Although Major General Gordon Bennett, officer commanding the 8th Australian Division, managed to avoid capture in Singapore, the hostile reception he met on his return home was worse. Like Kimmel, Short, Hutton and Smyth, he was never again given an active posting.

By early 1942 only one Allied 'star' still shone in the Far East – General Douglas MacArthur, Commander of US Army Forces Far East (USAFFE). MacArthur's success seems all the more dazzling set against the darkness which had descended on Kimmel, Short, Hutton and Smyth – men with whom, ironically, he had much in common. Like Kimmel and Short, MacArthur had been surprised by the Japanese and lost much of his air strength from the outset. His troops, like Perceval's and Hutton's, proved unequal to the Japanese and were soon in retreat. The sarcastic nickname given MacArthur by his men – 'Dugout Doug' – scarcely suggested confidence in his leadership. These doubts were shared by a number of Washington officials. Brigadier-General Dwight D Eisenhower, MacArthur's former aide, now head of the Pacific War Plans Division, General George Marshall, Army Chief of Staff, and President Franklin D

Roosevelt, all thought MacArthur even more culpable than Kimmel or Short given the nine hours warning between Japan's surprise attack on Pearl Harbor and their attack on the Philippines. Yet when, in March 1942, MacArthur escaped from Bataan, only weeks before its final fall, Australia gave him a hero's welcome – quite unlike the frosty reception met by their own general, Bennett, the previous month. Rewarded with his country's highest decoration, MacArthur was appointed commander of the newly-created South West Pacific Area.

The fall of the Philippines was the worst defeat yet suffered by the United States, a source of national humiliation. But instead of extinguishing MacArthur's star it added new lustre to it. American public opinion was almost uniformly on his side. It was widely believed that MacArthur's generalship had been brilliant; this alone had kept United States and Filipino troops fighting on long after the fall of Singapore, Rangoon and Java. Bataan and Corregidor became American household names. Blame was pointed at Roosevelt, Marshall and the United States Navy, the latter for timidity in failing to deliver to MacArthur the supplies promised by Washington. Some of MacArthur's more fanatical admirers considered Admiral King and General Marshall lucky to have escaped a Court Martial, and Roosevelt, impeachment and trial before the Senate. A Congressional Medal of Honor and command of a theatre were the very least MacArthur deserved.

Immediately after the war, MacArthur's role as a triumphant general ruling a conquered Japan rendered his reputation unassailable. Some high Washington officials and many former Philippine prisoners-of-war were unable to share in the adulation. But the hagiographic portrait of MacArthur produced in 1946 by his admiring successor in command, General Wainwright, immediately diminished the dangers of dissent. The first challenge to the 'received' version of the First Philippine Campaign came not from a former prisoner-of-war but from MacArthur's former airforce commander, General Lewis Brereton. *The Brereton Diaries*, published some months after *General Wainwright's Story*, raised some disturbing questions about MacArthur's handling of the campaign. Brereton implied that MacArthur's negligence was largely responsible for the success of the surprise Japanese bomber attack which had devastated American air bases at Luzon on the first day of the war. By now Louis Morton was compiling information for his official history of the First Philippine Campaign. His doubts about MacArthur's prewar defence plans were strong enough to furbish an article in *Military Affairs* (1948). A year later, the first book by a former prisoner-of-war, Colonel Ernest B Mullin's *Bataan Uncensored*, recounted a tale of ineptitude in high places. When Morton's *The Fall of the Philippines* appeared in 1953, it demanded a major critical re-evaluation of MacArthur's generalship.

This was slow to happen. By 1953, all eyes were focussed on MacArthur's recent conduct of the Korean War. On 11 April 1951 Truman had relieved MacArthur of command of the United States forces in Korea. Depending on one's political viewpoint, MacArthur's plans to expand the limited Korean War into China would have either purged the world of the evils of communism or plunged it into an atomic holocaust. Not surprisingly, during the 1950s and 1960s historians and political scientists were more interested in the postwar phase of MacArthur's controversial career than in dredging up the issue of the Philippines. But Volume 1 of Clayton James's definitive biography (1970) marked the start of a gradual shift in interest back to MacArthur's Second World War career.[1] Since then, younger historians such as Carol Petillo and Michael Schaller have followed up Clayton James' leads to develop a comprehensive critique of MacArthur's generalship during the Philippines campaign.[2] Numerous charges are levelled at MacArthur – failure to raise and train an effective army, failure to perceive the true nature of the threat, failure to respond with sufficient flexibility to changed circumstances. The catalogue of errors which emerges reads like a 'how-not-to' guide for would-be-generals.

Fifty years ago, MacArthur's defence of Bataan and Corregidor secured him a niche in America's pantheon of heroes. Recent scholarly scepticism has dislodged him from that niche, demoted him from superstar to failed actor, no better than Kimmel or Short. Or (to vary the metaphor) MacArthur looks less like a star than a supernova, a blaze of light without substance. But the new critique of MacArthur seems oddly uneven. It blames him for things over which he had no control, such as the effectiveness of the Philippine Army or shifts in US – Japanese relations, and exonerates him from failures for which he was personally responsible, such as the collapse of his administrative system in Bataan or the plummetting morale of his troops. Pendulums in historical scholarship always swing from one extreme to another before a balanced appraisal can be reached: it is the aim of this chapter to give the pendulum a backward nudge.

Douglas MacArthur took up the post of military adviser to the Commonwealth of the Philippines in December 1935. No-one could have been more delighted than the islands' president, Manuel Quezon. Ten years earlier, during MacArthur's second tour of duty as commander of the Philippines' American garrison, Quezon had been impressed by MacArthur's marked preference for the social company of prominent Filipinos rather than American expatriots. By 1935, MacArthur was America's most distinguished serving officer, having just completed five years as Army Chief of Staff in Washington. His controversial political reputation by no means deterred Quezon, since MacArthur's politics were sympathetic to the Philippines' interests. Roosevelt's newly-elected Democrat administration had ample reason to dislike MacArthur, who only three years before had enraged liberal America by clearing protesting ex-servicemen (the bonus marchers) from their encampments by the Anacostia

River outside Washington. MacArthur was closely associated with the Republican party. He was a personal friend of Herbert Hoover and John Rand, founder of the Sears Roebuck empire and major funder of Republican campaigns, and was even tipped within the party for presidential nomination. Quezon, worried that Roosevelt might thrust independence on the Philippines even before the projected date of 1946, had double reason to welcome MacArthur to Manila. Despite occasional disagreements, Quezon and MacArthur's friendship lasted for the six years the general spent on the Philippines. MacArthur's integration into the Filipino élite involved extensive business investments, high rank in the Masonic Lodge, and close family ties with Quezon, whom he requested to act as his baby son's godfather in 1938.

MacArthur's task between 1935 and 1941 was to create a defence for the Philippines. His own ideas about its scope and role differed radically from those held by the United States War Department and Navy, who, since the start of the century, had viewed America's possession of the Philippines as a strategic liability rather than an asset. In 1919 Japan's acquisition of German islands in the North Pacific which dominated communications between Hawaii and the Philippines heightened this sense of liability. The series of Orange (Japan) War Plans (WPO) developed by Washington steadily reduced the role of the United States garrison, the 'Philippine Department', from an active to a defensive one. In the event of war, the garrison would merely 'hold' the Bataan Peninsula and the forts dominating the entrance to Manila Bay while the United States Navy battled across the Pacific to the rescue. MacArthur's plans were far more ambitious. His national Philippine Army – some 200,000 men, annually trained and backed by a small airforce and a substantial force of torpedo boats – would be able to defend the entire archipelago.

The Army's War Plans Department voiced its reservations as early as the spring of 1936. They thought MacArthur's project at best unrealistic, at worst dangerous. The Philippine legislature was prepared to raise only an inadequate eight million dollars per year. Bureaucratic inefficiency and corruption (according to Eisenhower's diaries during his spell as MacArthur's aide between 1935–9) further reduced that sum.[3] Washington officials who feared insurrection from disaffected Filipino natives insisted that all modern weapons for Bataan's defence be stored on the fortress island of Corregidor: they saw the main danger to Philippine security as an internal one posed by Sakdalista guerrillas. They thought MacArthur's needs would be best served by a small, division-sized, highly-trained gendarmerie, one which could slot into existing American defence plans were war to break out before independence. This force could help defend the Bataan Peninsula alongside the Philippine Scouts and the small American garrison.

MacArthur's recent critics have asserted that Eisenhower and the War

Department were right at the time to censure his defence plans.[4] But criticisms made with the benefit of hindsight distort historical teleology: they presuppose that MacArthur was preparing for only one contingency, the full-scale Japanese invasion that actually occurred in 1941. In 1935, the threat of war with Japan seemed remote, even to the Japanese Navy, who thought conflict impossible before the early 1950s. Although Japan's subsequent involvement in China after July 1937 exacerbated US – Japanese relations, it made an attack on the Philippines seem less rather than more likely. In 1935, MacArthur was planning ahead for a post-independence army for the Philippines, one which would fulfil his classical ideals of military training as a prerequisite for citizenship. His National Army would train and meld the disparate ethnic, linguistic and racial groups on the islands into a distinct Philippine identity.

Clayton James, Schaller and others argue that the threat of war, even if remote in the late 1930s, was looming closer by the early summer of 1940. The defeat of France and Holland, coupled with Britain's apparent military impotence, now offered the Japanese the tempting target of vulnerable European Asian empires. An attack on the Philippines seemed an active possibility: this should, they assert, have prompted MacArthur to revert to a defence scheme which could fit in with the latest version of the Orange War Plan, WPO3.[5] But by this stage MacArthur's sense of personal identity was intimately bound up with the future of the Philippines. He had resigned from the United States Army in 1937, the year after he had accepted the role of Field Marshal of the new Philippine Army. The limited and defeatist implications of WPO3 were anathema to him; also to his supporters in the Philippine legislature, who would be reluctant to supply the same level of funding for a smaller, less nationalistic army. MacArthur's training in Washington military politics had alerted him to the potential conflict between narrowly-conceived defence plans and larger political issues.

Modern critics universally condemn the optimism with which MacArthur presented his defence plans to the Philippine legislature between 1936 and 1941. This could be excused as a necessary exercise to ensure the continued funding of his army, but unfortunately MacArthur used the same glowing terms in the reports he sent back to Washington. Historians of the Pacific War believe that the cumulative impetus of these unrealistic assessments led Roosevelt, in the wake of Japanese moves on Indo-China in early July 1941, to reverse American policy on the Philippines a few weeks later. MacArthur had repeatedly assured Washington that with just a little more help from the United States, his army could hold the Philippines. Between August and November, heavy bombers, modern fighters, thousands of tons of supplies and some 8,000 personnel were rushed across the Pacific. All that these last-minute efforts achieved, assert MacArthur's critics, was to increase the toll of the Bataan Death March.[6]

The theory that MacArthur was responsible for transforming American defence policy in the Western Pacific presupposes that within only a matter of weeks he had managed to convert Roosevelt, Marshall and the other Chiefs of Staff to his own views. But Washington was always fully briefed about the numerous shortcomings of MacArthur's Philippine Army. Eisenhower had spelt them out clearly to the War Department after returning from the islands in December 1939. On 4 June 1941, the Secretary of War and the Secretary of the Navy approved a new war plan (Rainbow 5) based on the assumption that the Philippines neither could nor should be defended.[7] The report Marshall received twelve days later from Major General Grunert, commander of the Philippine Department, analysed the state of the Philippine Army in terms which confirmed rather than dispelled Eisenhower's previous doubts.[8]

If Washington remained unconvinced by MacArthur's plans, what made the government change its policy? The concentration of scholarly interest on the stream of optimistic communiques flowing from Manila to Washington has diverted critical attention from some fundamental changes which were then taking place in the Administration's policy-making machinery. On 20 June, the disparate elements which had comprised the Army Air Corps had been formed into the United States Army Air Force. This was far more than a mere change of name – an important byproduct was the establishment of an independent Air War Plans Division.[9] On 23 June, Roosevelt signed an executive order authorising the acceleration and expansion of the production of heavy bombers – the B-17 and the B-24.[10] Any schemes the new Air War Plans Department now drew up could be very ambitious indeed.

On 2 July, attention was focussed on the Pacific when Japanese forces landed in southern Indo-China, a move which threatened not only the British and Dutch Asian empires but also the United States' supplies of rubber, tin and bauxite. For the next three weeks, various federal departments struggled to find an acceptable response. Defence plans for the Philippines were drawn up by the new Air War Plans Department, whose chief, Colonel Harold L George, had served as an observer on Dowding's staff during the Battle of Britain. George's division produced a blueprint for a defence of the Philippines by aircraft operating without the assistance of land or naval forces. What he called a 'strategical defensive' could be established, he argued, by the deployment of 340 heavy bombers and 130 fighters to Luzon. The commander of the Air Force, General 'Hap' Arnold, and the Secretary for War, Henry Stimson, took up the plan enthusiastically.[11] On 25 July, Stimson urged Roosevelt to authorise the despatch of large numbers of heavy bombers and fighters to the Philippines.[12] Two days later, Roosevelt announced a dramatic hardening in American policy towards Japan – the freezing of Japanese assets in the United States which, along with similar British and Dutch moves, cut off Japan's supplies of oil. On the same day, Marshall recalled MacArthur to the United States Army and appointed him Lieutenant General commanding a combined Philippine

Army-Philippine Department command, the United States Army Forces Far East. On 1 August Marshall told MacArthur of the official change in United States Pacific policy – the Philippines were now to be defended – and promised him substantial help. From that time until well after the Japanese attack on 8 December, Marshall always reassured MacArthur that help was on the way.

The sequence of events in June and July 1941 makes plain that the reversal of American policy on Philippine defence had nothing whatever to do with MacArthur's assurances about the efficiency of his troops. Contrary to the accepted version of events, the decision was made in Washington and *imposed* on MacArthur. The high class claims MacArthur had made for his Philippine Army later supplied Stimson, Roosevelt and Marshall with a convenient scapegoat when their own policy failed. MacArthur never realised he was not responsible for Washington's apparent change of heart. Obsessed with a land battle, he had in fact wanted military equipment and American advisers rather than aircraft. But when Brereton, commander of the new Far Eastern Air Force, arrived on 3 November, MacArthur greeted him warmly with the words, 'Lewis, you are just as welcome as the flowers in May'.[13] Between August and early December, an eight million dollar airfield improvement and construction programme gave the Philippines some forty completed and semi-completed airfields and the largest concentration of war planes outside the United States. Of the 8,000 American servicemen who arrived on the islands during this period, 5,600 were Army Air Force.[14] Impressive though the effort was it was all too little, too late. The Japanese struck on 8 December, nearly four months earlier than MacArthur had predicted.

Shortly after midday on 8 December, Japanese air attacks on Clark and Iba Fields in central Luzon wiped out many of the United States Air Force's heavy bombers and fighters. Manila, forewarned, but not forearmed, had received news of Pearl Harbor more than nine hours earlier. Finding the guilty party responsible for Luzon is a historical detective game only marginally less popular than solving the Pearl Harbor mystery. Was it MacArthur, or Brereton, his airforce commander, or Major General Sutherland, his new Chief of Staff? Or all three? Historians trying to reconstruct the events of those crucial nine hours have failed to reach a majority verdict. Brereton's diaries supply us with a seemingly unimpeachable defence. At 5.30 on the morning of the 8th, he sought an audience with MacArthur for permission to carry out an airstrike on Japanese airfields on Formosa. Sutherland refused him entry on the grounds that MacArthur was too busy. Brereton's urgent phone calls elicited MacArthur's belated approval for a photo reconnaissance mission over Formosa upon which any bombing mission would be based. Had that mission been authorised at 5.30 it might have pre-empted a Japanese strike and would have cleared Clark Field of the B-17s.

Although MacArthur, as Commander United States Army Forces Far East, was technically responsible, Brereton's defence for the days leading up to 8 December looks shaky. He delayed carrying out MacArthur's command to send the United States Air Force's heavy bombers to Del Monte Field in northern Mindanao (well out of Japanese range). Del Monte Field was still under construction and ground space was limited. But Brereton's motives for delay may have been more dubious. Notorious for his socialising, drinking and womanising, he had planned a party to end all parties for American air crews at the Manila Hotel on the night of 7 December, one which MacArthur's orders would have forced him to cancel. The party went ahead. Brereton did not get back until after 2 am. Woken by the news of Pearl Harbor at 3.30, he was almost certainly still drunk and probably not alone. Sutherland (on record as advising Brereton to down some coffee) may have refused him admittance to MacArthur for being the worse for wear. In any other context, MacArthur's decision to base an airstrike on evidence gathered from photo reconnaissance would have seemed prudent rather than over-cautious. The success of aerial bombing raids usually depended on an accurate knowledge of the target.

The argument about the delay in airstrike authorisation is a red herring: the real blame lay at Washington's door for allowing the latest American aircraft to gather in the Philippines without proper protection. On the day itself a number of chance factors coalesced to produce the disaster. Brereton, conscious of the vulnerability of his B-17s sitting stationary on the airfields, had ordered them up early that morning, covered by fighter protection. When authorisation for an airstrike came through at 12 pm, he ordered the B-17s and P-40s down for essential preparation and refuelling. In that brief period, when the skies over Luzon were clear, the Japanese bombers, whose take-off had been delayed for several hours by heavy fog over Formosa, flew over Clark and Iba Fields and could scarcely believe their luck; rows of American aircraft grouped on the fields while ground crews moved fuel lines and trailers of ammunition and bombs across the runways. It took them less than half an hour to break the back of the United States Far Eastern Air Force. Brereton should have kept a fighter screen aloft. But responsibility for the Luzon disaster ultimately points back to the Washington bureaucracy – Stimson, Marshall, Roosevelt, 'Hap' Arnold and the Air War Plans staff. In their rush to get the latest aircraft to Luzon as quickly as possible they had neglected the vital matter of protection. The heavy bombers, which could travel to Luzon independently, arrived well in advance of essential hardware such as radar sets, communication equipment and anti-aircraft guns. Under normal circumstances, the sequence would have been reversed: first air fields with bomb-proof hangers and anti-aircraft guns, then a radar and communications net tied to widely deployed fighter squadrons, last of all the heavy bombers. Washington and the Air War Plans Department took a gamble and lost.[15]

Although MacArthur can be exonerated for the Clark and Iba Field disasters, historians have argued that the islands' sudden dramatic loss of air power should have forced him to activate WPO3 at once.[16] But was the case so clear-cut on 8 December? If the decision depended solely on the state of his embryonic Philippine Army, then MacArthur was clearly in the wrong. Mobilisation, begun on 1 September, was due to be completed by 15 December. As the nine divisions finished their training, they were deployed in the three defensive commands into which MacArthur had divided the islands: three divisions to central and southern islands (the Visayas and Mindanao), two to southern Luzon, and four to north Luzon under Major General Wainwright's command. The Philippine troops were ragged at the seams. They had rifles and webbing but no proper uniforms. Their make-shift fatigues of denims, canvas shoes and straw hats barely distinguished them from ordinary Filipino peasants. Disciplined by NCOs only slightly less ignorant than themselves, their military training had not extended much beyond grasping basic commands and loading and firing weapons. Transport was minimal: any trucks beyond the paltry twenty assigned to each division had been requisitioned or stolen. The large shipments of equipment which arrived in Manila by early December proved mostly useless. Ammunition left over from 1918 was often defective, and the field guns lacked sights. The Philippine 'artillery regiments' were little more than gangs of curious peasants playing with obsolete guns.[17]

By December 1941, the regular strength of the USAFFE had grown to 30,000. Over half that number were tied up in service detachments and the Air Force: of the remaining 15,000 who served on the front line, 10,000 belonged to the Philippine Division. MacArthur concentrated them in a reserve position near Manila alongside two newly-arrived tank battalions and a field regiment of self-propelled guns, adding as leaven the best of his newly-raised divisions – 5,000 men drawn from the Philippine constabulary. MacArthur's reserve amounted to 20,000 well trained troops, supported by over a hundred tanks and about two hundred self-propelled guns and field-guns.

Was he wrong to risk pitting this force against the Japanese in manoeuvre warfare? Critics have suggested that by this stage MacArthur had retreated into a fantasy world, cushioned from reality by sycophantic staff and an imperious Sutherland who controlled access to his offices.[18] But MacArthur may have had perfectly good reasons (ones overlooked by historians) for his delay in activating WPO3. Although MacArthur's Philippine Army was far from ready, Marshall's radio message on 8 December had guaranteed him 'every possible assistance within our power'.[19] MacArthur believed that reinforcements would arrive any day. On 13 December, a convoy carrying 70 fighters and dive-bombers was re-routed from the Central Pacific to the Philippines via Australia under the protection of the United States Asiatic Fleet. Two days later, Marshall radioed MacArthur that another 160 fighters and dive-bombers were being loaded aboard two fast transports, and that an additional fifteen heavy bombers had been directed to the Philippines. On 22 December, he promised another 80 B-17s and B-24s via Africa and the Indian Ocean. He even allayed MacArthur's fears that the Japanese advance might cut the resupply link:

> The heavy bombers beginning to flow from this country via Africa to your theatre should be able to support you materially even if compelled initially to operate from distant bases. They will be valuable also in co-operating with naval forces and smaller aircraft in protecting your line of communications. The great range, speed and power of these bombers, should permit, under your direction, effective surprise concentrations against particularly favorable targets anywhere in the theater.[20]

Thus MacArthur had every reason to expect the imminent arrival of large numbers of war planes. Withdrawal to Bataan, with its one small airfield, would have seemed extremely premature. Had he abandoned the central Luzon airfields in mid-December, he would simultaneously have abandoned any chance of retrieving the situation. Resumption of an American command had not converted MacArthur to the advantages of WPO3. He was still a Philippine field marshal who knew that his mostly Filipino troops would interpret an American withdrawal as a sign that their commander was ready to sacrifice their families to the Japanese.

Although MacArthur rejected the cautionary policy of WPO3 he did not use his troops to try to ward off every single Japanese landing. He knew that the small Japanese landings at Vigan and Aparri on the north coast of Luzon (10 December) and at Legaspi in the extreme south east (14 December) were diversions. The only place on the Luzon coast where a large-scale landing was possible was Lingayen Gulf, about 100 miles north-west of Manila. It was here that he concentrated the divisions of Wainwright's North Luzon Force.

Morton and James, the two leading authorities on the campaign, have suggested that MacArthur harboured more reservations about the outcome of a battle between his own men and the Japanese invaders than is commonly supposed. On 13 December, MacArthur apparently told Quezon that he might need to activate WPO3 very quickly. Some of his officers inspecting defences at Lingayen seemed unduly concerned about the location of withdrawal routes.[21] This scarcely constitutes evidence. Substantial counter-evidence (overlooked by Morton and James) lies in the decisive nature of MacArthur's logistic arrangements, which can scarcely be open to misinterpretation. Since 8 December, trainload after trainload of supplies had been shifted from Manila to depots around Lingayen. On 18 December, when MacArthur's code-breakers gave him definite information that a large Japanese convoy was heading to Lingayen, he actually *increased* the supply flow to Lingayen rather than diverting it to Bataan. By 21 December, North Luzon's Force's depots were crammed with some 18,000 tons of supplies.

No general planning a token defence would have created advance depots on such a scale.[22] In addition MacArthur sent north from his reserve the crack 26th Cavalry of the Philippine Scouts and one of his newly-arrived tank battalions.

Would MacArthur have made a stand on Lingayen had he realised the disparity between his Philippine Army and the Japanese troops? He knew full well that his Filipinos weren't up to American standards, but neither, he thought, were the Japanese. All that he had heard about Japanese soldiers pointed to weakness and inefficiency: they had been unable to defeat the peasant militias of China after more than three years of war, and had been humiliated by the Red Army in the border clashes of 1938 and 1939, the same Red Army which was in turn humiliated by the militia of Finland in November 1939. The odds that a Japanese landing on Lingayen would succeed were not as high as they later appeared. By the third week in December, the Japanese had launched nine amphibious operations. Six of these had been successful because unopposed: of the three that had been opposed, two ended in defeat and one in near disaster.[23] A Japanese invasion force heading for Lingayen gulf would have to run the gauntlet of American submarines and aerial assault as well as coping with the high surf and uncertain weather conditions of December.

MacArthur could have amply justified his decision to stand at Lingayen. But in his *Reminiscences* he chose to skirt round the issue, devoting only two paragraphs to a suspiciously simplified account. According to MacArthur, on 22 December a large Japanese convoy entered the gulf and disgorged six divisions totalling 80,000 men – about twice the number of his 40,000 defenders. The Japanese already knew the locations of the defenders' strong points and easily avoided them. MacArthur claimed that what really prompted his decision to reactivate WPO3 was the news of a fresh Japanese landing at Lamon Bay, only forty miles south-east of Manila. He apparently suddenly realised that the Japanese commander General Homma intended 'to swing shut jaws of a great military pincer, one prong being the main force that had landed at Lingayen, the other the units that had landed at Atimonan'. Under these circumstances all he could do was pull back into Bataan to avoid a trap.[24]

What makes MacArthur's account so extraordinary is that it contradicts Louis Morton's meticulous historical analysis of the Lingayen landings published some twelve years earlier. Morton had pointed out that the Japanese landings had been far from easy. Although the United States Asiatic Fleet's submarines had proved only a minor deterrent, high winds and pounding surf had capsized landing craft and caused many of the Japanese invaders to swim ashore without arms or equipment. Moreover, Homma commanded not 80,000 men but only 43,000, about the same number that Wainwright had concentrated around Lingayen Gulf. Defending troops can rarely have been in such a favourable situation: mass slaughter of the Japanese should have been a likelihood. But after scrutinising dozens of unit diaries, Morton discovered only one instance of Filipino resistance.[25] The mere suspicion that the Japanese were coming was enough to panic the Filipinos, who by dawn were streaming south-east around the head of the gulf. Wainwright attempted a counter-attack, throwing the 26th Cavalry, elements of the provisional tank battalion, and Brigadier General Clyde Selleck's 71st Division of the Philippine Army against the Japanese. Never having trained together, the tanks and cavalry were unable to co-ordinate their activities. The Japanese drove both units back and by early afternoon of 23 December their patrol probes had produced widespread panic and chaos in Selleck's division.

It was this factor above all others that finally prompted MacArthur to activate WPO3. Although Lamon bay was only forty miles from Manila, the route between crossed country so rugged that it would have taken the advancing Japanese more than a week to get from one location to the other. The south-eastern jaw of MacArthur's 'great military pincer' would have closed so slowly that any potential prey would have had ample warning to escape.[26] It seems not insignificant that MacArthur punished the inept Selleck far more severely than any of his other failed divisional commanders. He was the only brigadier-general dismissed from command and reduced to the rank of colonel.

On 24 December the full implications of WPO3 came home to MacArthur. He was now no longer the commander of what had been, in effect, a theatre – he had been reduced to caretaker of a soon-to-be beleaguered fortress. Implementation of WPO3 entailed ordering Hart and Brereton to reduce their respective headquarters and withdraw to the south, Hart to Java and Brereton to Australia. MacArthur saw Hart go with little regret. Hart's small surface fleet had withdrawn at the outbreak of hostilities and his submarines had proved singularly ineffective. His dealings with MacArthur, which only just bordered on the civil, reflected the long-standing animosity between MacArthur and the United States Navy which had always precluded co-ordination of Philippine defence policy.[27]

MacArthur felt Brereton's loss more keenly. When his squadrons had first touched down on the islands, MacArthur had seen them as confirmation that after five years, Washington had at last decided to take his own plans for Philippine defence seriously. Even the disasters at Clark and Iba fields had not shaken MacArthur's confidence. Believing that Marshall's promised reinforcements would enable him to regain control of the air by early January, MacArthur dreamt of winning a land campaign against the Japanese in the Western Pacific while the United States Navy cowered in the Eastern. That dream now lay in ruins. Brereton's role was reduced to sustaining and developing aerial supply lines against the Japanese.

The relocation of HQ Asiatic Fleet and HQ USAAFFE were only two of the decisions MacArthur made on 24 December. Few generals have ever made as many sweeping command changes all on one day.[28] Apart from shutting down his naval and air headquarters, MacArthur shifted his own headquarters and the United States High Commission together with President Quezon and the entire Philippine Government to the Malinta tunnel complex on the fortress island of Corregidor. Simultaneously, he created two entirely new corps-level headquarters, one a rear-echelon HQ in Manila to oversee the withdrawal of forces to Bataan, the other on Bataan itself to organise the defenders. He also announced widespread changes in appointments: he sacked one divisional commander (Selleck), promoted another divisional commander (Jones) to the command of South Luzon Force, and transferred the South Luzon Force commander, General Parker, to the command of the Bataan Peninsula. Historians have acknowledged the confusion that inevitably ensued, but few have recognised its full implications.[29] It nearly led to the loss of one of MacArthur's corps, it certainly contributed to the ineffectiveness of supply movements to Bataan, and it seriously interfered with efforts to construct a sound defence scheme for the peninsular.

MacArthur's sweeping command changes have escaped censure because historians have focussed on the most successful single aspect of the operation: the carefully-planned and well-rehearsed withdrawal of Wainwright's North Luzon Force. This movement had been practised since the early 1920s: there could have been few officers with Philippine service who were not familiar with the phasing of the withdrawal from stop-line to stop-line. The retreat began on Christmas Day and by 31 December North Luzon Force reached the fifth and final stop line anchored on the Angat River at Baliug, a position about ten miles north of Manila Bay which covered the main road from Manila to Bataan as it wound round the head of the bay and bridged the wide, steeply-banked Pampanga River at Calumpit.

Apart from some minor skirmishes, the North Luzon withdrawal went like clockwork. But the parallel withdrawal of South Luzon Force gives a very different impression of MacArthur's generalship. MacArthur failed to give clear directives to Jones, who lacked the benefit of pre-planning for his extremely difficult task of co-ordinating a simultaneous retreat of three separate columns along three routes divided by lakes and jungle-clad mountains. The sudden withdrawal of any one force would leave the flanks of the other two exposed. This is precisely what happened at 3 am on 25 December when Japanese patrols penetrated the front of the middle column, the 1st Regiment of the 1st Philippine Division, who rapidly withdrew towards Manila. A furious Jones caught up with them a few hours later: but news of MacArthur's command changes had not yet filtered through and the regiment's Filipino commander refused to take orders from him.

By 28 December, South Luzon Force was holding the Japanese at bay at

Tiaong, still some forty miles south west of Manila. That same day MacArthur's Corregidor headquarters issued an order for the immediate withdrawal of South Luzon Force via Manila to Bataan. But the next day, 29 December, that order was countermanded by HQ Manila, which sent South Luzon Force back south-east again instructing them to hold the Japanese at bay for as long as possible. The Japanese had, of course, used the intervening hours to advance and occupy the Tiaong position. South Luzon Force grudgingly dug a new defence line. They were forced to abandon it the next day when HQ Corregidor ordered them to retreat north as quickly as possible and be across the Calumpit Bridges by 6 am on 1 January 1942.

As South Luzon Force rolled through Calumpit on New Year's Eve, MacArthur radioed Jones again to inform him that he was now to take charge of the Agnat River defence line and hold it until the last troops had pulled through Calumpit. He was then to withdraw over the bridges and blow them up behind him. Unfortunately, MacArthur forgot to relay this information to General Wainwright, the North Luzon Force commander. On the afternoon of 31 December, Wainwright arrived at Jones's new headquarters in Plaridel, a town just south of Baliuag, to conduct the final defence. Wainwright ordered Jones to pull back his troops: Jones replied that he was now in command and intended to fight the battle very differently. Brigadier General Stevens, commander of 91st Division, joined in the argument. The three generals were interrupted by news that the Japanese were now in Baliuag and that the defenders were retiring south. This unexpectedly solved the question. Just after 6 am the last of South Luzon Force passed over the Pampanga River blowing up behind them the bridges at Calumpit.

This complex operation was concluded successfully almost despite MacArthur, whose confusing last-minute changes in headquarters, commands and leadership nearly caused disaster. Within a five-day period, contradictory orders had had South Luzon force dancing up and down like a yo-yo: retreat, advance, retreat, advance, retreat. Even the most loyal Filipino private must have harboured a few doubts about his commander. Furthermore, MacArthur had inadvertently created a situation where two generals, Wainwright and Jones, each believed himself in command. Had events not overtaken them, they would have issued dangerously contradictory orders to troops about to fight the enemy.

Historians have been less forgiving of MacArthur's mishandling of WPO3's logistic aspects. WPO3 entailed withdrawal of supplies as well as troops – supplies intended to sustain some 43,000 men for the possible six months it would take before the United States Pacific Fleet came to the rescue. The town of Cabanatuan contained a vast rice depot on which civilian Manila depended. MacArthur's critics point out that its supplies would have fed Bataan for five years: MacArthur's threat to court-martial any logistic officer who laid a finger on them looks like another example of his readiness to sacrifice his troops' welfare to Filipino politics[29]. All this is another red herring. The Manila warehouses were always well-stocked, and there was no real shortage of supplies, only a difficulty in moving them. General Drake, MacArthur's Quartermaster, calculated on 8 December that it would take at least two weeks to move supplies to Bataan sufficient for WPO3. MacArthur refused to authorise the operation, instructing Drake instead to stock the depots in the Tarlac area in preparation for the anticipated battle for Lingayen Gulf. By 22 December, 35 trainloads, carrying 18,000 tons of supplies, had been shifted north.

Two days later, Drake learnt that WPO3 was now in effect. He faced the near impossible task of saving the contents of the depots as well as shifting to Bataan supplies for perhaps twice as many men in half the original time. The railway system was defunct; Japanese bombers had already destroyed rolling stock and scared away native train crews. Motor transport was by now out of the question. On 8 December, Drake had the foresight to requisition 1,000 civilian trucks for supply purposes, but by 24 December most had been commandeered by American and Filipino units during the move to Lingayen. Drake's only hope now was that troops retreating through big depots such as Tarlac or Fort Stotsenberg would have the sense to carry off with them some of the supplies to last for the projected six-month siege. Few did. But even fully loaded, they could not have carried away more than 30 per cent of the depot contents. They took only about 5 per cent: most of the residue fell into the hands of the advancing Japanese.[30]

Water transport was still a possibility. Even on 8 December, Drake had started to requisition supplies from merchant ships still docked in Manila Bay. Between Christmas Eve and the New Year, Drake scraped together a fleet of some 300 barges to carry supplies between Manila and Bataan. But docking facilities on Bataan limited unloading to six barges at a time. Manila dockyard's skilled Filipino stevedores had disappeared in terror of Japanese bomb attacks: their replacements, American and European civilian volunteers responding to radio broadcasts for help, were far slower. Few of the barges themselves could make more than 3 knots an hour. It took them more than ten hours to get to Bataan. Not surprisingly, most only managed one trip before the fall of Manila on 2 January 1942.[31]

In these circumstances, Drake's achievement in shifting more than 30,000 tons of supplies to Bataan and Corregidor was impressive. But the singular lack of communication between MacArthur and his quartermaster led to severe problems. Drake gave top priority to military supplies and ammunition. Corregidor never ran short of these, but men could scarcely eat bullets. When the first returns of unit strength came in, MacArthur had been amazed to read that he had some 80,000 troops on Bataan, with a further 26,000 civilians. He immediately suspected this was an exaggeration: the usual inflation of figures made by troops trying to secure ample rations.

When the figures proved correct, the ration situation looked grim. Drake calculated rations would last for fifty days at most. Even the most stringent exploitation of Bataan's natural resources – fish, rice and Caribou – would not secure adequate supplies for 180 days. The low priority given to medical supplies was equally worrying. The malaria that infested Bataan during the summer season did not seem a major threat in January: but by March the one month's supply of quinine and handful of mosquito nets would scarcely stave off an epidemic. MacArthur, who had suffered badly from malaria during his earlier service on Bataan in 1906, should have been more percipient.[32]

Historians seem to have assumed that defence lines on Bataan were adequate. But because MacArthur had forbidden any advance work on them (perhaps fearing the negative impact on Filipino morale), the task that faced General Parker on 24 December was formidable.[33] Speed was essential, but haste led to mistakes. The most serious was the abandonment of Fort Wint, an island outpost only marginally less important than Corregidor itself. Fort Wint dominated the entrance to Subic Bay, Bataan's north-western shore. Its guns, trained on the western side of the Bataan peninsula, would jeopardise any attempted landings. But on Christmas Eve Fort Wint's commander, Colonel Napoleon Boudreau, learnt that he had 24 hours in which to dismantle his guns and evacuate to Bataan. The task was impossible: on 25 December, the garrison withdrew, leaving the Japanese a Christmas present of all their fixed guns, some mobile guns, and several thousand rounds of 155 mm ammunition.[34]

United States Engineers began arriving on Bataan on 25 December. The peninsula had been thoroughly surveyed over the decades (MacArthur had assisted in the task as a junior officer) but too little time remained to make use of these detailed plans to construct man-made defence lines and obstacles. Bataan's excellent natural defences partly compensated: a tangle of steep jungle-clad mountains sandwiched between narrow coastal plains running down the eastern and western sides. The US Engineers, basing their calculations on the average capacity of their own troops, pronounced as impassible the rugged Mount Natib Massif in the centre of the peninsula's twenty-mile neck. They thought that a forward defence line across the eastern and western coastal plains would prove sufficient, the inland flanks of both lines anchored on the eastern and western slopes of Mount Natib. Mt. Natib's forbidding terrain would deter any Japanese from attempting the ten-mile gap between the eastern and westernmost American units. Some six miles south, the engineers began work on a rear battle line which, skirting the northern slopes of Mt. Samat, ran all the way across the peninsula. If and when the Japanese breached this, the battle for Bataan would be over.[35]

After establishing his new Corregidor headquarters, MacArthur began to reorganise the forces retreating into the peninsula. He placed Wainwright in charge of I Corps, three Philippine Divisions assigned to the rugged western side of the defence line. He assigned Parker to command II Corps (four Philippine Divisions and the Philippine Scouts) which he sent to the eastern side of the defence line. The ten mile front was defended by some 40,000 men, supported by about 100 guns. The Japanese commander on the spot, General Nara, attempted an assault on the Abucay line on 9 January, based on the false supposition made by Homma's intelligence that MacArthur's troops numbered only a demoralised 25,000. His own troops, reduced to 6,000 effectives by the demands of the southern campaign for the Indies, faced odds of 1 to 6: inevitably they failed to break through II Corps' position and were soon beaten back.

Carlos Romulo, MacArthur's press officer, described the battle for the Abucay line in these terms.

> MacArthur had set his wickedest trap and launched his first great attack against the Japanese at Abucay. He had set it with banked tiers of hidden artillery. He let the advancing Homma legions come on in a tremendous offensive, luring them into ambush. He did not fire until the Japanese army was in close range. Then thousands were fed to the hungry mouths of our guns at the slaughter of Abucay.[36]

Swashbuckling stuff: but Romulo's account, like most of MacArthur's press releases, oversimplifies and over-glamorises history. In reality the Japanese recovered rapidly from their initial reverse. Infiltrating through the jungle they located the Mount Natib gap, worked their way round the flanks of both Parker's and Wainwright's Corps, broke the cohesion of the Philippine Army Divisions, fought off American and Filipino counter-attacks and by 26 January had forced the defenders back to the Mount Samat line. General Nara then overplayed his hand. Now down to only 4,000 effectives, he attempted battalion-sized infiltration of the new defence line and battalion-sized landings near the southern tip of Bataan. The defenders now outnumbered the Japanese by 20 to 1. There was an unglamorous inevitability about Nara's decision to break off battle in the second week of February to await reinforcements.

The difference between Romulo's purple prose account of the Abucay line battle and the grey historical reality underscores the blurring of truth and fiction so characteristic of MacArthur's Philippine years. Historians have condemned as vulgar propaganda the stream of communiqués, despatches and press accounts flowing from Corregidor, all of which exaggerated and valorised MacArthur's central role as general leading his troops to victory[37]. Philippine jungle warfare was scarcely so heroic. But MacArthur, steeped in military history (he owned more than 4,000 volumes on the subject) may have been modelling himself, consciously or unconsciously, on great generals of the past, Napoleon, Washington and Lee. An avid film-goer, historical movies such as *The Buccaneer* may also have supplied MacArthur with the model for the bird's eye view sweep of the panoramic battle-field de-

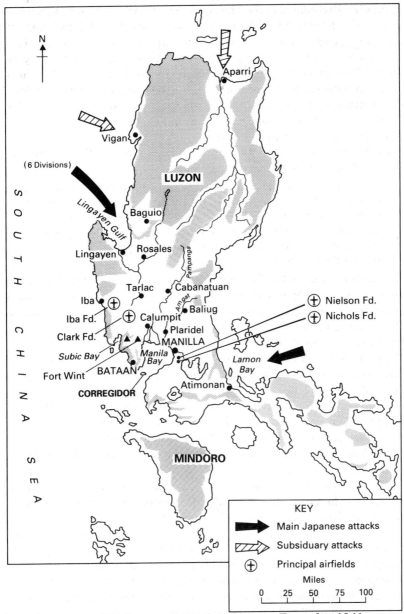

Map 7. *The Japanese Attack on Luzon - December 1941.*

Labels within the map:

N

South China Sea

Aparri

Vigan

(6 Divisions)

LUZON

Lingayen Gulf

Baguio

Lingayen

Rosales

Pampanga

Tarlac

Cabanatuan

Iba

Am gat

Baliug

Iba Fd.

Calumpit

Nielson Fd.

Nichols Fd.

Clark Fd.

Plaridel

MANILA

Subic Bay

Manila Bay

Fort Wint

BATAAN

Lamon Bay

CORREGIDOR

Atimonan

MINDORO

KEY

Main Japanese attacks

Subsiduary attacks

Principal airfields

Miles

0   25   50   75   100

scribed in his *Reminiscences*.

> Our headquarters, called 'Topside', occupied the flattened summit of the
> highest hill on the island. It gave a perfect view of the whole panorama of the
> siege area. As always, I had to see the enemy, or I could not fight him
> effectively. Reports, no matter how penetrating, have never been able to replace
> the picture shown to my eyes.[38]

Bataan proved a test of generalship, but not in the way MacArthur believed. Conditions in the Pacific and Asia rarely allowed generals to demonstrate their prowess with corps-sized thrusts and rapier-like ripostes. Battles
were won by junior officers and NCOs in bitter attritional slogging-matches.
Good generalship meant being able to inspire your men to fight that little
bit harder for that little bit longer. Often the only way a general could help
his men was by his morale-boosting presence. Vandegrift on Guadalcanal,
Moreshead in New Guinea and Slim in Burma all discovered this truth. So
in time did MacArthur, but not during the First Philippines Campaign.

Historians have paid too little attention to MacArthur's responsibility for
the administrative collapse on Bataan. The shortage of food and medical
supplies was made far worse by inefficient distribution: in such circumstances the usual formula applied – the closer to the front, the more distant
the supply source and the more inadequate the rations. Front-line troops
went short while rear echelons ate well. There was little MacArthur could
do to improve the supply lines themselves: rough tracks hacked out over
jungle-clad hills on which trucks often broke down. But he might have
cracked down far earlier on the problem of discipline in the rear areas which
enabled armed gangs of deserters to loot supplies. The Philippine Army
military police he sent to guard the depots proved infinitely corruptible. By
the time MacArthur considered publicly executing looters and deserters, the
problem was so widespread that such a solution would have been imposss-
ible to implement. Front line morale plummeted: empty bellies were bad
enough, but rumours that rear area troops never went hungry and that food
in Corregidor was ample, even luxurious, caused massive resentment. The
rumours were not entirely unfounded. The bacon, ham, fresh vegetables,
coffee, milk and jam which Wainwright found available in Corregidor when
he took over from MacArthur in March 1942 had long since disappeared
from Bataan.

Short rations led to low morale and severe malnutrition. After rations
were cut from January's barely adequate level of 2,800 calories a day to
March's starvation diet of 1,000, troops were forced to forage or die. Minor
ailments became major ailments and vitamin-deficiency diseases proved
debilitating. By 8 March, malaria affected over one third of all front-line
units. Lack of training in even elementary hygiene precautions meant that
common diarrhoea and dysentry ran rife through native Filipino troops
when they fell back to fixed positions. They drank stagnant water and failed

to sterilise their mess gear. Their latrines were neither properly constructed nor properly used. Once again, administrative inefficiency made the initial shortage of resources and supplies critical. As commander of the Philippines, MacArthur was ultimately responsible.

The swelling tide of complaints which reached Corregidor might have prompted MacArthur to go and see for himself but he ventured out of the underground labyrinth of his island fortress only once. Here he was most surely to blame. When his troops chanted the refrain 'Dugout Doug MacArthur lies ashaking on the Rock' (ironically to the tune of the 'Battle Hymn of the Republic') they were only acknowledging with bitter humour the absence of leadership which left them feeling as if they were fighting in a void. MacArthur might have made a world of difference to troop morale by a few unexpected tours of inspection, some unannounced appearances among his men. Simply the rumour that MacArthur was doing *something* to solve the problems of ration shortages, deserters and looters would have helped forge that vital link between high command and troops and sustained their fighting spirit. Instead he became a virtual recluse.

In a famous photograph taken in March 1942 of USAFFE HQ in the Malinta tunnel, MacArthur, wearing his cap of Field Marshal of the Philippine Army, leans back on his chair. The mask of stoic fortitude which fixes his features betrays more than a hint of boredom. How was MacArthur spending the long days, if not in active service? As he himself remarked wittily to Romulo, 'The sword may rest, but the pen never does'.[39] Historians have been fascinated by the stream of communiqués which flowed to Washington from Corregidor during the 78 days MacArthur was in residence. Like Lieutenant General Arthur Perceval signalling from Fort Canning to his superior General Sir Archibald Wavell in Java, MacArthur pleaded for reinforcements. Unlike Perceval, when he realised they were not in the offing, he refused to keep a respectful silence and began instead to play the role of arm-chair strategist, arbitrarily advising Washington on lofty matters of American defence policy. He urged the abandonment of the 'Europe first' strategy, suggested that America should press the Soviet Union to open up a front against Japan in Manchuria, and demanded that the Pacific Fleet abandon its timid defensive posture and launch a carrier strike against the Japanese home islands. Although immured on a remote Philippine island fortress, MacArthur found it difficult to stop behaving like the Chief of Staff he had been just six years earlier

Washington officials found MacArthur's 'advice' embarrassing but it made no difference to their policy. They could not ignore his more public manipulation of American opinion. It was no coincidence that of all the prominent journalists who gathered in Manila by 1941, Melville and Annalee Jacoby, correspondents for *Time* and *Life* magazines, should have been among those who ended up on Corregidor. MacArthur thoughtfully provided them with radio telephone links to the United States. He even wrote the copy which he broadcast on the radio station 'Voice of Freedom', set up soon after his arrival on Corregidor with the help of his friend Carlos Romulo. Romulo remembered MacArthur as a 'continual source of stimulation': he would pace up and down the headquarters lateral and then burst in upon his press officers:

> 'I have an idea!' That is one of his pet phrases. And he would go to his desk to scribble rapidly the suggestion for a broadcast or communiqué that had come to him. 'Think it over and see if you can improve upon it,' he would always say, tossing it across the desk.[40]

MacArthur either wrote or co-authored 140 communiqués – exciting, vivid and often wholly imaginary accounts of the campaign in which he always emerged as a military genius thwarting Japan's evil designs again and again. His troops on Bataan who knew the reality found the stream of propaganda nauseating. 'Voice of Freedom' broadcasts, ostensibly designed to boost Filipino morale, probably had the opposite effect. But enraptured American radio audiences hung on his every word. By the end of 1941, MacArthur was on the front cover of *Time*, and by early 1942 MacArthur-mania was sweeping the United States.

All this caused serious problems for Washington when it came to deciding what to do with MacArthur. Eisenhower was all for leaving him on Corregidor, where his histrionic talents equipped him perfectly for the role of heroic commander of a doomed fortress. This was a minority view (though one shared by the Navy).[41] Two other suggestions were raised – one that he should escape to Mindanao to lead resistance and perhaps become a guerilla chieftain, the other that he escape to Australia and take command of the United States forces assembling there.

Marshall really had only one option open to him. He simply could not allow MacArthur, a former Chief of Staff and a national hero, to fall into Japanese hands. On 4 February he first broached the subject of evacuating MacArthur from the Philippines.[42] The dispatch confirmed MacArthur's long-standing suspicions that Washington was preparing to abandon the Philippines. He embarked on a series of byzantine manoeuvres in a last attempt to manipulate American policy. On 8 February, Washington received three communications from Corregidor; one from Quezon, one from High Commissioner Sayre, one from MacArthur. Quezon proposed that the United States should grant immediate independence to the Philippines, which would then be neutralised. Japanese and United States forces would be withdrawn by mutual consent and the Philippine Army disbanded. Sayre and MacArthur endorsed Quezon's request, MacArthur adding that 'the temper of the Filipinos is one of almost violent resentment against the United States. Every one of them expected help, and when it has not been forthcoming, they believe they have been betrayed in favour of others.'[43]

The immediate reaction in Washington was one of shocked surprise. Recovering, Roosevelt and Marshall authorised Eisenhower, the one man in Washington with deep insights into MacArthur's psychology, to draft a reply under Roosevelt's signature which reached MacArthur on 9 February. Eisenhower hit MacArthur where he knew it would hurt most. He was instructed to capitulate his Filipino forces if necessary: but 'American forces will continue to keep the flag flying in the Philippines as long as there remains any possibility of resistance.' MacArthur should remember, continued Eisenhower, that 'the duty and the necessity of resisting Japanese aggression to the last transcends in importance any other obligation now facing us in the Philippines.' MacArthur probably never realised that this despatch was composed by his former aide: it would have heaped insult upon injury.[44] On 11 February, an angry MacArthur assured Roosevelt, 'I have not the slightest intention in the world of surrendering or capitulating the Filipino element of my command . . . there has never been the slightest wavering of my troops.' He firmly intended to fight 'to destruction' on Bataan and then Corregidor. He would arrange for the evacuation of Quezon and Sayre (they left by submarine a few weeks later) but he and his family would 'share the fate of the garrison.'

MacArthur had slammed the ball firmly back into Washington's court. The likely reaction of the American public to the death of their hero, his wife and baby son, gave Washington officials many sleepless nights. Marshall sent MacArthur a radiogram which urged him to reconsider. MacArthur ignored it. On 15 February, the day Perceval surrendered Singapore, MacArthur sent Marshall a despatch urging an immediate American naval offensive in the Pacific. This extraordinary game was brought to an end on 22 February when Roosevelt gave MacArthur a direct order to leave Corregidor for Australia where he would assume command of a new South-West Pacific theatre. This was one of the few orders MacArthur ever obeyed, but even then it was used as a basis for negotiations. MacArthur decreed that he would only leave when the situation was right, by which he meant not just the situation on Bataan but elsewhere. Significantly, his departure from Corregidor on 12 March came three days after the surrender of Java and the Japanese occupation of Rangoon. MacArthur knew the Japanese were pouring reinforcements into the Philippines and that the next assault would finish the Bataan garrison. It did, and Bataan surrendered on 9 April. A month later Corregidor also surrendered. By this time MacArthur, firmly ensconced in Melbourne as Commander in Chief of the new Southwest Pacific Area, was beginning his campaign to return to the Philippines.

Chapter Notes

1. D Clayton James, *The Years of MacArthur*, Vol. I, (London, 1970).
2. See Carol M Petillo, *Douglas MacArthur: The Philippine Years* (Bloomington, Indiana, 1981) and Michael Schaller, *Douglas MacArthur the Far Eastern General* (New York, 1989).
3. Robert Ferrell (ed.) *The Eisenhower Diaries* (New York, 1981), pp. 19–20.
4. See, e.g., James, I, 502–9; Schaller, p. 34.
5. Schaller, p. 45; James, I, 537; Ronald H Spector, *Eagle Against the Sun* (New York, 1985), pp. 72–4.
6. James, I, 609; Schaller, p. 49; Spector, p. 73.
7. W F Craven and J L Cate, *The Army Air Forces in World War II*, I, (Chicago, 1948), p. 139.
8. James, I, 581.
9. Craven and Gate, p. 145.
10. General HH Arnold, *Global Mission* (London, 1951), p. 159.
11. Craven and Cate, p. 178; Mark. S. Watson, *Chief of Staff Pre-War Plans and Preparations* (Washington, 1950), pp. 438–440.
12. Watson, pp. 445–6.
13. Louis Morton, *The Fall of the Philippines* (Washington, 1953), p. 67.
14. Morton, p. 49.
15. Lewis H Brereton, *The Brereton Diaries: The War in the Air in the Pacific, Middle East and Europe, 3 October 1941 – 8 May 1945* (New York, 1946), pp. 34–44; Craven and Cate, pp. 203–210; Arnold, pp. 271–3; Morton, pp. 80–90.
16. James, *The Years of MacArthur*, Vol. II (London, 1975), 27; Gavin Long, *MacArthur as Military Commander* (London, 1969), p. 67.
17. Morton, pp. 25–30.
18. Long, p. 67; James, II, 28.
19. Morton, p. 146.
20. Alfred D Chandler (ed.), *The Papers of Dwight David Eisenhower*, I (Baltimore, 1970), 21.
21. Morton, pp. 160–163; James, II, 27.
22. Alvin P Stauffer, *The Quartermaster Corps: Operation in the War Against Japan* (Washington, 1956), p. 6.
23. Unopposed: Patani, Singora (8 December); Guam, Vigan, Appari (10

December); Legaspi (12 December). Opposed: Kotabharu (8 December); Wake (12 December); Hong Kong (17 December).

24. General Douglas MacArthur, *Reminiscences* (London, 1964), p. 124.
25. Morton, p. 131.
26. Morton, pp. 195–202; Karl C Dod, *The Corps of Engineers: The War Against Japan* (Washington, 1966), pp. 80–82.
27. See e.g. Morton, pp. 164–6; James, II, 30; Long, p. 72; William Manchester, *American Caesar* (London, 1979), p. 218.
28. Morton, pp. 195–202.
29. Ernest B Miller, *Bataan Uncensored* (Long Prairie, Minnesota, 1949), p. 75; Stauffer, p. 9; James, II, 33; Manchester, p. 215.
30. Stauffer, pp. 11–13.
31. Stauffer, p. 12.
32. Morton, pp. 367–370.
33. The official history of the Corps of Engineers makes clear the extraordinary fact that the surveying of defence positions was not underway until 2 January (Dod, p. 87).
34. Morton, pp. 279–280.
35. Dod, pp. 85–9.
36. Carlos P Romulo, *I Saw the Fall of the Philippines* (London, 1943), p. 93.
37. See e.g. James, II, 89; Schaller, p. 61.
38. MacArthur, p. 130.
39. Romulo, p. 106.
40. Romulo, p. 107.
41. Ferrell, p. 49.
42. Chandler, pp. 97–8.
43. James, II, 94–6.
44. Chandler, pp. 104–6.

9

John Lucas and Anzio, 1944

Julian Thompson

The last entry in the Second World War diary of Major General John P Lucas includes the following passage:

> 'Message from Clark. He arrives today with eight generals. What the hell.
> General Clark sent for me at 8.00 pm. He was in his CP in the basement of the villa Borghese. He said I am to be relieved from command of the Corps. . . . I left Anzio the following day. I left the finest soldiers in the world when I lost VI Corps and the honour of having commanded them in the hour of their greatest travail cannot be taken from me.' [1]

When America entered the Second World War, Lucas had already been picked by General George C Marshall as a rising star. On taking over as Chief of Staff of the United States Army in September 1939, Marshall had prepared a list of those officers he intended for high command if America was committed to fighting; Lucas was one of them.

John P Lucas was born in West Virginia on 14 January 1890. He graduated from the United States Military Academy in 1911, and was commissioned into the cavalry. He took part in the Mexican Punitive Expedition of 1916–17 against Francisco (Pancho) Villa. In May 1917, one month after America's entry into the First World War, he was posted to the Infantry School of Arms as an instructor. In January 1918, he transferred to the Signal Corps and, as a temporary Major, served in France for a week before being wounded in action and evacuated to the United States. In 1920, he transferred to the field artillery. In the period leading up to the Second World War he attended the Command and General Staff School and the Army War College. He commanded field artillery battalions, a field artillery regiment and the divisional artillery of 2 (US) Infantry Division. By December 1941, he was a major general commanding 3 (US) Infantry Division, which was later to form part of his VI (US) Corps at Anzio. In March 1942, he was given command of III (US) Corps in the United

States. A year later Marshall sent him to North Africa to report personally on the situation in Tunisia and Algeria. In May 1943, two months after his return, he was on his way back to Algiers to join Eisenhower as his deputy, further proof of Marshall's regard for Lucas.[2] After six months, he was given II (US) Corps, which had no divisions under command. A month later in October 1943, General Mark Clark, commanding fifth US Army, having relieved Major General Dawley of command of VI (US) Corps, asked Eisenhower for Major General Ridgway as his replacement. At first Eisenhower agreed, but Marshall must have intervened, for Clark had to accept Lucas.[3]

Lucas was pitched straight into his first co-ordinated Corps battle, the crossing of the Volturno River, known to the Allies as the Winter Line. He performed competently in the four weeks of fighting that followed, a hard slog in which Fifth US Army advanced twenty miles with heavy casualties. Now nearly 54 years old, Lucas was, however, emotionally and physically exhausted by this short experience of command. His self-effacing manner, grey moustache, thinning white hair and habit of wearing a greatcoat and scarf in mild weather, did not inspire confidence. His American soldiers called him 'Foxy Grandpa'.

Throughout his diary, which he kept from the time he joined Eisenhower, Lucas comes across as a sensitive and compassionate man, with a faintly old-maidish quality. As deputy to Eisenhower, or Commander II (US) Corps with no operational responsibility, he is quick to criticise and air his school-mistressy views on the performance of others. Roving North Africa, he commented unfavourably on the morale of American troops, and irked Bedell-Smith, Eisenhower's chief of staff, by interference in minor administrative matters; such as the issue of cotton drawers to 34 (US) Infantry Division.[4] After meeting General Alexander for the first time, his comment was, 'a pleasant, meek looking little fellow'.[5] This from one whose battle experience consisted of chasing Mexican bandits and one week in France, about a man whose record in four years of fighting in the First World War and leadership during two disastrous retreats, France and Burma, were legendary. In Sicily, with a roving commission, Lucas comments on the lack of push to get off the beach, confusion and absence of grip.[6]

Later, under the pressure of command in battle and no longer the 'super-umpire', he writes:

'I am just a poor working girl trying to get ahead and am far from being a Napoleon.' [7]

and:

'I hope nothing goes wrong. If it does, my head will be the answer.' [8]

and:

'. . . to protect myself from criticism, however, I am moving a battalion of 504th [Paratroopers], now in Corps reserve, to the vicinity of Venafro.' [9]

These and other diary entries reveal an obsessive fear of failure and the effect on his reputation.

On 13 November 1943, Lucas first heard from Clark about Operation SHINGLE, the plan for an amphibious hook at Anzio: its purpose to outflank the Gustav Line. After the Allied landings in southern Italy, the Germans had fought a series of delaying battles, while preparing defence lines to their rear. The main German defensive barrier guarding the approaches to Rome was the Gustav Line, extending across the Italian peninsula from Minturno to Ortona. The Germans had reinforced the rugged mountainous terrain with a network of bunkers, wire and minefields. On 21 November 1943, Field Marshal Kesselring took over command of the Italian theatre. Under him, Army Group C was divided into two armies, the Tenth facing the Allies and also responsible for the defence of Rome, and the Fourteenth, guarding northern and central Italy.

Opposing the Germans was the Allied 15th Army Group, under General Alexander, with Clark's Fifth US Army on the western sector, and Montgomery's and subsequently General Leese's Eighth British Army on the eastern sector. By early January, fifth Army had broken through the Winter Line and occupied the high ground above the Garigliano and Rapido Rivers. From here they could look across to Mount Cassino, and Highway Number 6, curving round its base into the Liri Valley, the route through the mountains to Rome. The snow-tipped peaks, protected by the rain-swollen Garigliano and Rapido made the Gustav line a more formidable barrier than the Winter Line. Unless the Gustav Line could be turned, 15th Army Group faced another long and bitter mountain campaign.

Plans to outflank the Gustav Line had been under consideration from late October 1943, when it became clear that the Germans aimed to force the Allies to fight a slow, costly battle up the leg of Italy. The successful amphibious hook by Eighth Army at Termoli at the beginning of October 1943 seemed to provide a pattern for further operations of this kind.

In early November 1943, General Alexander ordered Clark to plan an amphibious landing on the west coast; with a D-Day of 20 December 1943: codename SHINGLE. The landing by a single division, was to form part of an Army Group offensive: Eighth Army to advance south-west astride Highway Number 5 from Pescara to the Adriatic coast to Rome; while Fifth Army punched north-west up the Liri valley to secure Frosinone. The purpose of the amphibious landing was to seize a beachhead south of Rome, secure the Colli Laziali (The Alban Hills), and link-up with Fifth Army advancing from the south. By 20 December 1943, because of the difficult terrain and the tenacious German defence, neither Army was near its objective and the amphibious operation was cancelled.

However, the slow progress of the Allied advance in Italy led to a revival of the idea of an amphibious landing south of Rome. On Christmas Day in Tunis, with the whole-hearted support of Churchill, who was present, plans

were drafted for a re-vitalised SHINGLE, but this time with over twice the
force – VI (US) Corps with two reinforced infantry divisions and part of an
armoured division.[10] D-Day was to be between 20 and 31 January, and the
amphibious operation was again to be co-ordinated with a drive from the
south which would begin some days earlier.

The majority of Landing Ships Tank (LSTs) in the Mediterranean
theatre were planned to sail for Britain by early 1944, in readiness for the
invasion of Normandy (Operation OVERLORD), and to India for use in
South East Asia Command. Thanks to Churchill's personal intervention, a
maximum of 88 LSTs were kept back for a limited time and made available
for SHINGLE. This was sufficient to lift only two divisions on D-Day, the rest
of VI Corps would have to land subsequently, which, depending on the
turn-round time of craft and ships, would not be before D plus 3.

When detailed planning started in early January 1944, some disagreements
and misconceptions began to surface. One in particular was to remain until
well after the landing took place. This concerned the aim or, in 1944 parlance,
the object, of the landing. Lucas had been given what he calls

> 'a tentative "planning" mission as follows: (1) To seize and secure a beachhead
> in the vicinity of Anzio, (2) Advance and secure Colli Lazialli, and, (3) Be
> prepared to advance on Rome.' [11]

These objectives were in accordance with Alexander's wishes at the time,
as he made clear in an interview after the war[12]. The purpose was to cut, or
at least threaten, the German line of communication to the formations
facing fifth Army on the Rapido and Garigliano. He hoped that the
Germans would react by pulling troops out of the line to face the new
threat, thereby enabling Fifth Army to break through.

Among Lucas's worries at the time was a concern that he did not have
sufficient force to fulfil the mission. Either at his instigation, or on his own
initiative, a British Lieutenant Colonel on VI Corps operations staff produced a one page minute, headed: 'Notes on Grouping of VI Corps for
SHINGLE'. This is an extremely interesting document, because it goes
further than the title would suggest. He starts:

> '1. The original object of the operation was to cut the L of C of the
> enemy troops opposing fifth Army. In view however of the limitations of
> craft it is clear that the expedition will not have the same scope. It is
> therefore necessary to re-examine the object. It is submitted that the
> new object is as follows:
>
> > "To land a force in area ANZIO; thereby threatening the enemy's L of
> > C and causing him to commit his reserves. To maintain this beach-
> > head secure against counterattack, and to raid and harass the L of C
> > therefrom."
>
> If these terms are accepted as the object of the expedition, it is submit-
> ted that the composition and grouping of the force is incorrect.'

2. There are two distinct requirements:

a. A strong force to secure the beachhead.

b. A powerful force to raid and harass.

It is important that the second force should be landed in the assault convoy, as the best, and possibly only, opportunity of exploitation will be in the early stages of the operation, before the enemy reaction has crystalized.'[12]

He lists the armoured and reconnaissance units available to VI Corps (many organic to the two infantry divisions): the equivalent of two tank regiments, a reconnaissance regiment, the equivalent of two regiments of SP artillery and two tank destroyer battalions. He argues that with the addition of infantry and engineers, a powerful mobile force could be constituted. He concludes by suggesting that this mobile force should be landed in the early stages, even at the expense of part of the two infantry divisions.

'Rapid exploitation and deep penetration will constitute the most effective method of dislocating the enemy's rear areas. His reaction will be more violent; more dispersed and consequently less concentrated against the beachhead. This will enable the beachhead troops to organize with the minimum of interference. Any successes by the mobile force will have results out of proportion to the effort and the cost.' [13]

There appears to be no record of what views Lucas had on the minute by his Assistant G-3. Clearly he disagreed with the mobile concept because his landing plan had his two infantry divisions, 3rd (US) commanded by Major General Truscott, and 1st (British) commanded by Major General Penney, landing in the first waves on D-Day. Combat Command A, part of 1st US Armored Division, would follow, but not for at least three days.

Clark certainly had misgivings about VI Corps advancing too far inland. This is confirmed by an interview in 1948.[14] In his orders for SHINGLE dated 12 January 1944 the mission is given as:

a. To seize and secure a beachhead in the vicinity of ANZIO.

b. Advance on COLLI LAZIALI.

There is a considerable difference betwen advancing on Colli Laziali and securing it. Expressing orders to a subordinate in such a way leaves them open for him to interpret as he sees fit. Any commander doing so has only himself to blame if a subordinate's view of what constitutes 'advancing on' a place differs from his. To the modern eye what Clark was giving in his orders was not a mission, of which there should only ever be one, ie; the purpose of the operation. He was giving Lucas his tasks. This is quite proper if they follow a clearly stated mission. In this operation there wasn't one, only a hope that by threatening the German rear, they would be panicked into pulling formations out from the force facing Fifth Army, or even withdrawing from the Gustav Line altogether.[15] After four years of war against the German Army, the Allies should have known better.

Clark's orders were delivered to Lucas by Fifth Army chief of staff, Major General Brann. He discussed the mission (tasks), with Lucas's Chief of Staff, Brigadier General Keiser, and his Assistant Chief of Staff G-3 (operations), Colonel Hill. He made it clear that Lucas's primary mission was to seize and secure a beachhead. He stated that much thought had been put on the wording of this order so as not to force Lucas to push on at the risk of sacrificing his Corps. Lucas was free to move to and seize Colli Laziali should it be possible. However, Lucas comments in his diary:

'Colli Laziali is the first terrain feature north of Anzio but is distant therefrom some twenty miles. The term "advance on" indicated in itself that the Army questioned my being able to reach this feature and, at the same time, hold a beachhead which would protect the port and beaches. It was perfectly obvious what the loss of my supply lines would do and it was also obvious that my little command would be in a tough spot if the enemy came in in force.' [16]

The ambiguous wording of Lucas's second task, as given to him by Clark filtered down the chain of command. In 1st (British) Division's operation order it emerged as; 'An avance to area Colli Laziali may take place.' [17]

Before receiving his orders from Fifth Army, Lucas had sent two senior staff officers to Allied Force Headquarters in Marrakech, Morocco. On arrival, Colonels Hill and O'Neill, Assistant Chief of Staff G-4 (logistics), having been told that they were not expected, were summoned to a meeting with Alexander and his Chief of Staff, Lieutenant General Harding. At first, to Hill and O'Neill's dismay, they were informed that the Corps was to land with only seven day's logistic maintenance, and no further resupply. O'Neill finally persuaded Alexander that the Corps would require 1,500 tons of supplies a day. The two staff officers were then summoned to see Admiral Sir John Cunningham, the new Commander-in-Chief Mediterranean Fleet, and senior Allied Naval Commander.[18] He said that he had based all his plans for shipping on the initial force landing with seven days maintenance and no resupply, and was surprised at Hill and O'Neill's insistence that the operation was impossible under such conditions.[19] Eventually he accepted that continued maintenance had to be planned, and reluctantly agreed to the figure of 1,500 tons a day.

Hill and O'Neill's next appointment was a high-powered conference, which included Alexander, Cunningham, General Wilson, the new Supreme Allied Commander in the Mediterranean, Lord Beaverbrook, several other senior officers, and chaired by Chruchill himself. He quizzed Hill and O'Neill on their reluctance to carry out SHINGLE with only seven days' maintenance. Alexander spoke up for the two staff officers, and Churchill accepted his explanation.

The question of how the force would be maintained prompted Cunningham to state that because of likely adverse weather, he could not guarantee to supply a formation of this size over beaches at this time of year. He added that the port of Anzio could not be used because the indications were that the Germans had sunk a vessel or two across the channel.

When O'Neill presented his innovative plan of supplying by trucks loaded on LSTs with empty trucks being returned to Naples for resupply, he was expressly forbidden to implement it by Churchill, Cunningham, and other senior officers. Requests for time for rehearsals and training for the two infantry divisions were equally brusquely dismissed. One can feel nothing but sympathy for these two colonels in the face of so much high-powered hindrance.

The conference re-convened after dinner, minus Churchill, Beaverbrook and Wilson, and ended well after midnight with very little progress. The next morning it was decided that 80 to 88 LSTs would be available until 3 February, 25 LSTs from 3–13 February, and 14 LSTs thereafter. To cater for the order that no empty trucks were to be returned to Naples for re-loading, 2,000 trucks would be found. The date of D-Day was confirmed as 22 January.[20]

From this vantage point, many years later, one can only express amazement at the way a higher headquarters could conduct the planning for an operation on which they pinned such high hopes. Prohibiting the plan to return empty trucks to Naples is an example. Leaving empty trucks standing idle in a beachhead is not only a waste of assets, but the problem of finding space to park in a congested area subjected to shelling is an unwelcome additional burden on the commander and his staff. Fortunately, in a rare show of spirit, Lucas disobeyed the AFHQ edict. Had he not done so, the logistic system would not have coped, with disastrous results.

Clark had been invited to the Marrakech conference, but excused himself on the grounds of the need to be in Italy. Either he or his Chief of Staff should have attended a meeting on such momentous matters affecting not only one of his subordinate formations, but the design for battle of his whole Army. It was fortunate that Lucas sent his staff officers, for without their contribution, subsequent events might have been very different.

Most of the area chosen as the beachhead for VI Corps was within a reclamation and resettlement project on a narrow coastal plain south-east of Rome. The Mussolini canal provided a ready-made protective barrier on the right flank of the beachhead. Its value as an obstacle was improved by the Germans' flooding of the land to the south and east. North of Anzio was a belt of woodland, the Bosco di Padiglione, through which the main road, the Via Anziate, ran due north through Carroceto and Campoleone to Albano and Highway 7. About seven miles north of Anzio, the road passed under a flyover carrying the Lateral Road over it, and south of Carraceto it went under an embankment. A secondary road ran from Nettuno through Le Ferriere to Cisterna and on to Velletri. Apart from these roads there was nothing but narrow paved roads and gravel tracks in the beachhead. The

3,100 foot Colli Laziali, lying about 20 miles north of Anzio, provide a grandstand view over most of the beachhead.

In the north-west the beachhead was bounded by the Moletta River and the Buonriposo and Vallelata ridges, which dominated the area. Between the lateral road and the Buonriposo Ridge, the farmland was interlaced with wide and deep ditches, whose banks were usually covered by brambles; 'the wadis' to soldiers lately from the desert. Although these were an obstacle to tanks, and offered some protection, they soon became water-filled trenches and avenues for enemy infiltration. At regular intervals there were small, two-story farmhouses built for settlers. The new community centre of Aprilia, dubbed the 'factory' by Allied troops, and the provincial capital of Littoria were modern model towns. The twin towns of Anzio and Nettuno in the centre of the beachhead were popular, prewar sea-side resorts.

As planning progressed, Lucas continued to worry about SHINGLE. Before he received his orders from Clark, he wrote:

> '. . . a failure now would ruin Clark, probably kill me, and certainly prolong the war. These are disagreeable contingencies, particularly the second, which has no appeal for me whatever.' [21]

He was also clearly exercised about commanding a combined Anglo-American force, and at one point confesses to being rather floored by the complications.[22] A week before D-Day he wrote; 'Fifty-four years today and I am afraid I feel every year of it'.[23] Perhaps his gloom showed, because at one meeting Admiral Cunningham said to him; 'the chances are 70/30 that by the time you reach Anzio, the Germans will be north of Rome'. A rather over-optimistic pronouncement from the same man who earlier had predicted that the Port of Anzio would not be available for use.

Despite Lucas's apprehension, the landing on the early morning of 23 January went unexpectedly well and without any serious opposition. By mid-morning over half the 40,000 men and 5,000 vehicles in the first lift had been landed. By midnight on D-Day about 36,000 troops and 3,200 vehicles were ashore. VI Corps had suffered 13 dead and 87 wounded, and taken 227 prisoners. Except for a few small coast artillery and anti-aircraft detachments, the only German troops in the area were scattered elements of 29th Panzer Grenadier Division. Only three engineer companies and the 2nd Battalion, 71st Panzer Grenadier Regiment, guarded the coast from the mouth of the River Tiber to the Mussolini Canal.

A further success was the capture of the port of Anzio intact. This was fortunate since the British beach north-west of Anzio proved to be too shallow, and British unloading was switched to the newly opened port.[24]

Having reached its first objectives by noon on D-Day, VI Corps advanced to occupy the ground within the planned initial beachhead. On the left, 1st British Division advanced towards the Moletta River and secured

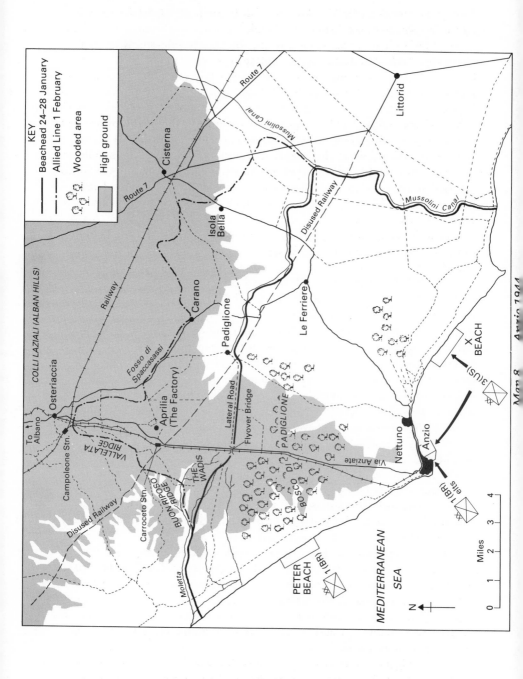

KEY

—— Beachead 24–28 January
—·— Allied Line 1 February

Wooded area

High ground

COLLI LAZIALI (ALBAN HILLS)

To Albano

Osteriaccia

Campoleone Stn.

Carroceto Stn.

BUON RIPOSO RIDGE

VALLELATA RIDGE

THE WADIS

Moletta

Aprilia (The Factory)

Fosso di Spaccasassi

Railway

Route 7

Carano

Isola Bella

Cisterna

Route 7

Padiglione

Lateral Road

Flyover Bridge

BOSCO DI PADIGLIONE

Le Ferriere

Disused Railway

Mussolini Canal

Mussolini Canal

Littorio

Disused Railway

Via Anziate

Nettuno

Anzio

1 (BR) sitd

1 (BR)

3 (US)

X BEACH

PETER BEACH

MEDITERRANEAN SEA

N

Miles

0 1 2 3 4

Map 8 Anzio 1944

about seven miles of the Via Anziate. On the right, 3rd US Division seized all the bridges over the Mussolini Canal, but lost most of them during the night of D/D plus 1 to aggressive attacks by the Hermann Goering Panzer Division, which had been resting in the area after a severe mauling at Cassino, and had been moved to Anzio as soon as news of the landings had reached Kesselring's headquarters. 3rd Division retook them by the end of D plus 1.

Both Clark and Alexander came ashore early on D-Day and were pleased to see the operation going so well. However, before Clark left to return to Naples, he said to Lucas; 'don't stick your neck out Johnny. I did at Salerno and got into trouble'.[25] Lucas had no intention of doing so, and dug in to consolidate the beachhead – his primary task. He did not intend advancing further until his build-up was complete, including Combat Command A of 1st Armoured Division.

It is at this stage in the operation that criticism of Lucas starts. There are those who believe that he should have dashed forward to seize the Colli Laziali. There is little doubt that he could have established forces there, but equally little doubt that they would have been dislodged or cut off by the German reaction. He could have seized and held Campoleone and Cisterna on D-Day, pre-empting the German occupation of these two towns. This might have made a great difference to the defence of the beachhead, although not to the eventual outcome of SHINGLE. If, in addition, had he acceded to his Assistant G-3's suggestion of forming a strong, mobile force, he might have kept the Germans guessing as to the true strength and extent of his bridgehead, and gained more time to build up a perimeter further out than he did. He certainly should have ordered a more vigorous patrol programme. However, given the emphasis Clark placed on securing the beachhead, and the vague 'advance on the Colli Laziali' order, Lucas was not actually wrong to stay where he was.

The Germans as usual responded quickly. 'However peaceful the scene, and apparently devoid of Germans, touch them in an area that is important to them, and their reaction is swift and violent', said a British officer who had ample experience of their remarkable ability to be quicker on the draw in a tactical sense most of the time.[26]

The German build-up rate by D plus 2 was nearly twice as fast as predicted by the Allies. By D plus 10 they had moved nearly 34,000 more troops into the area than the Allied figures for German strengths on D plus 16.[27] There are hints of wishful thinking in the Allied intelligence assessments produced at the time, including one which estimated that a maximum of two divisions would be available to reinforce German 10th Army defending southern Italy.[28]

The intelligence summaries (INTSUMS) in which these, and similarly optimistic predictions appear, were the product of assessments made at Allied Force Headquarters (AFHQ) in Algiers. Both Clark and General

Lemnitzer, who was Alexander's Deputy Chief of Staff at the time, later criticised the quality of the Allied and British intelligence in the Mediterranean Theatre of operations.[29] Although their comments could be judged as having been made with the wisdom of hindsight and possibly in self-defence, they both have a common theme: that behind the assessments was the assumption that eventually Hitler would do what was strategically correct and pull back to the Alps. This would enable him to keep the maximum force in France to await the Allies' impending attack. This is also Marshall's view.[30] If Allied intelligence took it for granted that Hitler believed that the main Allied invasion would be in France, and if they supposed he would therefore conclude that fighting forward in Italy in strength would be strategically unsound, it is a short step to postulating that forces to meet the Anzio landing would have to be drawn from 10th Army, not from elsewhere. Put crudely, the Germans would do what the Allies would if they were Germans.

The Germans did nothing of the kind. They had made plans under Case GERTRUDE to cope with several amphibious landings in Italy. Anzio was viewed as only the first of these, and despite its location on the Italian Southern Front, was seen as a major, independent landing. Case MARDER 1 (Western Italy), prepared on 20 December 1943, was put into effect and formations from southern France and the Balkans were ordered to reinforce Kesselring (114th Light and 715th Infantry Divisions from the Balkans and France respectively). These represented only part of the measures required by case MARDER, because the location of SHINGLE made it possible to reinforce with formations already under Kesselring's command, including Headquarters LXXVI Corps moved across from the Adriatic side of Italy. Indeed the move of three further divisions, 9th SS Panzer and 19th Luftwaffe Field from France, and an infantry division from the Balkans, was opposed by General Jodl.[31] Eventually eight-and-a-half German divisions opposed the Anzio beachhead, of which three came from northern Italy, one from France, one from the Balkans, two from opposite the Eighth Army, and a mere one-and-a-half divisions from the Cassino front.

Contrary to Allied expectations, the Germans were able to meet the new threat without major withdrawals from the Cassino front. At the time of the landing there were eight German divisions opposing Fifth Army. The break-out and link-up with Allied troops advancing from the Cassino front did not take place until 25 May. So it is fortunate that AFHQ's logistic plan for VI Corps to land with only seven days supplies and no resupply, was abandoned as a result of representations by Lucas's two staff officers at the Marrackech conference.

Lucas first came ashore on D plus two (24 January 1944). By this time the German build-up was evident. They had assembled the equivalent of about two divisions from units of nine divisions. Allied assessments had forecast this rate of build-up 'if Fifth or Eighth Army's prior attack failed to draw his (the Germans') reserves into the frontal battle' (ie on the Garigliano and Rapido).[32]

Unfortunately they did fail. Within a week the Germans had four divisions round the beachhead, and by the end of January, seven. The immediate defence of the area had been entrusted to General Schlemmer, the Commandant of Rome, but during D-Day, General der Flieger Schlemm, commanding I Parachute Corps, was recalled from the Garigliano front to take command. In Kesselring's words, Schlemm 'initially with only a limited staff, proved to be as capable as Schlemmer was incapable of establishing the basis for a sound defence'.[33] By 25 January, Kesselring, assessing that the position was now secure, ordered Von Mackensen, commander of Fourteenth Army, who had taken over from Schlemm, to strengthen the defensive cordon and eliminate the beachhead.[34]

Lucas commented in his diary, 'the strain of a thing like this is a terrible burden. Who the hell wants to be a general'.[35] A far cry from the hopeful soldier sent out by Marshall to North Africa less than a year before.

Probing patrols ordered by Lucas on 24 January towards Albano and Cisterna revealed that Aprilia (The Factory) was held by troops of the 3rd Panzer Grenadier Division, and Truscott's 3rd Division could make no progress beyond Le Ferriere. As a result of these patrols and intelligence, it was clear to Lucas that no major offensive to expand the beachhead was possible until he had more forces ashore. In the meantime, some limited attacks took place, securing the Factory and up to the area of the Embankment and Carroceto. Attempts to reach Cisterna were unsuccessful.

Lucas's main offensive on the night of 29/30 January only partially succeeded. On the right, 3rd Division failed to take Cisterna; in the process losing all but six men of two Ranger battalions who had spearheaded the attack. After a second attempt, Truscott, not the quitting type, ordered his Division to dig in to meet the anticipated counter-attack. On the left, Penney's 1st Division fought forward as far as the vicinity of Campoleone Station. The thrust by units of 1st Armored Division, which was planned to hook round Campoleone on Penney's left, bogged down in the flooded ditches of the 'wadi' country west of the Via Anziate. The attempt to take Campoleone failed. VI Corps was now pinned in a beachhead shaped like a right hand placed fist, palm downwards, with the second, third and fourth fingers clenched, and thumb and fore-finger extended. The Mussolini Canal ran along the right hand side towards the wrist. Cisterno was opposite the third and fourth knuckles. The second knuckle rested on Carano. The ball of the thumb lay on the Moletta River. Strung out in the forefinger pointing at Campoleone Station and Osteriaccia, an invitation to be chopped off, was the bulk of two brigades of 1st Division. At only two points was the beachhead as much as fifteen miles deep.

The whole of 45th US Infantry Division had now arrived in the beachhead, as had 168th British Infantry Brigade, detached from 56h British

Infantry Division on the Garigliano front. Lucas had constituted a reserve from 1st Armored Division and part of 45th Infantry Division, located in the area of the Bosco di Padiglione. Another arrival at the end of January was Clark's advanced command post, established in the grounds of the Prince Borghese Palace outside Nettuno. This had been planned at least ten days before the landing took place, to Lucas's dismay at the time:

> Clark says he is going to establish an advanced CP near mine. I wish to hell he wouldn't. I don't need any help.[36]

There is no record of Lucas protesting at this imposition of a one-over-one command arrangement, except in his diary. If Clark had considered Lucas did not need help, it was a curious step to take. In the event, although Clark did not spend all his time in the beachhead, he was well placed to see Lucas's performance at first hand, perhaps having nurtured doubts about him all along.

On 31 January, Alexander visited and stayed until 2 February. By the latter date, Lucas had ordered his Corps to dig in on the line they had reached, including leaving a great part of 1st British Division in their precarious salient. Had Lucas gone forward earlier (until 10 February, he never visited 1st Division), he might have appreciated the perilous position of the Division. Furthermore there was no tactical advantage in retaining the salient as the jumping-off position for future offensives, because armour could not deploy west of the Via Anziate. Apart from the considerable error of failing to withdraw 1st Division to a line just north of Carraceto, he was correct to go firm. Indeed, shortly after midnight 2/3 February, he received a message from Clark confirming this, and giving him the option of withdrawing 1st Division:

> Instructions issued to you to advance your left and to capture Cisterna are hereby rescinded. You should now consolidate your beachhead and make suitable dispositions to meet an attack. You may withdraw First Division farther to south if you consider that action advisable. Advance on our objectives will be resumed later . . .[37]

On the night of 3 February, a German assault aimed at pinching out the 1st Division salient was mounted. Von Mackensen had decided that the line of the Via Anziate was the best place from which to drive to the sea. After six days of bitter fighting, in which 3rd Brigade of 1st Division alone suffered nearly 1,400 casualties, the Division was driven back to a line just south of the Factory. 1st Division was now down to less than half strength, and Von Mackensen held the ground he wanted as a start line from which to punch through to the sea. Lucas sent two regiments of 45th Division to take over some of the front from 1st Division. Penney, realising that the Factory must be retaken as soon as possible to forestall the German build-up, called a conference at Headquarters 24th Guards Brigade.

Here, on the morning of 10 February, Lucas, visiting the Division for the first time, found both Penney and Major General William W Eagles, the commander of 45th Division discussing the counter-attack on the factory. At this juncture, with two of his divisional commanders present, Lucas, as their Corps Commander, should have grasped the reins and given orders for a co-ordinated attack. After listening to Penney's appreciation of the situation, and recommendation for a strong and immediate counter-attack, Lucas thought for a moment, and said to Eagles, 'OK Bill, you give 'em the works'. Soon afterwards he returned to the cellar in Nettuno from which he seldom emerged.

It seems that Lucas did not distinguish between conferences and giving orders. Conferences provide an opportunity for a commander to discuss forthcoming operations with his staff. He should retain firm control throughout and provide unambiguous guidelines for his staff to enable them to prepare orders to the formations and units under command. When giving orders, the commander should not confer with his subordinates – he tells them what he wants done. Lucas's conferences resembled debating societies, and giving clear, unequivocal orders was not his style.[38]

Lucas's order, which was no order at all, more like a throw-away line in an indifferent war movie, is an indictment of his competence as a corps commander. There was no co-ordinated plan, and insufficient artillery support. The outcome was an attack in too little strength, too late, which was thrown back.

Meanwhile, Alexander had ordered the remainder of 56th Division into the beachhead. 1st Division was pulled back into a second line of defence in the area of the Flyover, the initial line after the landing. There was to be no retreat from this position. VI Corps waited for the German attack, which was not long coming.

Kesselring and Mackensen, with direction from Hitler, aimed at a narrow thrust down the line of the Via Anziate between the Buonriposo Ridge and the Fossa di Spaccasassi in two phases: Phase One, breach the Allied defences; Phase Two, an armoured drive on Nettuno. A diversionary attack was to be made against 3rd Division in the Cisterna sector by the Herman Goering Panzer Division. The main attack was commanded by LXXVI Panzer Corps using 3rd Panzer Grenadier, 114th and 715th Divisions, and the Infantry Lehr Regiment in the first phase, and 29th Panzer Grenadier and 26th Panzer Divisions in the second. I Parachute Corps was given the task of protecting LXXVI Corps's flank.

The operation, FISCHFANG (catching fish), starting on 16 February, lasted until 20 February. It cost the Germans 5,389 casualties, and VI Corps few less, 45th Division alone suffered 2,400. On the first day, the Germans succeeded in penetrating about a mile in 45th Division's sector, and by the morning of 17 February, three German divisions with 50 tanks had forced the Allied line back into a salient two miles wide and one deep. Lucas sent 1st Armoured Division forward. In the afternoon, Von

Mackensen sent in his first phase reserves, but held back his second phase divisions. The salient became distended under the pressure of an attack by fourteen battalions supported by tanks. By the evening, the Germans were less than 1,000 yards from the Flyover.

All day on 18 February, the Germans mounted a maximum effort to gain the lateral road, but never quite made it. The Allied artillery pounded the Germans crammed into the narrow salient. Every yard of ground was bitterly contested. By last light, the attacks petered out in the face of 45th Division's stubborn defence. But throughout the night of 18/19 February, on the 19th, and on into the 20th the fighting continued.

On 17 February, Clark had ordered Truscott to move to VI Corps Headquarters as deputy commander. Truscott, the *beau sabreur*, whose courage was a byword in his division, and one of the outstanding generals of the war at the operational level, immediately made his cheerful presence felt in the dank cave at Nettuno; telling VI Corps's 'gloomy staff that nothing ever looked so bad on the ground as it did on a map at HQ', before going forward to see for himself, in marked contrast to Lucas.[39]

Early on 19 February, after much hesitation, but at Truscott's prompting, Lucas struck back. But not before Clark had to order him to take action. Lucas took 30th Infantry Regiment, 3rd Division's reserve, and 6th Armored Infantry from 1st Armored Division to form two task forces, telling Harmon, commanding 1st Armoured Division, to take these and however many tanks he needed, and attack from the south-east corner of the salient in a north-westerly direction. A complementary thrust by 169th British Infantry Brigade, under Brigadier Templer, commanding 56th Division, had to be drastically scaled down. 169th Bridgade's arrival in the beachhead was delayed by mines laid by the Luftwaffe in Anzio harbour. Nevertheless, the counter-attack took the Germans by surprise, and pushed them back about a mile, taking 500 prisoners. The beachhead had held, and although Kesselring mounted another attack on 29 February, VI Corps would never again be so near disaster.

Clark sent Lucas a message on the evening of 19 February:

> Congratulate Harmon on his success today. I want to tell you that your accomplishments today have been outstanding. Keep it up. I think your proposed dispositions of Harmon and one six nine brigade for possible counter-attack roles tomorrow are exactly correct. We have laid on an all out air program for tomorrow, the success of which is dependant on good weather. We are praying for that.[40]

Three days later, Lucas was relieved of command, and replaced by Truscott.

Lucas might have had some premonition of dismissal when Truscott was moved in from 3rd Division as Deputy Corps Commander. Nevertheless, it must have come as a shock after Clark's message of congratulation. It certainly cannot have surprised his divisional commanders, including

Truscott, who had been told by Clark on 18 January, that he would shortly be relieving Lucas.[41] Truscott was not 'blind to the fact that General Lucas lacked some of the qualities of positive leadership that engender confidence'.[42]

Lucas lashed out in his diary, principally blaming Alexander. For the wily Clark, despite his undoubted physical courage and ability, lacked the moral courage to take the responsibility for sacking Lucas. He unworthily resorted to the device of passing the blame upwards: to Alexander and to Devers, Deputy to General Wilson, Supreme Allied Commander Mediterranean. Lucas comments in his diary, 'I was not surprised at Alexander's attitude, he had been badly frightened, but what I heard about Devers was a great shock.'[43]

However critical one is about Alexander, and though one might accuse him, using late twentieth century argot, of being 'laid back', even his worst detractors, including Montgomery, have never hinted that he ever displayed fear. On the contrary, in situations with far more at stake than Anzio, his composure was, above all, what everyone around him remembered. Indeed, on a visit to Anzio on 14 February, Lucas found his attitude nonchalant and almost patronizing[44].

Although Lucas lays much of the blame for his dismissal on Alexander, what is really at issue is the whole concept of the operation. Anzio was a bluff that failed, and Alexander later admitted as much.[45] SHINGLE smacks of an operation that has not been thought through properly. Since October 1943, Alexander had held the view that the only way he could get to Rome was an amphibious hook by one division. Montgomery was scathing in his condemnation of the concept:

> ALEXANDER is trying hard to find a way out of the mess [the slow progress of the Italian campaign – *Author's note*]. But he won't do it by landing a Division at ROME; he will merely make it worse and the Division may well be written off by the Germans.[46]

In London, Washington, AFHQ, 15th Army Group and at Fifth Army, access to Ultra (intercepted and decrypted German radio traffic) must have made it clear that unless the Germans panicked, which in view of their track record was highly unlikely, any landing force would be quickly bottled up. These views had been put forward repeatedly by Clark's British Deputy Chief of Staff.[47] On the other hand, Field Marshal Alan Brooke, the British Chief of the General Staff (CIGS), was strongly in favour of going ahead[48]. While Eisenhower, still Supreme Allied Commander Mediterranean when SHINGLE was resurrected at Christmas 1943, claims in his memoirs that he opposed the operation[49]. This is a fabrication. The record of the Christmas Day 1943 meeting in Tunis quotes him:

> General Eisenhower said that he had not yet had an opportunity to study the OVERLORD operation. He felt strongly, however, that the right course was to

press on in Italy where the Germans were still full of fight. Nothing short of a bold venture such as SHINGLE would quicken up the successful prosecution of the campaign.

and later at the same meeting:

In his view there was no likelihood of the Germans suddenly breaking except under conditions which would be created by a successful SHINGLE.[50]

A signal from AFHQ Mediterranean to the Combined Chiefs of Staff in Washington and London, initiated by Eisenhower, having first mentioned the possible dangers to be encountered in landing at Anzio, continues:

'The conclusion reached was that in spite of SHINGLE being obviously a hazardous operation, the prize to be gained is so high that the risk may be worth taking'.[51]

When the operation started, he was in England, having been elevated to Supreme Allied Commander for the forthcoming invasion of France. At first his naval aide, Lieutenant Commander Butcher, excitedly referred in his diary (later published), to SHINGLE as 'a brilliant maneuver', hoping that eventually his master, rather than Alexander, would get the credit. When SHINGLE looked like ending in disaster, Butcher deleted his laudatory comments. With Eisenhower safely out from under, and no glory to be garnered from the operation, there was no point in crediting him with its conception. Alexander could carry the can.[52] However, it was Churchill who exerted the most influence on the decision to proceed. Unfortunately Alexander did not stand up to him.[53]

According to Lemnitzer, Alexander originally hoped to land five divisions at Anzio. He does not make clear whether they were all to land in the first few days. Nor does he discuss the provision of sufficient landing craft. However, he is specific that once the operation involved initially landing only two divisions, and not all of these on D-Day, there was no hope of holding the Alban Hills (Colli Laziali). He claims that Alexander was in full agreement with the Corps Commander's (Lucas's) decision not to push out far from Anzio.

Gen Alexander realized that we did not have the strength to hold the Hills even if we did take them. He thoroughly approved of the caution with which the Corps Commander was acting. Neither General Alexander nor Clark gave any sign that they thought Lucas had acted unwisely.[54]

This accords with Lucas's own comment:

My orders were, to me, very clear and did not include any rash, piece-meal effort. These orders were never changed although the Army and Army Group Commanders were constantly on the ground and could have changed them had they seen fit to do so.[55]

Although it is perfectly correct that his orders were never changed, it is clear that neither Alexander nor Clark were satisfied with Lucas's conduct of the battle from at least 25 January. On this occasion Alexander told Lucas that Cisterna should be taken. After this visit, and twice subsequently, Alexander told Clark that Lucas should be relieved but Clark was reluctant to do so. In response to telegrams from Churchill, prodding Alexander for explanations about the lack of progress at Anzio, the latter sent four messages to Churchill and two to the CIGS. All of these expressed his dissatisfaction with Lucas. On at least two occasions he ordered Lucas and Clark to produce a properly prepared Corps Plan[56].

Finally Alexander said to Clark in effect, 'You know what this Anzio beachhead will mean for both of us if there is a disaster here', and Clark agreed to the relief.[57] By 16 February, having sought and received CIGS's advice,[58] Alexander had arranged with Clark that Truscott would take over from Lucas.[59]

Despite Clark's declared reluctance at the time to relieve Lucas, he claimed later that it was necessary. According to his diary, he repeatedly told Lucas to push forward to Cisterna and Campoleone, but Lucas did not drive his divisional commanders hard enough.[60] He says that he warned Lucas that 'he would probably be relieved if he did not buck up'.[61] Lucas does not mention this warning in his diary. When the moment to sack him came, Clark claims that he took the responsibility,[62] although, as we have seen, this runs counter to what Lucas says. And Clark, when discussing the reason for the relief, throws the ball back into Alexander's court:

> Lucas was not relieved because he had done anything wrong, but because Alexander did not think he could stand up to the strain of further operations in the prolonged battle this promised to be.[63]

Yet in an interview for an oral history, he says that Keiser, Lucas's Chief of Staff, told him 'the man is really sick'.[64] And in his diary comments, 'Johnny Lucas was ill and tired physically and mentally from the long responsibilities of command in battle'.[65]

Whether the publicity-conscious Clark thought that relieving Lucas might reflect badly on him, particularly after sacking his predecessor only four months before, is hard to say. It is possible that Alexander's pointing out that Lucas was a millstone round both their necks helped to concentrate his mind on the question of his removal.

Neither Alexander nor Clark come out of Anzio well. Alexander's lack of grip of the Army Group battle was responsible for the operation and the manner in which it was mounted. His command style had worked in a one-over-one situation with Montgomery's Eighth Army in the Western Desert campaign, where no co-ordination was required. It was less successful in Italy where two armies, each commanded by a strong character, needed firm direction and, above all, a clear operational design. Anzio was a product of this lack of a proper design. If the beachhead was to be secured, what was its purpose? Surely not to provide a place where a force could sit contemplating the Germans? Yet the force was insufficient to do more, a fact that both Alexander and Clark seemed at times to be incapable of recognising. For as late as 29 January, both Fifth Army and 15th Army Group were producing over-optimistic forecasts of what they expected VIth Corps to achieve on 30 January, the day of Lucas's offensive. Clark's estimate of the situation on his Army front speaks of VI Corps advancing to Albano. While Lemnitzer, even further removed from reality, minutes the Chief of Staff of 15th Army Group:

> 6 Corps plan for 30 January 1944 is to attack at first light to seize the high ground in the vicinity of Colli Laziali to block the highway leading south-east of Rome.[66]

Wonderland indeed, and a clear indication of the lack of a firm concept and grip at 15th Army Group and Fifth Army.

If Clark was told by his Deputy Chief of Staff that Anzio had no chance of achieving its purpose, why did he not represent this to Alexander? Clark tried to help Lucas by giving him a firm primary mission of seizing and securing a beachhead but fudged it by the 'advance on Colli Laziali' part of his order. Once VI Corps was ashore, and before he established his forward command post, Clark visited frequently, often at great risk to himself. His personal courage was never in doubt. On a number of occasions he gave Lucas guidance, often tantamount to orders, but took no action when this was ignored.

In the end one comes to the conclusion that the overall situation at Anzio at the stage Lucas was relieved would not have been very different whoever had been in command of VI Corps. An attempt to push on to Rome, or even the Colli Laziali with the force at Lucas's disposal would have ended in disaster. What VI Corps did under his command was not fundamentally wrong, but his command style was so uninspiring that his superiors and subordinates lost faith in him. His removal was both necessary and timely, not for what had gone before, but for what was to come: three months of defensive battles, followed by hard fighting to break out. As his diary reveals, he was unfit for command in battle soon after he took over VI Corps. His conduct at Anzio was final proof of his inadequacy. Behind the scenes, Churchill was exerting pressure to obtain results from Anzio.[67] Lucas had to go anyway; he was the perfect scapegoat.

Although the primary purpose for which SHINGLE was mounted was not achieved, the operation was not a failure. On the Gustav Line, the Germans were defending the shortest line they ever held in the Italian campaign – 85 miles. By 30 January, because of SHINGLE, they had another 35 miles of front to contain. Alexander's primary task was to exert sufficient pressure on the Germans to prevent them withdrawing troops to reinforce their armies in North-West Europe. Anzio achieved more than that, the movement was the other way; German formations were drawn into Italy from France. 124 days of some of the most bitter and costly fighting of the Second World War was not in vain.

SHINGLE achieved something more. Adversity engenders a special quality in the human spirit. The American and British soldiers in the Anzio beachhead attained 'a camaraderie never closer in the Second World War'.[68]

Select Bibliography

Anzio Beachhead, (Historical Division Department of the Army of the United States, Washington DC, 1947).

1st Division, History of the First Division, Anzio Campaign, January-June 1944, (Alva Printing Press, Jerusalem, 1947).

Blumenson M, *United States Army in World War II; Mediterranean Theatre of Operations, Salerno to Cassino*, (Office of the Chief of Military History United States Army, Washington DC, 1969).

Eisenhower DD, *Crusade In Europe*, (William Heinemann, London, 1948).

Fraser DW, *And We Shall Shock Them, The British Army in the Second World War*, (Hodder & Stoughton, London, 1983).

Hamilton N, *Monty: Master of the Battlefield 1942–1944*, (Hamish Hamilton, London, 1983).

Hibbert C, *Anzio: the Bid for Rome*, (Purnell's History of the Second World War, Macdonald & Co, London, 1970).

Truscott LK, *Command Missions, a Personal Story*, (EP Dutton & Co Inc, New York, 1954).

Molony CJC, *The History of the Second World War, The Mediterranean and the Middle East*, Volume V, (HMSO London, 1973).

Morison SE, *History of United States Naval Operations in World War II, Vol 9, Sicily – Salerno – Anzio*, (Little Brown & Co, Boston, 1954).

Vaughan-Thomas W, *Anzio*, (Pan Books, London, 1963).

Verney P, *Anzio 1944; An Unexpected Fury*, (Batsford, London, 1978).

UNPUBLISHED SOURCES

Archives of the United States Army History Institute, Carlisle Barracks, Pa, USA:

The John P Lucas Papers:
The John P Lucas Diary, Parts I, II and III, including Annexes
Personal Papers, Correspondence and Memos Jan-Feb 1944
Maps Italy 1943–1944
Official Papers

Smythe Interviews
Interview with Major General Lyman Lemnitzer, 16 January 1948.

Mathews Interviews

(rank at time of interview – relevance to Anzio in brackets after name):
General Mark Clark (Fifth Army US Commander).
Field Marshal Alexander (Commander 15th Army Group).
Brigadier General Ralph H Tate (G-4 (logistics) Fifth Army).
Schram, OKW.
General Truscott (Commander 3rd US Infantry Division and VIth Corps).
General George Marshall (Chief of Staff, United States Army).
General Lyman Lemnitzer (Deputy Chief of Staff 15th Army Group).

The Senior Officers' Debriefing Programme:

Conversations between General Mark W Clark and Lieutenant Colonel Forest S
Rutgers Jr, 27 October 1972.

Histories and Lessons Learned (Allies and Axis) 1943–1944

The German Operation at Anzio:
Translation from German of Kesselring's Observations World War II 'Diary'.

Oral Histories:

Lieutenant General Robert J Wood, Staff of Fifth Army 1944.
Lieutenant General Hamilton Howze.
Lieutenant General Harrell, D/COS 3rd US Infantry Division and A/COS G-3 VI
Corps.
Lieutenant General Lemley.
Lieutenant General William B Rosson, Battalion Commander, 3rd US Infantry
Division and Assistant G-3 VI Corps.
Lieutenant General Heintges, Commanding 3rd Battalion, 7th Infantry Regiment,
3rd US Infantry Division.

Robert J Wood Papers:

Headquarters Fifth Army Outline Plan for Operation SHINGLE dated 12 January
1944, including Annexes and Appendices.

Headquarters Fifth Army

SHINGLE INTSUM Number 4 dated 30 December 1943.

Headquarters Fifth Army

SHINGLE INTSUM Number 8 dated 11 January 1944, including Beach Surveys.

Public Records Office Kew, England

Alexander Papers: Field Marshal Earl Alexander of Tunis

WO 214/8 Messages from Allied Force Headquarters Mediterranean to Combined
Chiefs of Staff 1 January to 29 February 1944.
WO 214/28 Operation SHINGLE
WO 214/14 Communications between General Sir Harold Alexander and Mr
Winston Churchill.
WO 214/30 Headquarters 15th Army Group operations staff and Army Group
Commander's papers.

British Formation War Diaries

WO 170/375 Headquarters 1st Infantry Division January 1944.
WO 170/376 Headquarters 1st Infantry Division February 1944.

Abbreviations and Notes

Abbreviations:

CCS – Combined Chiefs of Staff (The Chiefs of Staff of the United States and the United Kingdom).
AFHQ – Allied Force Headquarters (in the Mediterranean in the context of this chapter).
CIGS – Chief of the Imperial General Staff (British).

Notes

1. Lucas Diary, Part III, p. 101.
2. Lucas personal letter dated 25 May 1943, includes the passage, 'they told me that I had been picked above all the other Corps Commanders by General Marshall, McNair and (a secret) Eisenhower so it must be important. It means a great opportunity and I hope I can put it over'.
3. Senior Officers' Debriefing Program, conversations between General Mark Clark and Lieutenant Colonel Forest S Rutgers Jr, 12 October 1972, p. 65.
4. Lucas Diary, Pt. I, pp. 15–19.
5. Lucas Diary, Pt. I, p. 22.
6. Lucas Diary, Pt. I, p. 47.
7. Lucas Diary, Pt. II, p. 96.
8. Lucas Diary, Pt. II, p. 102.
9. Lucas Diary, Pt. II, p. 126.
10. Molony, C. J. C., *The History of the Second World War, the Mediterranean and the Middle East*, Volume V, (HMSO London, 1973), pp. 648–649, the VI Corps order of battle for the landing was:
    3rd US Infantry Division
    7th, 15th, and 30th Infantry Regiments (equivalent to British infantry brigade)
    504th Parachute Infantry Regiment
    509th Parachute Infantry Battalion
    1st, 3rd and 4th Ranger Infantry Battalions (equivalent to British commandos)

751st Tank Battalion (equivalent to British armoured regiment)
1st US Armored Division
Combat Command B
1st Armored Regiment (equivalent to British armoured brigade)
6th Armored Infantry Regiment (equivalent to British mechanised infantry brigade)
1st British Infantry Division
2nd and 3rd Infantry Brigades
24th Guards Brigade
46th Royal Tank Regiment
2nd Special Service Brigade (Commandos)
Number 9 Army Commando, and Number 43 Royal Marines Commando

11. Lucas Diary, Pt. III, p. 11.
12. Interview with Field Marshal Alexander by Dr. Sidney Mathews, p. 8.
13. Notes on Grouping of VI Corps for SHINGLE, by Lieutenant Colonel GS Assistant G-3 (British) HQ VI Corps, dated 3 January 1944, Lucas Papers.
14. Mathews interview with Clark, Part V, p. 6.
15. Mathews interview with Alexander, p. 8.
16. Lucas Diary, Pt. III, pp. 17–18.
17. WO 170/375 Headquarters 1st Infantry Division War Diary January 1944, Operation Order number 1, dated 12 January 1944.
18. The better known Admiral of the Fleet Sir Andrew Cunningham had returned to Britain to take over as First Sea Lord.
19. The figure of eight days maintenance is mentioned by both Eisenhower (WO 214/8 in AFHQ to Combined Chiefs of Staff message W9218/23209 of 031806A Jan 44), and by Alexander (WO214/28 file 13).
20. Report of Colonel William F. Hill and Colonel E. J. O'Neill on Conference Held in Marrakech, French Morocco on 7–8 January 1944.
21. Lucas Diary, Pt. III, p. 2.
22. Lucas Diary, Pt. III, p. 2.
23. Lucas Diary, Pt. III, p. 18.
24. The unsuitability of the British Beach (PETER Beach), should have come as no surprise. The Beach Survey Report contained in SHINGLE INTSUM Number 8 dated 11 January 1944, p. 5 is specific about the limitations.
25. Lucas Diary, Pt. III, p. 40.
26. General Sir John Hadcett, referring to Arnhem.
27. HQ Fifth Army INTSUM dated 30 December 1943, p. 3, gives the estimated build-up rates:

D-Day	14,300
D+1	19,300
D+2	22,300
D+3	31,300
D+16	61,000

The actual rates were:

| D-Day | 20,000 |
| D+1 | 24,400 |

D+2	40,400
D+3	41,100
D+10	95,000

28. Appendix Number 1 to Annex Number 1 to Outline Plan SHINGLE, p. 22, G-2 Estimate.
29. Mathews interview with Lemnitzer, p. 3.
30. Mathews interview with Marshall, part II.
31. Mathews interview with General Schram, OKW.
32. WO 214/8 W9218/23209 of 031806A Jan 44 from AFHQ to Combined Chiefs of Staff.
33. Translation from German of Kesselring's observations in his World War II 'diary', p. 37.
34. Kesselring, p. 37.
35. Lucas Diary, Pt. III, p. 35.
36. Lucas Diary, Pt. III, p. 18.
37. Fifth Army message 1128/022140A Feb.
38. Truscott, L. K. Command Missions, a Personal Story, (E. P. Dutton & Co. Inc., New York 1954), p. 329.
39. Truscott, p. 320.
40. Fifth Army message 3278/192234A Feb.
41. Truscott, p. 323.
42. Truscott, p. 320.
43. Lucas Diary, Pt. III, p. 101.
44. Blumenson, M. United States Army in World War II; Mediterranean Theatre of Operations, Salerno to Cassino, (Office of the Chief of Military History, United States Army, Washington DC, 1969), p. 424.
45. Mathews interview with Alexander.
46. Hamilton, N. Monty: Master of the Battlefield 1942–1944, (Hamish Hamilton, 1983), p. 441.
47. Hamilton, p. 441, n. 1.
48. Molony, p. 771.
49. Eisenhower, D. D. Crusade in Europe, (William Heinemann, London, 1948), pp. 232, 233 and 239.
50. WO 214/8 Record of Conference of Prime Minister with Commanders-in-Chief 25 December 1943, dated 26 December 1943.
51. WO 214/8 AFHQ to CCS W9218/23209 of 031806A Jan 44.
52. Hamilton, p. 515, the excised portion was only declassified by the United States Government in the 1970s.
53. Molony, p. 771.
54. Smythe interview with General Lemnitzer, 14 January 1948, pp. 9–10.
55. Lucas Diary, Pt. III, p. 49.
56. WO 214/14 Alexander to Churchill, 271820A Jan 44, 312235A Jan 44, 021955A Feb 44, and Alexander to CIGS 151700A Feb 44, and 161825A Feb 44. Also WO 214/30 15th Army Group to Fifth Army minute of 11 February 1944.
57. Mathews interview with Alexander, p. 8.

58. CIGS to Alexander 160110 Feb 44 includes the passage,

> 'Eisenhower's own personal selection (to replace Lucas), in order of priority, first Truscott, second Eagles, third Harmon. As an emergency measure could spare Patton for about a month'.

59. WO 214/14 Alexander to CIGS 161825A Feb 44.
60. Blumenson, p. 391, quoting Clark's diary for 30 January 1944.
61. Mathews interview with Clark, 10–21 May 1948, Pt. IV, pp. 9–10.
62. Mathews interview with Clark, Part V, p. 7.
63. Mathews interview with Clark, Part IV, pp. 9–10.
64. Senior Officers Debriefing Program, Clark, p. 66.
65. Molony, p. 739, here Clark is over-dramatic. Lucas had been commanding a corps for four months, not all the time in battle.
66. WO 214/30 Clark's estimate of the situation on Fifth Army front dated 29 January 1944, and Lemnitzer's minute of 29 January 1944.
67. Molony, pp. 737/738.
68. Verney, P. V. *Anzio 1944: An Unexpected Fury*, (Batsford, London 1978), p. 219.

10

Mutaguchi Renya and the Invasion of India, 1944

Louis Allen

Mutaguchi Renya was a man exuberantly confident of his own destiny. As if to emphasise by contrast the tragic depths to which his ambition later led him, his first two major interventions in the history of the Japanese Army were outstanding successes. It was he who exploited the Marco Polo Bridge incident in 1937, and brought fresh Army strength into China. It was he who led 18 Division from China to Malaya and, under the command of General Yamashita, drove the British out of Singapore. As commander of the 15 Army in Burma he intended to complete a hat-trick: he would lead the Japanese in the invasion of India, completing the downfall of the British in the East. The British would be driven out of the war in Asia, America would lose her closest ally and be forced to sue for peace. He, Mutaguchi, would achieve this consummation. How he failed is quite Chaucerian in its clarity of definition:

> *Tragedie is to seyn a certeyn storie,*
> *As olde bokes maken us memorie,*
> *Of him that stood in greet prosperitee*
> *And is y-fallen out of heigh degree,*
> *Into miserie, and endeth wrechedly . . .*[1]

* * *

Until March 1943, it had been Mutaguchi's firm belief that an invasion of India was impossible: the border mountains were not passable by a large force. Imperial General Headquarters in Tokyo and Southern Army General Headquarters in Singapore had suggested as far back as the summer of 1942 that the Japanese should not stop on the line of the Chindwin River, but press on into Assam, even as far as Dimapur and Tinsukia. This 'Operation 21' was studied in some detail from 22 July 1942 but the two divisional commanders involved – Mutaguchi, 18 Division; Sakurai, 33

Division – were unwilling to risk a venture across appallingly difficult country, with all the hazards of terrain and tropical diseases of the Indian frontier. When the GOC 15 Army, Lieutenant General Iida, who had successfully conquered the whole of Burma by the summer of 1942, heard their opinion, he advised against Operation 21. Southern Army agreed, and the idea was officially dropped on 25 October 1942.[2]

Then, in February and March 1943, news came to Mutaguchi and Sakurai that a British force had successfully crossed the uncrossable terrain, and had penetrated into north Burma under the noses of the Japanese. Mutaguchi reacted at once. He would mount an operation against the British base at Imphal.

There was something else. His first refusal to mount an expedition into Assam was, he thought, merely a rejection of an idea from a subordinate headquarters, i.e. 15 Army or Southern Army. Mutaguchi was promoted to GOC 15 Army on 18 March 1943, and set up his headquarters in the hill station of Maymyo. When he learned that the proposal had emanated from Imperial General Headquarters in Tokyo and that it might therefore be said to come from the Emperor himself, he was crestfallen. Had he, perhaps, done the unforgiveable thing, gone against the Emperor's personal wishes? Clearly, it was possible to go into India. With all the passion of the newly converted, at every conference, at every level, Mutaguchi and his staff tirelessly argued the case for pushing into Assam. Doubting voices were dismissed, including his Chief of Staff, Lieutenant General Obata, who was succeeded by Lieutenant General Kunomura. Or, if he had no power to dismiss them, their transfer was contrived by Mutaguchi's indefatigable string-pulling.

Supply was, naturally, the key to whatever scepticism lay on the Japanese side. Reinforcements would be available, within limits. Supplies would be available, within limits. When the Imphal operation began in March 1944, the Japanese had eight divisions in Burma, with two more to come in 1944; with an air division, a tank regiment, and an independent mixed brigade. The divisions earmarked for 15 Army and Imphal were 15, 31 and 33. Supplies would increase when the Burma–Siam Railway was completed in October 1943, ensuring that ammunition and rations did not have to come by the perilous sea-route between Saigon, Singapore and Rangoon, by this time at the mercy of Allied submarines. The line was finished at a terrible cost of lives among the Allied prisoners of war and native slave labour but it made a crucial difference to the Burma stockpile: whose monthly tonnage increased from 7,600 in November 1943 to 12,700 in May 1944.

It was one thing for supplies to reach Rangoon by rail. They had then to be transported to the divisional start lines, then across the hills into Manipur State. But Mutaguchi intended to short-circuit this particular problem. First, his soldiers would need meat. Genghis Khan had given him the answer to this. When he scoured the plains of Central Asia, Genghis

Khan had taken his meat rations with him. On the hoof. Mutaguchi would do the same.

Mutaguchi's other answer was the one he had learned as 18 Divisional commander in Malaya. The British had supplies galore. In preparation for a limited offensive across the Chindwin into Burma in 1943 (or early in 1944), they had accumulated vast stocks in the Imphal Plain, some of which had been pushed forward to 17 Division, at MS 109 on the road to Tiddim, or 20 Division, at Moreh, in the Kabaw Valley. The Japanese term for these supplies was '*Chāchiru kyūyō*' – 'Churchill rations' and they were the key to Mutaguchi's *real* supply plan. His men would carry on their backs enough food and ammunition for three weeks. By the time these ran out, say by mid-April, Mutaguchi expected his divisions to be in the Imphal Plain, within striking distance of Imphal itself, and in possession of enough captured British supplies to fuel his next stage onward into Assam. Here, too, his obstinate ignoring of the warning signs of change in British morale let him down. Because the British in Imphal had a plan of their own, into which Mutaguchi's offensive fitted perfectly.

Almost until the end of 1944, long after Mutaguchi's invasion of India had turned from a dream into a nightmare, the British higher command in London (the War Cabinet and Chiefs of Staff) and Ceylon (Mountbatten's Supreme Allied Command, South-East Asia, inaugurated in September 1943) shied away from the notion of an overland reconquest of Burma. The seaborne landing of forces to capture strategic airfields – Akyab, Rangoon, Moulmein – was sensible and would involve merely bottling up the Japanese forces in Burma and using the Burmese seaboard for an onward leap into Malaya and Singapore. The appointment of Lord Louis Mountbatten, a very junior admiral who had been a destroyer commander and then Chief of Combined Operations, was an indication that this strategy would be favoured.

Seaborne landings meant adequate numbers of landing craft, and these were never forthcoming. South-east Asia had low priority in contrast with Sicily, Italy and the Normandy landings. For everyone except the 14th Army commander, Lieutenant General William Slim, an overland reconquest of Burma was therefore only a strategic *pis-aller*. Even when it was envisaged, the notion was not – at first – to take forces beyond a limited advance across the Chindwin, to link with a double advance in north Burma from Ledo and Yunnan. But whatever the nature and extent of the advance across the Chindwin, the obvious storehouse was Imphal, the capital of Manipur State, essentially a basin in the hills, 30 miles long by 20 miles wide, from which the British-Indian forces could advance into Central Burma.

This is where the Japanese build-up for *their* advance provided Slim and his IV Corps commander, Lieutenant General Geoffrey Scoones, with a longed-for opportunity. If the Japanese came forward as Slim anticipated, they would stretch their L of C beyond the limits of endurance, across appalling country, precisely what the British would do if they moved first. When the Japanese divisions were drawn into the Imphal Plain, Slim could use tanks and massed artillery against them, winning his decisive battle before re-entering Burma. Slim and Scoones expected that one Japanese division would move against 17 Indian Division, using the Tiddim road to attack Imphal from the south, while another force would aim at the south-east corner of the Imphal Plain from the Kabaw Valley through the Shenam Saddle to the airfields at Palel. From the east across the Chindwin they expected another move, at divisional strength, through the Naga hills into the northern side of the Imphal Plain from Ukhrul. Lastly, they took it for granted that an attempt would be made to cut the road between Imphal and the British supply railhead at Dimapur. The obvious spot for this was at Kohima, 80 miles from Imphal and 46 miles from Dimapur. Given the difficulties of moving a really large force through this part of the Naga hills, both Slim and Scoones took it for granted that the Japanese would deploy nothing larger than a regiment against Kohima; an assumption which nearly proved fatal.

In this calculation, as in the timing of the offensive, both Slim and Scoones were wrong, and were caught on the hop. The southern claw of Mutaguchi's pincers closed in pretty much as Slim had foreseen: the main body of 33 Division (Lieutenant General Yanagida Motozō, leading two of his regiments, 214 and 215) came up from the south at Tiddim, while a separate force of 33 division troops, under the infantry group commander Major General Yamamoto Tsunoru, would attempt the breakthrough to Palel, using the tanks of 14 Tank Regiment. Yamamoto Force was probably the strongest unit, from the point of view of firepower, in Mutaguchi's 15 Army, and its route was the shortest. Further north, 15 Division (Lieutenant General Yamauchi) would make straight west for the Imphal Plain from their crossing points on the Chindwin. All this was predictable enough. But Mutaguchi did not intend to send merely a regiment against Kohima. The entire 31 Division (Lieutenant General Satō Kōtoku), was earmarked for this task because Mutaguchi had something else at the back of his mind besides interrupting the flow of supplies to the Imphal garrison and IV Corps. Every decision taken at the innumerable planning confer-ences, from Imperial General Headquarters down, had emphasised that the Imphal operation had a purely defensive purpose: to move the Japanese defence line forward from the Chindwin to the range of hills behind it, destroying or capturing British supplies as it went, and thereby forestall any British counter-offensive into Burma.

Such a limited aim was quite foreign to Mutaguchi's more grandiose conceptions. Although his superior in Rangoon, Lieutenant General Kawabe Masakazu, GOC of the newly created Burma Area Army, intended to keep Mutaguchi on a loose rein, because he valued his offensive spirit, he nonetheless kept in mind the strategic limitations of the offensive, 'Operation U' as it was termed. But once his forces were committed, Mutaguchi had no intention of halting on any line of defence. For him, the assault on Imphal was radically to change the course and outcome of the war. He wanted a whole division to take first Kohima and then push on to Dimapur. It would bring him right into India, to the banks of the Brahmaputra. Once there, he would unleash into India the renegade Indian forces which the Japanese had raised in Malaya against the British, and which had been reconstituted under a new leader in 1943.

That new leader was the former Lord Mayor of Calcutta and former President of the Congress Party, Subhas Chandra Bose.[4] He and Mutaguchi suited each other perfectly. Like most Japanese military commanders Tojo, the Prime Minister and War Minister, had not envisaged the Indian National Army as providing anything other than an ancillary force of scouts, interpreters and spies. Here was an Indian politician claiming co-belligerent rights. Tojo was sensitive on the Indian question. When Kawabe went to see him just before taking up his command in Burma, 'the measures we take in relation to Burma', Tojo told him, 'are really the first steps in our policy towards India. I'd like to stress that our main objective lies there, in India'.[5]

Mutaguchi's dream of knocking Great Britain out of the war would be achieved by using Bose. Once Mutaguchi was firmly established in Assam, Bose's men would spread anti-British propaganda throughout Bengal. The Indian Army – that most British of creations – would abandon its British masters and come over to him. The British position in India would become untenable. Britain would be unable to pursue her war against Japan, the United States would thereby lose its greatest ally, and be compelled to sue for peace. He, Mutaguchi, would have brought the war in Asia to a successful conclusion. This is no mere interpretation. He is quite explicit about this vision.[6]

What were the chances of any or all of this happening? Hindsight sees only a massive British victory, as the starving remnants of Mutaguchi's 15 Army, defeated and diseased, made their crestfallen way back across the Chindwin into Burma. Instead of driving the British, and later the United States of America, out of the war, and ensuring the triumph of the Imperial Japanese Army, Mutaguchi led it to the greatest defeat it had known in its history.

Yes. But was he ever within reach of success? Well into the post-war years, Mutaguchi was convinced that he could have achieved what he set out to do, had it not been for the feebleness, pusillanimity or stubborn shortsightedness of his divisional commanders. Yamauchi Motofumi (15 Division), Yanagida Motozo (33 Division) and Satō Kōtoku (31 Division).

Characteristic of Mutaguchi's determination to have his own way at all costs is his behaviour during the period of the planning conferences, in the summer and autumn of 1943. He had received a report from a group of Japanese intelligence officers, headed by Major Fujiwara Iwaichi, who had raised the 'Indian National Army' against the British in Malaya, that the terrain was more passable than they had suspected.

West of the Chindwin, Fujiwara had no information, but the report, which reached Mutaguchi in Maymyo in May 1943, was sufficient to allow him to make a strong appeal to Major General Inada, Vice-Chief of the General Staff at Southern Army, when he visited Maymyo on May 17.[7] 'You remember when you were on a tour of inspection in Manchuria in 1939?' Mutaguchi reminded him. 'I was Chief of Staff of 4 Army then, and I told you I felt deeply the responsibility of having, as regimental commander, fired the first shot at the Marco Polo Bridge two years before. I begged you to use me somewhere where I could die for my country. I feel now exactly as I did then. Let me go into Bengal! Let me die there!' Inada was not taken in. 'It might suit your book to go to Imphal and die there,' he drily replied, 'but what if Japan is overthrown in the process?'[8] Soon after, both Burma Area Army staff and 15 Army staff met in conference in Rangoon to discuss the proposal for a new defence line in north-west Burma, in the presence of the Emperor's brother, Prince Takeda. Not only did Major General Kunomura, Mutaguchi's chief of staff, try to pre-empt the conference decisions by presenting a plan of advance into Assam, without prior notice to Burma Area Army, his immediate superior, Mutaguchi also tried to nobble Prince Takeda the night before the conference in an attempt to win him over to his views. Since both these actions were offences against the principle of chain of command, Kawabe might have been expected to be furious at Mutaguchi going over his head. His diary (29 June 1943) shows no such reaction:

> I hear Mutaguchi has asked for an audience with HIH because he wanted to clarify to him personally how he saw the operation. I love that man's enthusiasm. You can't help admiring his almost religious fervour.[9]

The Imperial Prince was unimpressed. Rather, he was angry at having been got at, and was convinced by Inada's arguments that more thought should be given to supply, and that to attack with men carrying their food and ammunition and afterwards rely on stores captured from the enemy was 'to skin the raccoon before you caught him.'[10] He reported in this sense to Imperial General Headquarters in Tokyo. 'The army in the front line has no control of the situation in its rear. As things look, from the state of preparations, I think the Imphal operation is definitely not on.'[11] The report was made to Colonel Masada, chief of No. 1 Bureau, 2 Section (Operations) at Army GHQ, who, surprisingly, was not convinced. *Why* he was not convinced reflects the political reasons for elements in Tokyo deciding to back Mutaguchi. Japan was still smarting from defeats in the Pacific, at Midway and Guadalcanal. 'If we go into the rear set-up thoroughly' Masada thought, 'we can certainly get as far as Imphal.' [12] At Southern Army, in Singapore, the political element began to weigh more heavily than the logistic difficulties with Inada. 'Even if we do not carry out the Imphal operation to its fullest extent, we could set up Subhas Chandra Bose in a corner of India and raise the flag of free India. That alone would be an adequate political result. It will be an embellishment for Tojo's war leadership.' [13] At the level below this on the scale of command, Kawabe at Burma Area Army in Rangoon was sure he could delimit the operation as he thought fit, while giving Mutaguchi his head in the initial stages. 'Burma Area Army's job' he confided to his chief of staff, 'is to indicate to its subordinate commanders the objective they are to attain. How to achieve it is left to them. And Mutaguchi is a commander in whom I have the greatest confidence. We will make it clear that the object of the operation is to take the Imphal area. What happens after that remains in my hands. But there will be no mad rush into Assam'.[14] 15 Army was authorised to prepare for the operation in September 1943, and final approval was given by Imperial General Headquarters in Tokyo on 31 December 1943. It only remained for Tojo, in his dual capacity as Prime Minister and War Minister, to give the final consent.[15]

> For the defence of Burma, the Commander in Chief Southern Army shall destroy the enemy on that front at the appropriate juncture and occupy and secure a strategic zone in North-East India in the area of Imphal.[16]

This wording contained what were meant to be important limitations: 'for the defence of Burma', 'in the area of Imphal'. But Mutaguchi took it as the green light. He could now get on with his dream, the invasion of India.

There was to be a diversion. 28 Army, recently formed for the defence of the Arakan against a hypothetical Allied sea-borne assault, was to use 55 Division to mount an attack on 15 Corps in the Arakan, to draw attention from the Central Front, and ensure that the British commanders could not reinforce it from the five divisions in the Arakan (5, 7, 25, 26, 81 West African). Operation Ha-Go began on 4 February 1944. It was a brilliant stroke, an encircling move intended to penetrate behind 7 Indian Division, surround it, and destroy it. The force commander was Major General Sakurai Tokutarō, who intended, after putting an end to 7 Division, to cross the Mayu Range and destroy 5 Indian Division in the area of Maungdaw. Sakurai also intended to capture the 7 Indian Division commander.

He almost succeeded. Major General (later Lieutenant General Sir) Frank Messervy was caught in his headquarters, in his pyjamas, when the Japanese attack came in and narrowly managed to avoid capture by escaping to the supply dump at Sinzweya, known as the 'Admin Box', which now became a fortress. Sakurai applied the old and tried Japanese formula: encirclement, cutting communications, withering the enemy on the branch, filling him with terror by sudden night attacks. And although his orders were limited to holding the British reserves in the Arakan, Sakurai had much in common with Mutaguchi. 'It's child's play to smash the enemy in the Mayu Peninsula' he had said. 'Give me one battalion, I'll show you, I'd be in Chittagong by now.' [17]

But Sakurai was to come up against the same phenomenon that hit Mutaguchi and his plans over a month later. The British forces did not behave as they were supposed to. Instead of panicking when their L of C was cut, they stood and fought. Their supplies by road might be cut, but they received food and ammunition by air. There was ferocious close-quarter fighting in and around the Admin Box, but it was the tanks and guns massed inside it which decided the outcome. By 26 February 1944, Sakurai admitted defeat. He had failed to destroy 7 Indian Division, and his men were exhausted. The most important factor, as a later Japanese historian put it, was the altered geometry of the battlefield.[18] The flat encirclement by the Japanese of the Admin Box at Sinzweya, unaccompanied by adequate firepower, was countered by the cubic tactics (*rittai senpō*) of the British. Air supply made a multi-directional defence possible, which congealed the initial fluidity into a hardness which could only have been countered by stronger firepower, which the Japanese lacked. When the Japanese withdrew, they left 5,000 dead on the field. 'For the first time,' Slim was to write later, 'a British force had met, held and decisively defeated a major Japanese attack . . British and Indian soldiers had proved themselves, man for man, the masters of the best the Japanese could bring against them . . it was a victory about which there could be no argument, and its effect, not only on the troops engaged, but on the whole XIV Army, was immense'.[19]

There was something else. Sakurai's fringe feint had not lasted long enough. When Mutaguchi's offensive was planned, the date for the advance on Imphal was the first week in March. In the event, only 33 Division moved off on 7–8 March; 15 and 31 Divisions crossed the Chindwin and moved west on 15 March. The gap between the end of Sakurai's Arakan offensive and the start of the Imphal operation was therefore between one and two weeks, which gravely lessened its impact. 15 Division's slow arrival at the front was the cause of this. On the way through Thailand from China, Southern Army had press-ganged the division into road-making duties, which not only delayed its arrival at the Chindwin forming-up points, but ensured that the men would arrive exhausted. Not only that, they had to change their guns for more easily handled mountain-guns. And they had no anti-tank component. Not necessary, they were told by Lieutenant General Naka, Burma Area Army's Chief of Staff, the British would not be using tanks. Naka came up to 15 Division at the crossing point on 15 March 1944 and confessed he had been wrong. The British would be using tanks after all. But anti-tank guns were still not forthcoming. So 15 Division's offensive began under-strength – six battalions instead of nine –

and with quite inadequate artillery.

The supposition that Terauchi, at Southern Army HQ in Singapore, had consented to 15 Division's use in the Thailand road-building programme deliberately in order to put a brake on Mutaguchi's ambitions by limiting his offensive power has been hinted at. Perhaps. But there were other limiting factors beside manpower. One was airpower; another was the atmosphere of mistrust between Mutaguchi and his three divisional commanders.

The Japanese air strength in Burma by this time was ineffectual, though occasional damaging fighter sorties and bombing raids were made. By and large, the skies belonged to the Allies; necessarily so, for without that air supremacy the flight of innumerable transport planes – and the fate of the Admin Box battle – would have been quite different. Yamauchi, GOC 15 Division, was a sensitive and gentle-spirited individual who had served abroad as a military attaché, had lived in Washington, and acquired some western habits, including the preference for western-style latrines. He had a special wooden one made for him, which his orderly was instructed to carry about with him wherever they went. The change-over from lorried transport to pack transport imposed by the mountainous terrain between India and Burma can't have made this an easy task. What is more, Yamauchi was a dying man. Mortally ill of tuberculosis, he ended the operation in a military hospital in Maymyo, where he died in August 1944. He felt deeply Mutaguchi's contempt for his division, and dismissed the GOC as a 'blockhead' (*wakarazuya*), unfit to be in command of an army.[20] The GOC 33 Division, Yanagida, had also been a military attaché and regarded Mutaguchi (correctly) as a bully and a womanising bore. 'What's going to become of us,' he had been heard to say, 'with a moron like Mutaguchi as our Commander-in-Chief? (*Anna wake no wakaran gun-shireikan wa dōmo naran ne?*)'. The view was mutual. 'What can you do with a gutless bastard (*yowamushi*) like that?' was Mutaguchi's opinion of Yanagida.[21] Satō, GOC 31 Division, was an old political enemy from the days of army factional wrangling in the 1930s, and had already made it clear he had no confidence in Operation U and would do his duty and not a stroke more. All in all, the relations between Mutaguchi and his three most important subordinates were hardly promising at the outset of such a knife-edge operation.

As GOC 33 Division, Yanagida was to start his offensive a week earlier than 15 and 31 Division. His two infantry regiments, 214 and 215, were to cut off 17 Indian Division, prevent it withdrawing from Tiddim north to Imphal, hack it to pieces, and take its stores at the dump at Milestone 109. This needed dash and courage, and, in Mutaguchi's view, Yanagida lacked both.[22] Yanagida had no great faith in the Imphal operation. He had also, among his staff, a reputation for being squeamish at the sight of blood.

At the moment when 33 Division should have been dashing forward to Imphal, Yanagida deliberately slowed his advance. But it was a mistaken signal, not cowardice, that brought about this result. When 215 Regiment was attacked by 48 Brigade of 17 Indian Division on 22–25 March 1944, one of the battalion commanders signalled that he had lost half his battalion, that he and his men had burned the regimental flag and were fighting to the last man.

From this signal, Yanagida concluded not only that he had lost a field officer upon whom he relied, but that his whole advance had been blunted. His immediate reaction was to signal Mutaguchi his considered opinion that the Imphal operation should at once be brought to an end.

It is not difficult to sympathise with Mutaguchi's fury when he received that signal. Here was a divisional commander recommending the cessation of a whole operation on the basis of an initial setback. He sent off a staff officer, Major Fujiwara, to urge Yanagida on. Fujiwara pointed out that the operation on the other divisional fronts was going well, and if Yanagida kept up the pressure against 17 Division, Imphal would soon be in Japanese hands. But Yanagida had already made his decision. Henceforth there was to be no wild dash northwards. It was to be *tōsei zenshin*, a 'controlled advance'[23]. Fujiwara groaned when he heard the phrase. It meant the postponement of the capture of Imphal, whatever the other divisions were doing. At any rate, Mutaguchi was confirmed in his view that Yanagida was a coward, and from that moment on sent his orders to the division through its Chief of Staff, pointedly ignoring the divisional commander. In the end, Yanagida was dismissed on 22 May 1944, and succeeded by Lieutenant General Tanaka Nobuo, who took over in time to conduct a fighting retreat from the Imphal plain.

Yamauchi's offensive in the northern sectors started well. Two companies of the undermanned and undergunned 15 Division, moving over rough country to the south of 31 Division, and in more or less a straight line to Imphal, cut the Imphal–Kohima road, on 28 March 1944, at Kangpokpi (known to the Japanese from its church as 'Mission') effectively isolating IV Corps in the Imphal Plain. His right assault column crossed the Imphal road at Safarmaina and moved down on Imphal through the hills west of the road. By the end of March, Yamauchi's men, having cut the main road, were astride the hills looking down on IV Corps Headquarters in the Plain. With the capture of the heights of Nungshigum (Hill 3833 in Japanese accounts), overlooking the spread-out British encampments, Yamauchi was no more than six miles from the very heart of IV Corps. He was only prised off it by determined tank and infantry attacks in mid-April.

So, one by one, Mutaguchi's divisions were halted short of their targets. One by one, their ammunition ran out, their rations were exhausted. The onset of the monsoon completed their discomfiture. In thick glutinous mud, in pouring rain, the emaciated, tattered host fought on. In Slim's words, describing the retreat of Tanaka's 33 Division back to Tiddim and beyond,

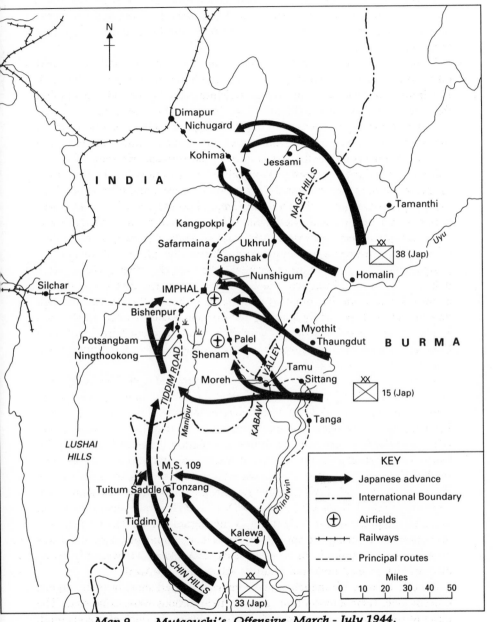

Map 9.   *Mutaguchi's Offensive, March - July 1944.*

There can have been few examples of a force as reduced, battered and exhausted as 33 Japanese Division delivering such furious assaults . . . Whatever one
may think of the military wisdom of thus pursuing a hopeless object, there can
be no question of the supreme courage and hardihood of the Japanese soldiers
who made the attempts. I know of no army that could have equalled them.[24]

They, and Mutaguchi, had come within an ace of winning. Their defeat
was correspondingly disastrous.

By early June, Mutaguchi was at the end of his tether, praying to his gods
for help, and trying to tell Kawabe that he thought the operation should be
terminated, but not being able to put it into words.[25]

Mutaguchi assumed Kawabe would understand him through *hara-gei*,
'belly talk' without any need for verbalisation.

I guessed Kawabe's real purpose in coming was to sound out my views on the
possibility – or otherwise – of continuing the Imphal operation. The sentence,
"The time has come to give up the operation as soon as possible" got as far as
my throat, but I could not force it out in words. But I wanted him to get it from
my expression. [26]

But military orders need to be verbalised, and Kawabe was as unable to
ask Southern Army to end the operation as Mutaguchi was to ask Kawabe
to order it.

The end came on 5 July 1944. Imperial General Headquarters accepted
defeat, and Southern Army, in its turn, ordered Burma Area Army to close
down the operation. It had not provided the embellishment for Tojo's
régime that had been hoped for. Two days later, Tojo's Cabinet fell, and he
was succeeded by General Koiso Kuniaki. The Imphal casualty figures,
though hard to pin down with accuracy, are instructive:

	Divisional Strengths	
	Before	After
15 Division	16,804	3,300
31 Division	16,666	6,400
33 Division	17,068	3,000
Totals:	50,538	12,700[27]

The totals do not include troops under direct command of 15 Army,
numbering around 36,000. Losses among them were not as heavy as among
the fighting divisions, but in both cases casualties described as 'sick and
wounded' were in many cases deaths, since the provisions for the wounded
were appalling. Slim calculates British casualties as roughly 15,000 killed
and 25,000 sick and wounded, but in the latter case hospital treatment was
often rapid and effective.

A Japanese historian of the Pacific War, Kojima Noboru, gives an even
lower survival rate than the one quoted above and works out the casualty
percentage per division as:

15 Division	78 per cent
31 Division	67 per cent
33 Division	84 per cent

the highest casualty percentages of any action fought by the Japanese during the war, the result, in his view, of a far from perfect plan and a far from perfect commander.[28] In his *Taiheiyō sensō* he reveals the total equipment losses to have been: guns 157 (80 per cent) and vehicles 1948 (70 per cent)[29]. The roll call of the dismissed is impressive too: GOC Burma Area Army; GOC 15 Army; Chief of Staff, Burma Area Army; all staff officers of 15 Army, save one; all three divisional commanders (by Mutaguchi himself).

Topographically and tactically, the various battles which went to make up the Imphal campaign are complex and disparate. Some were decided by hand-to-hand fighting of the most primitive kind, as at Sangshak and Kohima, some by the intervention of tanks, as at Kohima and Nungshigum, yet others by the use of fighter aircraft strikes, others again by air transport of troops and supplies, like the fly-in of 5 and 7 Indian Divisions from Arakan. The campaign extended from 8 March 1944, when 33 Division began its assault along the Tiddim road against 17 Indian Division, to 5 July 1944, when Mutaguchi was permitted by Kawabe to call it a day, a period of nearly five months. According to Lieutenant General (later Sir) Geoffrey Evans, first a brigadier (and commander of the Admin Box) and later a divisional commander (7 Indian Division), the crucial date was 4 April 1944, by which time 17 Indian Division had gathered at the entrance to Imphal Plain, bloody but intact, after surviving the Japanese attempt to cut it in two and destroy it.[30] 5 Division had been flown in, and one of its brigades sent to Dimapur. The Japanese put it at 19 April, when 15 Division had failed to break through at Sengmai, a village just north of Imphal, and was ordered on the defensive.[31] Whichever date we choose, the hinge of fate came early in the game, and the bloody slogging matches which followed, in the hills in and around Kohima, in the villages at the southern edge of the plain – Bishenpur, Ninthoukong, Potsambang – in the hunting down of the Japanese 15 Division in the hills and valleys north and east of Nungshigum, Yamamoto Force's vain efforts to break through to Palel against 20 Indian Division's stonewalling along the road between Palel and Shenam, all were really postludes which did not produce anything but partial and local success for Mutaguchi, once the initial triumphal impetus was exhausted. Once, that is, they were held at the entrances to the Imphal plain and their inadequate supplies began to run out.

But the direct thrust right into Bengal was to be the work of Satō's 31 Division, in Mutaguchi's mind. That was why he intended to send, not a regiment, but an entire division against Kohima. The key to Mutaguchi's failure lies in his relations with 31 Division.

Just how real were the prospects of success for Mutaguchi's invasion of

India? The evidence from the British side gives it a fair run. In particular, his order to Satō to leave Kohima and make for Dimapur could have presented the British command with an intolerable situation, as Mountbatten's Report makes clear.[32]

In *Defeat into Victory*, Slim, taking quite seriously this threat to India if Mutaguchi had broken through, both interprets and endorses Japanese expectations:

> Here [Burma] was the one place they could stage an offensive that might give them all they hoped. If it succeeded, the destruction of the British forces in Burma would be the least of its results.[33]

Similarly, Slim judges the impact of the possible loss of Dimapur:

> The loss of Kohima we could endure, but that of Dimapur, our only base and railhead, would have been crippling to an almost fatal degree. It would have pushed into the far distance our hopes of relieving Imphal, laid bare to the enemy the Brahmaputra Valley with its string of airfields, cut off Stilwell's Ledo Chinese, and stopped all supply to China.[34]

Arthur Swinson, author of a history of the Kohima battle, and of a study of Japanese generalship, is in no doubt that a push by Satō at that time would have succeeded. He refuses to accept censures such as Fujiwara's *tout court*:

> 'If Sato failed in his duty by retreating, then Mutaguchi and 15th Army had been failing for ten weeks, by not keeping him supplied . . . The 15th Army was brought to defeat by incompetent planning and incompetent staff work. The fault was Mutaguchi's. In the spirit of the true samurai he took unacceptable risks, and paid the penalty.[35]

This is putting a fine gloss on Mutaguchi's ambitions. Swinson continues:

> But could he have succeeded, had Sato sent a regiment straight for Dimapur without stopping to ask permission; in the view of this author – who happened to be in Dimapur at the critical period – he could have done. The whole place was in chaos and panic.[36]

Mutaguchi was still alive when Slim's and Mountbatten's statements appeared (1951 and 1956) but they do not seem to have come his way. What did come his way, and made a tremendous impact on him, were letters written to him in 1962 by AJ Barker, a military historian who was preparing a book to be called *The March on Delhi*, describing the attempted invasion of India in 1944.[37] With great good sense, he decided to approach Mutaguchi to put some questions to him, and incidentally revealed in correspondence that the British XXXIII Corps commander, Lieutenant General (later Sir) Montagu Stopford had no doubt that if Mutaguchi's forces had moved on Dimapur they would have succeeded. 'Your conviction that General Satō could have captured Dimapur is correct' wrote Barker (letter dated 11 September 1962). 'A few days ago I had the opportunity to ask General Stopford about this: if 31 Division had left a small unit behind to control Kohima and had continued to advance, he (Stopford) would have been placed in the gravest difficulties. It would have become very difficult to deploy 2 Division, and if fighting had broken out around Dimapur, Kohima would perhaps have fallen like a ripe fruit.' [38]

That sentence decided Mutaguchi to break a twenty-year silence, which he had maintained in tacit obedience to the Japanese proverb: 'a defeated general does not talk of war' (*Haigun no shō wa hei wo katarazu*).

The receipt of Barker's letter was a heaven-sent opportunity for Mutaguchi to justify himself. Since the end of the war he had been under a cloud, not merely as a prime proponent of militarist nationalism, but also, in the eyes of the ordinary Japanese soldier in Burma, as the author of their massacre by the British, the man who, with almost his entire staff, had been sacked at the end of the campaign. Now here was the British corps commander at Dimapur and Kohima agreeing with him. Had Satō pressed forward to Dimapur in April 1944, he would have found it a vast defenceless treasure-house of supplies, and could have wrought irreparable damage to a future British offensive. Mutaguchi issued Barker's letter with his own replies, as a privately printed pamphlet, on 23 April 1964 under the innocuous title *Explanatory materials in the National Diet Library concerning the U Operation in 1944*. The contents are less innocuous. Studded with exclamation marks, the pamphlet is Mutaguchi's counter-blast against Satō, who had, first, refused to go on to Dimapur and secondly, when, in his judgment, Mutaguchi had failed to supply his division with food, had brought his men out of the line and quit the Kohima front, leaving his infantry group commander, Miyazaki, with a small rearguard to delay 2 Division's advance from Kohima to the relief of Imphal. This was unparalleled insubordination.

What had happened with Satō is this. 31 Division was given the task of taking Kohima. Its infantry group commander, Major General Miyazaki Shigesaburō, a tiny cheerful creature who was one of the great characters of the Burma battlefield, chose to step aside en route to Kohima to take the village of Sangshak. It did not lie directly across his path, but his intelligence warned him that a British force of brigade strength was there, and he did not want to leave it lying on his flank. So, although Sangshak was outside his divisional area, and had been allocated as an operational task to 15 Division, Miyazaki devoted nearly a week's ferocious onslaught to it. The British defenders were 50 Indian Parachute Brigade, with a Mahratta battalion from 23 Division. After a dogged resistance, reminiscent of the worst days of trench warfare in World War I, 50 Parachute Brigade obeyed 23 Division's order to withdraw on Imphal, leaving Sangshak in Miyazaki's hands. His gains in matériel were considerable, but he had lost a number of junior company officers, which made a difference to the fighting at Kohima. And he had lost a week.[39] That week enabled a scratch defence to be raised in Kohima, under Colonel Hugh Richards (previously a Wingate column commander), who was later reinforced by a battalion of the Royal West Kents from 5 Division. So instead of walking into Kohima, as he might have done, he had to fight for it, house by house, hill by hill. He had occupied most of it by 18 April, when the advance group of British 2 Division, arriving in Dimapur from Central India, enabled 161 Brigade (5 Division) to relieve the garrison and begin to prise the Japanese away from the heights of Kohima. It took 2 Division nearly two months to do it, with much hard fighting; but their arrival ensured that the threat to Dimapur, and hence to the rest of Assam, was over. From his headquarters in Maymyo, and later in Indainggyi, Mutaguchi watched in anguish as his plans began to crumble. Why had Satō not gone forward from Kohima to take Dimapur, immediately, before the British had time to react and before Kawabe in Rangoon had time to put a spoke in Mutaguchi's ambitions?

Mutaguchi had tried. 'Advance on Dimapur at once!', he had signalled Satō as soon as he received news that 31 Division was in control of Kohima. That was sent on 8 April 1944. But Satō refused to budge. He knew that the Imphal plan was defensive in purpose, and contained no directive to move beyond Manipur. Besides, there was something else. In the pre-war jockeying for position among the various factions into which Japanese Army officers were split, Mutaguchi and Satō had been antagonists. In fact, on a number of occasions, Mutaguchi, then a colonel, had had Satō secretly followed and his movements reported. The net result was a deep hostility between the two men, compounded by Satō's conviction that the whole Imphal enterprise was a mistake anyway. He had no intention of sacrificing the men of his division in pursuit of the will o' the wisp of Mutaguchi's dreams of grandeur. As it happened, Mutaguchi's signal to Satō was intercepted at Burma Area Army headquarters in Rangoon. Reading it, Lieutenant Colonel Fuwa, an operations staff officer, realised at once that Mutaguchi was stepping beyond his brief, and took the signal to the GOC. Kawabe reacted at once. Another signal was sent, this time from Burma Area Army, instructing Mutaguchi to countermand the order for 31 Division to move on Dimapur. As Mutaguchi saw it, a vital opportunity was lost.

Later in the campaign, when Satō decided to withdraw from the front line to seek supplies for his men, Mutaguchi at first pleaded with him not to destroy his division's gallant reputation, so bitterly won in the fight for Kohima. When Satō proved obdurate, Mutaguchi sent his chief of staff, Kunomura, to reason with him. Kunomura asked Satō directly if he intended to obey Army orders. Satō was no fool and knew a trap was being laid for him (such disobedience in the face of the enemy was punishable by death).[40] 'There is no question of disobeying orders,' he replied, 'but first we must eat (*mazu kuu koto da*)'.[41] In the end, Satō was relieved of his command. Returning to Rangoon, he hoped his court-martial would bring Mutaguchi down with him and reveal the pitifully inadequate infrastructure of the whole Imphal operation. But neither Kawabe nor Mutaguchi wanted a scandal of those dimensions. Satō was described as mentally unstable and packed off to a remote command elsewhere. The Japanese official historians are guarded in their comments on Satō's withdrawal. Technically, it was not retreat in the face of the enemy, but the line between that and what Satō actually did with his division was a fine one. In the division's accounts of the episode, and in Satō's own memoir, there is no hesitation: had he not done what he did, many thousands more of his men would have perished, at a time when Mutaguchi's grand design had already failed.[42] As Mutaguchi sees it, Satō's behaviour provided the British with the victory which he, Mutaguchi, should have won.

On page 15 of his pamphlet, Mutaguchi writes: 'Colonel Barker's fourth paragraph has blown away at one fell swoop the dark clouds which have overshadowed me until this day. So I was not mistaken after all! I have nothing to be ashamed of! If my decisions had been followed, we would have won!'[43] The previous year, he went on, he had been visited by Lieutenant General Miyazaki, who had so nearly taken Kohima. Miyazaki said he had judged Satō would want to move on fast to Dimapur, taking advantage of the confused state of the enemy, and he had got ready two captured vehicles to go on ahead. 'Why did Satō not move on?' he asked Mutaguchi. 'I told him to,' Mutaguchi answered, 'but my order was countermanded by K, the GOC Burma Area Army.' 'Ah, is that so?' Miyazaki had replied, 'I had always wondered about it. What a great pity.' Mutaguchi did not refer to Kawabe by name, but merely used the initial K. No-one was in any doubt who was meant. So both Kawabe and Satō were covered by the indictment, twenty years after the event.[44]

One of Mutaguchi's staff officers (the only one not to be sacked in the aftermath of the defeat) resolutely continued to believe that Satō had wrecked the possibility of victory. This was Fujiwara Iwaichi, in 1944 a major on 15 Army staff, and in postwar Japan a lieutenant general in the Ground Self-Defence Force. 'The direct cause of the full-scale collapse of the Japanese Army on the Imphal front was brought about on 31 May 1944,' he wrote, 'by the disobedient conduct of Lieutenant General Kōtoku Satō, Divisional Commander of 31 Division, who withdrew and abandoned the Kohima line on his own responsibility. Most important, his was a treasonable action deliberately and with forethought put into execution against his superior, Army Commander Lieutenant General Mutaguchi of the 15 Army in order to bring about the collapse of the Imphal operations.[45]

Fujiwara's emphatic views are by no means characteristic of Japanese historiography, some of which is at least as critical of Mutaguchi as of Satō.

We should take into account the Japanese official historian's comment, that 15 Army's plan contained a clause to the effect that 31 Division was to send part of its force south to take part in the Imphal battle. To plan sending troops on to Dimapur was to ignore the spirit of this clause. And

Kohima was not occupied at this time. Only the village was taken, the surrounding heights were not yet in Japanese hands, and the struggle for Kohima *afterwards* shows that there could have been a hard slog, even if Dimapur had been taken.[46]

As a counterpoint to this, it should however be noted that the official Japanese history text from which this caveat is drawn, although anonymous, was in fact the work of Fuwa Hiroshi, a former officer on Kawabe's Burma Area Army staff; in fact the very officer who had notified Kawabe that a signal from Mutaguchi to Satō had been intercepted, ordering him to march on Dimapur. It was Kawabe's swift reaction to Fuwa's message that resulted in the signal to halt the advance on Dimapur being sent to Mutaguchi in the first place. So the 'anonymous' compiler of the Japanese official history is hardly a neutral observer.

In a postwar memoir, Satō presented his own case against Mutaguchi.

> I disagreed from the start with the Imphal operation, [he wrote] and I thought it unnecessary to run such risks. However, once the operation began, I expressed no dissatisfaction. As I had been ordered by Army, I rapidly occupied Kohima and consider I contributed greatly to the Army's operations.
>
> When the operations began, I advanced in command of the division, and occupied Kohima in three weeks, in accordance with Army orders. However, from then on, Army did not supply my division as it had promised at the beginning. The enemy counter-attacks were strong and on a large scale, and casualties increased.
>
> There was no food and no ammunition. In these circumstances, to keep on fighting, which was our prime duty, simply meant being annihilated. I never entertained any thought of annihilation.
>
> I thought we must stop the operation willy-nilly, and took emergency measures. If our division retreated, the front would collapse, and however much Mutaguchi wished to go on fighting, he would have to bring the operation to a halt.
>
> By doing this, I rescued my division from pointless annihilation, and by the same token I rescued 15 Army itself from a destruction equivalent to committing suicide.
>
> I carried out that decision alone, on my own responsibility.
>
> So when the retreat began, I did not notify 15 Division, and moreover even when we passed close to Sangshak during the withdrawal I did not call on Yamauchi, GOC 15 Division, although I passed close to his HQ.
>
> If 31 Division were to withdraw, then 15 Division also would have to cease fighting in its present front-line. Accordingly, 15 Division would have to withdraw together with our division. If that happened, 15 Division would not be responsible for withdrawing as I had done.
>
> Since I alone bore the burden of that responsibility, I kept silent as far as 15 Division was concerned. [47]

A recent study of Japanese failure in battle, entitled *Shippai no honshitsu* ('The essence of failure'), written by a group of six business analysts, concentrates on a method of analysis based on business management techniques, an interesting application of the methods of commerce to the field of military strategy. Imphal is one of the battles selected for analysis. After a brief account of the battle, the authors proceed to dissect it, and reach foregone conclusions about the crucial carelessness over the problem of supply. But they go on to say that Mutaguchi's basic culpability lay in the omission of contingency planning.[48]

If we add, to this refusal to have a contingency plan, Mutaguchi's absolute belief both in his own destiny and in the power of the Japanese spirit to overcome all obstacles, then the way was open to disaster.

Mutaguchi failed, first, because he was guilty of the oldest sin in the book: *hubris*. He was an over-reacher with a powerful sense of his own destiny, but he lacked two things, militarily, which might have swung the balance in his favour: intelligence and logistics. In fact these two were combined. He was cocksure about the supply problem because he under-estimated his enemy. His mind had not adjusted from the facile victories of 1942 to the very different enemy of 1944. The mistake the British had made, in 1941, of underestimating the Japanese, was repeated by Mutaguchi in reverse. When surrounded, he thought the British would cave in. They didn't. They stood and fought, so Mutaguchi failed to obtain his 'Churchill rations', and his men died in their thousands for lack of them, before he could bring himself to call a halt. That is why, of all the battles in South East Asia, the battle of Imphal remains most deeply embedded in the national historical consciousness of the Japanese.

There are three ancillary factors to be considered in relation to Imphal. The first is the air component; the second, linked to it, is Wingate; the third is Subhas Chandra Bose. Air supply was one of the major causes of Mutaguchi's defeat. In June 1944, the volume of air supplies to Allied forces on the central front reached 500 tons per day. Over 22,000 tons of supplies were delivered to IV Corps during the period when Imphal was cut off from railhead at Dimapur by road. Over 20,000 combatant troops were flown in and 35,000 useless mouths were evacuated. 'This achievement,' write the Indian historians, 'was probably the most important single factor in defeating the Japanese offensive. If it had failed, even partially, Imphal might have fallen to the Japanese and the course of the war would have been different.' [49] Raymond Callaghan's later historical study differs in some details from this assessment, but the order of magnitude is the same.[50]

The Allies had a clear superiority in fighters and bombers, too. Japanese 5 Air Division could only put up an average of 41 fighters a day in the period between 10 March and 31 March 1944, the first three weeks of Operation U. Against this, the Allies had 480 fighters, 224 bombers and 31 reconnaissance aircraft. The Japanese pilots may have been more experienced – they perforce had put in far more flying time – but they were overwhelmed.[51]

Air supremacy also guaranteed the success of the second ancillary factor, Wingate's second operation, which flew into North Burma ten days before Mutaguchi's divisions crossed the Chindwin in the opposite direction. It must be borne in mind that this operation had next to nothing to do, directly, with Slim's Imphal battle, though Wingate's base was for a time at Imphal, and 23 Brigade was detached from Wingate's force to operate on the flank of 7 Division in the re-taking of Kohima. The effect of the second Wingate operation on the Imphal battle is, of course, still a matter for debate. Michael Calvert, Wingate's most ardent doctrinal disciple, has written that the effect of the second incursion into Burma, according to the Japanese themselves, was to cut the supply lines leading to 31 and 15 Divisions' crossing points on the Chindwin and thereby ensure their supplies failed to come through.[52] It has been argued, on the other hand, that if the infantry strength allocated to Wingate – an entire army corps, in effect – had been used on the central front, it would have brought matters to a conclusion much more rapidly.

Mutaguchi himself was quite scornful of the threat posed by Wingate. When news reached him of the force's arrival by glider at landing grounds in North Burma, he was not unduly perturbed. The chief of the Japanese Army air forces in Burma, on the other hand, Major General Tazoe, was thunderstruck. In his view, the second Wingate expedition represented such a threat to the L of C in North Burma that, exactly like Yanagida a short time later, he recommended the cancellation of the whole Imphal operation. All available forces, he claimed, should be concentrated and sent against Wingate instead. He reasoned that, if Wingate succeeded, the Allies would in essence have forced a clear road right to Japan via North Burma and the airfields in China from which the American Major General Claire Chennault proposed to bomb the Osaka-Nagoya-Kobe complex, Japan's industrial heartland.

Mutaguchi simply poo-pooed this. Tazoe was an air general, and naturally stressed the air factor. Mutaguchi retorted that Wingate's base in the Imphal plain would soon be in Japanese hands, and when that happened his forces would simply wither on the vine, or, to put it in Japanese idiom, Wingate would be a 'mouse in a bag' (*fukuro no nezumi*).[53] Here, too, Mutaguchi was underestimating the forces sent against him. Wingate's first expedition had been land-borne and air-supplied, and was really only a foray, three thousand men strong. The second operation was different in kind as well as degree. It was – with the exception of one brigade – airborne and many times larger, carried its own mortars and artillery, flew out its wounded instead of leaving them behind, and intended to stay clamped to the Japanese L of C for a much longer period.

So the entire set-up was far more formidable than Mutaguchi realised, when he overrode Tazoe's objections; which were also dismissed by Kawabe in Rangoon.

Kawabe's role in relation to Mutaguchi is of great interest. He was perfectly well aware of the officially limited nature of Operation U, and knew that Mutaguchi's enthusiasm might well have to be restrained. On the other hand, as Mutaguchi's brigade commander in China, when Mutaguchi was regimental commander at the Marco Polo Bridge affair in 1937, he knew of Mutaguchi's great ambitions and the energy they fuelled.

So, in a sense, Kawabe was prepared to play it by ear and to see how successfully Mutaguchi's enthusiasm drove him forward. If he went too far, he could be checked. This left the initiative in Mutaguchi's hands, though Kawabe did intervene when he learned that Mutaguchi had ordered Satō to move on from Kohima to Dimapur: he realised Mutaguchi was determined to transform the operation from an attempt to ensure a new defence line into an invasion of India, against the intentions of the Japanese high command. Had Mutaguchi had a more pliant divisional commander than Satō at that moment in Kohima, one who, like Miyazaki, would not wait for orders but might on occasion anticipate them, then 31 Division might well have gone on to Dimapur, and changed the whole face of the war.

Which brings us to the third factor: Subhas Chandra Bose. His protagonists in modern Indian National Army historiography naturally emphasise the role of that Army in the final departure of the British. Many Japanese historians share these conclusions. In fact, the evidence seems to point to the military ineffectiveness of the INA, and to its political manipulation by Congress in 1945, when the INA trials and the mutiny of the Indian Navy provided ammunition for whoever wanted to throw things at the British. But there was no real *causality* here. The British were going to leave anyway, and the shrewd old observer Sardar Vallabhai Patel put it succinctly when he said 'instead of fighting the British, the time has come to help them roll up their bedding and depart.' [54] British withdrawal from India would have occurred sooner or later, and the extent to which the INA connection hastened the inevitable is a matter for debate. On the other hand, had Bose not been killed in that convenient air crash in Taiwan in August 1945, he might have proved to be a powerful rival to Nehru in the struggle for power after that power had been transferred. But by that time the connection with Mutaguchi and his plans for the invasion of India were so much vapour.[55]

By a strange final quirk of fate, Mutaguchi's foolhardy incursion into India served to consolidate British planning, just as Wingate's first expedition had been instructive to Mutaguchi. It was a curious reversal of fortune for the British high command. They had never really wanted to re-conquer Burma overland. Both at Cabinet level (Churchill) and theatre level (Mountbatten) it seemed infinitely preferable to put in sea-borne assaults across the Bay of Bengal to capture the airfields at Akyab and then put in another amphibious hook to take Rangoon from the sea and so avoid getting bogged down in the slow and painful slog across the jungles, rivers and hills of Burma. Slim was the exception. Like Stilwell, he had been run out of

Burma by the Japanese, and he was keen on administering to them a dose of
their own medicine. Slim had welcomed the Imphal battle as a means of
drawing Kawabe's forces into his own web and beating them in the Imphal
plain at the end of perilously overdrawn lines of communication, where he
could use aircraft and tanks at will. Slim's victory at Imphal transformed
the prospects for a Burma campaign. By August 1944 the Japanese were in
full flight towards the Chindwin, and streaming back into Burma. This was
a total contradiction of the gloomy views expressed in early February 1944
by Mountbatten's chief of staff, Lieutenant General Sir Henry Pownall:

> if . . . we are relegated to mucking about in Burma they may as well wind up
> this unlucky South-East Asia Command, leave here, if you like, a few figure-
> heads, a good deception staff and plenty of press men to write it up. Our
> practical value will disappear and the Burma operations turned back to India to
> run indifferently well.[56]

On 14 April, part of his diary entry reads:

> 'To try and recapture Burma from the north and north-west is a quite hopeless
> proposition . . .'[57]

It was this quite hopeless proposition that Slim put into effect from
autumn 1944 onwards, riding confidently on the shattering defeat of
Mutaguchi's attempt to invade India. Just as Wingate's example had
invited Mutaguchi into India, so Mutaguchi's attempt and its failure inexorably drew Slim back into Burma on the heels of the shattered 15 Army.
Within nine months he had almost cleared Burma of the Japanese.

Chapter Notes

1. Geoffrey Chaucer, *The Monkes Tale*, 'The mery wordes of the Host to the Monk'.
2. L Allen, *Burma – the Longest War*, (Dent, London, 1984), pp. 150–53.
3. N Kojima, *Taiheiyō Sensō* [The Pacific War], (Chūkō Shinsho, Tokyo, 1966), Vol. 2, p. 131.
4. On Bose and the Indian National Army, cf. inter alia, H Toye, *The Springing Tiger*, (Cassell, London, 1957); Hayashida Tatsuo, *Higeki no eiyū* [Tragic Hero], (Shinjusha, Tokyo, 1968); Joyce Lebra, *Jungle Alliance*, (Donald Moore, Singapore, 1971); K K Ghosh, *The Indian National Army*, (Meenakshi Prakashan, Meerut 1969); Milan Hauner, *India in Axis Strategy; Germany, Japan and Indian Nationalists in the Second World War*, (German Historical Institute, 1982); G. H. Corr, *The War of the Springing Tigers*, (Osprey, London, 1975); H. Toye, 'The Indian National Army 1941–1945', *Indo-British Review*, Vol. XVI – No. 1; Maruyama Shizuo, *Indo-Kokumin Gun* [The Indian National Army], (Iwanami Shinsho, 1985); N. Nagasaki, *Indo-Dokuritsu* [Indian Independence] (Asahi Shinbunsha, Tokyo, 1989).
5. Kawabe's diary, 22 March, 1944, in Defence Agency, Defence Research Centre, *Inpāru Sakusen* [The Imphal Operation], (Asagumo Shimbunsha, Tokyo, 1968), pp. 91–2.
6. Mutaguchi's diary, *Inpāru Sakusen*, pp. 90–91.
7. Conversation with Fujiwara, in L Allen, *Burma – The Longest War*, p. 157.
8. T. Takagi, *Kōmei* [Disobeying Orders], (Bungei Shunjū, Tokyo, 1966), p. 71.
9. ed. Rikusenshi Kenkyū Fukyūkai, *Inpāru Sakusen* [The Imphal Operation], Hara Shobō, Tokyo, 3rd edn., 1977, Vol. 1, p. 61.
10. 'Toranu tanuki no kawa sanyo de aru' in N. Kojima, *Eirei no tani* [Valley of Heroic Souls], (Kōdansha, Tokyo, 1970), p. 30.
11. *Ibid.*, p. 31.
12. *Ibid.*
13. *Ibid.*, p. 32.
14. Kawabe's post-war recollections, in Rikusenshi Kenkyu Fukyūkai, *Inpāru Sakusen*, I, pp. 61–62.
15. M. Itō, *Teikoku rikugun no saigo* [The last days of the Imperial Army], (Bungei Shunjū, Tokyo, 1st edn. 1959, 14th edn. 1969).
16. *Impāru Sakusen*, I, p. 109.

17. L Allen, *Burma – The Longest War*, p. 172.
18. Military History Staff of GDSF Staff College, *Arakan Sakusen* [The Arakan Operation], (Sanyōsha, Tokyo, 1970), pp. 245–6.
19. Slim, *Defeat into Victory*, (Cassell, London, 1956), pp. 246–7.
20. Yamauchi's Diary, in T. Takagi, *Funshi* [Death in Anger], (Bungei Shunjū, Tokyo, 1969), p. 63.
21. T Takagi, *Kōmei*, p. 65.
22. T Takagi, *Inparu* [Imphal], (Bungei Shunjū, Tokyo, 1968), p. 71.
23. N Kojima, *Eirei no tani*, p. 160.
24. Slim, op. cit., pp. 336–7.
25. Kawabe's Diary, Defence Agency Archives, Tokyo. On 5 June, Kawabe noted 'Mutaguchi was in good health, but his eyes were filled with tears'.
26. Mutaguchi's post-war recollections, in *Inpāru Sakusen*, Vol. 2, p. 112.
27. *Ibid.*, pp. 202–206.
28. N Kojima, *Eirei no tani*, pp. 317–318.
29. N Kojima, *Taiheiyō Sensō*, II, p. 172.
30. L Allen, *Burma – The Longest War*, p. 245.
31. S W Kirby, *The War Against Japan*, (HMSO, London, 1965), III, p. 310.
32. Vice-Admiral the Earl Mountbatten of Burma, *Report to the Combined Chiefs of Staff by the Supreme Allied Commander South-East Asia 1943–45*, (HMSO, London, 1951), p. 71, para. 200.
33. Slim, op. cit., p. 285.
34. *Ibid.*, p. 305.
35. A Swinson, *Four Samurai*, (Hutchinson, London, 1968), p. 250.
36. *Ibid.*, p. 251.
37. A J Barker, *The March on Delhi*, (Faber & Faber, London, 1963).
38. R Mutaguchi, *1944 – nen U-Go sakusen ni kansuru Kokkai Toshokan ni okeru setsumei shiryō* [Explanatory historical materials in the National Diet Library concerning Operation U in 1944], (privately printed by Inagaki Kikutarō, Tokyo, 1964), p. 12.
39. H Hammond-Seaman, *The Battle of Sangshak*, (Leo Cooper, London, 1989).
40. Rikugun Keihō [Japanese Army Penal Code], Article 42.
41. T Takagi, *Kōmei*, p. 209 et seq. and L. Allen, *Burma – The Longest War*, pp. 291–2.
42. In T Takagi, *Kōmei*, and *Biruma Sensen* [The Burma Front; Regimental History of 58 Infantry Regiment, 31 Division], (privately published, Tokyo, 1964).
43. R Mutaguchi, op. cit., p. 15.
44. Ibid., pp. 15–16. Defence Agency War History Centre, *Inpāru Sakusen – Biruma no bōei* [The Imphal Operation – The Defence of Burma], (Asagumo Shimbunsha, Tokyo, 1968), pp. 460–61.
45. I Fujiwara, 'Burma: The Japanese Verdict', *Purnell's History of the Second World War*, (London, 1975), p. 1706.
46. Defence Agency, *Inpāru Sakusen – Biruma no bōei*, p. 461.
47. *Ibid.* pp. 564–66.
48. Tobe Ryōichi et al., *Shippai no honshitsu* [The essence of failure], (Diayamondo-sha, Tokyo, 1984), pp. 92–119.
49. B Prasad et al., *Reconquest of Burma*, (Orient Longmans, Calcutta, 1954), Vol. 1, p. 265.

50. R Callaghan, *Burma 1942–1945*, (Davis-Poynter, London, 1978), p. 137.

51. N Kojima, *Taiheiyō sensō II*, pp. 159–60.

52. M Calvert, *Prisoners of Hope*, new edn., (Leo Cooper, London, 1971), pp. 297–98.

53. L Allen, *Burma – The Longest War*, pp. 327–28.

54. K L Panjabi, *The Indomitable Sardar: A Political Biography of Sardar Vallabhai Patel*, (Bombay 1962), p. 113.

55. N Kojima, *Taiheiyō Sensō*, Vol. II, p. 166.

56. B Bond, ed. Chief of Staff, *The Diaries of Lieutenant General Sir Henry Pownall*, Vol. 2, 1940–1944, (Leo Cooper, London 1973), p. 139.

57. *Ibid.*, p. 162.

Additional Sources

J H Boyle, *China and Japan at War 1937–1945* (Stamford UP, 1972), p. 185

Takumi Hiroshi, *Kotabaru tekizen jōriku* [Opposed landing at Kotu Bharu]

M Tsuji, *Singapore – the Japanese Version* (Constable, London, 1962), pp. 161–2

L Allen, *Singapore 1941–1942* (Davis-Poynter, London, 1977), p. 164

S L Falk, *Seventy Days to Singapore* (G.P. Putnam's & Sons, New York, 1975), p. 252

11

Gerd Von Rundstedt
1939–45

Charles Messenger

'*With his demonstrable achievements in every post and his whole personality, Oberlt v. Rundstedt justifies the certain belief of employment in the higher posts of the army in the future.*' So wrote von Rundstedt's corps commander at the end of 1905.[1] Some forty years later, an American journalist was calling him '*Germany's last hope*', [2] while Montgomery, in his notorious Ardennes press conference of 7 January 1945, spoke of him as '*the best German general I have come up against*'.[3] Yet, just over two months later, the doyen of the Prussian officer corps was removed from his command for the third time in just over three years. This time it was for good.

Von Rundstedt's family was part of the *Uradel*, the cream of the Prussian aristocracy that had documentary evidence of the family's existence prior to 1350 AD. It also had a strong military tradition. It was thus inevitable that von Rundstedt and his three brothers would become soldiers and be naturally imbued with the Prussian concept of Duty, Honour, Loyalty. His was a cadet branch of the family with no estates and little money. Consequently, his wish to be a cavalryman could not be fulfilled and he joined the infantry. His early promise was confirmed by entry to the *Kriegsakademie* in Berlin, stepping-stone to the *Grosse Generalstab*, itself the cream of the Royal Prussian Army. It was the power to influence rather than rank that counted in the *Grosse Generalstab* and it was thus as a Captain that 38 year-old Gerd von Rundstedt joined 22 Reserve Infantry Division at the end of July 1914 as its Chief of Operations. This formation was to be part of von Kluck's First Army on the extreme right flank of the great German wheel through Belgium and Northern France. It would play a crucial part in the Battle of the Marne which saw the end of von Moltke's dreams of shattering France in one blow. Von Rundstedt survived all this, but the strain proved too much and he was invalided and given a post in the military government at Antwerp in order to convalesce. He then went as

Chief of Staff to another division and found himself heavily involved in the bitter fighting on the River Narew in Poland in July 1915. His health again failed him and he was posted to the staff of the Military Governor of Poland. Fit again, he was appointed as Chief of Operations to a corps in November 1916 and, just under a year later, as corps Chief of Staff. Both these posts were on the Eastern Front, but in the late summer of 1918 he returned once more to the Western Front, again as a corps Chief of Staff in the German Nineteenth Army. These last few months of hostilities were undoubtedly the most frustrating and depressing period of the whole war for von Rundstedt. Nineteenth Army, which was deployed in Alsace, could only watch helplessly as the final Allied offensives to the north remorselessly drove back the German armies. The end of the war found von Rundstedt as a Major. He had been highly decorated and had been twice recommended, without success, for Prussia's highest military award, the *Pour Le Mérite*. Yet, with the abdication of the Kaiser and the growing anarchy in Germany, it seemed that von Rundstedt's world had been torn assunder.

The Versailles imposition of a 100,000-man long-service army on Germany and the government's attempts to democratise that army, were humiliations that some officers were unable to swallow. The result was the abortive Kapp Putsch of March 1920. This split the *Reichswehr* down the middle, but it is significant that the commander of *Wehrkreis* V, on whose staff von Rundstedt was then serving, was the first to declare for the government. As von Rundstedt himself later commented: 'It is a very ancient tradition that an officer does not concern himself with politics.' [4] Von Rundstedt's political reliability in this affair may have influenced his promotion to Lieutenant Colonel in October 1920, by which time he was serving as Chief of Staff to 3rd Cavalry Division. More so, it was probably his longstanding and growing reputation for sound judgement, tact, modesty, popularity and organisational abilities which brought his name to von Seeckt's notice. Von Seeckt himself had been appointed Chief of the Army Command (*Heeresleitung*) in the aftermath of the Kapp Putsch and among his objectives was to create a leadership framework on which a rapid expansion of the Army at some future date could be based. It was, in his eyes, essential to groom promising middle-piece officers for this and von Rundstedt was one of the chosen, the other four officers promoted with him being von Blomberg, von Bock, von Hammerstein-Equord, and von Leeb, all of whom would rise to the highest ranks.

For the next twelve years, von Rundstedt's path to the top rungs of the military ladder was remorseless – *Wehrkreis* Chief of staff, infantry regimental commander, *Gruppenkommando* Chief of Staff, cavalry divisional commander, *Wehrkreis* commander, and finally, on 1 October 1932, promotion to General of Infantry and appointment to the premier command, *Gruppenkommando* 1 in Berlin. Von Rundstedt was no intellect, indeed he himself once declared: 'I can hardly write my own name!'[5] Even so, his commonsense, balanced views, capacity for hard work, and his personal character which, in the eyes of his brother officers, epitomised all that was best in the Prussian officer corps, meant that he consistently stood high among his contemporaries.

Hitler's appointment as Chancellor in 1933 was not to von Rundstedt's taste. But, as far as he was concerned, Hitler had come to power legally, and von Hindenburg, whom von Rundstedt much admired, remained as Head of State. He certainly could not object to Hitler's pledge to expand the Armed Forces. Besides which, he still resolutely maintained that an officer should keep out of politics. Indeed, the one occasion when he had been pitchforked into the political arena, when, on von Papen's order, he had had to arrest the Prussian Cabinet in July 1932 and rule Berlin by military decree for a few days, had been a most uncomfortable experience for him. After von Hindenburg's death in August 1934, it was with von Blomberg's connivance that Hitler drew up a new oath for the Armed Forces, making them swear personal allegiance to him. Von Rundstedt made no public objection. As far as he was concerned, however much he abhorred National Socialism in private (he even scrawled 'Aryan Shit' on the cover of the file containing papers relating to proof of his non-Jewish ancestry)[6], his rigid observance of the traditional Prussian code meant that he could not take any unilateral action or step outside the chain of command. Von Fritsch, his immediate superior, thought likewise, despite his alienation from Hitler. Matters came to a head in November 1937 when Hitler made clear his preparedness to use the Wehrmacht offensively and both von Blomberg and von Fritsch made plain their objections. The result was their removal on the grounds of conduct unbecoming of an officer. Von Blomberg's dismissal provoked little sympathy, even his son-in-law, Wilhelm Keitel, doubtless disapproving of the new Frau von Blomberg, a woman with a conviction for immorality and the grounds for von Blomberg's dismissal, refused to support him. In contrast, the accusation that von Fritsch was a homosexual and that he was being investigated by the Gestapo rather than being brought before a military court of honour, caused deep anger within the Army. Von Rundstedt himself, summoned back from a map exercise in East Prussia for a private meeting with Hitler, demanded that von Fritsch be given the opportunity to defend himself in front of a military court. Hitler acceded to this and the subsequent court-martial, presided over by Goering and the proceedings interrupted by the *Anschluss*, quickly found the charges against him baseless. He was not, however, restored to the active list and retired a much embittered man, so much so that he handed von Rundstedt a written challenge to a duel for him to hand to Himmler. Von Rundstedt kept it in his pocket for some weeks, but in the end took no action. First, although duelling was still considered legally acceptable for settling matters of honour, von Rundstedt doubted, probably rightly, that Himmler would accept the challenge. He also believed there was a danger that it would do the Army as a whole little good in that it would stir up Nazi opinion against it. Nevertheless, the affair left a bitter taste in his mouth and enabled Hitler to increase his grip on the *Wehrmacht*. For a start he appointed himself Commander-in-Chief in von Blomberg's place. As for a replacement for von Fritsch as Commander-in-Chief of the Army, von Rundstedt would have been a natural choice and, indeed, his name was put forward to Hitler. He himself refused to be considered. He wanted to retire, but Hitler would not let him. He realised only too well von Rundstedt's high standing in the Army and had sought to cultivate him in a number of ways, including selecting him to represent the German Army at the funeral of King George V and giving him a signed portrait of himself on his 60th birthday. He did not, however, want von Rundstedt as Commander-in-Chief. He feared that he would only resist as von Fritsch had done. Instead he selected von Brauchitsch, who, on the surface, certainly had the right qualifications and was well regarded. What the Army did not know was that Hitler had been able to blackmail von Brauchitsch.

The *Anschluss*, in spite of showing up defects in the Army's logistic infrastructure, a symptom of too rapid expansion, served to encourage Hitler in his aim of removing the geopolitical injustices of Versailles. He now prepared to go to war with Czechoslovakia over the Sudetenland. Von Rundstedt was to command one of the four armies which would be formed from the existing *Heeresgruppen*, the new title for the *Gruppenkommando*, on mobilisation for the invasion. His Second Army was to attack from Silesia. Military resistance to Hitler was not, however, entirely dead. Halder, von Brauchitsch's Chief of Staff, was in touch with the resistance movement, which now believed that Hitler must be removed in order to avoid a disastrous European war. He was confident that von Rundstedt, among others, would support a coup.[7] In the event, Chamberlain's shuttle diplomacy averted the threat, although at grievous cost to the Czechs. A month later, on 1 November 1938, von Rundstedt was at last permitted to retire, but on the understanding that Hitler might recall him in an emergency.

Von Rundstedt and his wife settled in a rented apartment in Kassel, from where she originally came and where he had spent some years of his service. His return to active duty was not to be long in coming. Having dealt with the rump of Czechoslovakia and occupied the Baltic port of Memel, Hitler now turned his attention to Poland. In April 1939 he issued a three-part directive to the Wehrmacht. Part II was entitled *Fall Weiss* (Case White), the plan to destroy the Polish forces by surprise attack. Under the existing mobilisation plan the six peacetime *Heeresgruppen*, and a number of the *Wehrkreise* headquarters, were to form two operational army group headquarters and the army headquarters. One army group would be responsible for the West and the other the East. Preliminary studies on an attack on Poland had, however, revealed that two army groups should be employed, one to operate from Pomerania and East Prussia and the other from Silesia.

To earmark another *Heeresgruppe* to form the additional army group head-quarters would mean recasting the whole mobilisation plan. It was therefore decided to form a small unofficial planning group to do the detailed planning for the Silesia army group. Nominated to head it was von Rundstedt, and *Arbeitstab von Rundstedt* came into existence in May. He himself was based at home and the two other members were Major General Erich von Manstein, then commanding an infantry division, and Colonel Günther Blumentritt, who headed the Army's training branch. The planning was completed by mid June, when OKH* issued the final operation order. There then began the process of discreet mobilisation and deployment. Not until 12 August did von Rundstedt move to Silesia and six days later his staff gathered in Munich and then deployed to Silesia. Leaving Blumentritt to organise the largely untried staff, von Rundstedt and von Manstein were summoned to Obersalzberg, Hitler's Alpine retreat and where he was to address all his senior commanders. Hitler's announcement of the non-aggression pact with Russia came as a bolt out of the blue. Both von Rundstedt and von Manstein asserted after the war that this made them believe that Poland would cave in as Czechoslovakia had done.[8] Another source, however, quotes von Rundstedt saying to von Manstein: 'That crackpot wants war.' [9] Whatever they truly believed, the eleventh hour postponement on 25 August of the invasion did make it seem that a peaceful solution had been found. Their hopes were to be short-lived.

Von Rundstedt's Army Group South did all that was asked of it during the overrunning of Poland. This did not mean, though, that there were not anxious moments. Reinhardt's 4th Panzer Division made a spectacular dash to Warsaw, arriving there on the 8th. That evening von Rundstedt informed OKH that he had captured the city. It was premature; Reinhardt attempted to force his way through the streets and was bloodily repulsed, losing almost half his tanks in the process. His rapid advance exposed von Rundstedt's northern flank. Matters were not helped by the fact that his northern army commander, Blaskowitz, placed his one motorised element, the SS Leibstandarte, on his southern flank instead of using it to screen in the north as von Rundstedt had originally intended. The Polish Poznan Army struck one of Blaskowitz's divisions, which was spread out over 20 miles, and there were two days of heavy fighting before the situation was stabilised. It was, however, a blessing in disguise. Von Brauchitsch saw the opportunity to trap the Poznan Army and this was successfully executed by the two army groups acting in conjunction. The siege of Warsaw, which was finally brought to an end on the 27th, after the Luftwaffe had destroyed the public utilities, then occupied much of von Rundstedt's attention, as well as establishing a mutually agreeable demarcation line with the Russians who had invaded from the east on 17 September. Army Group South netted over

---

* *Oberkommando des Heeres* (Army High Command)

half a million prisoners alone during the campaign at a cost of some 31,000 killed, wounded and missing. It was an impressive performance and von Rundstedt was rewarded with the Knight's Cross to the Iron Cross and the appointment as Commander-in-Chief East and Military Governor of Poland. It soon became clear to him that he was powerless to prevent the atrocities being committed by the SS *Einsatzgruppen** on the Poles and that the reins of government were really in the hands of the soon to become notorious Karl Frank, head of civil administration. It was thus with relief that, on 20 October, he was ordered to hand over to Blaskowitz and to move, with his staff, to the Western Front where he was to take command of the newly formed Army Group A.

Much of the period of the Phoney War in the West was taken up on the German side with the debate on how and when to attack. On the one hand was Hitler, impatient to invade France and the Low Countries as soon as possible. On the other were his military commanders, who argued that the Western Allies were a very much more formidable enemy than Poland and that time was needed in order to prepare properly for the attack. This came to be overshadowed by the argument, initiated by von Manstein, over the plan itself. Von Rundstedt's wholehearted support for his Chief of Staff significantly contributed to the eventual acceptance of the weight of the attack being shifted from von Bock in the North and for the main thrust to come through the Ardennes. With his lengthy experience as a staff officer, von Rundstedt recognised that it was the staff's duty to present the options to the Commander and for him to select the preferred one and to take responsibility for it. After that, the staff should be allowed to see to the execution with minimum interference.

When the revised Plan Yellow was finally executed in May 1940, the results were devastating. In just six weeks, France was knocked out of the war and Britain stood alone. Even though he believed in maximum delegation, von Rundstedt was always prepared to go and see for himself. Guderian recorded how he came and visited him on the Meuse when the bridges over the river were under heavy air attack and marvelled at his coolness under fire.[10] Once across the Meuse, von Rundstedt's Panzer divisions made spectacular progress, but there was growing concern that the deeper they advanced the more extended and vulnerable their flanks would become. Hitler himself constantly emphasised to von Rundstedt the need to keep the southern flank well secured with infantry. French attempts to strike with armour against this flank were too ill coordinated to have much effect, but the British 1st Army Tank Brigade counter-attack at Arras on 21 May did produce more of a scare and caused von Rundstedt to halt the advance until the situation had been restored. The following night OKH ordered

---

* Literally 'Task Groups'. These units were most often responsible for atrocities committed in Hitler's name, particularly against the Jews.

him to continue the armoured drive to the Channel in order to cut off the norther Allied armies. By this time, though, the Panzer commanders themselves, with the noticeable exception of Guderian, were beginning to complain of the wear and tear on their vehicles and men and von Rundstedt ordered a day's halt on the 24th so that they could draw breath and the infantry could catch up. This was the origin of Hitler's famous Halt Order in front of Dunkirk. While Guderian condemned it at the time and von Rundstedt certainly did so after the war, there were sound military reasons for it. Von Rundstedt doubtless recalled Reinhardt's experience in trying to capture Warsaw single-handed. He was also well aware of the nature of the Flanders terrain from his tour at Antwerp some 25 years before, and there was no reason why the trapped Allies would not bitterly resist. It therefore made sense to pause while sufficient infantry were deployed in order to assist the armour. Where he, and everyone else who was not an airman, differed from Hitler was the latter's acceptance of Goering's boast that the Luftwaffe could destroy the forces trapped in the pocket of its own. Yet, in spite of the furore over this, the evacuation from Dunkirk marked the end of the first phase of the campaign. There now remained the rump of France, but this did not take long. Once bridgeheads across the Aisne had been established (the only difficult operation) and the Panzer divisions had been let loose, the end result was in no doubt.

Von Rundstedt's reputation stood higher than ever and tangible reward came in the form of promotion, together with eleven other Army and Luftwaffe generals, to the rank of Field Marshal. He was also appointed to command the German ground forces in the projected cross-Channel invasion of England. In spite of Halder's likening the operation to merely'a large-scale river crossing',[11] von Rundstedt did not take SEALION seriously, considering it a military impossibility. Hence he took the minimum interest in the preparations, even to the extent of going on leave during the critical period. The operation postponed indefinitely, he was appointed Commander-in-Chief West.

On 18 December 1940, Hitler issued Directive No 21 for the invasion of Russia. It came as no surprise to von Rundstedt; Hitler had spoken personally to him of his future intentions at the beginning of the previous June. Even so, the prospect filled von Rundstedt with gloom. The same team that had led the victorious army groups in France, von Bock, von Leeb, and von Rundstedt, was to do so in Russia. This time von Rundstedt was to command the southern army group. There was probably a particular reason for this. Operating with Army Group South was to be a sizeable Rumanian contingent, and later Hungarians (who had to be kept apart from the Rumanians since the latter resented having had to cede territory to Hungary under the terms of the September 1940 Vienna Award), Slovaks and Italians. It would require much tact in order to handle this polygot collection and von Rundstedt was the obvious candidate for it. It worked very well, especially in the case of the Rumanians. As von Rundstedt wrote to his wife: 'For political reasons Anton[escu]* appears as an independent commander although I am responsible for operations and he very nicely agrees to everything.' [12] Nevertheless, poor levels of equipment and training, by German standards, meant that the allied forces were of limited use and added to the burdens of an increasingly stretched logistics system.

Besides the fact that the invasion of Russia took place a month later than planned (although the lateness of the spring thaw played as great a part in that delay as Hitler's forays into the Balkans did), something that was to affect all three army groups, Army Group South had other particular problems. For a start, it was only given one Panzer group, unlike Army Group Centre, which had two and was very quickly able to create vast pockets of encirclement. Furthermore, the Russian resistance in the Ukraine was stiffer and better organised than elsewhere. Not until mid-July was von Rundstedt able to create a significant pocket, in the Uman area, which eventually yielded 100,000 prisoners. Further aggravation came from his northern flank, which was constantly harried by sizeable Russian forces operating from the Pripet Marshes. His troops also had to endure numerous thunderstorms, which quickly turned the terrain into glutinous black mud, so that movement virtually ground to a halt. Von Rundstedt recalled after the war that on one occasion it took a Panzer division 12 hours to traverse just 7 kilometres.[14] Increasing interference from Hitler's headquarters, the OKW,* did not help, especially since von Brauchitsch found it difficult to stand up to Hitler and keep him off the backs of his army group commanders. Von Rundstedt was prone to depression and also realised more than most, from his Great War experience on the Eastern Front, the enormous depth of the theatre. 'The vastness of Russia devours us', he exclaimed to his wife.[15]

Eventually, his forces crossed the Dnieper, but not before the Russians had destroyed all the railway bridges across it, which further aggravated the logistic problems. He now set about reducing the Russian forces around Kiev. With the assistance of Guderian's Second Panzer Army, temporarily transferred from Army Group Centre, the Ukrainian capital fell on 19 September, with no less than 600,000 Russian troops captured. Hitler, having lost interest in Moscow as a prime objective, now changed his mind and von Rundstedt was ordered to transfer troops to Army Group Centre for the final drive on the city which opened at the end of the month. In spite of this, he was still expected to continue his advance eastwards, notwithstanding the growing exhaustion of his troops and the fact that he had been ordered to capture Odessa and overrun the Crimea as well.

On 14 October, the autumn rains, prelude to winter, arrived in the

* General Ion Antonescu, the Rumanian dictator
* *Oberkommando der Wehrmacht* (the Supreme Headquarters of all the German Armed Forces)

Ukraine. Army Group South struggled on and secured the Donets Basin, but not before the Russians had been able to remove much of its industry to prepared locations behind the Urals. Von Rundstedt now proposed to von Brauchitsch that he halt for the winter and continue once more in the spring. This was rejected, for Hitler had now cast his eyes on Stalingrad and the Caucasus. The rain turned to snow and the temperature fell sharply. Von Rundstedt himself now suffered a heart attack, doubtless caused by the increasing strain, but insisted on remaining at duty.

Meanwhile, von Kleist's First Panzer Army struggled into Rostov-on-Don, gateway to the Caucasus, and secured it on 21 November, after fierce fighting. This left von Kleist's command dangerously extended. The Russians were quick to take advantage of it and launched bitter counter-attacks against First Panzer Army. On 28 November von Rundstedt ordered von Kleist to withdraw behind the River Mius, 50 miles to the West, in order to save him from being totally cut off and destroyed. Hitler was furious and on the 30th ordered von Brauchitsch to countermand von Rundstedt's order. This he did and von Rundstedt's immediate reaction was to ask von Brauchitsch to think again. If he did not von Rundstedt would tender his resignation. Early on the following morning, 1 December, Hitler signalled OKH that von Rundstedt was to be replaced by von Reichenau, who immediately assured OKH that he could hold east of the Mius, this in spite of von Kleist's objections. Within a few hours, von Reichenau was forced to eat his words when the Russians broke through the SS Leibstandarte, Hitler's own bodyguard, then under von Kleist's command. Hitler now acceded to von Reichenau's request to fall back behind the Mius. Two days later, he flew to the Ukraine to see for himself. Sepp Dietrich, the Leibstandarte commander, defended von Rundstedt's withdrawal decision. It so happened that bad weather forced Hitler to stage at HQ Army Group South on his return flight. Here he interviewed von Rundstedt, who had remained there pending instructions as to his future, and forgave him. He granted him sick leave and von Rundstedt departed for Germany. A few days later, as a further demonstration of Hitler's forgiveness, he arranged for von Rundstedt to be given a cheque for the large sum of 250,000 Reichmarks on his birthday in recognition of his distinguished services. He only cashed it under pressure and then refused to touch the money, terming it *Saugeld* (dirt money).[16]

Von Rundstedt was not the only leading military light to fall foul of Hitler at this time. Von Brauchitsch, von Leeb, Guderian and Hoepner all lost their jobs, and, except for Guderian, were never re-employed. Von Rundstedt, now aged 66 and having suffered a heart attack, might have also been expected to hang up his sword for good, but it was not to be. In early March 1942 he was summoned to Rastenburg, Hitler's headquarters in the East, and was told that he was to reassume as CinC West. His successor in this post, von Witzleben, had been admitted to hospital with haemorrhoids and von Rundstedt was told that his posting was merely in *locum tenens*. Hitler, however, then decided to retire von Witzleben and on 1 May 1942 von Rundstedt was confirmed in his post.

France might have produced less direct pressure for a Commander-in-Chief than an operational command on the Eastern Front, but this did not mean that von Rundstadt's new post was any sinecure. For a start, Hitler's 'divide and rule' policy for keeping his subordinates in check was very apparent. The various military governors, the Navy, Luftwaffe, SS and the German civil administration all had their separate links with Berlin and von Rundstedt only enjoyed absolute authority for preventing invasion of the coastline of Occupied Western Europe. Yet, because the focus of German attention was on the Eastern Front, the West was very much the poor relation when it came to force requirements. Too often von Rundstedt was sent cadres from shattered Eastern Front divisions. Once these had been restored to full strength he was ordered to release them back to Russia. The invasion of Sicily and the subsequent Italian armistice also meant the sudden loss of additional valuable formations to this theatre. Not until November 1943, when the only questions surrounding the Allied cross-Channel invasion were when and where, did Hitler finally take note of von Rundstedt's protests and give the West greater priority.

Among his measures was to despatch Rommel on a comprehensive tour of the coastline. The latter reported his findings to von Rundstedt just after Christmas 1943 and the two found themselves in broad agreement over the concept of defence. Nevertheless, von Rundstedt was suspicious of Rommel. 'Field Marshal Cub' he apparently called him,[17] considering that he was over-ambitious and played too much to the gallery with little justification since he had not experienced the 'real war' on the Eastern Front. He also viewed him as being too much in Hitler's pocket. This was especially since Rommel, although supposedly placed under von Rundstedt's command, had direct access to Hitler. Rommel, on the other hand, felt that von Rundstedt had little appreciation of the material strength of the Western Allies. Nevertheless, they did eventually, and shortly before the invasion, sink their mutual differences with one another.

Von Rundstedt also had worries of a different sort. A Francophile at heart, he was concerned about the future of France in the New Europe. He was, too, constantly pressured to take an active part in the plots against Hitler. He consistently viewed such a step as mutiny and in total contravention to his concept of loyalty and duty. Besides, as he pointed out more than once, he could not guarantee that his troops would support him. In any event, his growing old age and decreasing energy made him reluctant to become involved. As he said to one emissary 'Why always silly old me?', declaring that all he wanted to do was to die in harness.[18] The perpetual waiting for the Western Allies to invade also got him down; by his own admission, patience was never one of his strong points. Germany's increasingly grim overall situation also added to his depression. All these pressures drove him increasingly to rely on nicotine and alcohol. So concerned did his staff become about him that his son, who acted as his aide de camp during the last part of the war, had at one point to get him away for a cure at a sanatorium in Bavaria. In spite of all this, the German propaganda machine portrayed von Rundstedt as a 'guarantee for the security of Fortress Europe against all attempts by the Americans and British to infiltrate'.[19] This was reflected by the Allied media, one American commentator going as far as dubbing him the Allies' 'real Enemy No 1'.[20]

When the Allied forces finally came ashore on the Normandy beaches on 6 June 1944, they caught the German high command in the West by surprise, with Rommel snatching a brief leave in Germany and von Rundstedt planning to set off on an inspection tour of the Cotentin peninsula. Both Field Marshals had recognised that if the Allies could not be prevented from landing it was crucial to destroy their beachheads quickly before they could be consolidated. Armour was the most effective way of doing this, but two factors stood in the way of its prompt deployment. There was the belief, much encouraged by Allied deception measures, that the main landings were yet to come and would be in the Pas de Calais area. Rommel had three Panzer divisions under his command, one in the invasion area, which was committed, albeit piecemeal, on D-Day, and the other two north of the Seine, which neither he nor von Rundstedt were willing to redeploy immediately because of the Pas de Calais threat. Three further Panzer divisions were in the southern part of France, under Blaskowitz's Army Group G and would take time to redeploy. This left four mechanised formations, which von Rundstedt had formed into a mobile theatre reserve, but which Hitler insisted could not be used without his agreement. Von Rundstedt wanted to begin deploying these as soon as he heard of the landings, but Hitler refused to give him control of them and only allowed them to be moved to Normandy by degrees. As for the actual movement of the armour, this was delayed by both the Allied air and French Resistance attacks on communications in the weeks before the landings and the overwhelming air supremacy that the Allies enjoyed over North-Western France. The result of all this was that the German armour could only be committed piecemeal and no sooner did it arrive than it was forced to join the infantry divisions in desperately trying to contain the Allied beachhead.

Increasingly, Hitler clamoured for the Allies to be driven back into the sea, demanding at the same time that not an inch more ground must be surrendered. Von Rundstedt, who suspected that Keitel, Chief of Staff at OKW, only told Hitler what he wanted to hear, could only meet these demands if he received significant reinforcements from elsewhere to enable the Panzer formations to be withdrawn from the front line and concentrated for a counter-stroke. Even so, such an operation could only succeed if a limited withdrawal to beyond the range of the devastating Allied naval

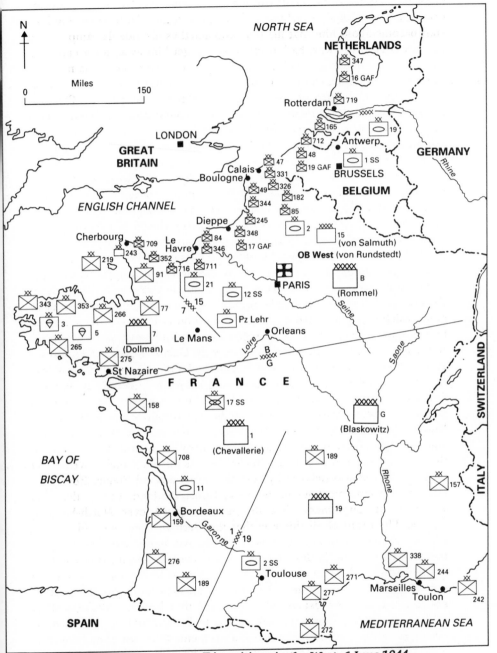

Map 10. *German Dispositions in the West, 6 June 1944.*

gunfire was permitted. Eventually, on 17 June Hitler came to France and von Rundstedt and Rommel had the opportunity to put their case to him in person. It cut little ice, Hitler being more interested in delivering them a lecture on the V-1 offensive against England, which had recently opened. Matters went from bad to worse, with Hitler continuing to insist on counter-strokes and von Rundstedt and Rommel replying that these were not poss-ible without reinforcement and withdrawals. Eventually, on 27 June, von Rundstedt demanded a 'free hand' for Rommel and himself. The response was a preremptory order from Hitler summoning both to Berchtesgaden. Forbidden to travel by air or train, they had to make the 600 mile journey by car. Once again they were subjected to a harangue on the new 'miracle' weapons. It was clear, too, that they could expect little in the way of reinforcement since the Russians had launched a devastating attack on the Eastern Front which was threatening to tear an enormous hole in the German line. They returned empty-handed to France on 30 June. Awaiting them was a fresh OKW order for an immediate counterstroke against Montgomery's EPSOM attack which had been launched for four days earlier. Again, von Rundstedt told OKW that this was not possible without with-drawals, but was told that this was forbidden. He got on the telephone to Keitel. What he said to him has been a matter for debate and variations exist, from the popular 'Make peace you fools!', which Milton Shulman says that Blumentritt told him,[21] to von Rundstedt's own postwar account that he merely advised Keitel to find a replacement for him if Hitler did not trust him any more.[22] Whatever he did say made no difference. Hitler had already decided to replace him and von Kluge had already arrived at Berchtesgaden on 30 June to be briefed prior to taking over. On 2 July, one of Hitler's adjutants arrived at von Rundstedt's headquarters. He had with him the Oakleaves to the Knight's Cross and a letter from Hitler, 'very cordial' according to von Rundstedt, stating that he was being replaced for health reasons.[23]

So for the second time in the war, von Rundstedt's star had fallen. Again Hitler had treated him with kid gloves. He knew that if he did so there was no danger of von Rundstedt straying from the strict confines of the Prussian code of loyalty. While he still had von Rundstedt not actively against him, the Field Marhal's high reputation in the German Army would help ensure that the German soldier continued to do his duty. Again, though, von Rundstedt was not to be left in peace for long.

On 20 July, von Stauffenburg's bomb exploded under the table during a Führer conference at Rastenburg. Retribution was swift. Among other measures, on 2 August Hitler ordered the setting up of a Court of Honour to investigate officers suspected of being implicated in the plot. If found guilty, they would be dismissed from the Service and put on trial by a civilian court. Among the members of the Court were Keitel and Guderian, who was now acting Army Chief of Staff. A week later, Hitler ordered von

Rundstedt, then taking another cure at Bad Tölz, to preside over it. Perhaps this was because Keitel and Guderian could not spare the time, but his appointment enhanced the status of the Court. Although this task was unpalateable to him, von Rundstedt had no truck with the plotters, whom he considered guilty of mutiny, and saw the role of the Court, as Guderian did, as serving to retain something of the Army's integrity. Even so, such now was Hitler's mistrust of the Army that there was no chance that he would allow his generals the freedom of action for which von Rundstedt had pressed so hard in June. This was another reason for von Rundstedt's lack of sympathy with the plotters.

Von Rundstedt's participation in the Court of Honour was to be mercifully short. On 1 September he was summoned to see Hitler who offered him overall command of the Western Front once more. Blumentritt claimed that this was at his instigation.[24] After von Rundstedt had left France at the beginning of July Rommel had been seriously wounded by a marauding Allied fighter and command of Army Group B was taken over by von Kluge, who remained as CinC West. He in turn had been sacked in mid-August and replaced by the more ideologically reliable Model. He soon found it nigh on impossible to both try and extricate Army Group B, whose shattered remnants were now being pursued by the Allies across northern France, as well as supervise the withdrawal of Army Group B from Southern France. Life was not made any easier by the fact that the headquarters of Army Group B and CinC West were some 60 miles apart. Blumentritt saw von Rundstedt's return as a means of easing the command and control dilemma and Model was delighted with the prospect. Jodl put the idea to Hitler, who agreed. Yet, von Rundstedt would have been justified, on grounds of age and health, to refuse the post. He did not because his strong sense of duty would not allow him to and, in any event, it would, in his eyes, have been deserting his troops at their hour of greatest need.

He arrived at his headquarters, now near Koblenz, on 5 September. The situation was grim. In the North, Montgomery's 21st Army Group was sweeping through Belgium and approaching the Dutch border. Bradley's 12th Army Group was advancing on the Saar, while Devers' 6th Army Group was making rapid progress up through Central France. Von Rundstedt's orders were turn a retreat into an aggressive delay in order to buy time for the West Wall to be prepared as a defensive line on which the Germans could anchor themselves. Von Rundstedt himself did not share Hitler's faith in the West Wall and saw the only feasible line as being on the Rhine. Throughout the winter, he would press Hitler to change his mind, but without success. None the less, he took care discreetly to secure all the crossings over the Rhine.

In the meantime, a problem on the Allied side worked in von Rundstedt's favour. Hitler's policy of turning the Channel ports into *Festungen* (fortresses) meant that the Allied supply lines still ran from Normandy. By the beginning of September they had become over-extended and the momentum of the advance began to slow. This provided valuable breathing space in which to restore some cohesion in the defence. Yet crises still arose. Within a few days of von Rundstedt's return to the West, American armour had entered Luxembourg and patrols had set foot on German soil for the first time. Von Rundstedt himself and his Chief of Staff, now Westphal, narrowly escaped capture. Next American tanks looked poised to break through the West Wall north of Trier and on the boundary between Army Groups B and G. So grave was the situation that von Rundstedt issued an order on 15 September which stated: 'It is no longer a question of operations on a large scale. The only task is to hold our positions until we are annihilated.' [25] Only through stripping the line to the south of men and mounting constant counter-attacks was the threat removed. Then came Montgomery's gamble at Arnhem and simultaneously a threat from Patton, who had established bridgeheads over the Moselle. Costly counter-attacks made no impression. So high were the casualties that von Rundstedt was forced to call them off, even though Hitler insisted that they should continue. Luckily, Eisenhower now ordered Patton to halt his offensive operations until the Scheldt had been cleared and the port of Antwerp opened. Then came the bloody battle for Aachen, which eventually fell on 21 October, and the fighting in the Hürtgen Forest. In the midst of this continuing pressure, Hitler revealed his intention to mount a major counter-offensive designed to split the British from the Americans.

The Allies, to von Rundstedt's fury, tended to call the Ardennes counter-offensive the 'Rundstedt Counter-offensive'. As he said after the war: 'If old von Moltke thought I had planned the offensive he would turn over in his grave.' [26] The truth was that he had no influence at all on the plan. Worse, Model's and his alternative and more modest proposal, the so-called Small Solution, was dismissed out of hand. All that he and Model could do was to try to prevent the Allies from breaking through, while simultaneously husbanding formations in the rear for the offensive itself. Insult to von Rundstedt's position was added when, on the eve of the offensive, Hitler and the OKW, together with such hangers-on as Martin Bormann, took up residence at the *Adlerhorst* (Eagle's Eyrie) just one kilometre from von Rundstedt's own headquarters. Furthermore, Hitler's final instructions for the offensive were issued direct to Model, bypassing von Rundstedt.

The course of the Ardennes counter-offensive is well enough known to need no description here. Suffice to say that it was not until 8 January that Hitler began to accept that it had failed, although this had been clear after the first few days. A week later, without informing von Rundstedt beforehand, he and his entourage boarded a special train and returned to Berlin. The Russian offensive across the Vistula had opened and demanded his attention. This did not mean, however, that von Rundstedt had finally been given any form of free hand. A Führer order issued on 21 January stated that any projected operations down to and including divisional level had to be referred to Hitler for his approval. While, by the end of January 1945, the Allies had made good their territorial losses incurred during the counter-offensive and were now once more pressing on towards the Rhine, Hitler still demanded that the West Wall should be held at all costs. Von Rundstedt himself remained convinced that no cohesive defence was possible west of the river, but was told that the Rhine had to be kept open for the transport of *materiel*. Even so, von Rundstedt realised that he could only hold the Allies for a short time and began a systematic programme of demolition of bridges over the Rhine, keeping to a minimum the number held open for his troops to use in their withdrawal.

His strategy seemed to be working. In the North, Schlemm's First Parachute Army was forcing the Canadians and British to fight for every inch of the path to the Rhine. In the centre, the Americans were also meeting staff resistance, aided by the numerous riverlines west of the Rhine, while in the extreme South, although Nineteenth Army had been forced out of the Colmar pocket, it was able to get back across the Rhine intact, Hitler having given his permission. The cliffs on both sides of the river in this region meant that it was most unlikely that the French and Americans would attempt an early crossing there. Hitler was pleased with von Rundstedt's performance and, on 18 February, awarded him the Swords to the Knight's Cross. Goebbels, too, noted with approval that von Rundstedt was gaining high marks in the enemy Press and that his tactic of drawing the Allies onto defence lines further in the rear would be 'highly disadvantageous to the attacking troops'.[27] By this time, though, the West Wall had been breached in several places and on 2 March the first Allied troops reached the Rhine, men from Simpson's Ninth US Army opposite Düsseldorf, but the bridge there had been blown. It was the same when Hodges' First US Army arrived opposite Cologne two days later. Von Rundstedt's contingency planning appeared successful. Schlemm's men continued their aggressive withdrawal and eventually the last elements crossed the Rhine on 9 March. Two days before this, however, disaster had struck.

At midday on 7 March, a task force from the US 9th Armored Division in First US Army secured high ground overlooking the small town of Remagen, which lies on the Rhine and south of Bonn. To their surprise, the Ludendorff railway bridge, which spanned the river here, appeared to be intact. Three hours later, having fought their way through the town, the Americans reached the bridge. The defenders tried to demolish it, but only succeeded in partially damaging the structure and the Americans charged across. What von Rundstedt had been desperately trying to prevent had now happened. The Allies had a crossing over the Rhine.

Not surprisingly, Hitler was furious when he heard the news and was determined that heads would roll. While von Rundstedt did everything possible, without success, to destroy the bridge, Hitler summoned Kesselring from Italy to report to him in Berlin. Goebbels commented in his diary that von Rundstedt had 'become too old and works too much on First World War ideas to master a situation such as is developing in the West'.[28] Kesselring saw Hitler on the 9th and was told that a 'younger more active commander' was needed in the West and he was to be appointed forthwith.[29] That same day, Hitler telephoned von Rundstedt and told him that he was to be relieved. According to von Rundstedt:

> 'As a camouflage, he said on the telephone that he wanted to save me the annoyance of flying courts martial, which could issue summary death penalties . . ., being active in my area. He said that he knew I did not want to participate in such a bloodbath.' [30]

The Field Marshal was then summoned to Berlin. Hitler presented him with The Swords and thanked him for his loyalty. That ended their last meeting.

Placed on the *Führer-Reserve* OKH for the third time in the war, von Rundstedt and his son now returned to Kassel, where they collected his wife. Then began a curious period of wandering about an ever-shrinking Germany until in mid-April 1945 the von Rundstedt family finally came to rest at the sanatorium at Bad Tölz. It was there, late in the evening of 1 May, that a patrol from the US 36th Infantry Division found and made him prisoner. The Allies heralded his capture as the 'biggest catch of the war',[31] but to von Rundstedt himself, as he told the patrol commander, it was 'a most disgraceful situation for a soldier to have to give himself up without resistance'.[32]

Von Rundstedt was an officer whose talents were recognised very early in his career and, from 1920 at least, he was specifically groomed for stardom. It was not so much military genius which placed him so high among his contemporaries, but dependability, common sense, and his officer qualities. Hitler quickly recognised these and saw in von Rundstedt a means of maintaining the loyalty of the officer corps to himself. Poland and France added to von Rundstedt's reputation and proved his ability for high command in war not only to his fellow Germans but also to Germany's enemies. In spite of Army Group South's particular difficulties in Russia, von Rundstedt again achieved some spectacular successes. However, his Great War experience in this theatre convinced him that Hitler was attempting to achieve too much too quickly. Eventually, his exasperation overrode his deeply ingrained sense of loyalty and duty. He disobeyed orders and suffered the inevitable penalty. One might have expected that, with his age and doubtful health, von Rundstedt's star had now finally set, but it was not to be. Hitler regarded him as a unique figurehead which he could not afford to throw onto the scrap heap. Thus he was recalled once more and his strong sense of duty would not allow him to refuse the summons, even though his energy was not what it was. His second downfall was similar to the first, namely that there was a limit to even his obedience when faced with orders which were militarily completely unsound and a situation in which he was permitted little or no initiative. Yet Hitler was careful not to extinguish his star. He might and did need von Rundstedt's services again. But while the Western Allies regarded him during his last period of active duty as the man most able to slow the rapid ebb in Germany's fortunes, Hitler continued to use him merely for his reputation, encasing him in an even tighter strait-jacket than before. His presence at the front was primarily to help ensure the German soldier's continued resistance and little more. In Hitler's eyes, his final dismissal was the only one that was brought about by failure, but by then the time for miracles was past and Germany's defeat imminent and inevitable. Strict observance of those three soldierly virtues of duty, honour and loyalty had largely gained von Rundstedt his high standing, but also served eventually to tarnish his star. For this he was to pay the penalty, not so much by virtue of his dismissal, but more in his postwar treatment.

Source Notes

This chapter is largely drawn on my recently published biography of von Rundstedt, *The Last Prussian* (Brassey's 1991).

1. Annual confidential report on von Rundstedt, Bundesarchiv Militärchiv, Freiburg, Pers 6/16.
2. Cort, David. *Life*, 25 December 1944.
3. *New York Times*, 8 January 1945.
4. *The Trial of Major War Criminals: Proceedings of the International Military Tribunal sitting at Nuremberg, Germany*, Part 21, p. 97 (HMSO, London, 1949).
5. Liddell Hart interview, 3 January 1946. Liddell Hart Centre for Military Archives, King's College, London, LH 9/24/132.
6. Author's interview with von Rundstedt's elder grandson, 4 November 1989.
7. Court testimony, September 1948, and quoted in Schall-Riancour, Heidemarie Grafin von, *Aufstand und Gehorsam Offizierstum und Generalstab im Umbruch: Leben und Wirken von Generloberst Franz Halder, Generalstabschef 1938–1942*, p. 244 (Wiesbaden, 1972).
8. Manstein. *Lost Victories*, pp. 30–31 (Arms & Armour, London, 1982 edition) and Von Rundstedt statement to the Commission of the International Military Tribunal Nuremberg, 19 June 1946, Institut für Zeitgeschichte, Munich, ZS 129.
9. Müller, K-J. *Das Heer und Hitler*, p. 411 (Stuttgart, 1969).
10. *Panzer Leader*, p. 105 (Michael Joseph, London, 1952).
11. Diary Entry 3 July 1940, Burdick, Charles & Jacobsen, Hans-Adolf, ed., *The Halder War Diary 1939–1942*, p. 219 (Greenhill Books, London, 1988).
12. Letter dated 8 August 1941, Bundesarchiv Militärarchiv MSg 1/1893.
13. Blumentritt, Günther. *Von Rundstedt: The Soldier and the Man*, pp. 103–4 (Odhams, London, 1952).
14. US Military Intelligence Service Report B-826 dated 6 September 1945.
15. Letter dated 12 August 1941, Bundesarchiv Militärarchiv MSg 1/1893.
16. The correspondence surrounding the cheque is to be found in Bundesarchiv, Koblenz under R 43 II/958a. The term *Saugeld* is from a letter written by Editha von Rundstedt, the Field Marshal's daughter-in-law to whom he gave control of the money, to Matthew Barry Sullivan, 26 March 1977, and confirmed in author's interview with von Rundstedt's two grandsons, 4 November 1989.

17. Comment by Blumentritt, who was von Rundstedt's Chief of Staff September 1943–July 1944, eavesdropped at Wilton Park POW Camp, England. CSDIC(UK) Report GRGG 344 dated 21 August 1945, Public Record Office (PRO), London WO 208/4178.

18. Tloke, Hildegard von, ed. *Heeres Adjutant bei Hitler 1939–1943: Aufseichnunge des Majores Engel*, p. 144 (Stuttgart, 1974).

19. *Pariser Zeitung*, 21 December 1943.

20. Reiss, Curt. *The Saturday Evening Post*, 2 October 1943.

21. Shulman. *Defeat in the West*, p. 137 (Secker & Warburg, London, 1985 edition).

22. Von Rundstedt interrogation by the Commission of the International Military Tribunal op cit.

23. *The Trial of Major War Criminals . . .*, Part 21, op. cit., p. 94.

24. Blumentritt, op. cit., pp. 241–2. Von Kluge had committed suicide after the failure of the bomb plot.

25. Bennett, Ralph. *Ultra in the West*, p. 133 (Hutchinson, London, 1979).

26. Gilbert, G. M. *Nuremberg Diary*, pp. 230–231 (Eyre & Spottiswoode, London, 1948).

27. Diary entries 28 February and 6 March 1945. Trevor-Roper, Hugh, ed., *The Geobbels Diaries: The Last Days* (Pan paperback edition, London, 1979).

28. 9 March 1945. *Ibid.*

29. Kesselring, Albert. *The Memoirs of Field Marshal Kesselring*, p. 237 (Kimber, London, 1953).

30. Interview with Dr. Freiherr von Ziegler, 26 November 1951, Institut für Zeitgeschichte, Munich, 311/52.

31. *London Evening Standard*, 2 May 1945 and *The Stars and Stripes*, 3 May 1945.

32. *T-Patch* (36 US Div's weekly newspaper), 8 May 1945.

Index